DATE DUE

DISASTER BY DECREE

THE SUPREME COURT DECISIONS
ON RACE AND THE SCHOOLS

DISASTER BY DECREE

THE SUPREME COURT DECISIONS
ON RACE AND THE SCHOOLS

LINO A. GRAGLIA

Cornell University Press

ITHACA AND LONDON

First published 1976 by Cornell University Press.

Published in the United Kingdom by Cornell University Press Ltd., 2–4 Brook Street, London W1Y 1AA.

Second printing 1977.

International Standard Book Number 0-8014-0980-2
Library of Congress Catalog Card Number 75-36997
Printed in the United States of America by Payne Printery, Inc.
Librarians: Library of Congress cataloging information
appears on the last page of the book.

TO KAY

Acknowledgments

For their help in bringing this book into being, I am deeply indebted to my wife, F. Carolyn Graglia, and to Albert W. Alschuler and William K. Jones. Each has read the manuscript at various stages and offered many valuable suggestions and criticisms of both style and substance. I am also grateful for the help given by my colleagues Mark G. Yudof and Lucas A. Powe, Jr. All these have, of course, been at least as helpful for their disagreements as for their agreements with various aspects of this work.

LINO A. GRAGLIA

Austin, Texas

Contents

Abbreviations

Calif. L. Rev.	*California Law Review*
Colum. L. Rev.	*Columbia Law Review*
Cong. Rec.	*Congressional Record*
Harv. L. Rev.	*Harvard Law Review*
HEW	Department of Health, Education, and Welfare
J. Politics	*Journal of Politics*
NAACP	National Association for the Advancement of Colored People
N.Y.U.L. Rev.	*New York University Law Review*
Va. L. Rev.	*Virginia Law Review*
W. Res. L. Rev.	*Western Reserve Law Review*
Yale L. J.	*Yale Law Journal*

DISASTER BY DECREE

THE SUPREME COURT DECISIONS
ON RACE AND THE SCHOOLS

I repeat, that I do not charge the Judges with wilful and ill-intentioned error; but honest error must be arrested, where its toleration leads to public ruin. As, for the safety of society, we commit honest maniacs to Bedlam, so judges should be withdrawn from their bench, whose erroneous biases are leading us to dissolution. It may, indeed, injure them in fame or in fortune; but it saves the Republic, which is the first and supreme law.

Thomas Jefferson, *Autobiography*

You seem . . . to consider the judges as the ultimate arbiters of all constitutional questions; a very dangerous doctrine indeed, and one which would place us under the despotism of an oligarchy. Our judges are as honest as other men, and not more so. They have, with others, the same passions for party, for power, and the privilege of their corps. Their maxim is *"boni judicis est ampliare jurisdictionem,"* and their power the more dangerous as they are in office for life, and not responsible, as the other functionaries are, to the elective control. The constitution has erected no such single tribunal, knowing that to whatever hands confided, with the corruptions of time and party, its members would become despots.

Thomas Jefferson to William C. Jarvis, September 28, 1820

At the same time, the candid citizen must confess that if the policy of the Government upon vital questions affecting the whole people is to be irrevocably fixed by decisions of the Supreme Court, the instant they are made in ordinary litigation between parties in personal actions the people will have ceased to be their own rulers, having to that extent practically resigned their Government into the hands of that eminent tribunal.

Abraham Lincoln, First Inaugural Address, March 4, 1861

The President, who exercises a limited power, may err without causing great mischief in the state. Congress may decide amiss without destroying the Union, because the electoral body in which Congress originated may cause it to retract its decision by changing its members. But if the Supreme Court is ever composed of imprudent or bad men, the Union may be plunged into anarchy or civil war.

Alexis de Tocqueville, *Democracy in America*

It's hell. It's just hell. What can we do? . . . In fact there's very little we can do and that's frightening. Sometimes it gets so bad I just sit down and cry.

A mother of school children in Boston; Washington *Post*, November 10, 1974

1 | *Introduction*

"Busing is, in important ways, the Vietnam of the 1970s. It is a quagmire; . . . a mistake; a tragedy; a breeder of endless demonstrations, riots, and dissent." Michael Novak wrote this in 1975. "Busing," Daniel Moynihan earlier predicted, and events seem almost daily to corroborate, "is an issue that can tear the 1970's apart." [1] Busing, the compulsory transportation of school children out of their neighborhoods to increase school racial mixing or "balance," may well have a potential for social disruption and dissolution unequaled by the Vietnam war at its height, for busing touches more directly and significantly the lives of larger numbers of average people.

Busing could not have become a serious issue, much less actually occur, in almost any community in America through the processes of accountable, representative government. It has become an issue and does occur only because it has been imposed by the United States Supreme Court—our least accountable and least representative institution of government—in the name of constitutional law. Constitutional law, it appears, is a powerful and amazing force. An understanding of its nature and source is urgently needed, but few subjects of comparable importance are less understood.

Constitutional law is in essence the product of the constitutional decisions of courts and, of course, ultimately of the Supreme Court. As Charles Evans Hughes, later chief justice, pointed out, "We are under a Constitution, but the Constitution is what the judges say it is." [2] Nothing better illustrates this, perhaps, than the fact that "the Constitution," without being relevantly amended, first permitted racial discrimination in public schools in order to separate the races, then prohibited such discrimination, and now often requires such discrimination in order to increase racial mixing. An understanding of the nature and source of constitutional law cannot be derived, however, from facile generalization about the Constitution, the Court, or the theoretical restraints on the Court's power. It can only be derived from careful observation of the Court's actual performance in specific areas of constitutional law, and no area serves so well as that concerning race and the schools. This is not only where the need of understanding constitutional law is most urgent, but also the area in which the modern expansion of the Court's power began and through which its current status in American life and government has largely been achieved.

In 1954, the Supreme Court in *Brown* v. *Board of Education of Topeka* took the apparently daring step of declaring public school racial segregation unconstitutional [3]—although it was not to insist on serious implementation of the prohibition for another decade. The decision, quickly applied to all racial segregation, gave great impetus to a revolution in race relations that was already well underway and that surely was destined to succeed. [4] Of even greater importance than the decision made was the fact that a decision of such magnitude could be made by the Court and could eventually prevail. The result was a drastic change in the perception, both inside and outside the Court, of the Court's role and power in the American system of government.

The Court had in past periods of judicial activism served to impede basic social change [5]—to provide, according to one rationalization, "a sober second thought" [6]—but rarely if ever had it served to initiate or expedite such change. As a consequence of the segregation decision, the Court increasingly became a tempting, willing, and seemingly omnipotent instrument for effecting fundamental social changes without obtaining the consent of the American people or their elected representatives. In the two decades since, the Court has intervened so frequently and decisively on so many issues affecting the essential nature of the American society that it has become, arguably, in domestic affairs at least, the most important institution of American government.

Brown v. *Board of Education* was the beginning. Subsequently, the Court declared Bible reading and all other religious exercises in public schools unconstitutional; it ordered the reapportionment of the national House of Representatives, of both houses of state legislatures, and of local government bodies on a one-man, one-vote basis; it reformed numerous aspects of state and federal criminal procedure, significantly enhancing the rights of the accused, . . . and it laid down a whole set of new rules governing . . . , in effect, the conduct of police throughout the country toward persons arrested on suspicion of crime.

The Court also—needless to say, this listing is not comprehensive—enlarged its own jurisdiction to hear cases challenging federal expenditures . . . and introduced a striking degree of permissiveness into the regulation—what is left of it—by state and federal authorities of material alleged to be obscene. In addition, the Court limited the power of state and federal government to forbid the use of birth-control devices, to restrict travel, to expatriate naturalized or native-born citizens, to deny employment to persons whose associations are deemed subversive, and to apply the laws of libel.

To this listing made by Alexander Bickel in 1970 there may now be added that the Court has severely limited the power of the states to control abortion and has effectively prohibited the use of capital punishment. [7]

On the issue of race and the schools, the Court's enhanced power and status emboldened it to move from *Brown*'s prohibition of segregation—the use of racial discrimination to separate the races—to a vastly more ambitious and questionable requirement of integration or "racial balance," the use of racial discrimination to increase racial mixing beyond the mixing that results from prohibition of racial discrimination. [8] While the *Brown* decision could be understood and justified—as it was at the time—as simply the prohibition of all racial discrimination by government officials, compulsory integration meant that the use of racial discrimination by government officials was not only permitted but, for the first time in our history, constitutionally required. The difficulty of explaining and justifying this new constitutional requirement is perhaps best demonstrated by the fact that the Court has never attempted to do so. Indeed, the Court has never openly stated that it does require school racial integration as such, that school racial separation or imbalance, however caused, is itself unconstitutional. The Court has, instead, continuously purported to require only "desegregation," the undoing or "remedying" of the segregation prohibited in *Brown*, of, that is, school racial separation caused by unconstitutional racial discrimination.

The Court's attempt to present compulsory integration as "desegregation" was greatly facilitated by the confusion as to the meaning of "desegregation" that had been engendered by the Court's unprincipled grant to the South of, in effect, a ten-year grace period in which to comply with *Brown*. The attempt had the enormous advantage for the Court of enabling it to require racial discrimination to integrate while purporting to continue to require only that all racial discrimination and school racial separation caused by school racial discrimination be eliminated. The attempt also obviated all need to justify compulsory integration on its own merits—in terms of any constitutional principle or of its actual or hoped-for effects. Finally, stating that the requirement was, not integration as such, but only desegregation, seemed to confine the applicability of the requirement to the South and, therefore, served to minimize, at first, national attention and concern. The Court's claim to be requiring only desegregation, the remedying of segregation made unconstitutional in *Brown*, had the disadvantage, however, that it did not comport with what the Court was actually doing. Each succeeding decision made clearer that the school racial separation being "remedied" could not be attributed to unconstitutional school segregation and that, in fact, it was simply school racial separation or imbalance itself, however caused, that had become unconstitutional. The increasing gap between what the Court was doing in fact and what it was required to say it was doing in order to maintain its "desegregation" or "remedy" justification for compulsory integration caused it increasingly to resort to methods of decision-making so unprincipled and unscrupulous, so heedless of both fact and reason, and disrespectful of federal statutory law (the 1964 Civil Rights Act) that they would not be tolerated by the American people if practiced by even the avowedly political institutions of American government. Even if compulsory school racial integration could somehow be defended, the performance of the Court in imposing it could not. If, as is often asserted, the Court's extraordinary power in American life rests ultimately on a moral foundation, its power to compel school racial integration rests ultimately on nothing.

Because of the high degree of residential racial separation throughout the nation, it was quickly discovered that a high degree of school racial mixing could not be achieved, especially in urban areas where a majority of blacks now live, except by the selection of children according to race for transportation out of their neighborhoods and away from their neighborhood schools to more distant neighborhoods and schools. The Supreme Court thereupon held that the Constitution so required.[9] This requirement, enormously costly, conferring no known benefit, and inconsistent with the most basic desires of parents to protect and provide for the welfare of their children, has been intensely opposed and resisted. It seems, indeed, to be favored on its own merits by very few, at least insofar as one's own children are involved. Its effects in actual operation have been not to lessen but to increase racial separation and hostility, to undermine support for our public schools, contribute to the deterioration of our cities, and seriously distort our political process.

In a later effort, the Court limited the requirement of busing for school racial balance by holding that a predominantly black urban school district and predominantly white suburban school districts did not have to be consolidated to create schools with a greater percentage of whites, and that the Constitution would be satisfied with busing for racial balance within the urban district alone.[10] While any limitation of a destructive and indefensible requirement must be welcomed, the irrational result was that a requirement whose real purpose is dispersal of black school children among predominantly white schools was found applicable to a school system already overwhelmingly black and certain to become thereby even more completely black more quickly.

Increasing recognition of the indefensibility of compulsory school racial integration or balance has left it with little support except the mistaken belief that it is somehow a requirement of the Constitution. "People have been taught to believe," Felix Frankfurter pointed out in 1937, "that when the Supreme Court speaks it is not they who speak but the Constitution, whereas, of course, in so many vital cases, it is *they* who speak and *not* the Constitution." "And I verily believe," he added, "that this is what the country needs most to understand."[11] What the country needs to understand today in regard to compulsory integration is that, not only has it been imposed by the Supreme Court and not by the Constitution, but it has been imposed by the Court most improperly. Nothing more than this understanding should be necessary to overcome the apparent paralysis that prevents our institutions of representative government from finding means to bring compulsory integration to an end.

2 | The First Revolution: The Supreme Court Prohibits Racial Segregation

In 1954, separation of school children according to race was required by statute in seventeen states and the District of Columbia and made a subject of local ordinance in four additional states. [1] Actions challenging such laws of four representative states and the District were argued before the United States Supreme Court in 1952, reargued in 1953, and decided in May 1954. [2] The state segregation laws were held unconstitutional in *Brown* v. *Board of Education of Topeka* and the District laws in *Bolling* v. *Sharpe*.[3]

Thus began the modern law of race and the schools. Although we have since come a very long way—the distance between prohibiting the use of racial discrimination to separate the races and requiring the use of racial discrimination to mix them— each step has been justified as an implementation of *Brown*. Voluminous scholarly and judicial debate has taken place on the question of "the meaning of *Brown*." The solution to present problems, it would appear, turns to a significant extent on the correct answer to this question.

The meaning of *Brown*, one is initially tempted to say, is simple and clear: laws requiring school assignment on the basis of race to keep the races separate are unconstitutional. The constitutionality of such laws was all that was before the Court for decision and therefore, in legal theory, all the Court could decide. More important, that was, as a practical matter, more than decision enough for that one day. There was little temptation indeed to decide or speak on anything more. The real question at the time was not whether the Court had decided more but whether that much would be accepted and prevail [4]—a question whose answer could be considered in doubt until the *Brown* decision was, in effect, ratified by the Civil Rights Act of 1964. [5] We have come so far so fast since the 1964 act that it has become difficult to remember where we began.

It must also be realized that, in further legal theory, judges do not simply decree a particular result in deciding a case but enunciate and apply principles or rules which determine that result and enable the prediction of future results. Discovery of the "true meaning" of *Brown* depends, therefore, on the discovery of its basic principle. But the theory is an ideal, not an achievable reality. Principles make law and life manageable, but our principles, like the interests they serve, are many and often conflicting—or there would be no difficulty in reaching decisions and, indeed, little to decide. A principle's capacity to determine the future is, therefore, limited. The meaning of a decision or opinion is not an existent entity to be discovered, like a vein of gold, by diligent search; it must, within limits, be supplied by later decision makers. The meaning of *Brown* at any time, at least where racial assignment to separate the races is not involved, is determined by the decisions of that time; those decisions are to a very limited extent determined by *Brown*. There is no escaping the need for making present decisions on the basis of present considerations. One of these considerations, in a legal system, is the existence of past decisions on the same or related problems, but the relevance of those decisions should depend not so much on the justifications given at the earlier time as on the justifications, if any, that can now be found. [6]

Legal theory and the lack of alternatives in seeking certainty or guidance lead to the reading of judicial opinions as scripture. It should be noted, however, at the outset of a detailed examination of judicial opinions, that judges, needing to get on with the business at hand, can no more than others trace the implications of their every word and sentence. Judges may, like others, decide better than they explain, and may, even more than others, be foreclosed from certain explanations. Judges usually may not, for example, officially notice that a constitutional ruling appropriate for Massachusetts may not be appropriate for Mississippi. Because appellate court opinions are to some extent committee products, arguments not entirely consistent with each other sometimes appear. As an unidentified justice of the Court was reported to have said, "It can be very difficult to get one Court opinion, even if people agree with the judgment. To write a Court opinion you have to sew a big enough umbrella for five guys to get under, and that can require some pretty fancy sewing." [7] The difficulty of obtaining a unanimous opinion, as in *Brown*, is, of course, even greater.

Most important, the Supreme Court, in deciding that a challenged governmental action is unconstitutional, is usually faced with an essentially impossible task. Because the Court has no recognized authority to enact its policy preferences into law, it cannot justify its decisions by openly stating and attempting to defend those preferences; it is expected to show that its decisions are derived from the Constitution. The fact is, however, that the provisions of the Constitution—for example, the provisions of the Fourteenth Amendment that "No State shall . . . deprive any person of life, liberty, or property without due process of law; nor deny to any person . . . the equal protection of the laws"—offer little or no guidance to resolution of most of the problems actually brought to the Court. This presents no difficulty, of course, where no finding of unconstitutionality is made. But where unconstitutionality is found, the Court must attempt to show that the decision follows logically from a constitutional provision, typically the Fourteenth Amendment, and that usually cannot be done. The necessary result is that Court opinions attempting to explain and justify its decisions of unconstitutionality often simply do not make sense but depart widely from the usual standards both of rationality and of fair and accurate factual statement. To a large extent, therefore, one who looks in the Court's opinions for an explanation and justification of the Court's decisions invalidating government action is looking for what cannot be found.

Finally, the legal ideal of continuity and stability impels judges to accommodate their decisions to the formulations of prior ones, even with some loss of clarity and candor. Maintaining the appearance of continuity has value, but the cost in rationality and realism can be high. One of the major disadvantages of the policy-making by judges that is inherent in constitutional law is, indeed, that the need to maintain the appearance of continuity and of principled decision-making often leads in particular cases to decisions that would not otherwise be preferred by even the judges that make them.

In technical legal terms, the question for decision in *Brown* was whether school assignment by race in order to separate the races constituted denial to "any person" of "the equal protection of the laws" within the meaning of the Fourteenth Amendment. The reargument of the case in 1953 was "largely devoted to the circumstances surrounding the adoption of the Fourteenth Amendment in 1868." The Court found the results of this search for historical intent to be "at best . . . inconclusive." [8] The fact, whatever its relevance, is that an argument that the Fourteenth Amendment prohibits school racial segregation would have seemed fanciful in 1868. Such segregation was later provided for in the District of Columbia by the very Congress that proposed the amendment, and it existed or was soon thereafter adopted in most or all states with a substantial black population. [9] The Fifteenth Amendment, prohibiting denial of the right to vote on account of race, seems to show that the Fourteenth was not understood as prohibiting even that.

The Court in *Brown* then turned to a review of its prior decisions. Its earliest decisions under the Fourteenth Amendment had interpreted it, the Court stated, as "proscribing all state-imposed discriminations against the Negro race." [10] The first of these, the *Slaughter-House Cases*, had found that the "one pervading purpose" of the Thirteenth, Fourteenth, and Fifteenth Amendments was "the freedom of the slave race, the security and firm establishment of that freedom, and the protection of the newly-made freeman and citizen from the oppressions of those who had formerly exercised unlimited dominion over him." [11] The best statement, perhaps, assigning a meaning to the Fourteenth Amendment was made in 1890 in *Strauder* v. *West Virginia*, quoted in a footnote to the *Brown* opinion and worth requoting.

It ordains that no State shall deprive any person of life, liberty, or property, without due process of law, or deny any person within its jurisdiction the equal protection of the laws. What is this but declaring that the law in the States shall be the same for the black as for the white; that all persons, whether colored or white, shall stand equal before the laws of the States, and, in regard to the colored race, for whose protection the amendment was primarily designed, that no discrimination shall be made against them by law because of their color? The words of the amendment, it is true, are prohibitory, but they contain a necessary implication of a positive immunity, or right, most valuable to the colored race,—the right to exemption from unfriendly legislation against them distinctively as colored,—exemption from legal discriminations, implying inferiority in civil society, lessening the security of their enjoyment of the rights which others enjoy, and discriminations which are steps toward reducing them to the condition of a subject race. [12]

Literally understood, this statement could well have been taken as explanation and justification enough for the *Brown* decision. Laws requiring segregation necessarily meant that "the law in the States" was not "the same for the black as for the white." Very little more was necessary in 1954 to show, with almost equal certainty, that such laws were in fact "unfriendly legislation against [blacks] distinctively as colored." [13] The difficulty, however, was that post-*Strauder* Supreme Court decisions had interpreted the Fourteenth Amendment as permitting segregation and, specifically, school segregation. These decisions, therefore, had to be dealt with by the Court in *Brown*. The Court's attempt to do so without explicitly overruling them and to establish continuity with later pre-*Brown* decisions accounts for the reasoning used by the Court in the remainder of its *Brown* opinion. Because it is this reasoning that much later became the source of dispute as to the meaning of *Brown*, the pre-*Brown* school segregation cases must be briefly considered.

"Separate but Equal": The Early Cases

That racial segregation did not offend the Constitution was first established in a case not concerned with schools. In 1896, in *Plessy* v. *Ferguson*, [14] the Court upheld a Louisiana statute requiring "equal but separate accommodations for the white and colored races" in passenger trains. The Court agreed with the earlier cases that "the object of the [fourteenth] amendment was undoubtedly to enforce the absolute equality of the two races before the law," but no legally enforced inequality was found: If "enforced separation of the two races stamps the colored race with a badge of inferiority, . . .

it is not by reason of anything found in the act, but solely because the colored race chooses to put that construction upon it." Although *Plessy* was not a school case, the Court relied on state court decisions upholding school segregation under state constitutions. It also found the Louisiana law no more objectionable than the "acts of Congress requiring separate schools for colored children in the District of Columbia"[15]—the obverse of the reasoning to be used in *Bolling* v. *Sharpe* when those acts of Congress were invalidated on the basis of the invalidation of the state segregation laws in *Brown*. [16] Only Justice John Marshall Harlan dissented, arguing in his famous opinion that "our Constitution is color-blind." [17]

A case involving school segregation itself came to the Court three years later, in 1899, in a procedurally complex setting, in *Cumming* v. *Richmond County Board of Education*. The Court found no violation of the Fourteenth Amendment in the refusal of the Georgia courts to enjoin the operation of a public high school only for whites until one should be provided for blacks. [18] Despite his *Plessy* dissent, Justice Harlan wrote the opinion of a unanimous Court. [19] In *Berea College* v. *Kentucky* (1908), the Court upheld a state statute requiring segregation even by private schools. [20]

The third and last school segregation case to deny all relief to an objecting plaintiff was *Gong Lum* v. *Rice*, decided in 1927. A girl of Chinese ancestry, "of good moral character . . . a citizen and an educable child," sought admission to the white rather than the black school for her area. The Court, in a unanimous opinion written by Chief Justice William Howard Taft, treated the constitutionality of school racial segregation as settled. "Were this a new question," he said, "it would call for very full argument and consideration, but we think that it is the same question which has been many times decided to be within the constitutional power of the state legislature to settle without intervention of the federal courts under the Federal Constitution." "Assuming" the many state and lower federal court cases on the question "to be rightly decided," he said, school racial segregation "does not conflict with the Fourteenth Amendment." *Plessy*, indeed, settled "a more difficult question." [21]

"Separate but Equal": The Graduate School Cases

In the 1930s, the National Association for the Advancement of

Colored People (NAACP) initiated and led a campaign against school segregation by financing and otherwise assisting litigation in the federal courts. The decision was made to begin with higher education, especially law schools, where, it was hoped, the near impossibility of attaining equality and the absence of any valid need for segregation would be most easily seen by judges. [22] The campaign bore fruit in the Court's next decision on the question of segregation, *Missouri* ex rel. *Canada* v. *Gaines*, in 1938. [23]

Missouri maintained a law school for whites and, "pending" establishment of a law school for blacks, offered qualified blacks tuition payments in law schools in adjacent states. The Court, in a somewhat confusing opinion by Chief Justice Charles Evans Hughes, with two justices dissenting, held that this arrangement was unconstitutional. The equality of the legal education offered blacks and whites was, he wrote,"beside the point." The question was not the quality of the training supplied the plaintiff by the state, but "its duty when it provides such training to furnish it to the residents of the State upon the basis of an equality of right. By the operation of the laws of Missouri a privilege has been created for white law students which is denied to negroes because of their race." [24] If court opinions were exercises in logic, it would appear that the doctrine of "separate but equal" had been rejected, at least with regard to education. If the issue of equality is irrelevant and a black cannot "by reason of race" be denied a "privilege" offered whites regardless of the quality of what he is offered, it is racial discrimination itself that is impermissible. There is no peculiar or necessary inequality in the fact that the offered facilities are outside the state; they might, in fact, be more convenient or otherwise superior for an individual applicant.

The relief actually granted the plaintiff by the Court, however, in effect affirmed the "separate but equal" doctrine even for law schools. The state was not required to admit the plaintiff to the white law school, but only "to furnish him within its borders facilities for legal education substantially equal to those which the State there afforded for persons of the white race." [25] Ten years later, in 1948, in *Sipuel* v. *Board of Regents*, the Court held, *per curiam* (by the Court, without an opinion by an individual justice), that Oklahoma must provide legal education for blacks "as soon" as it provided it for whites. [26] In a later opinion in the case, the Court refused to order admission of the plaintiff to the white law school, noting that the case did not "present the issue whether a state might not satisfy the equal protection clause of the Fourteenth Amendment by establishing a separate law school for Negroes." [27]

The Court next confronted the question of school segregation, for the last time before *Brown*, in two cases decided together in 1950. In *Sweatt* v. *Painter* the plaintiff was a qualified black applicant who was refused admission to the University of Texas Law School because of race but was offered admission, some years later, to a separate facility created during the course of the litigation. Confining its decision "as narrowly as possible," the Court refused to reconsider *Plessy* or its application to law school education. Instead, unlike the Court in *Gaines*, it considered the question of whether the alternative offered the plaintiff was in fact equal. The new law school was found to be unequal to the University of Texas Law School not only in physical and material respects but, "what is more important," in "those qualities which are incapable of objective measurement but which make for greatness in a law school." These intangible qualities included "reputation of the faculty, experience of the administration, position and influence of the alumni, standing in the community, traditions and prestige." [28]

The other case, *McLaurin* v. *Oklahoma State Regents*, involved a black who had been admitted, pursuant to court order, to a graduate school of the University of Oklahoma but subjected to a series of gradually diminishing restrictions. He was, for example, first required to "sit apart at a designated desk in an anteroom adjoining the classroom, " then in a railed-off section of the classroom marked "Reserved for Colored," and, at the time of the decision, was assigned to a separate table in the library and the cafeteria. The Court found that these restrictions handicapped him in "his pursuit of effective graduate instruction," "his ability to study, to engage in discussions and exchange views with other students, and, in general, to learn his profession." It held that "under these circumstances the Fourteenth Amendment precludes differences in treatment by the state based upon race. Appellant, having been admitted to a state-supported graduate school, must receive the same treatment at the hands of the state as students of other races." [29]

The Court's Basis for *Brown*

Pursuant to the judicial tradition of creating an appearance of continuity even while effecting a complete reversal of direction, the Court in *Brown* made a weak attempt to show that its decision could be reconciled with those from *Plessy* to *Gaines* and made to follow from those beginning with *Gaines.* Instead of openly overruling *Plessy*'s permission for segregation as inconsistent with *Strauder* and other early decisions and with any semblance of racial equality in law or fact, the Court seemingly distinguished it from *Brown* (found its principle inapplicable) because it involved "not education, but transportation." *Cumming* and *Gong Lum*, which did involve education, were disposed of with the statement that in them "the validity of the [*Plessy*] doctrine itself was not challenged," and *Berea College* was merely cited with a "See also" in a footnote. The Court then undertook to show that its decision was based on the later cases. The "intangible considerations" relied on in *Sweatt* and *McLaurin* to show inequality between graduate schools applied, the Court said, "with added force to children in grade and high schools." [30] This contention was unnecessary except to find support in *Sweatt* and *McLaurin*, and it is questionable as a statement of fact—the intangibles relied on in *Sweatt* and *McLaurin* would seem more important in distinguishing between graduate schools than in distinguishing between grade and high schools. Nonetheless, it is the Court's explanation of this contention that has given rise to most of the subsequent controversy about the "meaning" of *Brown*.

"To separate" grade and high school children, the Court said, "from others of similar age and qualifications solely because of their race generates a feeling of inferiority as to their status in the community that may affect their hearts and minds in a way unlikely ever to be undone." The effect "on their educational opportunities was well stated by a finding" by a district court in one of the cases:

Segregation of white and colored children in public schools has a detrimental effect upon the colored children. The impact is greater when it has the sanction of the law; for the policy of separating the races is usually interpreted as denoting the inferiority of the negro group. A sense of inferiority affects the motivation of a child to learn. Segregation with the sanction of law, therefore, has a tendency to [retard] the educational and mental development of negro children and to deprive them of some of the benefits they would receive in a racial[ly] integrated school system.

"Whatever may have been the extent of psychological knowledge at the time of *Plessy* v. *Ferguson*," the Court continued, this district court "finding is amply supported by modern authority." The Court then cited, in its famous footnote 11, several psychological and sociological writings on questions of race. [31]

This conventional effort by the Court to support its decision by showing continuity with prior ones was in this instance badly mistaken for several reasons. If it is taken at all seriously, it must be taken as showing a serious misapprehension by the justices of the limits of their competence and the competence of the quoted district judge. Judges in constitutional cases typically assume an expertise on questions of American ideals or values, but rarely had they assumed the expertise necessary to decide so difficult and controverted a question of empirical or scientific fact. For judges to presume to decide such questions as the determinant of "the motivation of a child to learn" or of the "educational and mental development of negro children" is to be disrespectful of both the difficulty and the possibility of gaining useful knowledge about such matters. The dangers involved in such presumption could hardly be better illustrated than by *Brown* itself. As many commentators—both those supporting and those attacking the decision—quickly pointed out, the "finding" that school segregation had adverse educational effects on blacks was not in fact "amply supported," if supported at all, by scientific knowledge. [32]

The "modern authority" primarily relied on by the Court for its statement of the psychological effects of segregation on black children was social psychologist Kenneth B. Clark, who was the author first cited by the Court in footnote 11, who had prepared a statement signed by thirty-two social scientists that was made an appendix to the NAACP's brief for the plaintiffs in *Brown*, [33] and who had testified as an expert witness for the NAACP at the trial of several of the cases consolidated in *Brown*. Clark's published statements and testimony on the psychological effects of segregation on black children were based on an experiment he conducted with groups of black children aged three to seven in segregated southern schools and unsegregated northern schools. Clark showed the children a brown doll with black hair and a light-colored doll with blonde hair and asked them to pick the one that is "nice" and the one that "looks like you." He found that many of the black children in segregated schools picked the white doll, and he testified that this showed that "a fundamental effect of segregation is basic confusion in individuals and their concepts about themselves" and that the black children had "been definitely harmed in the development of their personalities." Clark's own data showed, however, that a *smaller* percentage of black children picked the white doll in segregated schools than in unsegregated schools. As Ernest Van den Haag pointed out, Clark had testified that "he was proving that 'segregation inflicts injuries upon the Negro' by the very tests which, if they prove anything—which is doubtful—prove the opposite!" [34] Hadley Arkes later noted that "it was not until after the *Brown* case had been decided that Clark took note of this embarrassment in the data," that "if the injury was shown in the tendency of black children to reject their blackness, then it was the children in the North, in the less segregated settings, who had exhibited these injuries to the greatest degree." Clark's explanation was: "The apparent emotional stability of the Southern Negro child may be indicative only of the fact that through rigid racial segregation and isolation he has accepted as normal the fact of his inferior social status. Such an acceptance is not symptomatic of a healthy personality." Arkes commented:

This was, several years before *Catch-22*, a minor advance on the times. The Negro child showed injury to his personality either way—if he rejected his color or if he accepted it. This kind of flexibility might be quite admirable at times, but it only raised here a serious question about the grounds on which the decision in *Brown* had been justified. [35]

The fact seems to be, as a strong supporter of integration stated, referring to the "evidence on the educational impact of desegregation," that "there was none at the time of *Brown*." The evidence that has become available since *Brown*, it might be added, still does not show that racial mixing in schools is an aid to black educational achievement. [36] If justification of the *Brown* decision depended on the Court's explanation of why segregated schools were necessarily unequal, the decision would still lack justification.

The lack of support for the Court's statement that segregation had adverse educational effects on black children led to denunciation of *Brown*, not only as applied social science rather than law, but as bad social science, and it nourished the hope, or at least the argument, that further consideration of the evidence or of new evidence would lead to permitting segregation again. No further consideration of evidence, however, was to be allowed. [37] But the *Brown* decision did not in fact turn on a finding of educational harm from grade school segregation, as was in effect at once admitted in *Bolling* v. *Sharpe*, [38] which involved the District of Columbia and was decided the same day as *Brown*. Because the Fourteenth Amendment applies only to the states and not to the federal government, the "equal protection" clause was not available to the Court. Because constitutional provisions have little to do with constitutional law, however, this presented no difficulty. The "due process" clause of the Fifth Amendment [39] is applicable to the federal government, and school segregation in the District was found to violate that. Although *Plessy* had purportedly not been overruled but only "distinguished" as not involving education, the prohibition of school segregation was now based on a simple prohibition of racial discrimination, on the "principle 'that the Constitution of the United States, in its present form, forbids, so far as civil and political rights are concerned, discrimination by the General Government or by the States against any citizen because of his race.' "[40]

That *Brown* did not turn on a finding of educational harm to black children and was seen by the Court as simply a prohibition of racial discrimination was further shown seven days later when the Court, *per curiam*, reversed and remanded "for consideration in the light" of *Brown* a group of decisions upholding racial segregation in a state law school, a state university, and a public park. [41] Within a year, the Court, simply citing *Brown*, invalidated racial segregation in recreation facilities and, within two years, in transportation itself. [42]

In these circumstances, the Court's attempts to avoid overruling *Plessy*'s permission for racial discrimination on the ground that *Plessy* did not involve education and to show that *Brown* followed from *Sweatt* and *McLaurin* because "intangible considerations" of educational equality "apply with added force" to grade school segregation served not to strengthen but only to obfuscate the *Brown* decision. The attempts undermined the relatively simple, clear, and defensible justification for the decision with which the Court started: the Fourteenth Amendment should be interpreted as "proscribing all state-imposed discrimination against the Negro race." To depart from this justification was unnecessarily to provide arguments for opponents of the decision and handicap its defenders.

The Justification for the *Brown* Decision

Because there are no eternal certainties, the justification for a decision is, like all explanations, a matter of adequacy rather than of absoluteness. A decision is adequately justified if it is or can be based on a principle whose validity and applicability few will openly or persuasively challenge. No principle is more generally accepted, appealing on its face, or basic to American ideals than that a human being or, at least, an American citizen in America should not be disadvantaged by government because of his race or ancestry. It is no use to pretend that even this principle is an absolute, that it answers all racial questions and obviates the need for further thought, but it may be as close to a useful absolute as any we have.

If one accepts this principle, as nearly all do, no more is required to justify the *Brown* decision—assuming that the issue was a proper one for the Court to decide—than to show that the individuals involved were in fact disadvantaged by school segregation. No resort to psychology is necessary to show this. The psychological argument— that segregation "generates a feeling of inferiority"—seems to suggest, as *Plessy* noted, that the difficulty lies in black attitudes, misapprehension, or, perhaps, excessive sensitivity. [48] An individual is necessarily disadvantaged when he is confined to association with only a part of the society. Each white was also so confined, but a disadvantage is not removed by making it universal, and even if the general disadvantage of segregation was relevant, the black is clearly more disadvantaged than the white, as a matter of arithmetic, by being confined to association with the smaller group— and the group with less than even a proportionate share of wealth and influence.

Apart from numbers, school segregation under conditions of equality is often not economically feasible or physically possible. Segregation was possible in the South for so long only because the supposed requirement of equality was, as the *Cumming* case illustrates, often virtually ignored. [44] Funds may not be available for two effective school systems; the number of interested persons necessary for many activities or programs may also not be available in a divided school system. There is no way that a trip of ten, five, or even two miles can be made no more disadvantageous than a trip of only one mile. A serious insistence on equality in education would make segregation impractical or impossible in enough situations to defeat segregation in principle, make efforts to maintain it seem not worthwhile, and amount to prohibition by an alternative route. There is no need to consider either psychological effects or legislative motives to show as an empirical fact, as demonstrable and certain as nearly any, that segregation is disadvantageous to at least some of the individuals involved; the contrary is rarely asserted. That is the justification for the *Brown* decision, and few constitutional decisions can be justified so well. [45]

The *Brown* decision, it is interesting to note in light of later developments, was urged upon the Court by the NAACP on the ground that "The Fourteenth Amendment prevents states from according differential treatment to American children on the basis of their color or race." Justice Felix Frankfurter asked Thurgood Marshall, the general counsel of the NAACP, who was arguing for some of the plaintiffs in *Brown*, "You mean, if we reverse, it will not entitle every mother to have her child go to a nonsegregated school?" Marshall replied, "The school board, I assume, would find some other method of distributing the children, a recognizable method, by drawing district lines." He later stated to the Court: "The only thing that the Court is dealing with . . . [is] whether or not race can be used. . . . What we want from the Court is the striking down of race. . . . Put the dumb colored children in with the dumb white children, and put the smart colored children with the smart white children—that is no problem." [46] Unfortunately, the NAACP and Marshall, when he was appointed a justice of the Court, were later to argue, not that race could not be used in assigning children to school, but that the *Brown* decision, properly understood, required that it be used.

The appeal and general acceptance of a simple prohibition of all official racial discrimination are so great, indeed, that it is hardly possible to quarrel with the *Brown* decision—as distinct from the opinion—except on the ground that so important a social change should not have been made by unelected, lifetime appointees. The *Brown* case was less a traditional law suit than a call for a social revolution, and in a healthy democracy social revolutions are made by elected representatives authorized to effectuate their political views and accountable for the results. The fact that this revolution was made, or greatly advanced, by judges soon led to many other revolutions, much less justifiable, being made in the same way.

3 | *"With All Deliberate Speed":*
A Time for Caution

A Reprieve for Segregation

The limited, almost tentative, approach of the Court to its decision invalidating school segregation is best illustrated by the fact that the Court failed to grant effective relief, even with regard to the nominal plaintiffs, individual black school children. If racial discrimination in the assignment of pupils to schools is unconstitutional, the remedy seems obvious and simple: assignment not based on race. The Court, however, found the question sufficiently difficult to require further argument the following year. Reargument resulted in a further disappointment for plaintiffs in 1955. The Court, in *Brown* II, again failed to grant specific immediate relief, remanding the question instead, but providing very little guidance, to the district courts. The ultimate objective was clear: admission to public schools "on a racially nondiscriminatory basis." But it was first necessary, the Court found, "to achieve a system of determining admission" on such a basis, and such "a system" was to be instituted, not at once, but "as soon as practicable" and "with all deliberate speed." Although a year had already elapsed since *Brown* I, the Court required, not full compliance with that decision, but only "a prompt and reasonable start toward full compliance." The Court continued:

Once such a start has been made, the courts may find that additional time is necessary to carry out the ruling in an effective manner. The burden rests upon the defendants to establish that such time is necessary in the public interest and is consistent with good faith compliance at the earliest practicable date. To that end, the courts may consider problems related to administration, arising from the physical condition of the school plant, the school transportation system, personnel, revision of school districts and attendance areas into compact units to achieve a system of determining admission to the public schools on a nonracial basis, and revision of local laws and regulations which may be necessary in solving the foregoing problems. They will also consider the adequacy of any plans the defendants may propose to meet these problems and to effectuate a transition to a racially nondiscriminatory school system. [1]

Despite this explicit authorization of delay in effectuating a constitutional right, the Court declared that "it should go without saying that the vitality of these constitutional principles cannot be allowed to yield simply because of disagreement with them." [2] There was, however, little reason for this unprecedented allowance of delay except anticipated disagreement and resistance. There was never any danger that *Brown* I would be effectuated sooner than "practicable." Where dissatisfaction with a court decision is great, as it was here, there is always available as a source of delay the argument that the decision applies only to the parties before the court. More important, undesired laws do not enforce themselves; money, time, and initiative are required, and the resources of the NAACP, which for many years bore almost the whole burden of seeking compliance, were not without limit. In law, "at once" ordinarily means "as soon as practicable," with no further dispensation necessary. No one argued or imagined that children still in segregated schools in May 1955, when *Brown* II was decided, would be assigned without regard to race sooner than the following September, at the beginning of the next school year. That the problems the district courts were authorized to consider did not usually require still more time was evident from the effective steps to end segregation quickly taken by the border states and the District of Columbia. "By the opening of the [1955] fall term in the following year only eight states remained completely segregated in their system of public schools; and more than a quarter of a million Negro children were attending desegregated schools in states which had the year before *required* segregation." [3]

The assignment of children on a nonracial basis to their neighborhood schools is not usually an exceptionally difficult or time-consuming process. It seems that the "re-districting, reassigning of students and mapping new school bus routes" that would have been necessary for the school systems involved in the cases decided in *Brown* "could mostly have been solved in a few weeks or months." [4] The reasons for delay cited by the Court are not impressive. Concern with "the physical condition of the school plant" suggested that whites could not be expected to go to the schools previously provided for blacks; nonracial assignment would ordinarily require less, not more, in the way of transportation and personnel; enforcement of *Brown* certainly would not require awaiting revisions of inconsistent "local laws and regulations." There was certainly no thought at the time that anything more than neighborhood assignment might be required: The Court had explicitly set for reargument in *Brown* II the question whether "within the limits set by normal geographic school districting, Negro children should forthwith be admitted to schools of their choice." [5] The Court thus contemplated that not even assignment to neighborhood schools would be required, but that a free choice of schools would be enough, and even freedom of choice was not required "forthwith," but was to be made available with "all deliberate speed"—that is, gradually.

The Court's refusal to grant relief, even to the parties before it, was unfortunate for several reasons. First, it was likely to be interpreted—and it was—as vacillation, as uncertainty on the part of the Court that its new law would prevail. The refusal seemed to promise, despite the Court's disclaimer, that opposition would prove successful in achieving at least a more lengthy delay.

From across the South came slightly suppressed expressions of elation from officials at the nature of the decree. Of particular joy was the failure of the Supreme Court to set a deadline for compliance. Some even called it "a victory for the South" and felt that the decree was the "mildest" possible without the high court's actually reversing itself. [6]

If a bitter pill is to be swallowed, it is probably better to require that it be swallowed at once. [7] There was undoubtedly ground for the Court to fear, as Alexander Bickel has argued in defense of its authorization of delay, that its new law could not be made to prevail for some time, [8] but it is nonetheless a mistake for a lawmaking institution to make its uncertainty and indecision manifest. The appearance of confidence and finality, even when the reality is lacking, can breed respect and acceptance.

Second, leaving the question of relief to the district courts with an explicit authorization of delay depending on "good faith" and "the public interest" put those courts in an untenable position. Familiarity with, and responsiveness to, local conditions are valuable in decision-making, but the relevant local condition in this context was the intensity of the opposition to ending segregation. The only defense a local judge could have had for ending segregation was the clear and irresistible mandate of higher authority, and that mandate the Court did not provide. [9]

Third, the Court's decision lost sight of the individual plaintiffs, whose rights, in legal theory, provided the Court's only warrant for making a decision. The Court, according to the theory, may invalidate legislation, not in order to substitute the social policy it prefers, but only as incidental to enforcing the constitutional rights of the parties before it. The theory is hardly tenable and had long been abandoned in practice, but never so openly. Louis Lusky noted:

> Conceptually, the "deliberate speed" formula is impossible to justify. . . . Since [its beginning] judicial review has been founded in the judicial duty to give a *litigant* his rights under the Constitution. But the apparently successful plaintiff in the *Brown* case got no more than a promise that, some time in the indefinite future, other people would be given the rights which the Court said he had. [10]

Individual interests, it is true, must often be subordinated to the interests of effective legal administration; despite the ideal of individual worth, classification—the treatment of an individual as part of a group—is necessary. Again, no absolute can be stated. The Court's refusal to grant plaintiffs individual relief, however, in effect utilized the very classification by race it began by condemning. The most charitable interpretation is that the Court chose to ignore the interests of the individual blacks before it in favor of a supposed interest of racial groups—an approach that, as in *Plessy*, has been a major source of injustice to blacks throughout our history.

> One of the subtler manifestations of this viewpoint [the group stereotype of blacks] is the notion that Negroes (unlike whites) possess rights as a race rather than as individuals, so that a particular Negro can rightly be delayed in the enjoyment of his established rights if progress is being made in improving the legal status of Negroes generally. . . .
> It is hard to avoid the conclusion that this premise infects the so-called "deliberate speed" formula. . . . The Court had determined to deal with the problem as involving the rights of the Negro race rather than the rights of individuals. Citing the traditional power of courts of equity to shape remedies so as to reconcile public and private needs, the Court applied that power in a way that is believed to be unprecedented. It

left open the possibility that the plaintiffs themselves would be denied any relief from the legal wrong they were found to have suffered, if only steps were taken to protect other Negroes—at some later date—from similar harm. [11]

Even when practiced with the most benign motives, racism has undesirable effects. If the Court's later reimposition of racial classification can find support in *Brown* II, as the Court was to state, [12] it is in this racist element of *Brown* II.

By far the most unfortunate consequence of the Court's refusal to decree relief, however, was that it enormously complicated and confused the issues. Instead of a relatively simple requirement of "immediate" assignment to schools without regard to race, the Court introduced the ultimate complexities and uncertainties of an inquiry into "good faith" and "the public interest." In place of nonracial assignment, the requirement became the production of a "desegregation plan." The issue for litigation thereafter was not simply whether assignment was in fact nonracial, but when this type of assignment would be required and under what circumstances something less would suffice. This issue—the acceptability of different desegregation plans—was to be litigated for more than a decade. Under cover of the resulting confusion and delay, the original prohibition of segregation was metamorphosed into a requirement of integration. The time for ending racial assignment to separate the races eventually came, but the requirement of the desegregation plan remained, and racial assignment—this time, to integrate—returned. That this drastic change had been made was never openly admitted and, therefore, did not have to be justified. The discussion continued in terms of desegregation and desegregation plans, but the change was not less complete because of that.

A Decade of Hesitation by the Court

For a decade after *Brown*, the most remarkable thing about the Supreme Court's action with respect to school segregation is that it acted so little. Having declared the war, it largely withdrew from the battle. The prohibition of racial segregation in grade and high school education was rapidly extended to segregation in all areas of public life, but without further discussion by the Court. [13] As to grade and high school segregation, the Court denied all applications for review until 1958, when it broke its silence in two cases, *Cooper* v. *Aaron*—the famous Little Rock case—and *Shuttlesworth* v. *Birmingham Board of Education.* [14]

Compliance with *Brown*, in varying degrees, was fairly prompt in the District of Columbia and nine of the seventeen states that had racial segregation in 1954. As early as 1955, some blacks had been assigned to schools on a nonracial basis in all but eight states. In these eight, however, *Brown* met strong resistance. After much talk of "nullification," "interposition," and "massive resistance," the chief means soon settled upon for minimizing or avoiding compliance were the so-called pupil placement laws. [15]

The usual method of assignment to schools when a school district is large enough to have more than one is the creation of geographic attendance zones around each school; all students who live in a zone are assigned to the school in their zone. To maintain school segregation where there was some residential integration, as was common in the South, a dual zone system, with separate but overlapping zones for each race, was necessary. Assignment according to race could have been ended by simply abolishing this dual system and assigning children to schools strictly on the basis of neighborhood—although the fact that the schools had been built and situated for a segregated system would often make their location and capacity less than ideal. Substantial racial mixing, however, would have resulted, and means to avoid this were sought. There was no doubt at the time that, although racial discrimination was to be gradually ended, there was no requirement of racial mixing as such. The most frequently quoted statement was that of the highly respected Circuit Judge John Parker, writing for a three-judge court on the remand of one of the cases decided in *Brown:*

[The Supreme Court] has not decided that the states must mix persons of different races in the schools or must require them to attend schools or must deprive them of the right of choosing the schools they attend. What it has decided, and all that it has decided, is that a state may not deny to any person on account of race the right to attend any school that it maintains. . . . The Constitution, in other words, does not require integration. It merely forbids discrimination. [16]

Children already in a school at the time of *Brown*, although originally assigned because of their race, presumably could be reassigned to that school for the nonracial reason of maintaining educational continuity. Similarly, they might be assigned to a higher school on the basis of the lower school attended or to a school being attended by a sibling, even though the original assignments were on a racial basis. A difficult problem arose, however, with regard to students new to the school system—beginning students and students who had recently moved into the school district. Pupil placement laws were rapidly enacted throughout the deep South to overcome this difficulty by abolishing all attendance zones and requiring the assignment of children individually on the basis of several ostensibly nonracial factors.

Assignment based on individual consideration of each child, however, is hardly feasible, and, in practice, racial assignment of new students simply continued according to the dual zone system. The pupil placement laws typically set up administrative procedures whereby reassignment according to the factors specified in the law could be requested. In 1956, the Fourth Circuit found the North Carolina Pupil Placement Act not unconstitutional on its face and held that the plaintiff black children, still assigned to the school formerly for blacks, fifteen miles out of the town, could not challenge the constitutionality of their assignment until they had exhausted their administrative remedies under the act. In 1957, the Supreme Court let this decision stand.[17]

Arkansas had not yet enacted a pupil placement law when the Little Rock school board—somewhat a model of expedition at the time—adopted a plan in 1955 that was later approved by a district court and a court of appeals. Racial assignment was to be replaced by geographic assignment in 1957 at the senior high school level, and at lower levels in successive years—the "stair-step" method—until, as the Supreme Court noted, "complete desegregation would be accomplished by 1963." After the disturbances that followed Governor Orval Faubus' use of the National Guard to keep black children from entering the formerly white high school, the board petitioned for permission to delay implementation of the plan. In *Cooper* v. *Aaron,* decided September 1958, the Court held that conditions "directly traceable to the actions of legislators and executive officials of the State" were not grounds for additional delay. Reviewing the "prompt and reasonable start" and "all deliberate speed" requirements of *Brown* II, the Court said:

> Of course, in many locations, obedience to the duty of desegregation would require the immediate general admission of Negro children, otherwise qualified as students for their appropriate classes, at particular schools. On the other hand, a District Court, after analysis of the relevant factors (which, of course, excludes hostility to racial desegregation), might conclude that justification existed for not requiring the present nonsegregated admission of all qualified Negro children.[18]

Thus, although the principle of *Brown* I was reaffirmed, it was also made clear that, even after four years, the time for the end of racial assignment had not yet come.[19]

Two months later, in *Shuttlesworth* v. *Birmingham Board of Education*,[20] the Court passed upon the Alabama School Placement Act, a law which had become a model for other states. The act provided that pupils were to be assigned and transferred to schools and to classes within schools on the basis of sixteen vague factors that were apparently sufficient to ensure that no integration would occur. They included

> the psychological qualification of the pupil for the type of teaching and association involved; . . . the psychological effect upon the pupil of attendance at a particular school; the possibility of threat of friction or disorder among pupils or others; the possibility of breaches of the peace or ill will or economic retaliation within the community; . . . the maintenance or severance of established social and psychological relationships with other pupils and with teachers.[21]

As if to remove any doubt, the act explicitly provided that, upon the written objection of a parent or guardian, "no child shall be compelled to attend any school in which the races are commingled."[22] Under the act, no black in Alabama had been assigned to attend the same school as a white.[23] In a suit by black school children, alleging that racial assignment continued as before, a three-judge district court denied relief, finding that the plaintiffs had not proved the existence of racial discrimination and holding the law constitutional *"upon its face."*[24] The Supreme Court granted certiorari (that is, agreed to review the decision) and, in a one-sentence *per curiam* opinion, affirmed "upon the limited ground on which the District Court rested its decision."[25]

A sigh of relief almost audible arose in many quarters of the

land. If Alabama had discovered the answer to compliance with
Brown, the terrors of *Brown* had indeed been greatly overstated.
Legal analysts could argue that the decision, properly understood,
was very limited. But its impact was unmistakable. There is
more justification than some legal scholars care to admit for the
unscholarly belief that the significance of a Supreme Court
decision lies more in the immediate result reached—who wins
and who loses—than in the explanation given. A close observer
of this area of the law stated at the time:

> While not so dramatic as the running Little Rock tragedy, with its
> federal troops, international publicity, and special session of the Court,
> this case in many ways seems the most significant event since the
> *Brown* decision. For here the Court authoritatively stamped an assignment
> law, passed for the specific purpose of meeting *Brown*, as at least
> not illegal per se. This was a real victory for moderation, orderly
> processes, and perhaps for undisrupted operation of southern schools.
> Surely the judges know that an assignment law will retard widespread,
> indiscriminate mixing of races, which some people interpret "desegrega-
> tion" to mean. Surely the judiciary understands that desegregation
> under those laws will come slowly and only after state or local officials
> have had full opportunity to consider the case of each pupil.
> And the judges undoubtedly realize it was the hope of the state
> legislators that the assignment statutes would do just these things
> and perhaps more. [26]

The decision, in the words of the United States Civil Rights
Commission, "gave great impetus to reliance on pupil placement
plans by Southern States as a means of meeting legal requirements
with little or no actual desegregation." [27]

Pupil placement laws amounted to little more than invitations
to litigation. The requirement that plaintiffs follow the administrative procedures provided by such laws meant that the validity
of a challenged assignment was more likely to be made moot, by
the challenging pupil's graduation from the school, than decided.
Limits imposed on class actions meant that relief, if obtainable,
would apply only to individual complainants. Because segregation
had to be ended only gradually—not in all grades at once—there
was usually the question of what speed should be required as
well as questions about the administration of the pupil placement
laws in the grades for which the time to end segregation had come.
Cooper's further authorization of delay and *Shuttlesworth*'s apparent

endorsement of pupil placement as a means of ending segregation ensured that litigation of these issues would long occupy the lower federal courts; it did occupy them into the early 1960s. By about 1962, however, the procedural obstacles to effective litigation challenging segregation were largely overcome, and it was generally established that making the pupil placement system applicable to pupils initially assigned according to race was not a permissible means of ending segregation in any school or grade when the time to do so had come. [28] This eventual insistence that the dual zone system of initial assignment by race be abolished meant that the usefulness of pupil placement laws had ended.

Aside from its response to Governor Faubus' defiance, the Court did not issue another signed opinion on school segregation until 1963, when it decided *Goss* v. *Board of Education of Knoxville, Tennessee.* The lower courts had approved desegregation plans providing for school assignment according to nonracial attendance zones but authorizing transfer upon the request of any student who would as a result of assignment by neighborhood be assigned to a school formerly serving the other race or where he would be in the racial minority—this is known as a minority-to-majority transfer. Reaffirming *Brown* as a case "in which racial classifications" were "held to be invalid," a unanimous Court, in an opinion by Justice Tom Clark, reversed the decision of the lower courts. The use of race as a criterion for granting transfers was "no less unconstitutional than its use for original admission or subsequent assignment to public schools." The Court twice noted, however, that transfer provisions not explicitly based on race would present "an entirely different case."[29]

The result was to corroborate further that *Brown* I meant simply a prohibition of the use of race in making school assignments. The Court also took the occasion, however, to indicate that the time for delay under *Brown* II was running out: "Now, however, eight years after this decree was rendered and over nine years after the first *Brown* decision, the context in which we must interpret and apply this language ['earliest practicable date' and 'all deliberate speed'] to plans for desegregation has been significantly altered."[30]

The pace of the Court's decisions now quickened. The following year brought to the Court the particularly provocative situation in *Griffin* v. *County School Board of Prince Edward County*. The county had been a defendant in one of the original cases consolidated in *Brown* and became thereafter a focus of Virginia's policy of "massive resistance" to ending segregation.[31] The "successful" plaintiffs in the original suit had, of course, never been assigned to schools on a nonracial basis. When admission without regard to race was finally ordered by the district court in 1959, the county, acting under state authorization and with the avowed purpose of avoiding integration, closed its public schools. State and county tuition grants and tax credits were provided to assist attendance at "private" schools, none of which, of course, admitted both blacks and whites.

The district court enjoined the county officials from providing such support while the public schools remained closed. There was little difficulty with the proposition that a prohibition of school racial discrimination by the state includes prohibition of direct and substantial state financial support of racially discriminatory schools, and the Supreme Court unanimously affirmed the district court's holding. The Court went on to state, however, with Justices Clark and John Marshall Harlan (the second) dissenting, that the district court was also authorized to require county officials to levy taxes and operate and maintain a public school system like that of other Virginia counties "if necessary to prevent further racial discrimination." How a prohibition of racial discrimination could require maintaining a public school system was not explained. The Court announced, instead, that "the time for mere 'deliberate speed' has run out, and that phrase can no longer justify denying these Prince Edward County school children their constitutional rights to an education equal to that afforded by the public schools in the other parts of Virginia."[32]

There had surely been time enough for compliance with *Brown* I, but the suggestion that compliance required public schools to be maintained was nothing more than the Court's first utilization of the confusion engendered by *Brown* II. Passage of the 1964 Civil Rights Act was now less than two months away, and the position of the Court had very much changed. No longer fearing that *Brown* would not prevail, the Court now became, and thereafter remained, indignant at the delay and recalcitrance that its ten years of hesitancy had done much to authorize and encourage. It now adopted a decisiveness that would, it seemed, sweep every difficulty away. [33] It is probably inherent in Supreme Court lawmaking that the remedy for one excess will be another. As Alexander Bickel has noted, the Court either "rushes forward too fast or it lags; its pace hardly ever seems just right," making it "in a vast, complex, changeable society, a most unsuitable instrument for the formation of policy." [34]

That the time for compliance with *Brown* I had come was reiterated in two 1965 *per curiam* decisions passing on desegregation plans: "Delays in desegregating public school systems are no longer tolerable." [35] In fact, however, delay continued to be tolerated. The plan in one of the cases did not call for the end of racial assignment in all grades until the 1968-1969 school year. Plaintiffs sought to have this advanced to 1965-1966. The Court held that individual blacks were to be allowed "immediate transfer" upon request to a school with a "more extensive curriculum and from which they are excluded because of race," but otherwise a "general plan consistent with [the] principle" of no further delay could be carried out. [36] Thereafter, the courts of appeals accelerated time schedules, but delay was still accepted in some cases. [37] The definitive answer to the question of delay came with the Court's pronouncement in 1969, in *Alexander* v. *Holmes County Board of Education*, that "every school district is to terminate dual school systems at once and to operate now and hereafter only unitary schools." [38]

Thus the answer was finally given to what should have never been in question; present compliance with *Brown* I would be required. The passage of the 1964 Civil Rights Act had removed all doubt. But the question was answered too late for a return to the apparent simplicity of the *Brown* I requirement. By this time the federal courts at all levels had become long-accustomed to formulating and supervising methods of school assignment and to prodding school boards to ever more vigorous efforts. The courts' exertions had gained not only acceptance but endorsement and applause; the moral superiority of the judicial to the political process came to be widely recognized. Full compliance with *Brown* could now be achieved, but judicial withdrawal from control of the schools could no longer be expected. Moreover, the results of compliance with *Brown*, it soon became obvious, would be, for those who had endured the struggle, far from thoroughly satisfying: schools largely black and largely white would continue to exist in the South, as in the North. As Alexander Bickel had written in 1964, the "likely—and anticlimactic—outcome of all the litigating and all the striving" to end segregation was that "a number of Negro children are admitted to white schools. Some few whites go to Negro schools; most flee to other homes, or out of the public school system altogether." St. Louis, for example, was "desegregated in 1954-1955. The city was rezoned geographically, without regard to racial considerations." The "result as of 1962" was that roughly 70 percent of the black secondary students and 85 percent of the black elementary students attended schools "whose student bodies were 90 to 100 percent Negro." [39] The racial millennium would not come. Settling the question of the time for compliance with *Brown* easily led, therefore, to redefinition of what compliance meant. In the guise of merely continuing to insist upon compliance with the requirement of *Brown*, a very different requirement was created.

4 | The First Revolution Succeeds— and Brings a Call for a New Crusade

The 1964 Civil Rights Act: The Triumph of *Brown*

That the Court's *Brown* gamble had been successful was established by the enactment of the Civil Rights Act of 1964. [1] *Brown*'s prohibition of racial discrimination was adopted as a comprehensive national legislative policy and applied by the act's several titles not only to education but to employment, public accommodations, public facilities, and federally assisted programs. Because the act became the essential means by which the prohibition of school segregation was converted to a requirement of school integration, its relevant provisions and their legislative history must be reviewed in some detail.

Public education was the subject of Title IV, "Desegregation of Public Education." Section 407 authorizes the attorney general of the United States to initiate school desegregation actions on behalf of complaining individuals in certain circumstances. Section 401, the first section of the title, defines "desegregation" as follows: " 'Desegregation' means the assignment of students to public schools and within such schools without regard to their race, color, religion, or national origin, but 'desegregation' shall not mean the assignment of students to public schools in order to overcome racial imbalance." This limitation of "desegregation" to nonracial assignment reappears as a proviso to section 407: "Nothing herein shall empower any official or court of the United States to issue any order seeking to achieve a racial balance in any school by requiring the transportation of pupils or students from one school to another or one school district to another in order to achieve such racial balance." Finally, as evidence of treble or quadruple caution, the limitation appears yet again, as section

410: "Nothing in this title shall prohibit classification and assignment for reasons other than race, color, religion, or national origin."[2]

Title VI of the act, "Nondiscrimination in Federally Assisted Programs," states (section 601): "No person in the United States shall, on the ground of race, color, or national origin, be excluded from participation in, be denied the benefits of, or be subjected to discrimination under any program or activity receiving Federal financial assistance." Section 602 provides that federal departments and agencies authorized to grant federal financial assistance under any program or for any activity are to issue "rules, regulations, or orders . . . consistent with achievement of the objectives" of the act. These are not to "become effective," however, "unless and until approved by the President." Failure to comply with such rules can result in the cutoff of federal funds. Section 603 provides for court review of any department or agency action taken in accordance with section 602.[3]

The importance of Title VI for school desegregation derived from the fact that in fiscal 1964 the federal government provided, under a variety of programs, some $176,000,000 to the public school systems of the seventeen states that had practiced racial segregation. Its importance was multiplied with the passage of the Elementary and Secondary Education Act the following year, pursuant to which additional funds exceeding half a billion dollars have been made available to those states.[4] These vast sums are distributed by the Office of Education of the Department of Health, Education, and Welfare (HEW).

The legislative history of Titles IV and VI is extensive and unambiguous as to the meaning of "desegregation," although, given the above-quoted provisions of Title IV, additional certainty is hardly possible. Every title of the act, indeed, was defended by its proponents, with what proved to be irresistible force, on the ground that it did no more than prohibit racial discrimination. The possibility that a requirement of racial discrimination to achieve integration or racial balance might somehow result from the act was the strongest argument of its opponents and was repeatedly and emphatically denied by its proponents. Belief in the impossibility of such a result was regarded as crucial to the act's passage, and every attempt was made to allay the opponents' fear. For example, Congressman Emanuel Celler of New York, the floor manager in the House of the bill that became the act, said: "Thus, the bill would simply implement the law of the land and hasten the enjoyment by all our citizens of their constitutional rights. There is no authorization for either the Attorney General or the Commissioner of Education to work toward achieving racial balance in given schools." Senator Hubert Humphrey of Minnesota, the floor manager of the bill in the Senate, said that Title IV would "create no new rights" and "impose no new duties on local officials, since such officials are already under a long-declared constitutional duty not to segregate or otherwise discriminate." He declared, furthermore, that Title VI would grant no power except to require that "the local school authority refrain from racial discrimination in treatment of pupils and teachers. . . . This bill cannot be attacked on its merits. Instead, bogeymen and hobgoblins have been raised to frighten well-meaning Americans." Senator Thomas Kuchel of California said:

Other equally invalid scare charges have been made. For instance some have erroneously implied that Title IV would provide funds to secure racial balance in all schools throughout America and thus overcome racial imbalance. The House specifically provided in section 401(b) of the bill that "desegregation" shall not mean the assignment of students to public schools in order to overcome racial imbalance. Let this be thoroughly understood. [5]

Senator Humphrey, a leading proponent of the act, analyzed it for the Senate title by title. Coming to Title IV, he stated:

Changes are made to resolve doubts that have been expressed about the impact of the bill on the problem of correcting alleged racial imbalance in public schools. The version enacted by the House was not intended to permit the Attorney General to bring suits to correct such a situation, and, indeed, said as much in section 401(b). However, to make this doubly clear, two amendments dealing with this matter are proposed.

The first of these additional assurances was, he said, the proviso to section 407, which he quoted. This provision "should serve to soothe

fears that title IV might be read to empower the Federal Government
to order the busing of children around a city in order to achieve
a certain racial balance or mix in schools." The second
additional assurance was "a new section 410 [that] would
explicitly declare that 'nothing in this title shall prohibit
classification and assignment for reasons other than race, color,
religion, or national origin.' Thus, classification along bona
fide neighborhood school lines, or for any other legitimate reason
which local school boards might see fit to adopt, would not be affected by title IV, so long as such classification was bona fide." [6]

When Senator Humphrey came to his analysis of Title VI,
Senator Robert Byrd of West Virginia, an opponent of the act,
asked him if he could give assurance that "school children may
not be bused from one end of the community to another end
of the community at the taxpayers' expense to relieve so-called
racial imbalance in the schools." Humphrey replied, "I do," and
he again quoted the proviso to section 407. That proviso,
he continued, "merely quotes the substance of a recent court decision,
which I have with me and which I desire to include in the Record
today, the so-called Gary case." [7] The case referred to is *Bell* v.
School City of Gary, Indiana, the then most recent court of appeals
decision holding that the Constitution did not require school
racial balance: "Desegregation does not mean that there must be
intermingling of the races in all school districts. It means only that
they may not be prevented from intermingling or going to school
together because of race or color." The court had approved
school assignment by neighborhood even though "the resulting
effect is to have a racial imbalance in certain schools where
the district is populated almost entirely by Negroes or whites." [8]
Senator Byrd persisted: would section 407, however, "preclude
the Office of Education, under section 602 of title VI, from
establishing a requirement that school boards and school districts
shall take action to relieve racial imbalance wherever it may
be deemed to exist?" "Yes," Senator Humphrey replied, "I do
not believe in duplicity"; section 407 "must apply throughout
the act," and, he pointed out, the *Gary* case was particularly
significant "as to racial balancing" because "the Supreme Court
refused to grant certiorari in this case. In effect, the ruling
of the circuit court has been upheld." [9]

Senator Byrd then agreed that no court could order school racial balance pursuant to the act, but he was not satisfied that the Office of Education might not seek to require it by threatening to cut off funds:

Suppose the Office of Education establishes a regulation that there shall be no racial imbalance in the schools of any district which receives Federal assistance. Cannot the Office of Education, pursuant to carrying out this regulation, deny assistance to school districts wherein racial imbalance exists?

Senator Humphrey again quoted the proviso to section 407 that nothing in the act empowered any federal "official or court to issue any order" requiring racial balance, and section 602, he pointed out, provides that for funds to be cut off "the President would have to issue the order." But, Byrd asked, "what assurance does the Senator give me that the President will not approve such a requirement?" "Because," Humphrey answered, "I do not believe the President will violate the law. . . . I cannot go to the White House and take a blood oath from him, but the President can read." When Senator Byrd declared that he was still "not convinced" that the Office of Education would not nonetheless "seek to achieve an objective of racial balance in the schools," Senator Humphrey replied, "I want to set the troubled mind of the distinguished Senator at rest"; he pointed out, "I am manager of the bill"; therefore, his assurance to Byrd that racial balance could not be required would be of "some importance" in any interpretation or application of the act. Furthermore:

I shall be glad to accept an amendment to clarify that point to make it more precise. One cannot get anything more definite than that.

.   .   .   .   .   .

I cannot believe the Senator's worries are well grounded. We are willing to listen to the Senator's arguments or his amendment, for I think he would probably secure great support. [10]

At this point in the discussion, Senator Jacob Javits of New York interjected that he had "had a great deal to do with drafting" section 602 of the act, relating to the grant or cutoff of federal funds, and he added his assurance that there was no "danger of envisaging the rule or regulation relating to racial imbalance," because "it is negated expressly in the bill."

Therefore, there is no case in which the thrust of the statute under which the money would be given would be directed toward restoring or bringing about a racial balance in the schools. If such a rule were adopted or promulgated by a bureaucrat, and approved by the President, the Senator's State would have an open and shut case under section 603. That is why we have provided for judicial review.

Senator Javits assured Senator Byrd that "any Government official" who sought to require racial balance pursuant to the act would be "making a fool of himself." [11]

Senator Humphrey then gave Senator Byrd the ultimate assurance that the act could not be used to require racial balance because, in any event, such a requirement would be unconstitutional:

[The *Gary*] case makes it quite clear that while the Constitution prohibits segregation, it does not require integration. The busing of children to achieve racial balance would be an act to effect the integration of schools. In fact, if the bill were to compel it, it would be a violation, because it would be handling the matter on the basis of race and we would be transporting children because of race. The bill does not attempt to integrate the schools, but it does attempt to eliminate segregation in the school systems. [12]

Despite this legislative history and the repeated provisions of the 1964 Civil Rights Act that racial discrimination was prohibited and that no requirement of integration or racial balance was to be imposed pursuant to the act, just such a requirement was soon imposed by the Office of Education and upheld by the courts. A clearer illustration of administrative and judicial perversion of legislative purpose would be difficult to find.

Every assurance written into the act and reiterated by its sponsors and supporters that it could not be made the basis of a requirement of integration proved to be worthless. The act's provision that "no rule, regulation, or order" would become effective without presidential approval afforded no protection against the Office of Education. The Office issued, not "rules, regulations, or orders," but merely "administrative guidelines" which, it determined, did not require presidential approval. [13]

If, as Senator Humphrey believed, ability to read precluded using the act to require integration, illiteracy soon proved widespread. If, as Senator Javits believed, only a "fool" could argue for compulsory integration under the act, giving his opponent an "open and shut case," fools enough were soon to be found both on and off the bench. If Congress, like Senator Humphrey, did not "believe in duplicity," it failed to reckon with the existing realities of the relevant administrative agencies and courts.

The Civil Rights Commission and the Office of Education: The Perversion of the 1964 Civil Rights Act

Pursuant to Title VI of the 1964 Civil Rights Act, the Department of Health, Education, and Welfare issued regulations applicable to federally assisted programs in general. Responsibility for determining compliance by school districts was given to HEW's Office of Education. [14] In April 1965, the Office of Education issued a detailed "General Statement of Policies" that soon became known as the "guidelines." [15] The Office interpreted the act as requiring no more than the Supreme Court required in *Brown* II: that is, only that segregation be ended gradually. The complexity and confusion inherent in *Brown* II were, therefore, transferred to the administration of the act. The question continued to be not simply whether assignment to schools on the basis of race had ceased, but what, short of a complete cessation, would be acceptable.

The guidelines provided three "methods of compliance" with Title VI by school districts. Districts could submit written assurance that racial discrimination was not being practiced; [16] submit a final order of a federal court requiring "the elimination of a dual or segregated system of schools"; or submit an "adequate" desegregation plan. The conditions of adequacy were set forth in detail. The guidelines did not require simple nonracial assignment according to geographic attendance zones; permitting "freedom of choice" was also acceptable if various requirements were met. The fall of 1967 was set as the "target date for the extension of desegregation to all grades" of any school system not desegregated sooner.

Freedom-of-choice plans evolved out of, and generally were substituted for, pupil placement plans as the latter became unworkable because of increasing insistence by the courts that initial assignments be nonracial. Assignment was to be on the nonracial basis of individual choice by the student (or his parents) of any school of his level within the school district or within a geographic zone that included his residence. In accepting freedom-of-choice plans as a means of compliance with the act, the Office of Education followed, but with generally stricter and more specific requirements, the many court decisions that had accepted these plans as constituting compliance with *Brown*.[17] The courts, in turn, then relied heavily on the requirements of the guidelines in passing on the constitutionality of such plans under *Brown*. The Court of Appeals for the Fifth Circuit, by far the most important court of appeals in school segregation litigation because of its jurisdiction over most of the deep South, quickly accepted the guidelines as establishing not only administrative requirements but also minimum constitutional requirements.[18] Consequently, the decisions of the judicial and the administrative institutions thereafter had a cumulative and accelerating effect on the development of school segregation law.

Another institution concerned with school segregation was the United States Civil Rights Commission. The Commission had been created by the Civil Rights Act of 1957 to serve as a general overseer in matters related to race.[19] Although it had only investigatory and advisory powers, it naturally saw its function to be the spurring of greater achievements in race relations. In February 1966, the Commission issued a report on the progress of "desegregation" and showed itself much displeased.[20] The results of ending assignment to schools according to race, which were bound to be disappointing to some members of the judiciary, were totally unacceptable to members of the Commission and would certainly be no less so to the "desegregation" specialists of the Office of Education. To professional "desegregators" merely ending racial discrimination was far too small a task and too limited a goal. As Nathan Glazer has written:

It is the fate of any social reform in the United States—perhaps anywhere—that, instituted by enthusiasts, men of vision, politicians, statesmen, it is soon put into the keeping of full-time professionals. This has two consequences. On the one hand, the job is done well. The enthusiasts move on to new causes while the professionals continue working in the area of reform left behind by public attention. But there is a second consequence. The professionals, concentrating exclusively on their area of reform, may become more and more remote from' public opinion, and indeed from common sense. They end up at a point that seems perfectly logical and necessary to them—but which seems perfectly outrageous to almost everyone else. This is the story of school desegregation in the United States.[21]

The task, as the Commission saw it, regarding "southern school desegregation" was nothing less than to devise methods of assigning pupils to schools "so as to eradicate the effects of 100 years or more of dual and racially segregated school systems."[22] "Desegregation," as used by the Commission, was to be a potent tool.

The Commission recommended that the Office of Education "make it clear" that means of "desegregation" other than nonracial assignment to schools were "permissible" if a greater degree of integration would result. For example, a school district "may wish," the Commission helpfully suggested, "to construct a single large new school, or educational center, for all students in the district." The guidelines for freedom-of-choice plans should be revised, the Commission said, "to insure" that such plans were "adequate" not merely to "disestablish dual, racially segregated school systems," but "to achieve substantial integration within such systems."[23] This goal the Office of Education was authorized to achieve, according to the Commission, through its control of funds under a statute that trebly insists that desegregation means no more than nonracial assignment.

The Commission, deeply dissatisfied with the fact that Congress had limited the 1964 act to ending segregation, recommended in essence that the Office of Education abuse its authority and nonetheless impose a requirement of integration. The recommendation was more than welcome to the Office of Education. Sufficient conviction of good intentions readily grants self-exemption from the requirements of good faith. The

Commission's recommendations and objectives were promptly incorporated by the Office in a new and much more extensive set of guidelines issued in April 1966.[24] Imposing a requirement of integration in the face of the language of the act was a delicate task, but the Office of Education, following the lead of the Commission, was equal to it. The Office, unlike the Commission, did not find it necessary to mention "integration" or "racial balance," and those terms did not appear in the revised guidelines. Nothing else was necessary than that "segregation" and "desegregation" be given new meanings. Despite the act's definition of "desegregation" as nonracial assignment, the new guidelines found that an inadequate standard for determining compliance. "No single type of plan," they stated, "is appropriate for all school systems"; assignment according to "nonracial attendance zones" may not be sufficient for "the purposes of Title VI." On the contrary, in some cases "the most expeditious means of desegregation" might be to "close the schools originally established for students of one race." The reorganization of "the grade structure of schools" would be "another appropriate method." Indeed, "desegregation" not only no longer meant nonracial assignment, but could mean racial assignment, despite the act, if greater integration would thereby result: "A school system may (1) permit any student to transfer from a school where students of his race are a majority to any other school, within the system, where students of his race are a minority, or (2) assign students on such basis." The earlier exemplary statement that "any educational opportunity offered by a school system must be available to students without regard to race, color, or national origin" was, like the act itself, to be ignored; students could be transferred and assigned according to race when the result was to increase racial mixing.[25]

This extraordinary feat of turning the act against itself was accomplished, in part, under cover of the continuing confusion resulting from the persistence of the need for a "desegregation plan." The 1966 guidelines, unlike the 1965 ones, set no "target date" for desegregation. Since the Supreme Court had by now decided that delay was no longer tolerable, segregation was presumably to end in all schools and all grades at once—that is, in the following (1966-1967) school year. Because its basis had been removed, the day of the desegregation plan should have been over, and the question in segregation litigation should have finally been reduced to whether assignment to schools was in fact nonracial. By now, however, the question of the time for compliance had been so long and so thoroughly confused with the question of the meaning of compliance that the "desegregation plan" could be given a new life on a different footing. Only the function of the plan had to be changed—from permitting delay in ending segregation to requiring integration.

Apparent justification for the guidelines' continuing to speak of "desegregation plans" rather than simply following the act's mandate of nonracial assignment was provided by the widespread adoption of freedom-of-choice assignment by southern school districts. Geographic assignment, relatively simple and clear-cut, would have provided the Office of Education with few opportunities, in 1966, for the formulation of detailed regulations and requirements other than those ensuring that geographic zones were drawn without regard to race—although the Office did venture to suggest, as has been noted, that assignment based on geography would not be "appropriate" in all cases and that assignment according to race in order to increase integration was "permitted." Assignment according to choice, however, was a very different matter; opportunities for abuse by school officials or others, and therefore for additional regulation, were abundant. Although such a method of assignment was generally permitted by the courts during the *Brown* II era of gradualism in ending racial assignment, a good case could have been made for a simple prohibition now that the period of gradualism was over. The Civil Rights Commission recommended, and the Office of Education adopted, however, the "lesser" restriction of conditional permission. As is often the case, supposed leniency became the path to greater severity.

The Office of Education's allowance of freedom-of-choice assignment provided a perfect vehicle for requiring integration despite the act. Permission for so unusual and often complex a method of assignment could properly be limited to cases in which it could be shown to be "operating fairly" or "working." Given the objectives of the Civil Rights Commission and the Office of Education, "working" could be and was taken to mean, not that choices were uncoerced, but that substantial integration was produced. The test under the revised guidelines for "determining whether a free choice plan is operating fairly and effectively, so as to materially further the orderly achievement of desegregation" and "actually working to eliminate the dual school structure" was "the extent to which Negro or other minority group students have in fact been transferred from segregated schools." A free-choice plan is not "operating effectively" if it "results in little or no actual desegregation" or, if, after "having already produced some degree of desegregation, it does not result in substantial progress." "Actual desegregation," of course, meant integration, and "progress," the guidelines stated quite specifically, was to be rapid. If, for example, "8 percent or 9 percent" of the students in a school system "transferred from segregated schools for the 1965-66 school year, total transfers on the order of at least twice that percentage would normally be expected" in the following year.[26]

The act the Office of Education was purportedly enforcing defined "desegregation" as nonracial assignment and prohibited the Office from requiring assignment "in order to overcome racial imbalance." Congress, however, had neglected to define "actual desegregation" or to prohibit the requiring of racial balance to ensure that freedom-of-choice assignment was "operating fairly and effectively." The act's limitations and prohibitions could therefore be easily escaped. Secretary of HEW John Gardner was able to assure Congress that the contention that racial balance was being required by the Office of Education "misconceives the purpose of the percentages," which were only "used to assure true freedom of choice." The Commissioner of Education, Harold Howe II, corroborated that "the guidelines do not mention and do not require 'racial balance' or the correction of racial 'imbalance.' Racial imbalance certainly means the notion of trying to establish some proportion of youngsters that must be in each and every school. We are not about such an enterprise. We are trying to give the effect of free choices . . . in having pupils enter into whatever school they may wish to attend." [27] In fact, however, very definite proportions were established to determine whether a sufficient number of blacks were in schools with whites, and the freedom with which choices of school had been made by blacks and whites was irrelevant if the specified percentages had not been met.

Thus was the use of racial percentages or quotas introduced into the law of "desegregation," and, like the "desegregation plan," it proved to have a vitality that extended far beyond the need that called it forth. Freedom of choice could and would come to an end, but the racial quota to achieve "desegregation" would remain and prosper.

"An Idea Whose Time Has Come":
The Court of Appeals for the Fifth Circuit

Any expectation that such a blatant perversion of the 1964 Civil Rights Act as the Office of Education's 1966 guidelines would not, as Senator Jacob Javits had argued, be countenanced by any court was quickly shown to be baseless. In *United States* v. *Jefferson County Board of Education,* decided in 1966, a panel of the Court of Appeals for the Fifth Circuit, reversing several district court decisions, held, with one judge dissenting, that the revised guidelines not only were authorized by the 1964 act but set forth "minimum standards" as a matter of constitutional law. "No army is stronger than an idea whose time has come," quoted Judge John Minor Wisdom on behalf of himself and Judge Homer Thorneberry,[28] and for them, as previously for the Civil Rights Commission and the Office of Education, the time had come for the idea of compulsory integration. Whatever may be the case with armies, the provisions of the 1964 act, its legislative history, and all prior decisions of the Fifth Circuit and other courts of appeals to the contrary did not prove stronger.

"We approach decision-making here with humility," Judge Wisdom said, and proceeded to deliver a fifty-seven-page demonstration of his determination to work his will in spite of all obstacles. He found widespread moral and intellectual shortcomings in others. There were "determined opponents of desegregation" who "flee to the suburbs" and "would scuttle public education rather than send their children to school with Negro children." The courts that had for twelve years distinguished prohibiting segregation from requiring integration had been fooled by a "mystique that has developed." Congress had been most derelict: the "one reason more than any other" that had "held back desegregation of public schools on a large scale" was "the lack, until 1964, of effective congressional statutory recognition of school desegregation as the law of the land." [29] The 1964 Civil Rights Act, the statute that Congress finally did enact, explicitly perpetuating this "mystique," was then so misused as to support those who contended that Congress had acted all too soon.

The 1966 guidelines imposed a requirement of integration without ever using the term. The Fifth Circuit, however, not limited to enforcing the 1964 act, and armed with "the United States Constitution," could be explicit: "In this opinion we use the words 'integration' and 'desegregation' interchangeably." The distinction between the two was, the court said, "a quibble devised over ten years ago by a misreading of *Brown*." It followed that "the United States Constitution, as construed in *Brown*, requires public school systems to integrate students, faculties, facilities, and activities"; "the law imposes an absolute duty to integrate, that is, disestablish segregation"; the "racial mixing of students is a high priority educational goal." [30] Requiring integration was, according to this reasoning, no change at all from *Brown*; therefore, no serious attempt at justification was necessary. Thus, by means of nothing more than wordplay, the constitutional mandate was changed from a prohibition of racial discrimination to separate the races to a requirement of racial discrimination to mix them.

Wordplay is inevitable in judicial decision-making; the meaning of words is not unalterably fixed. The essence of rational decision-making lies, nonetheless, in consideration of the conflicting interests involved and not merely in the possibility of giving words new meanings. The ease with which the latter could be done had already been demonstrated by the Civil Rights

Commission and the Office of Education. To "prohibit segregation" may be said to be the same as to "require desegregation"—although the mere change from the negative to the affirmative has at least rhetorical significance—but the meaning of the terms is obviously not the same if the first means, as in *Brown*, the prohibition of racial assignment to separate the races and the latter means, as in the 1966 guidelines, the closing and restructuring of schools and the use of racial assignment and racial quotas. Consideration and justification of the wisdom and propriety of the change are avoided, but it is made no less drastic a change because of that. No better example can be found of decision-making in which the judges, in Learned Hand's words, "win the game by sweeping all the chessmen off the table." [31]

To hold, as the court did, that a requirement of integration followed from *Brown*'s prohibition of segregation is to change radically, if not to reverse, a constitutional requirement without acknowledging or justifying the change. To hold, however, as the court also did, that a requirement of integration was authorized by the 1964 act is to fail to keep faith with the Congress. Proclaiming "the judiciary's duty to the nation to cooperate with the two other coordinate branches of government in carrying out the national policy expressed in the Civil Rights Act of 1964," the court proceeded to defeat that policy and turn the act against itself. Congress had indeed, as the court said, "decided that the time had come for a sweeping civil rights advance," [32] but the essence and basis of that advance, enabling it to overcome all opposition, was the principle that racial discrimination was an evil. That was the "idea whose time had come." [33] To find in the act authorization for the racial discrimination necessarily involved in compulsory integration was to violate that principle and thereby remove from the act its source of strength. It was also to make the act's proponents seem charlatans, its opponents prophets, and the legislative process hapless. *Brown*, too, was deprived of its source of strength by finding in it a constitutional requirement of racial discrimination, but the Constitution says nothing of segregation, desegregation, or integration. The act could not be more explicit as to the meaning of "desegregation." However that word may be defined and redefined for the purposes of constitutional law, to interpret it in the act as requiring or authorizing a requirement of integration is to undermine the usefulness of language for communication and make legislative deliberations and assurances futile.

Undertaking to show that the 1964 act authorized a requirement of integration, the court first quoted section 401 of the act: "'Desegregation' means the assignment of students to public schools and within such schools without regard to their race, color, religion, or national origin, but 'desegregation' shall not mean the assignment of students to public schools in order to overcome racial imbalance." The court then stated:

The affirmative portion of this definition, down to the "but" clause, describes the assignment provision necessary in a plan for conversion of a de jure dual system to a unitary, integrated system. The negative portion, starting with "but," excludes assignment to overcome racial imbalance, that is acts to overcome de facto segregation. As used in the Act, therefore, "desegregation" refers only to the disestablishment of segregation in de jure segregated schools. [34]

The court's reasoning is sufficiently illogical and obscure to defy explanation. It seems to be: the "affirmative portion" of the act's definition of desegregation requires nonracial assignment; but, the "negative portion," prohibiting "assignment . . . to overcome racial imbalance," somehow limits that requirement to "de jure segregated schools"; therefore, the court and the Office of Education were authorized by the act to require racial assignment after all and to require it even in cases, such as those before the court, involving schools that *had been* "de jure segregated." In effect, a double prohibition of racial assignment was found to authorize such assignment.

The language of section 401 of the act prohibiting assignment to overcome racial imbalance (the "negative portion") had been added to the section's definition of "desegregation" by an amendment offered by Congressman William Cramer of Florida, a member of the House Judiciary Committee which reported the bill that became the 1964 act. Like Senator Byrd of West Virginia, Cramer, along with other southern congressmen, had repeatedly expressed the fear that "desegregation," despite its definition in the act as nonracial assignment, might somehow be redefined to require or permit requiring racial balance, [35] and he offered his amendment to insure doubly against any such possibility. "The purpose," he stated, "is to prevent any semblance of congressional acceptance or approval of the concept of 'de facto' segregation or to include in the definition of 'desegregation' any balancing of school attendance by moving students across school district lines to level off percentages where one race outweighs another."[36] Incredibly, the court relied on this amendment and quoted this statement by Cramer—not mentioning that he was from Florida—to support its interpretation of the act as authorizing a requirement of integration in the South but not in the North. Congressman Cramer's successful insistence that an explicit prohibition against seeking racial balance be added to the act had the effect, according to this "interpretation," of confining the act's limited definition of "desegregation" to the North and authorizing a requirement of racial balance in the South. [37]

Equally incredible is the court's treatment of Senator Humphrey's assurance to Senator Byrd of West Virginia that "classification along bona fide neighborhood school lines, or for any other legitimate reason which local school boards might see fit to adopt, would not be affected by Title IV" and that the bill "does not attempt to integrate the schools, but it does attempt to eliminate segregation in the schools." Senator Humphrey's "references to *Bell*" v. *School City of Gary, Indiana,* the court stated, "indicate that the restrictions in the Act were pointed at the Gary, Indiana, de facto type segregation." [38] That is, Humphrey's assurances were, to Byrd of West Virginia, a state that had had the "*de jure*" "type segregation," no assurances at all. Senator Humphrey believed that *Bell*, the most recent case dealing with the issue, had been "in effect . . . upheld by the Supreme Court" and that this showed that action to achieve racial balance was not only not constitutionally required but was constitutionally prohibited. [39] But because *Bell* arose in the North, the court found the act and Senator Humphrey's assurances to Senator Byrd consistent with the view that compulsory integration was authorized for the South. The fact that Gary, Indiana, had racially segregated schools until 1949, as was explicitly pointed out by the district court in *Bell*,[40] adds a touch of irony to the court's argument. Nothing, however, can make the court's conclusion more baseless or its treatment of the act more reprehensible.

District Judge William Cox, sitting on the court of appeals "by designation" (special, temporary appointment) dissented. He noted the many decisions of the Fifth Circuit—which the panel had in effect overruled although it was not authorized to do so—holding that the Constitution does not require school racial integration. Quoting from the 1964 act, he found: "The English language simply could not be summoned to state any more clearly than does that very positive enactment of Congress, that these so-called 'guidelines' of this administrative agency . . . are actually promulgated and being used in opposition to and in violation of this positive statute." "The majority opinion herein," he said, "is the first to say that the *Brown* case, together with the Civil Rights Act of 1964, makes it necessary that these public schools must now integrate and mix these schools and their facilities, 'lock, stock and barrel.' That view comes as a strange construction of the Fourteenth Amendment rights of colored children." He predicted: "If the majority opinion in these cases is permitted to stand, it will, in the name of protecting civil rights of some, destroy civil rights and constitutional liberties of all our citizens, their children and their children's children."[41]

On rehearing *en banc* (by all members of the court), the panel's decision was affirmed by a vote of 8 to 4, and its opinion was adopted "subject to the clarifying statements" of a two-page *per curiam* opinion. In effect the panel's opinion was fully endorsed. The many prior decisions of the court "distinguishing between integration and desegregation" were overruled.[42] The court affirmed that the South was to be distinguished from the North in applying the 1964 Civil Rights Act and the Constitution.[43] In the South, integration would be required in order to overcome "the effects of the dual school system." The Office of Education's guidelines were found to "establish minimum standards" of "desegregation" and to "comply with the letter and spirit of the Civil Rights Act of 1964" and were to be given "great weight" by the district courts of the circuit, whatever their applicability might be "in some other circuits" where only "state tolerance of *de facto* segregation" was involved. [44]

Each of the four dissenting judges wrote a separate opinion. Judge Walter Gewin pointed out that the effect of the decision was to "dichotomize the union of states into two separate and distinct parts." In the South "there must be a mixing of the races according to majority philosophy even if such mixing can only be achieved under the lash of compulsion." But

there is no constitutional requirement of proportional representation in the schools according to race. . . . When our concepts as to proportions and percentages are imposed on school systems, notwithstanding free choices actually made, we have destroyed freedom and liberty by judicial fiat; and even worse, we have done so in the very name of that liberty and freedom we so avidly claim to espouse and embrace. . . . Both proportional representation and proportional limitation are equally unconstitutional. [45]

"Throughout the opinion" of the majority, Judge Gewin stated, "there appear a tangled conglomeration of words and phrases of various shades of meaning, all of which are equated with each other to reach the conclusion desired by the majority that school boards in this Circuit must adopt and implement a plan of forced integration." "In order to escape the clear meaning of the 1964 act and the unquestioned intent of Congress as illustrated by the legislative history, the opinion summarily obliterates any distinction between desegregation and integration." He showed that Judge Wisdom's attempt to distinguish *Bell* v. *School City of Gary*—the decision relied on by Senator Humphrey to show that integration could not be required—as involving "de facto segregation" was invalid because, as the district court had stated in that case, Gary had followed "the separate but equal policy, then permitted by Indiana law," up to 1949. "If the majority is correct," Judge Gewin concluded, that there is no distinction between desegregation and integration, "it is entirely likely that never before have so many judges been misled . . . for so long." [46]

Judge Griffin Bell argued that "mandatory assignment of students based on race" is a "new and drastic doctrine" that adds "new fuel in a field where the old fire has not been brought under control." He found that "the restrictions in the Civil Rights Act of 1964 against requiring school racial balances by assignment and transportation are written out of the law with respect to the de jure states." He believed that "legally compelled integration" should not "be substituted for legally compelled segregation. It is unthinkable that our Constitution does not contemplate a middle ground—no compulsion one way or the other." [47]

Judge James Coleman pointed out:

Prior to 1954, racially separate, if equal, schools had not been condemned as unconstitutional. One is not to be punished or harassed for an act which was lawful when it was done. Indeed, such condemnation in this instance would inferentially include some of the most highly respected Judges who ever graced the Supreme Court. . . . As I understand it, an Omnipotent God does not change yesterday when it is past and gone. Certainly this Court cannot do it. [48]

By the majority decision,

the freedom of the Negro child to attend any public school without regard to his race or color, first secured in the *Brown* cases, is again lost to him after a short life of less than thirteen years. . . . Because of his race he can be assigned to a particular school to achieve a result satisfactory to someone who probably does not even live in the district but who wishes to make a racial point. . . . We are not freeing these children of racial chains. We are compounding and prolonging the difficulty. [49]

Judge John Godbold noted that the brief for the United States on the rehearing *en banc* argued that the original panel had not "held that the Constitution imposes an absolute duty to achieve a racial mixing of students so as to eliminate a disproportionate concentration of Negroes in certain schools within a system." Judge Godbold stated that he wished he could read the majority opinion as so limited and that "if the language of mandatory mixing is indeed a mere aside we shall all await with interest to see whether the courts are the prisoners of their own slogans and the dictum of today is to be asserted as the law of tomorrow."[50]

Despite the enormous importance of this rewriting of both the act and constitutional law, the Supreme Court declined to review the decision, permitting it to stand.[51]

There was, it appears, no way for Congress to legislate the end of school racial discrimination in 1964, however greatly desired or desirable that end might be. Given the institutions and circumstances of the time, it was probably inevitable that those who would come forth to administer and enforce such legislation would find this objective unacceptably limited. However much Congress might insist to the contrary, any such legislation was destined to become the means, not of ending, but of requiring racial discrimination. And because this requirement, once administratively imposed, would be raised by the courts to the level of a constitutional requirement, Congress would lose the power to eliminate it, even by repealing the original legislation. There was, the opponents of the act were proved correct in contending, no way to combat a recognized evil without bringing about a possibly greater one.

The Fifth Circuit's ruling that some degree of racial balance was now required in formerly segregated schools was rejected by the other three courts of appeals—those for the Fourth, Sixth, and Eighth Circuits—primarily concerned with segregation law.[52] Although it declined to review *Jefferson County*, the Supreme Court granted certiorari in a case from each of these other courts and, reversing the decision in each, quickly established the Fifth Circuit's ruling as the one to be followed. Thus were rendered worthless the assurances by the supporters of the 1964 Civil Rights Act that its provision for court review obviated fears of administrative misuse for the purpose of requiring integration. Instead of providing a restraint on the excesses of other government officials—a traditional justification for the Supreme Court's extraordinary power in our system— the Court proved itself to be the most dangerous source of excess.

5 | The Second Revolution: The Supreme Court Requires School Racial Integration in the South

Although not generally realized at the time, the Supreme Court's 1968 decision in *Green* v. *County School Board of New Kent County*[1] and companion cases worked a revolution in the law of school segregation comparable to, indeed more drastic than, that effected by *Brown*. The *Green* opinion was only the Court's fourth signed opinion on school segregation in the thirteen years since *Brown* and the first to return directly to the basic question of method of school assignment. With the *Green* decision, however, the *Brown* era was brought to a close. Purporting to do no more than apply the holding of *Brown* to the cases at hand, the Court changed the constitutional mandate from a prohibition to a requirement of racial discrimination in school assignment.

The *Green* Trilogy

The factual situation presented in *Green* was unusually simple and clear-cut. New Kent County, in rural Virginia, had only two schools, each a combination elementary and high school. One (New Kent) was located in the eastern part of the county, the other (Watkins) in the western part. The county population was half black and half white and was mixed residentially throughout the county. The school population, however, was predominantly black—740 blacks to 550 whites. Prior to *Brown*, the schools were racially segregated; Watkins was for blacks and New Kent for whites. After the bluster of "massive resistance" to ending segregation,[2] Virginia adopted a pupil placement plan in 1956, which was repealed in 1966. Until 1965, Watkins continued to have all black students, faculty, and staff, and New Kent remained all white. No white had applied for admission to Watkins and no black for admission to New Kent. In 1965, while litigation challenging this situation was pending, the school board, in order to continue to receive federal financial aid, adopted a freedom-of-choice plan acceptable to the Office of Education. The plan, as filed with the district court in May 1966 and supplemented in June 1966, provided that all students would be assigned to the schools of their choice and that free transportation would be provided. Pupils beginning elementary and high school were required to make a choice; thereafter, attendance at the chosen school would continue unless a transfer was requested at the beginning of any school year. In the event of overcrowding at either school— which had not yet occurred—priority would be granted on the basis of geographic proximity to the school. The plan provided that there was to be no racial discrimination in any element of the operation of the school system, including the assignment of faculty, administrators, and other school employees.[3] Thirty-five black students chose, and were admitted to, New Kent in 1965, 111 in 1966, and 115 in 1967; no white student chose Watkins. In 1967, one white teacher was assigned to Watkins, and a black teacher was assigned, on a part-time basis, to New Kent.[4]

The plan was approved by the district court and, with a minor change, by the Court of Appeals for the Fourth Circuit sitting en banc. The Fourth Circuit held that "compulsive assignments to achieve a greater intermixture of the races" were not required. It stated: "Since the plaintiffs here concede that their annual choice is unrestricted and unencumbered, we find in its existence no denial of any constitutional right not to be subjected to racial discrimination."[5]

The Supreme Court unanimously reversed the Fourth Circuit's decision. The opinion, by Justice William Brennan, is a masterwork of indirection, requiring careful attention. The Court was unable to find racial discrimination in violation of Brown I, but it found unconstitutionality nonetheless and purported to find it on the basis of Brown II. Following the lead of the Office of Education and the Fifth Circuit, the Court made Brown II's authorization of delay in compliance with Brown I and the consequent development of the "desegregation plan" the means of converting Brown I's prohibition of segregation to a requirement of integration without openly admitting that a change had been made. *Brown I* had converted *Plessy*'s permission for segregation to a prohibition of segregation without expressly overruling *Plessy; Green* performed the much more difficult feat of converting a prohibition of racial discrimination to a requirement of racial discrimination while purporting to enforce the prohibition.

The Court began its opinion by quoting *Brown II* and quoted it extensively throughout. *Brown I* almost disappeared from view; it was mentioned only in connection with *Brown II* and never quoted. The Court even omitted any reference to where the *Brown I* opinion could be found in the United States Reports; another example of the Court's mentioning a case without this reference would be difficult to find. *Green* was made to appear to present the *Brown II* question, although no question of delay was in fact now involved. The 1964 Civil Rights Act was mentioned only in a footnote, which quoted Title VI as showing, the Court said, that Congress was "concerned with the lack of progress in school desegregation." Congress' actual treatment of the specific subject—the meaning of "desegregation"—in Title IV was ignored.

The question for decision as stated by the Court was not whether the school board was in compliance with *Brown I* but whether there had been "adequate compliance with the Board's responsibility 'to achieve a system of determining admission to the public schools on a nonracial basis . . .' " under *Brown II*.[6] In fact, there was, or should have been, no question of "achieving a system of determining admission . . . on a nonracial basis"; nonracial admission itself, the lower courts had found and the Supreme Court did not dispute, had been achieved. After a selective recital of the facts, the Court stated:

> The pattern of separate "white" and "Negro" schools in the New Kent County school system established under compulsion of state laws is precisely the pattern of segregation to which *Brown I* and *Brown II* were particularly addressed, and which *Brown I* declared unconstitutionally denied Negro school children equal protection of the laws. Racial identification of the system's schools was complete, extending not just to the composition of student bodies at the two schools but to every facet of school operations—faculty, staff, transportation, extracurricular activities and facilities. In short, the State, acting through the local

school board and school officials, organized and operated a dual system, part "white" and part "Negro."[7]

The point of this review of a prior situation not now before the Court is not immediately clear. Speaking of the *Brown* decisions as "particularly addressed" to a "pattern of separate" racial schools seems a strange circumlocution, but accurate enough, perhaps, once "under compulsion of state laws" is added. That *Brown* I prohibited such school separation was not, however, in dispute. There was also no dispute about the facts that New Kent County, along with the rest of Virginia, once had a "pattern of separate" schools, that the "racial identification of the system's schools was [at that earlier time] complete," or that there had been, "in short," a "dual system." If the suggestion was, however, that "the racial identification of the system's schools was complete" in the system now before the Court, it was incorrect. One hundred and fifteen blacks, the Court was later to note, were attending schools with 550 whites, and—the Court found no occasion to note—neither school any longer had a completely one-race faculty and the school board had prohibited racial discrimination in all phases of the system's operation. It is difficult to escape the impression that the Court was blurring the facts of the past and the facts of the present after a general blurring of what *Brown* held.

The opinion becomes progressively more elusive. "It was such dual systems," the Court next said, "that 14 years ago *Brown I* held unconstitutional and a year later *Brown II* held must be abolished." Such a system, one is left to wonder, as New Kent once had but did not now have?

School boards operating such school systems were *required* by *Brown II* "to effectuate a transition to a racially nondiscriminatory school system." It is of course true that for the time immediately after *Brown II* the concern was with making an initial break in a long-established pattern of excluding Negro children from schools attended by white children. . . . Under *Brown II* that immediate goal was only the first step, however. The transition to a unitary, nonracial system of public education was and is the ultimate end to be brought about; it was because of the "complexities arising from the transition to a system of public education freed of racial discrimination" that we provided for "all deliberate speed" in the implementation of the principles of *Brown I*.[8]

The Court then quoted further from *Brown* II's statement of reasons for permitting delay; the Court emphasized here and throughout the opinion that delay (as was to be expected) had in fact occurred.[9] Again, literally understood, the above quoted passage seems no more than a convoluted way of stating what was not in dispute: that *Brown* II authorized delay ("making an initial break") in ending segregation (the "established pattern of excluding Negro children from schools attended by white children") but that the *Brown* I requirement of nonracial assignment ("a unitary, nonracial system of public education") remained (was "the ultimate end"). Again, however, no question of delay was before the Court; the school board was not asking for further time, and the Court did not dispute (except by invariably placing the words "freedom of choice" between quotation marks) the fact that nonracial assignment was then in effect for all grades. The relevance of *Brown* II and the basis for a possible constitutional objection were, therefore, not apparent.

The Court nonetheless showed, by a rarely equaled feat of sophistry, that *Brown* II required the conclusion that the New Kent County school system was constitutionally defective. "*Brown II* commanded," the Court said, "the abolition of dual systems." But the school board contended that that had been accomplished, since, as the Court put it, "every student, regardless of race, may 'freely' choose the school he will attend" and that it could, therefore, "be faulted only by reading the Fourteenth Amendment as universally requiring 'compulsory integration,' a reading it insists the wording of the Amendment will not support." "But that argument," the Court answered, "ignores the thrust of *Brown II*."

In the light of the command of that case, what is involved here is the question whether the Board has achieved the "racially non-discriminatory school system" *Brown II* held must be effectuated in order to remedy the established unconstitutional deficiencies of its segregated system. In the context of the state-imposed segregated pattern of long standing, the fact that in 1965 the Board opened the doors of the former "white" school to Negro children merely begins, not ends, our inquiry whether the Board has taken steps adequate to abolish its dual segregated system. *Brown II* was a call for the dismantling of well-entrenched dual systems tempered by an awareness that complex and multifaceted problems would arise which would require time and flexibility for a successful resolution. School boards such as the respondent then operating state-compelled dual systems were nevertheless clearly charged with the affirmative duty to take whatever steps might be necessary to convert to a unitary system in which racial discrimination would be eliminated root and branch.

It was "relevant" that the board did not adopt "its 'freedom-of-choice' plan . . . until some 11 years after *Brown I* was decided and 10 years after *Brown II.* . . . Such delays are no longer tolerable." Therefore, "the burden on a school board today is to come forward with a plan that promises realistically to work, and promises realistically to work *now*." [10]

Obfuscation was now complete. There was an "affirmative duty" to eliminate "racial discrimination" "root and branch," which, on the surface, was no more than the requirement of *Brown* I. But, contradictorily, to "open the doors" of the schools to the races equally and to prohibit, as the school board had, all other racial discrimination was not enough. A requirement of eliminating racial discrimination must be distinguished, apparently, from an "affirmative" requirement of eliminating it "root and branch," and the latter may require, not the elimination, but the practice of racial discrimination. It was not *Brown* II, of course, but *Brown* I that "commanded the abolition of dual systems" and required a "racially nondiscriminatory system"; *Brown* II made immediate compliance unnecessary. *Brown* II's "remedy" for the "unconstitutional deficiencies" of segregation was to permit it to be ended gradually. In any event, the lower courts had found that a "racially nondiscriminatory system" had been achieved in New Kent County, and the Supreme Court did not disturb that finding. Assignment to schools was according to choice, and choice, the plaintiffs conceded, was "unrestricted and unencumbered." New Kent County had finally, after fourteen years of turmoil, ended racial assignment only to learn that that was no longer the requirement and that racial assignment, now to increase integration, was to begin again.

"The New Kent School Board's 'freedom-of-choice' plan," the Court concluded, "cannot be accepted as a sufficient step to 'effectuate a transition' to a unitary system." The board, of course, had not offered any plan as a "step" to "effectuate a transition" to a "unitary system"; it had established a "unitary system" by eliminating all racial discrimination. "Dual system" meant the maintenance of separate schools to which students were assigned according to race. The board now maintained only one system of schools, to which all students were assigned without regard to race. The Court, however, found a new meaning for "dual system":

In three years of operation not a single white child has chosen to attend Watkins school and although 115 Negro children enrolled in New Kent school in 1967 (up from 35 in 1965 and 111 in 1966) 85% of the Negro children in the system still attend the all-Negro Watkins school. In other words, the school system remains a dual system.[11]

"Dual system" now meant, "in other words," not assignment by race to separate schools but simply insufficient racial mixing. The Fifth Circuit had shown in *Jefferson County* that a shift from a prohibition to a requirement of racial discrimination was only a matter of redefining words. The Supreme Court was even more subtle. It found no need to speak, as had the Fifth Circuit, of requiring "integration"; requiring only "desegregation" and the "disestablishment of the dual system" would serve as well. It was only necessary to understand that the establishment of a nonracial system, as had been found here, was "no universal answer" to this new requirement of "desegregation" and "disestablishment of the dual system" and that, indeed, the reintroduction of racial discrimination could be the answer.

A constitutional requirement of racial discrimination to increase integration could not, of course, be openly admitted and would have been most difficult to justify as such. Instead of attempting such justification, the Court imposed the requirement—by what it actually did—while insisting that it was requiring only that all racial discrimination be eliminated. It was thus able to retain the enormous advantage of seeming to combat racism, as in *Brown,* while in fact imposing a racist requirement. Humpty-Dumpty, of Lewis Carroll's *Through the Looking-Glass,* who insisted that when he used words they meant exactly what he intended them to mean, no more and no less, would have approved. The district court was instructed to see, on remand, "that state-imposed segregation has been completely removed" even though that court had found that all segregation had already been removed and though that court's real task now was to see that racial discrimination was reinstituted. The school board, the Court said finally, "must be required to formulate a new plan and, in light of other courses which appear open to the Board, fashion steps which promise realistically to convert promptly to a system without a 'white' school and a 'Negro' school but just schools." [12] In fact, the requirement was not "just schools" but racially mixed schools, and racially mixed to a greater degree than results from ending segregation.

Raney v. *Board of Education of the Gould School District,* decided with *Green,* presented a very similar situation. [13] Again, there were only two schools, each a combination elementary and high school that had formerly been segregated, and a racially mixed population throughout the school district (Gould, Arkansas). The county had a majority of blacks—1,800 to 1,200 whites—and the schools, therefore, were even more predominantly black—580 to 300—than those involved in *Green.* In 1965 the board, with the approval of the Office of Education, adopted a system of annual free choice. No white chose the formerly black school, and between eighty and eighty-five blacks chose the formerly white school. The Court of Appeals for the Eighth Circuit, affirming the decision of the district court, found that "the Constitution" was "unquestionably satisfied." [14] The Supreme Court again reversed, holding that "the plan" was "inadequate to convert to a unitary, nonracial system" and that the "school system remains a dual system." The board, therefore, was, like the board in *Green,* to "convert promptly to a system [with] just schools." [15]

Monroe v. *Board of Commissioners of the City of Jackson,* also decided with *Green,* presented a very different situation. [16] The city of Jackson, Tennessee, had eight elementary schools, three junior high schools, and two high schools, all formerly segregated, and a school population of 7,650, about 40 percent of which was black. The blacks were not dispersed throughout the city; the "great majority" lived in the central area. Token integration had occurred as early as 1961, when, pursuant to the Tennessee pupil placement law, three blacks were admitted to formerly white schools. In 1963, under a court order to end all racial assignment, the school board had adopted assignment according to geographic zones. The board provided, as was apparently permissible under

Goss, that any student could transfer to any other school where space was available; priority was granted to zone residents in the event of overcrowding.

The three junior high schools, with which the appeal was concerned, were in an east-to-west alignment and, accordingly, each was given a north-to-south attendance zone. The schools in the eastern and western zones were those formerly designated for whites, and the one in the central zone, where the great majority of blacks lived, for blacks. In the 1967-1968 school year, the central junior high school was all black and had approximately 80 percent of the system's black junior high school students; all white students resident in the zone had chosen to transfer. The western junior high school, with 819 students, was nearly all white; all but 7 blacks resident in the zone had chosen to transfer. The eastern junior high school had 349 whites and 135 blacks. The situation in the elementary schools was similar; no whites chose to remain in, or transfer to, the three formerly black schools. The Court of Appeals for the Sixth Circuit, affirming the district court, upheld the method of assignment. Explicitly rejecting *Jefferson County,* the court reaffirmed that the Constitution required the ending of racial discrimination, not the taking of steps beyond that in order to increase integration.[17]

Again the Supreme Court reversed. The school board had not met its "affirmative duty" under *Green* "to convert to a unitary system in which racial discrimination would be eliminated root and branch." Although initial assignment was geographic, the allowance of "free-transfer" (always put between quotation marks by the Court) "operated," like the free-choice method of *Green,* "simply to burden children and their parents with a responsibility which *Brown II* placed squarely on the School Board." How a system of assignment to neighborhood schools combined with the grant of an option to transfer placed a burden on anyone or failed to eliminate racial discrimination, even "affirmatively" and "root and branch," was not explained. The inability to show racial discrimination was apparently overcome by simply assuming that the board had acted in bad faith. An intent to achieve a "minimal disruption of the old pattern" was "evident" from the board's "long delay in making any effort whatsoever to desegregate" and from past discrimination by the same or earlier board members.

The transfer option, the Court said, was an "implicit invitation" by the board to return "to the comfortable security of the old, established discriminatory pattern," which "patently operates as a device to allow *resegregation* of the races to the extent that desegregation would be achieved by geographically drawn zones."[18]

That freedom to transfer allowed the great majority of blacks, who lived in the central area, to attend school outside that area was not mentioned; nor was it shown that, given the residential concentration, greater "desegregation would be achieved" in fact by eliminating the option. The board had argued that the free-transfer provision operated to achieve as much integration as could be achieved, because whites assigned to predominantly black schools in the black area would otherwise leave the school system. Without disputing the validity of this contention, the Court treated it as further evidence of the board's bad faith.[19]

The Court thus completed its review of the decisions of the courts of appeals primarily concerned with school segregation litigation. Only the Fifth Circuit's *Jefferson County* decision was left standing.

Freedom of Choice

The situations in *Green, Raney* and *Monroe* demonstrated the futility of any hope that the end of school racial discrimination would quickly mean the end of school racial separation. Segregation had at last ended, but, unless further steps were taken, substantial separation would continue. It almost seemed as if the former segregationists, having been pursued with so great an effort down so many trails, were now to be permitted to prevail. Surely a victory as great as *Brown* had now become should be more satisfying to the victorious and costly to the defeated.

In imposing racial segregation for so long, the southern states had, nearly all now agreed, acted indefensibly. After the invalidation of segregation by *Brown* I, those states greedily accepted *Brown* II's reprieve to delay its end as long as possible. When, finally, racial assignment to schools had to be ended, they adopted unusual methods—free choice and free transfer—that were likely to minimize the degree of integration. Racial discrimination had ended, as far as was apparent in the cases before the Court, but the effects of past discrimination clearly had not. Wrongs should not only be prevented but rectified. The races had been wrongfully separated by law in the past. Why should they not now be intermixed by law, at least as a corrective? The answer, of course, is or should be that, despite the ease with which words can be redefined and confused, compelling integration obviously involves very different considerations than does prohibiting segregation; it involves, for example, the requirement rather than the prohibition of the use of racial discrimination by government officials. Unsatisfying and therefore unpersuasive as the realization always is to the thoroughly committed, there are limits to effective social action, some things that cannot be done at any acceptable cost. Prohibition of an evil without correction of its continuing effects may in this imperfect world be all the progress and justice achievable at one time.

More can be said in favor of the result reached by the Court in *Green* and in *Raney*, if not in *Monroe*, than of the Court's method of reaching it. Requiring integration and a return to racial considerations in the assignment of students to schools was not necessary to invalidate the adoption of free-choice or free-transfer assignment by a school board immediately upon ending segregation. Such assignment practices could have been invalidated as racially discriminatory in themselves or because they offered many opportunities for racial discrimination that would be difficult to detect.

Where there was segregation, schools were officially designated as for blacks or for whites and were operated on a racial basis in all respects—in the assignment of students, faculty, and staff and the provision of activities and services. There should have been no question after *Brown* I that the racial assignment of faculty and staff, as well as of students, was impermissible, but because of *Brown* II, the ending of this racial discrimination was allowed to await the gradual elimination of the racial assignment of students. The racial identifiability of the schools, therefore, did not end immediately upon the adoption of nonracial assignment. It is clearly racially discriminatory for a state to designate individual schools as appropriate or intended for blacks or for whites—that is, to offer or attempt to offer students a choice of a school that is all, or nearly all, black or white—even though assignment is nonracial. To the extent that a school continued to have a faculty, staff, and student body all or nearly all of one race, freedom of choice came close to doing just that. What was, in effect, the offering of a choice on racial grounds could have been ended by the school boards in *Green* and *Raney* simply by their requiring geographic (neighborhood) assignment; integration, at least at first, would have been complete. The resulting student-body integration would have facilitated the elimination of racial assignment of faculty and staff; at least they would have no longer been offered a clear racial choice. Racial classification of students by the board would not be required, and the limitation of the prohibition of freedom of choice to formerly dual systems would be clearly justified.

Freedom of choice in school selection was a method very rarely employed except in districts required to end segregation. In operation it is cumbersome and expensive—often to the point of unworkability.[20] As favored schools become overcrowded, it usually becomes necessary to revert to some degree of geographic assignment, with the result that little freedom of choice is in fact provided. Assignment to neighborhood schools, on the other hand, was nearly universal, simple, and efficient. Freedom of choice, however, often, as in the districts involved in *Green* and *Raney,* resulted in a lesser degree of integration at first than neigborhood assignment would have. Because a search for the motive of official action is usually meaningless or futile, the law ordinarily treats a challenged action according to its effects. To show adoption of a course of action inferior in all respects to an alternative course but with different racial effects is to show racial discrimination and, where that is prohibited, the invalidity of the action.

This argument for invalidating freedom of choice and freedom to transfer may, however, be pursued on several levels. One may argue that their adoption does not constitute racial discrimination because, apart from their racial effects, they are not inferior to neighborhood assignment in all respects. Some have argued, indeed, that freedom of choice in school selection should be the ideal.[21] Freedom of choice itself, after all, is generally considered a positive value. The Supreme Court found the free-transfer provision in *Monroe* an "implied invitation" from the school board to the students to return "to the comfortable security of the old, established discriminatory pattern," but even if that was so, such comfort and security as are available are ordinarily not to be lightly denied. Even the personal freedom to choose, to discriminate, on a racial basis is ordinarily protected in the absence of some overriding injury to others.[22]

The usual answer to this, of course, is that the choice of schools by blacks just emerging from segregation cannot be "truly" free. The Court so implied in *Green*, presumably, by always putting "freedom of choice" in quotation marks.[23] Debate on the nature of free will is always possible, but the law, for the best of practical reasons, generally accepts the choices of competent adults as valid and responsible, except when coercion of a physical or perhaps economic nature is found. It is generally well to resist the temptation to think that we know better than others what is in their interest and to reject as irresponsible the choice we do not favor. As it was cynical to believe, in 1883, that blacks had been "the special favorite of the laws,"[24] it may be condescending to believe today that blacks cannot know and protect their own interests. The law at last is no longer antiblack; the 1964 Civil Rights Act, 1965 Voting Rights Act, and 1968 Civil Rights Act may in good conscience be taken as bases for a lessening of paternalism and an increase of respect.[25]

Be that as it may, the fact remains that freedom-of-choice school selection provides many opportunities for abuse by school administrators and others. Resentment against individuals by opponents of integration may be enhanced by the knowledge that integration results from personal choice rather than impersonal assignment. They may be tempted to make the integrated school unattractive, and even unsubtle physical and economic pressures may be difficult to detect and prevent. Furthermore, the mechanics of effecting freedom of choice assignment are often sufficiently complex to make proper implementation difficult to ensure. No improper consideration of motive, imputation of bad faith, or acceptance of black helplessness is necessarily involved in the recognition that integration is strongly opposed by many and that, therefore, legal requirements should be set so as to minimize opportunities for, and facilitate prevention of, wrongdoing. Given the availability of geographic assignment as an alternative, a general prohibition of free choice of schools by students may be justifiable on the ground that more specific methods of control are not administratively feasible.[26]

Taking the argument still one step farther, however, one might urge that freedom of choice, with certain minimal procedural protections,[27] should be permitted for any school district willing to assume its burdens, because it may provide the maximum amount of integration that is, as a practical matter, likely to be achieved. To expect school districts, such as New Kent County, Virginia, and Gould, Arkansas, with preponderantly black school populations to be able to achieve and maintain racially balanced schools may be to make the wish the father to the thought. The Civil Rights Commission had already pointed out at the time of *Green* that "there is evidence to suggest that once a school becomes almost half—or majority—Negro, it tends rapidly to become nearly all-Negro."[28] Prince Edward County, Virginia, the Court had seen, preferred closing its public schools to permitting any degree of integration; ordering the schools reopened and the end of state tuition grants for attending private schools resulted only in a school system very nearly all black.[29] Realistically viewed, the result of freedom of choice in New Kent County, Virginia—115 of 740 blacks attending school with whites and the number increasing each year—and in Gould, Arkansas,[30] may be regarded as not entirely deplorable. A system of freedom of choice, fairly administered, means that all blacks who wish to attend school with whites will do so, and those who do not wish to, will not. The motivation and willingness involved should contribute substantially to the value and success of integration. Opponents, white or black, of greater integration should find it in their interest to make any predominantly black school as attractive as possible, and blacks should be in a position to make certain that this is done.[31] The result, though some may think it imperfect, may satisfy nearly everyone immediately involved and, in any event, may be as much integration as can in fact be brought about. As Christopher Jencks has written:

Such a system does not ensure that every black child will attend school with whites or vice versa. Blacks will only attend school with whites if they apply to schools where whites are enrolled. Whites can escape attending school with blacks if they can find schools that have no black applicants. . . . The "liberal" alternative, which is widely viewed as the road to racial equality, seems to be compulsory busing of blacks to white neighborhoods, and vice versa. This implies that black parents cannot send their children to all-black schools, even if they want to, because all-black schools are *by definition* inferior. This position strikes us as both racist and politically unworkable over the long haul.[32]

An even stronger case for allowing freedom of choice might be made in the situation presented in *Monroe,* where the great majority of blacks were residentially concentrated in a single area. The free-transfer provision which the Court found objectionable permitted any black living in the black area to attend a predominantly white school in a different area. Geographic assignment with freedom to transfer resulted, at the junior high level, in one school that was all black, one that was nearly all white, and one that had 349 whites and 135 blacks. It was not shown that greater integration would have resulted from nonracial geographic assignment without freedom to transfer, although the Court apparently sought to create the impression that some increase, at least in the system as a whole, would take place. It was not clear, therefore, that the school board could "formulate a new plan" that would result in greater integration in, as the Court purported to require, a "nonracial, nondiscriminatory school system."[33]

The board argued in *Monroe* that any increase in integration that might be achieved by abolishing the free-transfer provision "would be a fleeting victory—a victory that lasted only long enough for those whites who are in a predominantly Negro zone to locate their residence elsewhere."[34] The Court's answer to this introduction of reality was to treat it as a virtual confession of guilt by the board, making the need to abolish freedom to transfer even clearer:

Respondent's argument in this Court reveals its [the free-transfer provision's] purpose. We are frankly told in the Brief that without the transfer option it is apprehended that white students will flee the school system altogether. "But it should go without saying that the vitality of these constitutional principles cannot be allowed to yield simply because of disagreement with them." *Brown II,* at 300.[35]

The language quoted from *Brown* II is certainly stirring rhetoric, but it is nothing more, and as has been shown above, it was not applied in *Brown* II itself. The Constitution, as Justice Robert Jackson has said, is not a suicide pact; it does not require self-defeating acts.[36] Insistence on principle and legality in the face of threatened lawlessness can be justified even where great immediate costs are involved, but to ignore the existence of perfectly legal means of avoiding a requirement is to bury one's head in the sand. The board, concerned with maintaining a viable school system, could not, like the Court, enjoy this luxury.

Perhaps it was enough for the decisions in *Green, Raney,* and *Monroe* that free choice and free transfer can be considered generally objectionable for the reasons given above. In the interest of stating a general rule, at some point consideration of the particulars of a given case and of the possible ramifications of a decision must cease. The phenomenon cited by the board in *Monroe,* however, was not a peculiarity of that case but was widespread if not universal, and the self-defeating potential of the decision was immediate and clear.

Whatever might be said in favor of the decisions reached in *Green, Raney,* and perhaps even *Monroe* as a simple prohibition of freedom of choice and freedom of transfer in the circumstances of those cases, the Court did not base the decisions on that ground, and, given the temper of the times and of the Fifth Circuit, there could be no reasonable expectation that the decisions would be understood as limited to such a prohibition. The Court's use of *Brown* II, its redefinition of "dual system," and its finding of unconstitutionality despite the undisputed fact that racial discrimination had been eliminated in the operation of the school systems involved left little doubt that the constitutional mandate had changed from a prohibition of racial discrimination to separate the races to a requirement of racial discrimination to increase integration. Enormous confusion and uncertainty would undoubtedly result from the Supreme Court's requiring racial discrimination while purporting to require its elimination, but a constitutional requirement of racial discrimination could not be openly admitted and defended. The all-important Fifth Circuit would understand that what the Court now wanted was not what it was forced to say, and the Fifth Circuit could be depended on to instruct the school boards and lower courts of the South.

Compulsory Integration: Principle and Other Considerations

The *Green* rationale that integration was not constitutionally required for its own sake but only as "desegregation," to "remedy" the segregation prohibited in *Brown*, seemed to mean that the requirement could be applied only in the South. This served to minimize national attention and concern and, consequently, opposition and to make the decision seem but another step taken by a patient Court to counteract still another attempt by the recalcitrant South to evade the requirement of *Brown*. Confinement of compulsory integration to the South on this rationale is difficult to justify, however, for several reasons. First, many areas outside the South had school racial segregation at one time—often, as in the case of Gary, Indiana, almost until the time of *Brown*.[37] In addition, nearly all states had laws—for example, antimiscegenation laws—that required racial discrimination and impeded integration and that might therefore provide a reason for compulsory integration as a "remedy." Furthermore, all racial separation can be said to be "by law," because the law permits, or does not require steps to eliminate, such separation; that is, the "by law-not by law" distinction and its equivalents (the "*de jure—de facto*" and "state action-private action" distinctions) can be easily broken down, as has often been shown.[38]

Most important, although segregation—assignment of children to separate schools according to race—made racial separation mandatory and complete, a substantial amount of school racial separation obviously occurs and persists, as the result of social and economic factors, in all areas with a large biracial population, regardless of the absence or presence of segregation in the past.[39] Steps to correct a condition existing everywhere regardless of whether or not segregation existed in the past are not easily justifiable as a remedy for the effects of past segregation. Indeed, to the extent that school segregation made residential integration more acceptable and common in the South than would otherwise have been the case, a simple prohibition of racial discrimination will result in more integration in the South than would have otherwise occurred.

The confinement of compulsory school racial integration to the South therefore requires some rationale other than that it is a remedy for school racial separation that, except for segregation in the past, would not exist. [40] Another rationale might be that the South is where school racial separation was explicitly imposed by law most recently and in a generally segregated society, with, it may be assumed, particularly demoralizing effects. Additionally, the South may be said to be the region whose history shows it is least to be trusted to abide by a simple prohibition of racial discrimination in situations where integration would result. Compulsory integration may be confined to the South, therefore, not because segregation in the past caused the present school racial separation, but because recent and general earlier segregation makes the present school racial separation a greater evil or because compulsory integration is required as a prophylactic measure. Because, however, it is no longer possible, owing to the passage of time, to require integrated schooling for those individuals who were explicitly and generally segregated or who imposed segregation, the "remedy" has the aspect of attempting to benefit some to atone for injury to others and of disadvantaging some because of the wrongs perpetrated by others. As segregation in the South becomes less and less "recent," the basis for a drastically different treatment becomes more and more difficult to see, especially when southern schools become, as they now have, the most integrated in the nation. [41] The suspicion becomes unavoidable that the South's minority position in national politics is being taken advantage of and that the present inhabitants of the South are being punished for the sins of others and used as scapegoats for racial problems that exist everywhere. It appears, therefore, that a requirement of integration must be of nationwide application and justified, on its own merits, as such. The Supreme Court has never attempted to justify compulsory integration for its own sake, to explain why it is a wise choice of social policy. It has avoided the need by simply claiming that integration is not required for its own sake but only in order to "remedy" the segregation prohibited in *Brown*—a claim that became more obviously fictional with each succeeding case.

A problem of social choice is a problem and justification of the choice made is needed because interests come into conflict. School racial integration, even that which results from merely ending segregation, conflicts with real and substantial interests, if for no reason other than that economic and cultural or social class differences are almost invariably involved. [42] The almost universal desire to avoid and to have one's children avoid intimate association with those of a lower economic and cultural level may be deplored, but it cannot realistically be ignored. Compulsory integration, usually involving greater economic and cultural differences, conflicts with these interests in a magnified form and, depending on the means employed, with other interests as well. No matter how highly school racial integration is valued, or how firmly it is made a matter of constitutional right, further steps to advance it must at some point so disserve other values as to be seen as not worthwhile. [43] No calculus exists for determining this point as to any interest, but it is reached and justification fails when the cooperation or acquiescence needed for further advance is not available or obtainable. It is reached more quickly the more a system is democratic and cooperation is therefore less readily coerced. Despite *Green*'s fatuous command to integrate by "whatever steps might be necessary," we have not, in school racial integration, finally found the absolute good. Other values exist and conflict, and justification and acceptance are therefore necessary.

Whether or not a requirement of school racial integration can be sufficiently justified to gain needed acceptance—a question later to be discussed—it clearly cannot be justified, as was attempted in *Jefferson County* and *Green*, on the basis of the principle that most easily justifies *Brown*'s prohibition of segregation—that all racial discrimination by government is prohibited. The force of that principle must, on the contrary, be overcome; some racial discrimination by government must be not only permitted but required. That it was overcome by what the Court did in *Green* may prove, if it has not already proved, the greatest loss, in terms of injury to the national political health, resulting from that decision.

The demand for principled judicial decision-making can, given the variety of the world and of the interests almost always involved, easily be overdone. But the legal system's need to formulate and maintain meaningful principles is nonetheless one of the most important interests involved in every decision, and other, more immediate, interests are often rightly sacrificed to it. Principles, to the extent that they are available, provide a starting place and guide for thought, making the resolution of problems more manageable. They can lead rapidly to desired results in a large enough proportion of similar cases to outweigh the loss of flexibility adherence to principle necessarily involves. They provide, in addition, at least the appearance of clarity, certainty, and evenhandedness that is needed to make regulation by law effective. Perhaps most important, principles, in law as in ethics, provide a means of persuasion to the acceptance of immediate disadvantage in the hope of longer-term advantage by asking that the more remote consequences of actions or policies be taken into account.

Finally, judicial adherence to generally accepted principles serves the important value, involved in all judicial decision-making and particularly in constitutional decision-making by the Supreme Court, of helping to maintain a system of self-government. No matter how desirable a social change may be, it is more easily justified, nearly all would agree, if it is brought about by elected representatives rather than by judges. The availability of an accepted principle to support judicial action helps maintain the distinction between the legislative and judicial functions. The need to maintain this distinction is most important in Supreme Court constitutional decision-making because it is in such decisions that the danger to self-government and the potential for injury to the social and political fabric from unacceptable but extremely difficult-to-change policy choices is greatest.

No principle better served all these purposes, proved more valuable in its overall and long-range consequences, or—at least by 1964—had more nearly acquired moral status than the principle that racial discrimination by government is a constitutionally prohibited evil. It may well have been our best hope for holding racial claims and animosities within bounds and of ultimately achieving racial equality. It proved sufficient in 1964 to overcome all the interests opposed to ending segregation in the schools and elsewhere. To gain acceptance, compulsory integration must not only overcome those interests, now magnified, and others as well, but also the very principle by which they had been successfully overcome. There is little reason to think the effort can succeed or that it should. As John Kaplan has argued:

> Probably the most serious drawback to [a requirement of integration is that it] would require governmental authorities to re-enter the field of racial classification. This is exactly what the plaintiffs' attorneys urged the Supreme Court to prohibit in the *Brown* case, and for good reason. Although today a court might rule that the state is required to consider race in a benign way, tomorrow this might well prove a precedent for a much less happy result. Moreover, even today it is not easy to decide whether a given racial classification is benign. [44]

Compulsory integration not only requires the abandonment or major qualification of the principle that racial discrimination by government is prohibited but substitutes no meaningful alternative principle. The result is that the requirement is not only difficult to accept but difficult to understand. The "dual system" is to be abolished, but the removal of racial discrimination as its defining characteristic left it wholly undefined. Greater racial mixing in each school or in some proportion of the schools in a system was apparently the objective, but no indication was given of the degree of mixing that would suffice or of the obstacles that would have to be overcome in order to achieve it. *Green*'s "whatever steps might be necessary" was not the statement of, but a refusal to state, an intelligible requirement. In reality, considerations of time, distance, expense, and other factors are always at some point determinative of what can and must be done.

The real question school boards and lower courts faced was what losses and costs should or must be borne in order to achieve any given degree of increased racial mixing—whether, for example, spending $10,000 or $100,000 or 1 percent or 10 percent of a school budget or requiring pupils to travel one mile or five miles farther from home is justified or required in order to convert one or more predominantly black schools to schools less predominantly black or to schools predominantly white. "How can the courts weigh the value of a 30 per cent increase in integration against a requirement that students cross a dangerous traffic artery or walk five extra blocks? How could the courts weigh the achievement of integration through bussing children against the greater cost and a somewhat larger class size?" [45] The variables are infinite. *Green* provided no rule or guide other than that integration or racial balance was to be heavily favored. The result was to require essentially *ad hoc*, subjective decision-making by judges in passing on school board actions, to make the acquiescence of opponents because of respect for law difficult to obtain, and to create an inexhaustible source of conflict and litigation. More than a decade of litigation resulted from the unprincipled requirement of "all deliberate speed" in *Brown* II; just when that source of dispute was removed, this new unprincipled requirement of *Green* was introduced, as if to ensure that segregation litigation would never come to an end.

The enormous implications of the Court's decision in *Green* to depart from a simple prohibition of racial discrimination, just firmly established by the civil rights acts, and the patent speciousness of its use of *Brown* II as the justification require that an explanation be sought outside the bounds of the Court's opinion. Analysis of that opinion reveals little more than what a leading scholar of constitutional history, referring to another decision regarding race, has called a "desperate earnestness" [46] to achieve the desired result and a confidence by the Court that its power and support were now sufficient to make inapplicable the restraints imposed by the need to offer justification. The decision is perhaps ultimately explicable only in terms of the "spirit of the times," the social upheavals and rendings of the 1960s and the continuing momentum of what had gone before. Nothing, it had come to seem, especially to the Supreme Court,.

could not be dared and nothing could not be defied by those with a vision of social equality.

The 1964 act had removed all doubt that *Brown* was a great achievement and would prevail. That act, which had been thought hardly possible a very short time before, was the greatest legislative step on the road to racial equality in a century. It was soon supplemented by two additional great steps, the Voting Rights Act of 1965 and the Civil Rights Act of 1968. The march of progress had surely become irresistible. One might have hoped, in a coldly rational world, that the Court, seeing its great and dangerous decision crowned with success and the cause of racial equality finally taken up by the other arms of government, would contentedly relinquish the vanguard. A frequent justification of the Court's extraordinary power in our system—usually offered by those whose views could in no other way prevail—is that the Court, though undemocratic itself, can serve to overcome other impediments to democracy and protect the interests of politically voiceless minorities. But now that the impediments to political action had been overcome and the minority had been given its political voice, the Court determined to march to new frontiers. Success and acclamation are not, among mortals, a prescription for self-restraint.

The forces favoring the *Green* decision were overwhelming. The position of the NAACP, the moving force, was officially supported by the United States government, acting through the Civil Rights Division of the Department of Justice, which, as in every case since *Gaines*, had filed an *amicus* (friend of the court) brief. [47] The Office of Education, the Civil Rights Commission, and the Fifth Circuit all favored moving on to a requirement of integration. It was not to be expected that the Supreme Court, which had sparked the revolution, would call a halt. Those who had fought so long, so well, and so successfully to end racial discrimination sought another victory; only former segregationists, it seemed, were opposed. The fact that the parties had switched positions on the basic principle involved—the NAACP now urging and the school boards opposing racial discrimination—was not enough for the latter now to prevail.

6 | *Caution Turns to Wrath:*
Racial Integration "at Once"

Green marked the end of the Supreme Court's reticence on questions of race and the schools. Decisions now came rapidly and easily. No obstacle to greater integration, it seemed, could longer exist; no further requirement to achieve integration could be too severe or too soon imposed.

Montgomery County

The Court spoke next in *United States* v. *Montgomery County Board of Education*, decided in 1969, one year after *Green*. As part of an overall desegregation plan, the district court had ordered the Montgomery County, Alabama, school board to assign faculty to schools so that the ratio of white teachers to black in each school would eventually be "substantially the same" as in the system as a whole. [1] As a first step, each school was to have at least one faculty member of each race, and schools with faculties of more than twelve were to have at least one black for every five whites, or vice versa. On appeal by the board, a panel of the Court of Appeals for the Fifth Circuit affirmed the district court's order in all respects but one. The court found, in regard to faculty integration, that "compliance should not be decided solely by whether" the system "has achieved the requisite ratios" and that it was enough at first that the ratio be "*substantially* or *approximately* five to one." [2] The constitutionality of mandatory racial assignment was not otherwise discussed.

On appeal by the United States government, the Supreme Court, in an opinion by Justice Hugo Black, reversed the court of appeals' modification of the district court's order, reinstating it in all respects. Again, mandatory racial assignment did not merit discussion; the only question was whether the court of appeals erred in finding a fixed ratio too rigid. In place of the *Green* requirement to "convert to a unitary system in which racial discrimination has been eliminated root and branch," the Court now openly spoke of the board's "responsibility to achieve integration as rapidly as practicable." [3] The reference was made, however, only in passing, as if the responsibility were well established and presented no significant question.

Sufficient justification for requiring racial ratios was provided, apparently, by Montgomery County's and Alabama's history. The Court stated that "neither Montgomery County nor any other area in Alabama voluntarily took any effective steps to integrate the public schools for about 10 years after our *Brown I* opinion." State and school officials had operated "racially segregated schools in defiance of our repeated unanimous holdings that such a system violated the United States Constitution" and, until the 1964 district court desegregation order in the present case, had operated them, "so far as actual racial integration was concerned, as though our *Brown* cases had never been decided." The "repeated unanimous holdings" are not specified, but the only decisions after *Brown* and before 1964 involving school segregation are *Cooper* v. *Aaron* and *Shuttlesworth* v. *Birmingham.* In its 1958 *Shuttlesworth* decision, the Court, as noted above, had found Alabama's 1955 pupil placement law constitutionally unobjectionable. A requirement of "steps to integrate" was, of course, unheard of in the Supreme Court prior to *Green*, one year before, and even in *Green* it was not openly stated. Whatever its relevance, the charge of "defiance," which now became a theme with the Court, seems, therefore, subject to question. On no apparent basis except that charge, however, the Court concluded that the district judge's requirement of faculty racial quotas "was adopted in the spirit" of *Green*, since "his plan 'promises realistically to work, and promises realistically to work *now*.' " [4]

The Court found the case refreshingly simple: "It is good to be able to decide a case with the feelings we have about this one. The differences between the parties are exceedingly narrow." The United States, Justice Black noted, argued only that the district court's order was proper "as a *remedy for* past racial assignment" and not that "racially balanced faculties are constitutionally or legally required." The school board, on the other hand, recognized its "affirmative responsibility to provide a desegregated, unitary and nonracial school system" and "to assign teachers without regard to race so that schools throughout the system are not racially identifiable by their faculties." In fact, of course, the government's argument and the board's statement of its duty were diametrically opposite. The requirement the government urged and the Court imposed on the board was to assign faculties *with* regard to race. The result was to establish the principle, without discussion and without justification other than Alabama's "defiance," that the use of racial discrimination and racial quotas to integrate was, at least with regard to faculty, constitutionally not only permissible but sometimes mandatory. To make very clear that measures imposed by lower courts to advance integration were not likely to meet disapproval, Justice Black carefully noted that the plaintiffs "with some reason argued" that the district judge "should have gone farther to protect their rights than he did."[5]

Alexander

Four months later the Court spoke again, in *Alexander* v. *Holmes County Board of Education.* Self-righteousness now turned to wrath. A Fifth Circuit Court of Appeals decision involving thirty-three school districts in Mississippi was peremptorily reversed in a one-paragraph *per curiam* opinion, and the Fifth Circuit was in effect severely chastised, as if it had been lax and unreliable in following the Court's directives in this area of the law. The question was, the Court said, "one of paramount importance, involving as it does the denial of fundamental rights to many thousands of school children, who are presently attending Mississippi schools under segregated conditions contrary to the applicable decisions of this Court." The Fifth Circuit had erred in granting a motion for additional time because, it apparently failed to realize, "all deliberate speed" was "no longer constitutionally permissible." With that the Court concluded its opinion except for the following statement, citing *Griffin* and *Green*: "Under explicit holdings of this Court the obligation of every school district is to terminate dual school systems at once and to operate now and hereafter only unitary schools." [6] The question involved was not further stated or discussed.

The question was not, however, as suggested by the Court's indignant opinion, whether "all deliberate speed" was still constitutionally permissible. On July 3, 1969, the Fifth Circuit, applying *Green*, had held that the freedom-of-choice plans of thirty-three Mississippi school districts, which had previously been approved by that court, were no longer constitutionally sufficient. The districts were ordered to formulate and submit new plans to produce greater integration for the school year beginning in September 1969, two months later.[7] The Department of Justice, representing the United States as plaintiff or intervenor in most of the cases, then requested the Fifth Circuit to extend the time for compliance with this new requirement. This motion was referred to the district court for a hearing. The Department of Justice and the Department of Health, Education, and Welfare argued that new plans could not be prepared and put into operation by the beginning of September; the district court so found, and on August 28, 1969, the Fifth Circuit approved an extension of time to December 1, 1969.[8]

NAACP lawyers representing individual plaintiffs then presented a motion to Justice Black, as circuit justice, asking that he vacate the Fifth Circuit's order. Justice Black was of the opinion that "there is no reason why such a wholesale deprivation of constitutional rights should be tolerated another minute." He was, however, "unable to say" that the evidence did not support the lower courts' findings that the "time was too short and the administrative problems too difficult to accomplish a complete and orderly implementation of the desegregation plans before the beginning of the 1969-1970 school year." He therefore denied the motion but expressed the "hope" that "these applicants will present the issue to the full Court at the earliest possible opportunity" and assured them that he would, despite the lower-court findings, require action "not only promptly but at once—*now*."[9] This advice was taken, and on October 9, 1969, the Court, as stated above, reversed the Fifth Circuit. It directed the Fifth Circuit to issue an order, "effective immediately, declaring that each of the school districts here involved may no longer operate a dual school system based on race or color, and directing that they begin immediately to operate as unitary school systems within which no person is to be effectively excluded from any school because of race or color." [10]

This instruction and the summary reversal of the Fifth Circuit on the ground that *Brown* II's authorization of delay had ended, seem, in the circumstances, little more than cruel jokes. There was, of course, no issue of prohibiting the operation of schools "based on race or color" or of excluding any person "from any school because of race or color." On the contrary, the school districts had been ordered to operate their systems racially and to exclude blacks and whites, regardless of their choice, from schools predominantly of their race. That order, however, was no longer in dispute. The only question before the Court was whether the Fifth Circuit erred in allowing the school districts three months in addition to two summer months to abandon their previously approved methods of operation, to formulate new methods producing greater integration, and to put these new methods into operation. Although it reversed the lower courts' grant of additional time, the Court did not hold that those courts were mistaken in finding, or that the Department of Justice and HEW were mistaken in insisting, that reorganization of the school districts could not be accomplished in a shorter time. The question was not even discussed. Reality had now become irrelevant. For the Court it was enough to insist that "dual systems" must be eliminated "at once." This is behavior possible only for those who need answer to no one. It is not decision-making according to law but lawless tyranny, not the action of the public servants of a sovereign people but the application of the lash.

Carter

Even the Fifth Circuit, however, seemed unable to believe what the Supreme Court now required. On December 1, 1969, it decided, unanimously and *en banc*, the consolidated appeals of sixteen school cases from several states. It recognized *Alexander* as having "supervened all existing authority to the contrary" and that under that decision "the shift is from a status of litigation to one of unitary operation pending litigation." It was "apparent" that "converting to a unitary system involved basically the merger of faculty and staff, students, transportation, services, athletics and other extracurricular school activities." Plans for achieving such "merger," however, had not yet been "originated" for some of the school districts by either the Office of Education or the school boards. The question, therefore, was whether "merger" should be required "during the present school term" and "despite the absence of plans." The Fifth Circuit held that this was indeed the requirement as to everything but student bodies and that it was to be accomplished by February 1, 1970, while the school term was in progress and despite the absence of plans. The "merger of student bodies into unitary systems," however, was found "difficult to arrange" during a school term "in the absence of merger plans." The court noted: "Many students must transfer. Buildings will be put to new use. In some instances it may be necessary to transfer equipment, supplies, or libraries. School bus routes must be reconstituted." [11] Students, therefore, the court held, did not have to be reassigned until the following term. In allowing this the Fifth Circuit was found to have erred. The Supreme Court granted certiorari to plaintiffs in three of the cases, and the Fifth Circuit was again summarily reversed, on January 14, 1970, in *Carter v. West Feliciana Parish School Board*: "Insofar as the Court of Appeals authorized deferral of student desegregation beyond February 1, 1970, that court misconstrued our holding in *Alexander*." [12] Believable or not, the midterm transfer of students without regard to school board preparation was constitutionally required. The possibility of doing what the Court ordered to be done and the educational effects of attempting to do it were irrelevant; all that was relevant was that the races be mixed.

Justice Harlan, joined by Justice Byron White, concurred separately. They agreed that *Alexander* had not been complied with, but felt that "further guidance" as to the meaning of *Alexander* was called for. As they understood it, *Alexander* entitled plaintiffs in school segregation cases to "immediate relief" to achieve "disestablishment of segregated school systems" upon "a prima facie showing of noncompliance" with *Green*. If an HEW plan is available, the district courts should order that it be adopted unless the school board demonstrates "beyond question" its "unworkability." In any event, the district court should order "such measures [as] will tend to accomplish the goals set forth in *Green*, and, if they are less than educationally perfect, proposals for amendments may thereafter be made." The measures should be put into "actual operative effect" within, at the most, "a period of approximately eight weeks" after a finding of noncompliance with *Green*, "including the time for judicial approval and review." The required procedure, unique in American law, was apparently first to grant plaintiffs relief, to the extent of reorganizing entire school systems, if necessary, within at most eight weeks, and then to consider the defendants' objections. Justices Black, William Douglas, William Brennan, and Thurgood Marshall, however, objected that this procedure was too lenient. "Those views," they said, "retreat from our holding in *Alexander*" that "dual school systems" are to be terminated "at once." [13]

Chief Justice Warren Burger and Justice Potter Stewart dissented. They "would not peremptorily reverse the judgments" of the Fifth Circuit "sitting *en banc* and acting unanimously": "That court is far more familiar than we with the various situations of these several school districts, some large, some small, some rural, and some metropolitan, and has exhibited responsibility and fidelity to the objectives of our holdings in school desegregation cases." Summary reversal, therefore, "without argument and without opportunity for exploration of the varying problems of individual school districts, seems unsound to us." [14]

The Fifth Circuit, it should be added, finally understood what was now required. Upon remand, sitting *en banc*, it disposed of fourteen cases in a one-paragraph *per curiam* opinion ordering midterm reassignment of students in all the cases. Only Judge Charles Clark, recently appointed to the court, joined by Judge James Coleman, was willing to consider and state what was actually involved. In a powerful dissenting opinion, he found that the court's decision, dealing "with the central lives of literally hundreds of thousands of children, parents, teachers and others," "lacks even the smallest spark of compassionate understanding." It is justified neither with reason nor logic, nor is it supported by the slightest attempt at persuasion. We do not show the District Court or the litigants how to get this case out of the courts. We do not point out where the new concept of mid-term student body merger has been applied with success. We do not demonstrate the shortcomings or defects of other more reasonable options available. We simply issue another cryptic edict.

. . . . .

All of what we do here is based upon granting equal protection to citizens. When the calm, bright light of history illuminates what has been done, it is bound to show that too great a haste for "equal" played a major part in destroying the protection we sought to provide. . . . For it cannot be rightly said that the blame for the lack of all deliberate speed belongs upon the school children of either race or upon their parents, yet it is they who are being equally *punished* by being deprived of one of the most vital and fundamental of the protections encompassed by the Fourteenth Amendment—a viable public education. For some of these children it is their last year in school. For all of them it's their most important. Reorganization of their districts in mid-year not only separates them from their friends and classmates, destroys their close identity with their school, interrupts months of training in difficult subjects with teachers they understand and to whom they respond; it also drains their districts of already thin financial resources and sends them packing across town or across the county or parish to strange environs with new classmates, new teachers, possibly to a different curriculum, with different or no equipment.

. . . . .

The precipitate haste with which complex actions are demanded in the midst of a school year, the brief unexplained command by which it is ordered and the failure to consider separate varying district problems on an individual basis combine to deprive the litigants before us of due process and to destroy the very protection we seek to make equal. [15]

Northcross

In the context of apparently unyielding insistence on integration "at once" regardless of cost, the Court's decision in *Northcross* v. *Board of Education of the Memphis, Tennessee, City Schools*, [16] two months

later, appears on the surface somewhat confusing. Certiorari
had been granted to the plaintiffs in a school "desegregation"
case, and the Court found, as was to be expected, that the
court of appeals, which had denied the relief sought, had seriously
erred. Suprisingly, however, the denial was affirmed in all respects,
and a relatively limited "desegregation" order was left standing.

The case involved the latest phase of long-continuing litigation
in Memphis. In May 1969 the district court had ordered the
Memphis school board to submit a plan by January 1970
based on geographic assignment. After the Court's *Alexander*
decision in October 1969, the plaintiffs naturally concluded that
much greater speed and effort to mix the races were now
constitutionally required. The district court, however, denied a
motion for further relief and continued to require only a geographic
plan by January. The plaintiffs appealed this denial to the Court
of Appeals for the Sixth Circuit and also moved for an
injunction directing the district court to require "a plan for the
operation of the City of Memphis Public Schools as a unitary
system during the current 1969-70 school year." A "unitary
system" was defined by plaintiffs as one that "would require
that in every public school in Memphis there would have to be
55% Negroes and 45% whites. Departures of 5% to 10% from
such rule would be tolerated." [17]

The Sixth Circuit affirmed the denial of further relief and
denied the injunction. It pointed out that the "unitary system"
required by *Alexander* was, as the Court had said in that case,
one in "which no person is to be effectively excluded from any
school because of race or color" and that the Court had
"exposed the question" in *Alexander* as involving children "presently
attending . . . schools under segregated conditions." This, the Sixth
Circuit said, "is not descriptive of the present situation of
Memphis." Memphis was "not now operating a 'dual school
system'" and would have "converted its pre-*Brown* dual system
into a unitary system" upon compliance with the district
court's order. The Supreme Court, the Sixth Circuit correctly
pointed out, had "not announced" that each school in a system
was to be racially balanced. [18]

The Sixth Circuit thus avoided the clear import of what

the Court had done in *Green* and later cases by focusing on what the Court had said. There was no doubt that the Court now required some degree of racial balance but found it prudent to continue to speak, inconsistently, of "desegregation" and the end of racial discrimination. The Sixth Circuit, which did not, at the time, share the Court's objectives, was able, quite properly, to comply only with what the Court was willing to say. It in effect challenged the Court either to state openly that it was requiring racial balance or to make clear that it was not. The Court decided not to ignore the challenge, but neither would it have its hand prematurely forced.

The Court granted certiorari and, *per curiam*, "held" that "the Court of Appeals erred" in several respects: in finding that Memphis was "not now operating a 'dual school system,'" that Memphis would, upon compliance with the district court's order, have converted to a unitary system, and that *Alexander* was "inapplicable to this case." [19] Despite its finding of so much error, the Court immediately concluded its opinion by affirming all that the Sixth Circuit had done. The Sixth Circuit was permitted to prevail in this case, but not, in effect, without a warning that the Court's requirements were not always to be so easily escaped.

Northcross was notable at the time primarily because the newly appointed chief justice, Warren Burger, concurred separately. He took the occasion to urge that the Court "as soon as possible" resolve "the basic practical problems" involved in the requirement of a "unitary system." [20] In the context of *Alexander* and *Carter* the mere realization that problems could exist was significant. To recognize problems was to realize that limits to compulsory integration would eventually have to be found. For the Court, however, this was no time to speak of either problems or limits, for to do so would serve, as Chief Justice Burger's opinion did, as a basis for hope and argument by opponents of compulsory integration. [21] This was a time to speak of absolutes, of the need to take "whatever steps might be necessary" and "at once." Fear, it seemed, was to be struck in the hearts of the opponents so that limits, should they ever be found, would, no matter how wide, be gratefully accepted as a reprieve rather than resisted as a new imposition. [22]

The chief justice's call for some recognition of reality was seriously weakened, however, by his acceptance of the pretense that the Court still required the elimination of racial discrimination. "The suggestion that the Court has not defined a unitary school system," he said, "is not supportable," for in *Alexander*, "we stated, albeit perhaps too cryptically, that a unitary system was one 'within which no person is to be effectively excluded from any school because of race or color.' "[23] In fact, however, whatever a "unitary system" might require, it was *not* the elimination of racial exclusion. No such exclusion had been found in *Green* or any later case. On the contrary, it was apparent that the Court, despite what it continued to say, was *requiring* racial discrimination and exclusion in order to increase integration. The statement quoted by the chief justice not only failed to define "unitary system," "cryptically" or otherwise, as it was actually being used by the Court, but was inconsistent with that usage. The inconsistency between *Alexander*'s definition of "unitary system" and the requirement imposed in its name in practice had already been pointed out by Judge Clark:

> Nobody knows what constitutes "[a unitary school system] within which no person is to be effectively excluded from any school because of race or color." . . .
> The assignment of specific racial quotas and the establishment of minimum, acceptable, percentage, racial guidelines for students, most assuredly cannot be the terms of definition, for when a child of any race wishes to attend a school because of its location close to home, because of the deemed excellence of its faculty or facilities, because it is attended by brothers or sisters or close friends or because it is on Dad's way to work or in Mother's car pool, and his wishes accord with valid educational policy, yet that child winds up being excluded from that school solely because the color of his or her skin doesn't conform to a predetermined arbitrary racial quota or percentage guideline, that child's right to be free of racial distinctions is gone. By the very wording of the phrase to be defined, a school system can't be "unitary" if a child is effectively excluded from any school because of his or her race or color. It's easy to see what it isn't, the challenge is to show what it is.[24]

The Lower Courts' Search for the Meaning of *Green*

At the time of *Green*, the great majority of school districts in the South were operating, after much litigation and negotiation, under freedom-of-choice plans approved by, or pursuant to the requirements of, the courts and the Office of Education. *Green*, of course, was the signal for litigation to begin anew. The litigation machine constructed by the NAACP in the 1930s, supplemented, as a result of the 1964 Civil Rights Act, by the Department of Justice and the Office of Education, was now capable of mass production. Cases could now be brought to court and disposed of wholesale. [25]

Although the Court's opinions continued to speak of eliminating racial discrimination and ending racial exclusion, its actual decisions left little doubt that it now required some degree of integration. *Green, Raney,* and *Monroe* indicated that systems with 80 to 85 percent of the blacks attending all black schools were, at least in the circumstances of those cases, not "unitary." *Monroe* further indicated that the likelihood of the flight of whites from a system could not be taken into account. *Montgomery* established the principle that racial assignments and quotas were at least permissible with respect to faculty. *Alexander* and *Carter*, finally, indicated that whatever was required was required "at once," regardless of educational disruption. The ideal, presumably, if not the requirement, was a perfectly racially balanced school system—that is, one in which the racial ratios of students, faculty, and staff were the same in each school as in the system as a whole. The "basic practical problem" for the lower courts was to determine what lesser degree of racial balance, if any, would suffice in a given situation.

More specifically, the task in each case was to determine the racial composition of the system as a whole and of each school within it, determine whether any existing racial imbalance was constitutionally permissible in light of the measures that would be necessary to lessen it, and determine the further measures, if any, to be required. In practice, the principal considerations became the number of all black or "nearly" all black schools in a system, the percentage of the system's blacks in such schools, and the possible means of reducing this number or percentage. The task was made more difficult for some judges by the knowlege—irrelevant under *Monroe*—that many of the possible steps that could be taken would probably result in a white exodus, leaving the system still blacker. [26] A most unfortunate aspect of the whole process was the creation of the unavoidable impression that black students constituted an imperfection to be diluted and white students a resource to be exploited. The real objective, each succeeding Supreme Court decision up to 1974 made clearer, was to disperse the blacks as thinly as possible.

The Fifth Circuit, vindicated by *Green,* quickly gave it and later cases a broad reading. The court quickly ruled that racial quotas for faculty and staff were everywhere required, that "majority-to-minority" transfer provisions (allowing students to transfer from schools in which they were in the racial majority to schools in which they would be in the minority) were required, and that the location and capacity of new schools were to be selected, under district court supervision, so as to increase integration.[27] Achieving racially balanced student bodies, however, proved a more serious problem. Judge Wisdom's immediate post-*Green* ruling, for a panel of the court, that any school district where "there are still all-Negro schools or only a small fraction of Negroes enrolled in white schools" fails "as a matter of law" to "meet constitutional standards as established in *Green*"[28] was found very difficult to apply and was not in fact followed by other judges of the Fifth Circuit. More and more drastic restructuring of school systems was ordered, but some all black schools almost always remained.

School districts in the circuit had the good fortune, during much of 1970, to have school "desegregation" appeals come before a three-judge panel that included two of the dissenters in *Jefferson County.*[29] This panel, tacitly rejecting Judge Wisdom's view, did not read *Green* as requiring some degree of racial balance in all schools, but as permitting geographic assignment and the preservation of neighborhood schools. The panel began by requiring only strictly geographic assignment even though some all black schools would remain.[30] It quickly moved, however, to requiring the "pairing" of schools in "close proximity"[31] and then to requiring the closing of some schools and to the pairing of schools not in very close proximity.[32]

Later panels of the court, less committed to preserving neighborhood schools, rapidly went further. School districts were required to rezone according to explicit racial lines, to pair ever more distant schools, and to "cluster" groups of schools.[33] Even these panels, however, hesitated to require school districts to abandon completely the neighborhood concept and to provide extensive transportation of pupils. The fact that a plan "involves some bussing" was not found necessarily to "defeat it until the extent of bussing and the cost of the increase are known," and only "impractical attendance zones or inordinate transportation problems" would be considered obstacles,[34] but the restructurings actually ordered were apparently limited to schools within contiguous zones. The result was that some all black or nearly all black schools almost always remained and had to be tolerated.[35] It soon became clear that, because of residential racial concentration, such schools could not be completely eliminated in most nonrural areas without a requirement of racial busing throughout the school district. Such a requirement was a very different matter from the disallowing of freedom of choice in the circumstances of *Green*. Even on the Court of Appeals for the Fifth Circuit, most judges found it hard to believe that *Green* could or would be carried so far. *Alexander* and *Carter* were indeed drastic decisions but, on the face of the opinions, only in insisting that what was required by *Green* was required "at once." Surely, one could hope, reality would dictate that cross-district busing to achieve racial balance was not the requirement.

7 | *"And Even Bizarre": The Supreme Court Requires Busing to Achieve School Racial Balance in the South*

Green pointed the law of race and the schools toward the precipice; *Swann* v. *Charlotte-Mecklenburg Board of Education* and *Davis* v. *Board of School Commissioners of Mobile County*,[1] three years later, in 1971, took it over the edge. The worst fears concerning what compulsory integration might mean were fully confirmed. Racial balance was indeed required, and cross-district busing was required where necessary to achieve it. The defeat of hope was made more complete by the fact that the opinion was written by Chief Justice Burger and made unanimous by the concurrence of the newly appointed Justice Harry Blackmun. If, as is often claimed, presidential elections and new court appointments can to some extent reconcile the Court's power and democratic government, it would obviously take more elections than one and more appointments than two.

Swann v. *Charlotte-Mecklenburg*

The facts of *Swann* bore little resemblance to those of *Green*. The Charlotte-Mecklenburg School District, consisting of Mecklenburg County, North Carolina, with the city of Charlotte at its center, was one of the largest in the nation in area—550 square miles, 22 miles from east to west and 36 miles from north to south; in the number of schools—107; and in the number of students—over 84,000 in the 1968-1969 school year and increasing at the rate of about 3,000 a year.[2] The black school population, 29 percent of the total, was heavily concentrated in the city (21,000 out of 24,000), and 95 percent of this population in a single section of the city.[3]

The delay and recalcitrance emphasized in *Green* were here much less evident. Unlike Virginia, North Carolina never adopted a policy of "massive resistance." It was the first state to seek accommodation with *Brown* by adopting, in 1955, the technique of pupil placement, thereby accepting integration, at least in principle. And unlike Alabama's Pupil Placement Act, which the Court found constitutionally unobjectionable on its face in 1958,[4] North Carolina's did result in some integration. Token integration existed in Charlotte as early as the late 1950s.[5] In 1962, the school board voluntarily adopted a plan of nonracial geographic assignment to be implemented concurrently with a five-year, thirty-million-dollar school construction program. Over 2,000 blacks attended schools with a majority of whites by the 1965 school year, and geographic zoning was put into effect for all schools by the 1966 school year.[6]

The operation of this plan was challenged by plaintiffs in 1965. After extensive litigation, it was approved, with minor modifications, by the district court and the Court of Appeals for the Fourth Circuit, sitting *en banc*.[7] School "desegregation" cases, however, neither die nor fade away, but begin again on a larger scale.

The District Court: Compulsory Integration to Improve Black Academic Performance

The district court having retained jurisdiction, the plaintiffs, after *Green*, instituted a new round of litigation. The matter came this time before a newly appointed district court judge whose opinions show great confidence in his ability to prescribe for social ills and a deep belief that the prescriptions were constitutional commands. The judge did not find that the board had failed to comply with the 1965 order under which it was operating. Indeed, he praised the board for having "achieved a degree and volume of desegregation of schools apparently unsurpassed in these parts," and for having "exceeded the performance of any school board whose actions have been reviewed in appellate court decisions. The Charlotte-Mecklenburg schools in many respects are models for others. They are attractive to outside teachers and offer good education."[8] He specifically found that there had been "no racial discrimination or inequality" in eleven elements of the operation of the system challenged by the plaintiffs.[9] The only "racial discrimination" he found consisted simply of the use of neighborhood schools and the grant of freedom to transfer in a situation of black residential concentration.[10] The district judge was quite candid in stating that "the difference between 1965 and 1969 is simply the difference between *Brown* of 1955 and *Green* v. *New Kent County* of 1968. The rules of the game have changed, and the methods and philosophies which in good faith the Board has followed are no longer adequate to complete the job which the courts now say must be done 'now.' " Under the new "rules of the game," as the judge understood them, the Charlotte-Mecklenburg schools were "not yet desegregated" because they were not racially balanced—"approximately 14,000 of the 24,000 Negro students still attend schools that are all black, or very nearly all black, and most of the 24,000 have no white teachers"—and black students were not doing well academically.[11]

The *Green* theory, however, was that racial balance was not constitutionally required as such wherever racial imbalance exists, but only as a "remedy" for unconstitutional segregation, to "disestablish the dual system" that *Brown* had prohibited in 1954. Many of Charlotte-Mecklenburg's schools that were predominantly black in 1968 had never been black schools under the dual system, but had been white or were new schools that had become predominantly black as the result of an increase in the black school-age population from 7,500 in 1954 to 24,000 in 1968. These predominantly black schools were, of course, indistinguishable from such schools in the North and West, and the *Green* theory of removing the racial identification they had under the dual system was, therefore, inapplicable. Ignoring these doctrinal refinements, the district judge proceeded on a quite different theory which made the former racial designation of the schools irrelevant. The need and justification for compulsory integration as he saw it was simply that "as a group Negro students score quite low on school achievement tests . . . , and the results are not improving under present conditions." There was, he later pointed out, an "alarming contrast in performance" between black and white students which, he thought, was "obviously not known to school patrons generally"; at least, "it was not fully known to the court before he studied the evidence in the case." [12] This contrast, which, however, is nation-wide, [13] he demonstrated with respect to Charlotte-Mecklenburg by using detailed tables. The relatively poor performance of blacks, he felt competent to determine, "cannot be explained solely in terms of cultural, racial or family background without honestly facing the impact of segregation": "It is painfully apparent that 'quality education' cannot live in a segregated school; *segregation itself is the greatest barrier to quality education.*" The "experts [three professors from Rhode Island College called as witnesses by the plaintiffs] all agree (and the statistics tend to bear them out)" that "a racial mix in which black students heavily predominate tends to retard the progress of the whole group." [14] The solution was clear and simple: a "dramatic improvement" in black performance could be "produced" "without material detriment to the whites" by "transferring underprivileged black children from black schools into schools with 70% or more white students." [15] On this basis, an article of faith in the 1960s, now almost totally discredited, [16] the racial busing of school children was brought to Charlotte-Mecklenburg and, thereby, to the nation. Racial balance was required by the district judge, not to "disestablish the dual system" according to the *Green* theory, but simply because he believed that majority-white schools were necessary to improve academic performance by blacks.

The district judge repeatedly denied that he accepted the plaintiffs' argument that the board should be required to "assign the children on a basis 70% white and 30% black, and bus them to all the schools," but he accepted it nonetheless. The board, he pointed out, had "the power to establish a formula and provide transportation; and if this could be done, it would be a great benefit to the community." [17] How it could be done, however, was a matter of no great concern to the judge. "Cost," he said, "is not a valid, legal reason for continued denial of constitutional rights." The board had the "assets and experience" to deal with the problem involved. For the judge, the desirability of neighborhood schools was no more than a "theory." He had his own "philosophy of education," according to which "educators should concentrate on planning schools as educational institutions rather than as neighborhood proprietorships." He could see "no reason except emotion . . . why school buses cannot be used by the Board to provide the flexibility and economy necessary to desegregate the schools. Buses are cheaper than new buildings; using them might even keep property taxes down." [18]

The practical difficulties were, nonetheless, enormous, but the judge was equal to them.[19] After rejecting or only temporarily approving several board plans as inadequate, the judge, in December 1969, appointed one of the plaintiffs' "expert" witnesses, John Finger, a professor of education from Rhode Island College, as a consultant to prepare an additional plan. Finger was instructed that "all the black and predominantly black schools in the system are illegally segregated"; that "efforts should be made to reach a 71-29 ratio in the various schools so that there will be no basis for contending that one school is racially different from the others," although "variations from that norm may be unavoidable"; that "bus transportation . . . may validly be employed"; and that the "alleged high cost of desegregating schools (which the court does not find to be a fact) would not be a valid, legal argument against desegregation." [20]

In February 1970, the board and Finger each submitted a plan to the court. Under the board's plan, seven predominantly black schools were to be closed, the faculty of every school in the system was to be racially balanced according to the ratio of the races in the system as a whole and only majority-to-minority (integration-increasing) transfers were to be allowed. Utilizing computers, the board attempted to disperse the blacks throughout the system to the greatest extent possible by redrawing attendance-zone lines. The result, for the system's ten high schools, was that none would have a black majority, nine would have a black population of from 17 to 36 percent, and the tenth a black population of 2 percent. Of the twenty-one junior high schools, twenty would be no more than 38 percent black, and one would be 90 percent black. Of the seventy-six elementary schools, nine would be predominantly (83 to 100 percent) black and would have approximately half of the system's black elementary school students.[21] Few, if any, school systems of the nation's larger cities with substantial black populations could show a comparable racial balance.[22] Furthermore, and of crucial importance according to the *Green* "disestablishment" rationale for requiring racial balance, the high school that would have been left 98 percent white under the board's plan had never been a segregated school, a part of the dual system, but had been built after 1965; the one junior high school that would have been left predominantly black had never been a segregated school for blacks but had been a segregated white school that became black, after segregation ended, because of the growth of the black population in the area of the school; and at least two of the nine elementary schools that would have been left predominantly black under the board's plan had never been segregated schools for blacks.[23] There could be no question, therefore, of requiring a change in the racial composition of these schools in order to remove the racial identification they had under the dual system. But these facts were irrelevant, of course, under the district judge's very different rationale that racial balance was required to improve black academic performance.

Despite the high degree of racial balance that would have been achieved under the board's plan, Finger was able to suggest several improvements. Although the board's plan left no high school more than 36 percent black, he recommended transporting three hundred black students from the central city to the suburban high school that would otherwise be 98 percent white. He further recommended that the one junior high school left with a black majority under the board's plan be eliminated by creating nine "satellite zones" in black residential areas from which blacks would be transported to nine outlying junior high schools.[24]

Finally, he recommended that the nine majority-black elementary schools remaining in the inner city under the board's plan be eliminated by "grouping" them with twenty-four suburban, predominantly white schools. Blacks assigned to grades 1 to 4 in these nine schools under the board's plan were, under Finger's plan, to report to them daily in order to be transported to one of the twenty-four suburban schools; whites assigned to grades 5 and 6 in the twenty-four suburban schools were to report to them in order to be transported to one of the nine city schools. Under this plan, no school in the system would be less than 9 percent or more than 39 percent black, except for one elementary school that would be 3 percent black.[25] Although the judge insisted that *"it is still to this day the local School Board and not the court, which has the duty to assign pupils and operate the schools, subject to the requirements of the Constitution,"* he rejected the board's plan for each of the three levels of schools and ordered the board to put Finger's plan into effect.[26]

Upon objection by the board that implementation of the Finger plan would involve inordinate costs, additional hearings were held on the question and supplemental findings were made by the judge in March 1970. The costs, number of children, distances, and riding times involved in busing proposals are extremely difficult to estimate and invariably a source of much dispute. The board estimated that under its plan 4,935 additional children would be bused, 104 additional buses would be required, $144,600 would be added to annual operating costs, and the total first-year busing cost, including the purchase price of buses at $5,400 each, drivers' salaries, parking and other expenses, would be $864,700. It estimated that under the Finger plan the additional requirements would be, instead, the busing of 19,285 children, 442 buses, $586,800 in annual operating costs, and $3,406,700 in first-year costs. The judge found, however, that various "discount factors" were to be applied to the board's figures: for example, not all eligible children would use the bus (private transportation costs could, apparently, be ignored), not all children go to school every day, the hours of opening and closing a school could be staggered to utilize buses better, the minimum distance for which transportation would be provided could be increased from one and a half to one and three-quarters miles, and buses could "be operated at a 25 percent figure overload."[27] Taking these "discount factors" into account, the judge found that the Finger plan would add only 13,300 children to be bused, 138 buses, an annual operating cost of $532,000, and a first year cost of $1,011,200.[28]

The judge found the additional costs involved, according to his computations, insignificant and the available resources ample. An additional annual operating cost of $400,000, for example, would, given the $45,000,000 school budget, "add less than 1 per cent to the local cost of operating the schools."[29] The $745,200 cost of 138 additional buses was "much less than one week's portion of the Mecklenburg school budget." As for resources, "there had been a sizeable operating surplus in the state [school] budget for every biennium since 1959-60"; "the state replaces [buses] when they are worn out"; and "the North Carolina Board of Education has approximately 400 new school buses and 375 used buses in storage." To ease further the board's concern about costs, the judge noted that half ($255,000) of the additional annual operating cost of transportation that he computed the local system would have to pay was "at current rates . . . only slightly more than the annual interest on the value of the $3,000,000 worth of school property" already abandoned by the board by closing schools to further racial balance.[30]

Despite his rejection of the board's plan—even the provisions concerning the high schools, none of which would have been more than 36 percent black—the judge continued to insist that his order was "not based on any requirement of 'racial balance.' "[31] In fact, however, the judge required not only that racial balance be achieved but that it thereafter be permanently maintained. He ordered that "the defendants maintain a continuing control over the race of children in each school, just as was done for many decades before Brown v. Board of Education, and maintain the racial make-up of each school (including any new and any reopened schools) to prevent any school from becoming racially identifiable," and that "the Board adopt and implement a continuing program, computerized or otherwise, of assigning pupils and teachers during the school year as well as at the start of each year for the conscious purpose of maintaining each school and each faculty in a condition of desegregation."[32] These requirements followed as a matter of course from the basis on which he decided the case— predominantly white schools were constitutionally required because they were necessary for "quality education" for blacks.

The Court of Appeals: Compulsory Integration to Overcome Residential Racial Concentration

On appeal by the board, the Court of Appeals for the Fourth Circuit, sitting en banc, split three ways. The prevailing opinion of three judges affirmed the district court's order except that it remanded for further consideration the question whether the elementary schools could be sufficiently balanced with less busing.

Two judges, each writing an opinion in which he was joined by the other, dissented from the remand and would have affirmed in all respects. The remaining judge would have reversed on the ground that "busing to prevent racial imbalance is not as yet a constitutional obligation."[33] The result was a decision that went far beyond not only *Green* but anything the Fifth Circuit had done in its many decisions since *Green*.[34] This decision from a court that, unlike the Fifth Circuit, had not been noted for daring advances, but had consistently sought to limit "desegregation" law to established requirements, is difficult to explain.

Perhaps, as often happens, the majority saw the decision as something of a compromise with the still more extreme views of the district court and two of its own members. Judge John Butzner, who wrote the prevailing opinion, joined by Chief Judge Clement Haynsworth and Judge Herbert Boreman, had been appointed since the court's last decision upholding the Charlotte-Mecklenburg school system. Judge J. Braxton Craven, a source of intellectual leadership on the court, had, unfortunately, disqualified himself on the ground that he had approved the Charlotte-Mecklenburg school system in 1965 as a district judge. Chief Judge Haynsworth, one of the ablest federal judges, who usually wrote the court's *en banc* opinions on questions of race and the schools, had just been through the process culminating in his rejection as a Supreme Court nominee. The elderly Judge Albert Bryan, who would have reversed, wrote a very brief opinion providing little exposition and analysis. Judge Bryan did, however, cogently point out that the 1964 Civil Rights Act indicated, at the least, "Congress' hostile attitude toward the concept of achieving racial balance by busing."[35]

The Fourth Circuit's substantial affirmance of the district court's decision is all the more surprising in that none of the judges, including those who would have completely affirmed, accepted the district judge's basis for decision. The district judge, as has been noted, rejected the board's plan for each of the three school levels because, in his view, majority-white schools were constitutionally required simply to improve black academic performance. The Fourth Circuit, nowhere mentioning black performance, did not accept this theory and thereby avoided, as the Supreme Court had done and would do, that potentially explosive issue. The

Fourth Circuit, however, also made the inapplicability of the *Green* theory irrelevant by adopting still a third theory: that residential racial concentration could be found, and had been found by the district judge, to be the result of official racial discrimination. Assignment of children to neighborhood schools was, therefore, constitutionally impermissible where, owing to such concentration, racially imbalanced schools would result. "The district judge found," the court stated, "that residential patterns leading to segregation in the schools resulted in part from federal, state, and local governmental action. These findings are supported by the evidence and we accept them under familiar principles of appellate review."

The "evidence" noted by the court in support of these "findings" included the facts that "North Carolina courts, in common with many courts elsewhere, enforced racially restrictive covenants on real property" until 1948, when the Supreme Court "prohibited this discriminatory practice," and that "urban renewal projects, supported by heavy federal financing and the active participation of local government, contributed to the city's racially segregated housing patterns. The school board, for its part, located schools in black residential areas and fixed the size of the schools to accommodate the needs of immediate neighborhoods. Predominantly black schools were the inevitable result." The court realized that such "evidence" is everywhere available, but found that "the fact that similar forces operate in cities throughout the nation under the mask of *de facto* segregation provides no justification for allowing us to ignore the part that government plays in creating segregated neighborhood schools."

If the facts cited by the court are what justified a requirement of racially balanced schools in Charlotte-Mecklenburg, the requirement was, of course, applicable nationally, a conclusion that was by no means unacceptable in the South. *Green* notwithstanding, there was in fact no tenable basis, as the court recognized, for imposing the requirement on the South alone:

The necessity of dealing with segregation that exists because governmental policies foster segregated neighborhood schools is not confined to the Charlotte-Mecklenburg School District. Similar segregation occurs in many other cities throughout the nation, and constitutional principles dealing with it should be applied nationally.[36]

It was not difficult to believe at this time that resistance to the imposition of increasingly harsh requirements on southern school systems was no longer possible and would cease only if the requirements were made applicable nationally. As Congressman Jack Edwards of Alabama argued in a debate in the House of Representatives in November 1971 on antibusing measures: "We are busing all over the First District of Alabama, as far as you can imagine. Buses are everywhere. People say to me, 'How in the world are we ever going to stop this madness?' I say, 'It will stop the day it starts taking place across the country, in the North, in the East, in the West, and yes, even in Michigan.' "[37] The court would have, almost off-handedly in a single paragraph, worked another revolution in the law of school segregation. The court had found a rationale for requiring racial balance, but it was not the rationale of the district court or of *Green*, and it would have made obvious, all too soon for the Supreme Court, that school racial balance was required everywhere.

The court then proceeded to reach substantially the same result as the district judge had, except with regard to the elementary schools. In contrast to the district judge, however, it found that "not every school in a unitary school system need be integrated." "Some cities have black ghettos so large that integration of every school is an improbable, if not an unattainable goal. . . . An intractable remnant of segregation, we believe, should not void an otherwise exemplary plan for the creation of a unitary school system."[38] The court said nothing of continually maintaining racial balance once it had been achieved. Adopting "the test of reasonableness" and accepting as "not clearly erroneous" the district court's estimates of the amount and cost of the busing that would be involved, the court affirmed the rejection of the board's plan for all schools and the requirement that the Finger plan be adopted for high schools and junior high schools. As to the two groups of secondary schools, the court found that the increase in the number of pupils bused would be only "about 17% of all pupils now being bused"; older pupils were involved, and "the routes they must travel do not vary appreciably in length from the average route of the systems' buses." Rejection of the board's plan for the high schools, though it left no school more than 36 percent black, and the requirement that three hundred blacks be transported from the city to a suburban high school that was 98 percent white were justified because the requirement would "tend to stabilize the system by eliminating an almost totally white school in a zone to which other whites might move with consequent 'tipping' or resegregation of other schools." [39]

As to the elementary schools, however, while the board's plan was "properly disapproved," the Finger plan should also have been disapproved, because too great an increase in busing was required. It would have required transporting an additional 9,300 elementary school children (an increase of 39 percent) in ninety additional buses (an increase of 32 percent). If the elementary school part of the Finger plan were adopted, operation of the plan as a whole would increase the number of children bused by 56 percent and the number of buses needed by 49 percent. "The board," the court said, "should not be required to undertake such extensive additional busing to discharge its obligation to create a unitary school system." [40]

The court's approach to limiting busing was clearly unsatisfactory. It was based, as the judges who would have simply affirmed pointed out, on a purely "subjective assessment" defining no rule. [41] The court could have and should have simply found that no further "remedy" was required, because its 1966 order had been fully complied with and the racial imbalance in the system was not due to former segregation. It also might have rejected a requirement of busing as incompatible with the 1964 act. Even if some busing was to be required, the court could have refused to require "satellite" zoning; that is, the "remedy" could have been limited to the pairing and clustering of schools within contiguous zones. This was, apparently, the limitation that the United States, appearing as *amicus curiae*, had urged and that the Fifth Circuit's decisions had established. In any event, the board's plan should have been accepted because it more than met all then established constitutional requirements and because the district judge's rejection of that plan was based on the clearly erroneous theory that majority-white schools were constitutionally required to improve black academic performance. The district court's rejection of the part of the board's plan concerning the secondary

schools was erroneous beyond question, under the *Green* "disestablishment" theory, because the plan would have produced a very high
degree of racial balance in all secondary schools except two that
had either never been segregated or had not been segregated for the
race that now predominated. The Fourth Circuit, however,
was proceeding on an erroneous theory of its own, based on the
existence of residential racial concentration, that would have made
the racial balance requirement applicable in the North as well as
the South.

The Supreme Court: Compulsory Integration to "Dismantle the Dual System"

The Supreme Court granted petitions for certiorari by both
sides.[42] The task, it stated, was to define "in more precise terms
than heretofore the scope of the duty of school authorities and
district courts in implementing *Brown I* and the mandate to
eliminate dual systems and establish unitary systems at once."
The Court then rendered an opinion which bore almost no
relation to the facts of the case before it and which, when considered in light of those facts and of the decision reached, succeeded
only in establishing a requirement of almost perfectly racially
balanced schools regardless of cost. Reversing the Fourth Circuit's
remand regarding elementary schools, it reinstated the district
court's order in all respects. Cross-district busing for racial
balance in a large metropolitan school system was indeed what the
Constitution required. "There are limits," the Court assured,
to "how far a court can go,"[43] but its holding that they had not
been exceeded by the district court's decision in this case showed
that they must be remote indeed.

Perhaps the most striking feature of the story of Charlotte-
Mecklenburg's ordeal is that, although the school board lost in
each court it came before, it lost each time on the basis of a
different theory. The Supreme Court stated that "we must of
necessity rely to a large extent" on the "informed judgment" of
the lower courts, but, with regard to the basic theory of unconstitutionality, it relied in fact on neither of the lower courts. Racial
balance was constitutionally required by the district court to
improve the academic performance of blacks and by the Fourth

Circuit to counteract the effects of racial residential patterns thought to be the result of official racial discrimination. The Supreme Court held that racial balance was required to "dismantle the dual system."[44] This approach had the advantages of maintaining continuity with *Green*, of avoiding the question of black school performance, and of appearing to limit the requirement to the South, but the disadvantage—which, however, gave the Court little difficulty—of requiring the Court to ignore or misstate the facts of the case.

Following the example of *Green*, the Court began with the claim that compulsory integration follows from *Brown* II. "The objective today," the Court stated, "remains to eliminate from the public schools all vestiges of state-imposed segregation." Alleged sins in the past—not necessarily those of North Carolina or Charlotte-Mecklenburg—were again made to lend support to new requirements in the present. There had been the "deliberate resistance of some to the Court's mandates" and the "dilatory tactics . . . noted frequently by this Court and other courts," as a result of which, "by the time" of *Green* "in 1968, very little progress had been made in many areas where dual systems had historically been maintained by operation of state laws." Further steps were necessary because, despite the "plain language of *Green*," "the 1969 Term of Court brought fresh evidence of the dilatory tactics of many school authorities." For this evidence, the Court cited *Alexander*. "The failure of local authorities to meet their constitutional obligations aggravated the massive problem of converting from the state-enforced discrimination of racially separate school systems."[45] In fact, by 1968 progress in eliminating school racial discrimination was very great and was rapidly increasing as a result of the 1964 Civil Rights Act. To cite *Alexander* as an example of "dilatory tactics" and berate "school authorities" for a "failure . . . to meet their constitutional obligations" when the obvious fact, illustrated by both *Alexander* and the present case, was that those obligations were no sooner met than changed, was only to add insult to injury. Most important, whatever basis there might have been for the Court's statements, they did not apply to the present case, the one the Court was supposed to be deciding. The Charlotte-Mecklenburg school authorities, at least, the Court failed to note, had fully met their "constitutional obligations" as explicitly laid down in a 1965 court order and were condemned again only because, as the more disingenuous district judge had stated, "the rules of the game have changed."

Having thus established *Green* as its basis for requiring racial balancing and busing, the Court turned to the effect to be given the 1964 act's proscriptions of such requirements. "It is important to remember," the Court began, "that judicial powers may be exercised only on the basis of a constitutional violation. Remedial judicial authority does not put judges automatically in the shoes of school authorities whose powers are plenary. Judicial authority enters only when local authority defaults." "Absent a finding of a constitutional violation," it "would not be within the authority of a federal court" to require a "prescribed ratio of Negro to white students." The Court itself was apparently unable to remember this, however, in deciding the case before it; the constitutional deficiency, according to the *Green* theory, of the board's plan, at least for the high schools and junior high schools, the Court nowhere showed. Chief Justice Burger was concerned, however, with combating the theories of the lower courts that would have made racial balance a general constitutional requirement, while he would, in effect, have made the proscriptions of the 1964 act inapplicable only in the South. In the course of this effort, he casually observed that it would be "within the broad discretionary powers of school authorities" to institute the policy that "each school should have a prescribed ratio of Negro to white students reflecting the proportion for the district as a whole."[46] The question of the constitutional validity of such a policy was not presented for decision, and if it should be presented it should either be one of great difficulty or easily be decided in the negative, on the ground that such a policy would grossly disadvantage individuals on the basis of their race. It is often the case, however, that in the combating of error much error is approved.

The Court then quoted section 401(b) of the act, which states that "desegregation" means the assignment of students to schools "without regard to their race," and "shall not mean" assignment "to overcome racial imbalance," and the proviso to section 407 that "nothing herein shall empower any official or court of the United States to issue any order seeking to achieve a racial balance in any school by requiring the transportation of pupils or students from one school to another or one school district to another in order to achieve such racial balance."[47] The Court's present usage of "desegregation" was, of course, directly contrary to the act's definition, and requiring the transportation of pupils to achieve racial balance was precisely what was involved in the case. The Court found, however, that "the language and the history of Title IV show that it was enacted not to limit but to define the role of the Federal Government in the implementation of the *Brown I* decision." It then disposed of the act in one paragraph:

On their face, the sections quoted purport only to insure that the provisions of Title IV of the Civil Rights Act of 1964 will not be read as granting new powers. The proviso in [section 407] is in terms designed to foreclose any interpretation of the Act as expanding the *existing* powers of federal courts to enforce the Equal Protection Clause. There is no suggestion of an intention to restrict those powers or withdraw from courts their historic equitable remedial powers. The legislative history of Title IV indicates that Congress was concerned that the Act might be read as creating a right of action under the Fourteenth Amendment in the situation of so-called "de facto segregation," where racial imbalance exists in the schools but with no showing that this was brought about by discriminatory action of state authorities. In short, there is nothing in the Act which provides us material assistance in answering the question of remedy for state-imposed segregation in violation of *Brown I.*[48]

The Court's distinction between "define" and "limit" is not clear —to define is to limit—but, as has been indicated above, there can be no doubt, in any event, that the quoted provisions were intended as limits or that, as such, they were essential to the passage of the act. There is no way to read either the language or the history of Title IV without concluding that Congress meant to provide the most complete assurance possible that the act would not become a means of requiring school racial balance, and specifically, busing to achieve racial balance. The Court's assertion that "the legislative history of Title IV indicates that Congress was concerned" with prohibiting a requirement of racial balance only "in the situation of so-called 'de facto segregation,' where racial imbalance exists in the schools but with no showing that this was brought about by discriminatory action of state authorities" is simply baseless.[49] Congress was assured in 1964 by proponents of the act that "the busing of children to achieve racial balance" would be unconstitutional because "we would be transporting children because of race" and that the Supreme Court had "in effect" recently so held.[50] The objective of the quoted provisions, insisted upon by representatives of the South, was to preclude a requirement of racial balance in districts where a showing of "discriminatory action by school authorities" in the past most assuredly could be made.

The Court did not, like the Fifth Circuit in *Jefferson County*, find that the act supports a requirement of racial balance, but only that it does not preclude it, but the perversion of the act is hardly less. Without the act, *Brown*'s prohibition of school racial segregation would have still been a long way from effectuation, and a requirement of busing to achieve racial balance would have been inconceivable. If the act does not "in terms" preclude the Court from imposing such a requirement under the rubric of constitutional law, the conclusion is nonetheless inescapable that the effect of the Court's ingenious but disingenuous interpretation was to turn the act against itself and against the clear will and understanding of the Congress and the electorate that made the act possible.[51]

The Court next offered a gratuitous and confusing discussion of the "construction of new schools and the closing of old ones." "In the past," it found, the placing of schools had been a "potent weapon for creating or maintaining a state-segregated school system." And, "since *Brown*," school authorities have sometimes "closed schools which appeared likely to become racially mixed through changes in neighborhood residential patterns" and constructed schools in white areas far "from Negro population centers in order to maintain the separation of the races." Therefore, the Court concluded, "it is the responsibility of local authorities and district courts to see to it that future school construction and abandonment are not used and do not serve to perpetuate or re-establish the dual system."[52]

The meaning and relevance of these observations in an opinion purportedly concerned, like *Brown* and *Green*, with "dismantling the dual system" are unclear. "In the past" (prior to *Brown*), areas with a dual system had no need for any devious "potent weapon" to maintain segregation; students were simply assigned to school on a racial basis, as was then constitutionally permissible.[53]

Since *Brown*, racially discriminatory school construction practices are no doubt unconstitutional, but the applicability of the *Green* "remedy" requires no showing of present racial discrimination where a school district that had the dual system is involved. In any event, the Court cited no evidence and none appears in the record that any school was closed or built in Mecklenburg County since *Brown* to avoid or impede integration. On the contrary, many schools had become racially mixed without being closed, and many predominantly black schools were closed—$3,000,000 worth in 1969 alone—in order to disperse the blacks for better racial balance.[54] Again, the Court must have been talking about some other case.

The Court then turned to the "central issue" of the case, student assignment, and found "essentially four problem areas":

(1) to what extent racial balance or racial quotas may be used as an implement in a remedial order to correct a previously segregated system;

(2) whether every all-Negro and all-white school must be eliminated as an indispensable part of a remedial process of desegregation;

(3) what the limits are, if any, on the rearrangement of school districts and attendance zones, as a remedial measure; and

(4) what the limits are, if any, on the use of transportation facilities to correct state-enforced racial school segregation.[55]

These problem areas were separately discussed on a generally high level of abstraction, and little or no effort was made to tie the principles announced to the decision reached. As to each area, limitations or qualifications were stated in theory but ignored in application.

The Court began the discussion by insisting again, in the face of what was actually involved, that its concern continued to be, as in "every holding from *Brown I* to date," "to dismantle dual school systems." The "objective" was only to ensure that "school authorities exclude no pupil of a racial minority from any school, directly or indirectly, on account of race."[56] The Court was apparently oblivious to the fact that a requirement of racial balance and the use of racial quotas necessarily means that some pupils of each race, minority as well as majority, will be excluded from certain schools because of their race. As in the case of its earlier approval of a requirement of faculty racial quotas, a requirement of racial exclusion was justified only by reiterating that racial exclusion is prohibited. This justification must suffice because the Court is subject to no review, but there is nothing that entitles it to respect.

Coming to the question of requiring racial balance and the use of racial quotas, the Court saw an important distinction between a requirement of a "fixed mathematical racial balance" and what the district judge had done. If the district judge had required, "as a matter of constitutional right, any particular degree of racial balance or mixing," the Court would, it said, "be obliged to reverse." The district judge, however, it found, had approved only a "very limited use of mathematical ratios" as "no more than a starting point in the process of shaping a remedy, rather than [as] an inflexible requirement."Admittedly, the district judge had instructed Finger that "efforts should be made to reach a 71-29 ratio in the various schools so that there will be no basis for contending that one school is racially different from the others." But the "claim" that this "imposed a racial balance requirement of 71%-29% on individual schools" was "blunted" by "the fact that no such objective was actually achieved—and would appear to be impossible." Furthermore, "the District Judge went on to acknowledge that variation 'from that norm may be unavoidable.' "[57] But the Finger plan had "actually achieved," although the Court did not here mention the fact, a school system in which none of the 107 schools was less than 3 (9 except for one school) or more than 39 percent black. To require this was not, apparently, to require "any particular degree of racial balance or mixing." Why the achievement of a still more precise racial balance "would appear to be impossible" was not explained. No reason appears why Finger could not have racially balanced each school down to the last pupil, using no more than the techniques the Court went on to approve.

As further justification for its approval of the district judge's "very limited use of mathematical ratios," the Court stated:

The predicate for the District Court's use of the 71%–29% ratio was twofold: first, its express finding, approved by the Court of Appeals and not challenged here, that a dual school system had been maintained by the school authorities at least until 1969; second, its finding, also approved by the Court of Appeals, that the school board had totally defaulted in its acknowledged duty to come forward with an acceptable plan of its own, notwithstanding the patient efforts of the District Judge who, on at least three occasions, urged the board to submit plans.[58]

The Court's statement is inaccurate in several respects. First, the board had not maintained an unconstitutional dual system until 1969; the district court in 1965 and the Fourth Circuit, *en banc*, in 1966 held that the board had achieved a constitutional system by 1965 at least. In the present round of litigation, the district court explicitly found that the board had complied in good faith with those earlier decisions. The Court's implication that new requirements were justified by a failure to comply with prior ones was, therefore, baseless. Second, the board had not "totally defaulted" in its "duty to come forward with an acceptable plan" unless its offering a plan that would have eliminated all majority-black senior high schools and all such junior high schools except one that had not been a black school under the dual system can be described as a total default. The constitutional deficiency of at least these parts of the board's plan is not apparent even with the aid of the Court's decision that they were properly rejected. Finally, it does not appear that the district court found that the board had "totally defaulted" in presenting its plan,[59] and, in any event, the court of appeals clearly had not "approved" any such finding. On the contrary, the two court of appeals judges who would have affirmed the district court's decision in all respects complained that "the majority implies that the actions of this Board have been exemplary."[60] Even when he did refer to the case before him, Chief Justice Burger seemed to be referring to some other case.

The Court's short discussion of the matter of eliminating one-race schools seems to change direction with each sentence and, in any event, has little bearing on what the Court did. The Court began by noting "the familiar phenomenon that in metropolitan areas minority groups are often found concentrated in one part of the city. In some circumstances certain schools may remain all or largely of one race until new schools can be provided or neighborhood patterns change." Nonetheless, "schools all or predominantly of one race in a district of mixed population will require close scrutiny to determine that school

assignments are not part of state-enforced segregation."[61] "In
light of the above," however, "it should be clear that the
existence of some small number of one-race, or virtually one-race,
schools within a district is not in and of itself the mark of a
system that still practices segregation by law." But "the district
judge or school authorities should make every effort to achieve
the greatest possible degree of actual desegregation and will thus
necessarily be concerned with the elimination of one-race
schools." [62]

The net result "in a system with a history of segregation" is
"a presumption against schools that are substantially disproportionate in their racial composition." School authorities have the
burden to show as to such schools that "school assignments are
genuinely non-discriminatory" and that "their racial composition
is not the result of present or past discriminatory action on their
part." [63] Although the announced purpose of the opinion was to
define "in more precise terms than heretofore the scope of the
duty of school authorities" under *Green*, a requirement of "every
effort to achieve the greatest possible degree of actual desegregation" seems very little improvement on *Green*'s "whatever steps
may be necessary." Nor does the requirement seem consistent
with the Court's assurances, in its present opinion, that "there
are limits."

If "some small number of one-race, or virtually one-race,
schools within a district is not in and of itself" impermissible,
it is difficult to understand, and the Court did not undertake to
explain, why the board's plan, at least for the high schools and
junior high schools, should have been rejected. If the facts as to
these schools (almost perfect racial balance except for one 98
percent white high school that had never been segregated and
one majority-black junior high school that had never been a
segregated black school) were not sufficient to show that the
racial imbalance that would have remained under the board's
plan was "not the result of past or present discriminatory action"
by school authorities and, therefore, to rebut the "presumption"
of unconstitutionality, it does not seem that the presumption
can ever be rebutted. Despite the Court's assurances, the decision
it reached indicated, in light of the facts of the case, an

unqualified requirement of nearly complete racial balance in every school of a formerly segregated system. Whether or not such a requirement could have been justified, it is not consistent with what the Court said it was requiring.

Turning to the "tools employed by school planners and by courts to break up the dual system," the Court approved the use of "frank—and sometimes drastic—gerrymandering of school districts and attendance zones" and the "additional step" of "pairing, 'clustering,' or 'grouping' of schools with attendance assignments made deliberately to accomplish the transfer of Negro students out of formerly segregated Negro schools and transfer of white students to formerly all-Negro schools." That the zones may be "neither compact nor contiguous" but "on opposite ends of the city" is no obstacle to their use "as an interim corrective measure"; that they may be "administratively awkward, inconvenient and even bizarre in some situations" does not mean that their use can "be avoided in the interim period." " 'Racially neutral' assignment plans . . . may fail to counteract the continuing effects of past school segregation resulting" from the discriminatory placement and sizing of the schools.[64]

Nonetheless, the Court assured, "it must be recognized that there are limits" as to "how far a court can go."[65] What these might be, given what the Court actually did, was not suggested except by repeating that "the objective is to dismantle the dual school system" and by referring to "what is said" earlier in the opinion. What the Court actually did was approve the requirement that the board adopt the Finger plan. The Finger plan required the busing of three hundred inner-city black high school students thirteen to fifteen miles to a suburban high school to make it less white, the busing of blacks from nine satellite zones to nine suburban junior high schools to eliminate one majority-black junior high school, and the restructuring of elementary school grade levels and the exchange of elementary students between nine central-city elementary schools and twenty-four suburban elementary schools. It made no difference that the required plan would *not*, as to the high schools, the junior high schools, and at least two of the nine city elementary schools, "accomplish the transfer of Negro students

out of formerly segregated Negro schools and the transfer of
white students to formerly all-Negro schools," but instead would
transfer students to schools that had not been segregated schools
for students of the other race or that had not been segregated
at all. As throughout the opinion, the Court's explanation of what
was required was, apart from its merits, inapplicable to the
situation actually involved.

The Court's discussion of the busing issue, for which the
case is chiefly noted, is very brief. Busing, it found, "has
been an integral part of the public education system for years. . . .
Eighteen million of the Nation's public school children,
approximately 39%, were transported to their schools by bus
in 1969-1970 in all parts of the country." Busing was "a
normal and accepted tool of educational policy."

> The Charlotte school authorities did not purport to assign students
> on the basis of geographically drawn zones until 1965 and then they
> allowed almost unlimited transfer privileges. The District Court's
> conclusion that assignment of children to the school nearest their
> home serving their grade would not produce an effective dismantling
> of the dual system is supported by the record.

Busing, therefore, is an appropriate "remedial technique."
"Desegregation plans cannot be limited to the walk-in school." [66]

The extensive evidence and argument in the case about the
additional number of children to be bused and the cost of
busing under the different proposals proved to have been largely
unnecessary. The Court mentioned neither consideration except
to note that the amount of transportation required by the
Finger plan "compares favorably" with Charlotte's transportation
at that time of 23,600 children a day and that "the school
system would have to employ 138 more buses that it had
previously operated. But 105 of these were already available
and the others could easily be obtained." [67] As to time and
distance, the district judge had found, the Court noted, that
"the trips for elementary school pupils average about seven
miles and . . . would take 'not over 35 minutes at the most.'"
Under the "transportation plan previously operated in Charlotte,"
students were transported "an average of 15 miles one way
for an average trip requiring over an hour." Objection to busing

"may," however, "have validity when the time or distance of travel is so great as to either risk the health of the children or significantly impinge on the educational process." [68] Expense, apparently, is never a valid objection.

The losses involved in abandoning the neighborhood school were not considered except for the statement that "All things being equal, with no history of discrimination, it might well be desirable to assign pupils to schools nearest their homes." [69] The supposed benefits from achieving racially balanced schools were, of course, also not considered. It was enough for the Court to repeat the claim, patently untenable on the facts of the case, that racial balance was not being required for any reason except to "dismantle the dual system." Consideration of the question whether busing to achieve racial balance would drive from the school system and the city many who are necessary to their continued well-being and lead to greater school and residential racial separation was, under *Monroe*, not even permissible.

"On the facts of this case," the final section of the opinion states, "we are unable to conclude that the order of the District Court is not reasonable, feasible and workable." It is well that reasonableness is the test, but the reasons given for affirming the district court's order and "the facts of this case" bear almost no relation to each other. The issue, in any event, was, as the Court earlier purported to recognize, not whether the district court's plan was "reasonable," but whether the board's plan, even the parts that applied to the high schools and junior high schools, was unconstitutional. [70] In its eagerness to "formulate guidelines" for other cases, the Court forgot the issue in the case before it and neglected to apply the "guidelines" it formulated.

The result is that no practical limit on the degree of racial balance required or on the means to be used to achieve it was in fact found. Elsewhere in the opinion, however, the Court suggested that there are limits in regard to time and place—that racially balanced schools will not be required everywhere and forever. The Court explicitly rejected the district judge's view, which followed from the different basis of his decision, that racial balance must be not only achieved but permanently maintained.

At some point, these school authorities and others like them should have achieved full compliance with this Court's decision in *Brown I.* The systems will then be "unitary" in the sense required by our decisions in *Green* and *Alexander.*

It does not follow that the communities served by such systems will remain demographically stable, for in a growing, mobile society, few will do so. Neither school authorities nor district courts are constitutionally required to make year-by-year adjustments of the racial composition of student bodies once the affirmative duty to desegregate has been accomplished and racial discrimination through official action is eliminated from the system.[71]

The Court also explicitly refused to adopt the Fourth Circuit's theory that would have, in effect, required school racial balance everywhere because racial imbalance is the result of residential racial concentration that was presumably caused by some official racial discrimination in the past. After an early reference to *Green* as concerned with "areas where dual school systems had historically been maintained by operation of state laws," the Court stated:

We are concerned in these cases with the elimination of the discrimination inherent in the dual school systems, not with myriad factors of human existence which can cause discrimination in a multitude of ways on racial, religious, or ethnic grounds. The target of the cases from *Brown I* to the present was the dual school system. The elimination of racial discrimination in public schools is a large task and one that should not be retarded by efforts to achieve broader purposes lying beyond the jurisdiction of school authorities. One vehicle can carry only a limited amount of baggage. It would not serve the important objective of *Brown I* to seek to use school desegregation cases for purposes beyond their scope, although desegregation of schools ultimately will have impact on other forms of discrimination. We do not reach in this case the question whether a showing that school segregation is a consequence of other types of state action, without any discriminatory action by the school authorities, is a constitutional violation requiring remedial action by a school desegregation decree. This case does not present that question and we therefore do not decide it.

Our objective . . . does not and cannot embrace all the problems of racial prejudice, even when those problems contribute to disproportionate racial concentrations in some schools.[72]

It is difficult to know what to make of this. The intent to limit the busing requirement to formerly dual systems is strongly and repeatedly intimated, but the question, in the end, is simply left open. As in his *Northcross* concurrence, Chief Justice Burger appeared anxious to find limits on the requirement of racial balance but, enmeshed in the Court's debased terminology and restrained here, no doubt, by his concurring colleagues—the last two sentences of the first paragraph are almost certainly by a different author—he was unable to arrive at a clear and meaningful statement. The result, again, as was soon to be seen by the Court's application of the requirement, with Chief Justice Burger's concurrence, to Denver, an area that had never had the dual system of the South,[73] was to state no practical limit at all.

The apparent limitation of the balancing requirement to achieving but not permanently maintaining school racial balance is also largely illusory. The racial balance contemplated by an approved busing plan may not be achievable even once. American communities are indeed not "demographically stable" when they are engaged in compulsory racial integration by busing. Some of the white parents, particularly the economically better-off, whose children are to be transported to the black inner city will invariably decline to have them go, preferring to withdraw them from the system. The system will consequently have a greater proportion of blacks and will often become sufficiently less attractive to still other whites to induce their departure—and so on. The inner-city schools with a predominance of blacks may never be adequately balanced racially, and a new busing plan may always be necessary.

We do nothing but delude ourselves when we adopt . . . a premise [that some degree of school racial balance must be achieved]. Like chasing the pot of gold at the end of the rainbow, this reasoning embarks us on a course without an end. Unless someone would be boldly foolish enough to assert that courts can deprive school district patrons of their freedom, then it follows as the night follows the day that the courts will never finish litigating such "numbers game" cases.[74]

Even if an adequate balance is once achieved by a particular busing plan, when, if ever, may that busing cease? Clearly it will not be sufficient for a school system to bus for just one or two school years and then revert to neighborhood assignment with its consequent racial imbalance. On the other hand, busing presumably need not continue after it no longer serves to increase racial balance—when, for example, the schools to which blacks are being bused have become, owing to the departure of whites, as predominantly black or more so than the neighborhood schools from which the blacks have been taken. Constant adjustments will be necessary, and room for continuing disputes and litigation will be ample.

The point, if any, prior to the time the system becomes all or nearly all black at which busing for racial balance may cease will probably depend only on when a particular district judge decides to abandon the quest. This is well illustrated by the further proceedings in this very case. Nothing the Court had said about the need to "dismantle the dual system" was sufficient to dissuade the district judge from his view that "the essential reason segregation in public schools is unconstitutional" is that "segregated education is inferior education." He therefore simply ignored the Court's admonition that school boards would not be required to overcome the effects of population movements, and he continuously reiterated that the Charlotte-Mecklenburg board would be required to do so.[75] Any attempt to limit the balancing requirement must, nonetheless, be welcomed, even if it is not likely to be very effective. Perhaps the Court's assurance that the requirement has a limited duration will encourage some other district judges, less convinced of the value of racial balance, finally to terminate the continuous upheaval of school systems.

The effects of the quest for racially balanced schools—and, incidentally, the baselessness of the Court's continuing charge of "defiance" by southern school boards—may perhaps best be seen in what two district court judges have called "the annual agony of Atlanta." Those judges have so well summarized Atlanta's experience up to 1971 as to warrant lengthy quotation.

This case is now in its thirteenth year before this court, having been filed in 1958. Atlanta in 1961-62 was one of the first major southern cities officially abandoning the dual school system. In its court experience, the original desegregation order was one of the few unappealed and assented to. Periodically as each new specific to Brown v. Topeka was belatedly developed by the higher courts, the School Board has been returned to court and given new directions. . . . Each has been accepted and promptly implemented. In the interim, the system voluntarily accelerated from the early concept of grade-by-grade annual integration to systemwide integration; it voluntarily and studiously located new schools and rezoned so as to maximize integration; it voluntarily liberalized its pupil-transfer plan; and in various ways increased responsibility for its black teaching personnel, principals, and area superintendents. Through court order, it has advanced from the initial requirement of two teachers of opposite race to each school to a computerized mathematical distribution of its faculty by race throughout the city; and from historical and traditional attendance zones to a court-supervised optimum [integration] plan. No one has successfully challenged the good faith of its elected Board of Education, the appointed Superintendent, . . . or of its administrative personnel throughout this uncertain decade. . . . Each change has produced convulsive implosions within the system and what has now become the annual agony of Atlanta has caused significant change in the character of the system, both physically and psychologically.

When this suit began, Atlanta had a pupil ratio of 70% white and 30% black and a predominantly white faculty; today, its racial complexion has reversed to 70% black and 30% white and its 4,800 teachers are 60% black and 40% white. From an enrollment of 115,000 students it has dropped to 100,000 in the school year 1970-71, during which it lost 7,000 whites and gained 1,000 blacks. . . . Since 1961, it has annually achieved substantial temporary integration by the establishment or construction of "line schools." However, 34 of those schools have gone from all-white to 90% or more black during that period. This "tipping process" is so rapid that it sometimes occurs by the time a facility deliberately located to increase integration can be completed and occupied. Seldom does it last longer than two years. . . .

The cause of such frustrating results lies in factors completely beyond the control of school authorities. Segregated housing, whether impelled by school changes or not, remains the unconquerable foe of the racial ideal of integrated public schools in the cities. The white flight to the suburbs and private schools continues. . . .

Of paramount significance, however, is the obvious result. Atlanta now stands on the brink of becoming an all-black city. A fruit-basket turnover through bussing to create a 30% white - 70% black uniformity throughout the system would unquestionably cause such a result in a few months time. Intelligent black and white leadership in the community realizes and fears it. Responsible citizens both in and out of the school system are deeply concerned with preservation of the biracial identity of the city. Without it, the ultimate goal of equality in all its aspects is doomed and Atlanta's position of leadership is severely threatened. [76]

The experience of school districts outside the South with compulsory integration has been shorter, but not otherwise different. For example, the seventeen schools of the school district of Inglewood, a suburb of Los Angeles, were 60 percent "European-American" in 1970 when a state judge ordered busing for racial balance. Five years later, when the district had spent $300,000 on busing and the schools were 80 percent "minority," the judge, over the protest of the local branch of the NAACP, decided that busing could cease. "As a practical matter," he stated, "we are now busing black children from predominantly black schools to other predominantly black schools." The schools of Pasadena, however, another Los Angeles suburb operating under a busing order, had by this time become only 41 percent black, and all efforts by its school board for relief from the order were denied. [77] In 1970, majority-black schools were eliminated in Pasadena by busing; by 1973, however, five such schools had reappeared because of further white withdrawals from the school system. Denying the board's application for relief, the federal district judge stated, "At least during my lifetime there would be no majority of any minority in any school in Pasadena." Despite *Swann*'s assurance that racial balance had to be achieved only once, the Court of Appeals for the Ninth Circuit affirmed this decision. It found that racial balance in Pasadena was at most "a transitory and temporary achievement, enduring for a period of the utmost brevity." One of the judges stated: "This is a sad business. . . . We cannot perpetually homogenize school children every September," but he concurred nonetheless. One judge dissented. [78]

Lest There Be Doubt or Hope

Davis v. *Board of School Commissioners of Mobile County*, a companion case to *Swann*, removed any hope that *Swann* might be explained or limited by the alleged "necessity" for the Court to "rely to a large extent" on the "informed judgment of district courts in the first instance and on courts of appeals." [79] It also demonstrated that busing to achieve racial balance would be required in a situation even more intractable than that of *Swann*.

Mobile County, Alabama, containing the city of Mobile and its suburbs (the "metropolitan area") and many rural communities, was 1,248 square miles in size, even larger than Mecklenburg County.[80] Blacks made up a much larger proportion of the school population—42 percent—than in Mecklenburg and a still larger proportion in the metropolitan area—49.5 percent. Owing primarily to the departure of whites as the system became increasingly integrated, these proportions were growing.[81] The great majority of the black population was residentially concentrated in a portion of the metropolitan area east of a major north–south highway (Interstate 65). At the beginning of the 1969 school year, the system had 73,500 students in ninety-one schools.

The litigation had a very long history. In the current round, the district court ordered a plan involving school pairing and rezoning that would have left nineteen schools, with 60 percent of the blacks, entirely or almost entirely black. A high degree of integration would have been achieved in the rural parts of the system and in the western section of the metropolitan area but not in the heavily black eastern section. On appeal by plaintiffs, the Fifth Circuit rejected the district court's plan in favor of one submitted by the Department of Justice which provided for greater integration. The Fifth Circuit further "improved" this plan by requiring that an all black elementary school be closed and an all black high school be rezoned. On the basis of the facts before the court, these measures would have completely eliminated the all black or nearly all black high schools and junior high schools and all but eight such elementary schools, which would have had 25 percent of the total black school population. The court noted that the remaining such schools were "the result of neighborhood patterns" and that the situation would be "further alleviated" by a majority-to-minority transfer provision which would permit any black who so desired to transfer to a majority-white school, with free transportation to be provided.[82] After further orders by the court, the number of majority-black schools was reduced to six (one all black and five at least 90 percent black), which would have 5310 students and 17 percent of the black school population. [83]

The Supreme Court, with Chief Justice Burger again writing the opinion, unanimously reversed. As always, the Court began by attempting to establish that the board had been derelict. "The present desegregation plan evolved," the Court stated, from an earlier one, and "the Court of Appeals held that that earlier plan had 'ignored the unequivocal directive to make a conscious effort in locating attendance zones to desegregate and eliminate past segregation.' " [84] Whether the approved plan under review had in any sense "evolved" from the earlier, very different plan is debatable, but the Court's research had uncovered a harsh-sounding criticism, albeit one actually made at an earlier stage of the case by a different panel of the court of appeals, and directed, not to the board, but to the district court. [85] The Court further pointed out that the Fifth Circuit, this time in the opinion under review, had "concluded that with respect to faculty and staff desegregation the board had 'almost totally failed to comply' with earlier orders." The facts regarding this issue are that the district court had ordered the board to balance the faculty racially in each school, "as far as is educationally feasible" to "reflect substantially" the racial ratio (60 white to 40 black) of faculty members in the system as a whole. The Fifth Circuit found that as of June 1970, "only a few schools approached the 60–40 faculty ratio." For the 1970-1971 school year, however, which the Court later considered relevant in passing on the adequacy of student racial balance, no school had a faculty in which more than two-thirds were of one race. [86] Perhaps the court of appeals chose this relatively minor issue to demonstrate its strictness, fearing, as proved to be the case, that it might be found, regarding student balance, to have been not strict enough, but the result was only to provide the Supreme Court with a finding of "total failure" upon which to rely.

Having laid this foundation, the Court proceeded, still rather indirectly, to the question before it, the adequacy of the plan approved by the court of appeals. The district court's plan, it pointed out, would have left seven senior and junior high schools and twelve elementary schools with student bodies completely or almost completely black. The court of appeals' plan, however—the one supposedly under review—was to have eliminated all such schools except for six of the elementary schools, which, that court had found, would have only 17 percent of the system's black school-age population. The Supreme Court, without mentioning the percentage relied on by the court of appeals, found a much higher percentage more relevant. These six schools, it stated, were "projected to serve 5,310 students, or about 50% of the Negro elementary students in the metropolitan area."[87] This higher percentage was obtained by considering, first, only metropolitan-area schools rather than all the schools in the system and, then, only elementary schools— that is, by comparing the number of blacks in the six schools in question, not with the number of blacks in all schools in the entire system, but with only the number of blacks in elementary schools in the metropolitan area.[88]

Although the court of appeals' plan reduced the number of nearly all black schools from the nineteen left by the district court's plan to six, the Supreme Court found that the plan was "like the District Court's plan" in that it "was based on treating the western section in isolation from the eastern. There were unified geographic zones, and no transportation of students for purposes of desegregation." The court of appeals, however, had explicitly recognized that black residential concentration east of the highway made it "necessary to go to the west to aid in reducing the number of all Negro schools,"[89] and the extensive pairing and rezoning that it ordered *did* require substantial "transportation of students for purposes of desegregation."

Whatever the merits or shortcomings of the court of appeals' plan on the basis of the evidence in the record that was before that court, the Supreme Court did not confine itself to that record, but permitted petitioners to file a "supplemental brief" introducing new evidence at the Supreme Court level. This evidence, consisting of figures on actual enrollment for the

1970-1971 school year, showed "that the projections on which
the Court of Appeals based its plan for metropolitan Mobile
were inaccurate." [90] Under the plan, "as actually implemented,"
not six but nine elementary schools that were over 90 percent
black remained, and "over half" of the black senior and junior
high school students in the metropolitan area were in all black
or nearly all black schools.

Such results, of course, were virtually inevitable in a system 42
percent black. The court of appeals could and did assign
whites to predominantly black schools, but it could not,
unfortunately for its plan, require them to attend those schools, [91]
and, under *Monroe*, was prohibited from considering the likelihood
that many would not attend them. If the fact that many
whites will not attend a predominantly black school is a
reason for invalidating a plan, few plans will prove acceptable
in a system with a large proportion of blacks. "The measure of any
desegregation plan," the Court said, "is its effectiveness," [92]
but this measure, it seems, is applicable not in determining
whether racial balance should be ordered but only to show
that still another order is required.

" 'Neighborhood school zoning,' " the Court concluded,

is not the only constitutionally permissible remedy; nor is it *per se*
adequate to meet the remedial responsibilities of local boards. Having
once found a violation, the district judge or school authorities should
make every effort to achieve the greatest possible degree of actual
desegregation, taking into account the practicalities of the situation.
A district court may and should consider the use of all available
techniques including restructuring of attendance zones. [93]

The result, of course, is that "neighborhood school zoning"
is constitutionally *im*permissible and per se *in*adequate where
the "greatest possible degree of actual desegregation" (racial
balance) is not achieved—as it will not be when blacks
are residentially concentrated. And the likelihood that racial
assignment will not achieve balance because whites will leave
the school system is not one of the "practicalities" to be
taken into account.

The court of appeals must be reversed, the Court said finally,
because "inadequate consideration was given to the possible

use of bus transportation and split zoning" (attendance zones separated from the assigned school). Both the district court and the court of appeals, however, had before them and considered several split-zoning plans, and bus transportation was in fact required by the plans they adopted. The "inadequacy," therefore, was not in a failure to consider but in the failure to adopt split zoning and cross-district busing. [94] Busing, the Court said in another case decided that day, is "absolutely essential to fulfillment of [the] constitutional obligation to eliminate existing dual school systems." [95]

The Chief Justice Has Second Thoughts

Because of the Court's actions and, perhaps more important, its attitude, beginning with *Green*, on questions of race and the schools, its decisions in *Swann* and *Davis* could not have been wholly unexpected. Chief Justice Burger's performance, however, seems to defy understanding. Did he call in *Northcross* for early consideration of "basic practical problems" only to make clear in *Swann* and *Davis* that racial balance was required and all problems were irrelevant? The mystery deepened when, four months after *Swann*, he again addressed himself to the integration requirement in *Winston-Salem/Forsyth County Board of Education* v. *Scott*, [96] passing on behalf of himself alone, as circuit justice, on an application for a stay, pending a petition for certiorari, of a district court "desegregation" order.

The Forsyth County school system was strikingly similar to that of Charlotte-Mecklenburg except that racial imbalance in the Forsyth County system and, presumably, therefore the need for "desegregation" by "all available techniques" were very much greater. In 1969 the system had 50,000 students, 27.5 percent black, in 67 schools. Fifteen of the schools were all black, 7 were all white, and 31 were 95 percent or more of one race. The district court had, prior to *Swann*, approved, with minor modifications, a board plan that did not use satellite (split) zoning and apparently would have changed the racial situation very little. After the Supreme Court's decisions in *Swann* and *Davis*, the Court of Appeals for the Fourth Circuit reversed the lower court's decision and remanded the case, along with several others, for reconsideration in light of those decisions. The district judge was instructed, in the language of *Davis*, to make and to require that the school board make "every effort to achieve the greatest possible degree of actual desegregation, taking into account the practicalities of the situation" and to give "adequate consideration" to "the possible use of bus transportation and split zoning."[97] The district court then found it "apparent that it is as 'practicable' to desegregate all the public schools in the Winston-Salem/Forsyth County system as in the Charlotte-Mecklenburg system and that the appellate courts will accept no less."[98] The court therefore ordered the board to adopt substantially the plan submitted by the plaintiffs, which, Chief Justice Burger noted, "employed satellite zoning and extensive cross-district busing."

Although he apparently found it a difficult decision to make, Chief Justice Burger denied the application for a stay because the record before him was "inadequate" for "such extraordinary relief," the schools involved were to open in four days, no application had been made to the court of appeals, and "no reasons appear" why application was not made to him earlier. He took the opportunity, however, to issue an eleven-page opinion discussing the requirements and limitations of *Swann*. The author of *Swann* was now difficult to recognize. The district court, it appeared, may well have erred in approving the busing plan. Indeed, Chief Justice Burger was far from sure that the plan originally approved by the district court was not in fact adequate despite the great amount of racial imbalance it would have left. That plan had "retained geographic zoning and freedom-of-choice transfer provisions, but with certain modifications allowing priority to majority-to-minority transfers and increasing the racial balance of several schools." The district court had found, Chief Justice Burger pointed out, that "the boundaries of the attendance zones had been drawn in good faith and without regard to racial considerations, and to ensure that, so far as possible, pupils attended the schools nearest their home, taking into account physical barriers, boundaries, and obstacles that might endanger children in the course of reaching their schools" and that "the racial concentration of

Negroes was not caused by public or private discrimination or state action but by economic factors and the desire of Negroes to live in their own neighborhoods rather than in predominantly white neighborhoods." [99] It was indeed surprising to learn that these remained important, or even relevant, considerations after *Swann* and *Davis*, for those decisions are then inexplicable. If the continued existence of a large number of virtually one-race schools can be so justified, the need for *Swann*'s "bizarre" attendance zones "on the opposite ends of the city" should never occur again.

The Fourth Circuit had instructed the district court to order a plan meeting the requirements of *Swann* and *Davis*. This was "interpreted" by the district judge, Chief Justice Burger said, as meaning that "because the State of North Carolina formerly had state-enforced dual school systems, declared unconstitutional in *Brown* . . . , the pupil assignment plan in Forsyth County had to be substantially revised to 'achieve the greatest possible degree of desegregation.' " For this interpretation, the judge was chastised: "Just why the District Judge undertook an independent, subjective analysis of how his case compared factually with the *Swann* case—something he could not do adequately without an examination of a comprehensive record not before him—is not clear." [100] The district judge, of course, had no choice. His first decision showed him unenthusiastic about compulsory integration, but, having been reversed and ordered by the Fourth Circuit to require compliance with *Swann* and *Davis*, he could not in good faith have failed to order busing. If *Swann* cannot be applied by lower courts without an examination of its "comprehensive record," it cannot be applied at all, and Chief Justice Burger's elaborate attempt in *Swann* to provide "guidelines" was a futile exercise. As pointed out above, his opinion in *Swann* gives little evidence that he ever examined that record himself.

The "school authorities" also erred, the chief justice found, in believing they were required to adopt "a revised pupil assignment plan which was expressly designed *'to achieve a racial balance throughout the system which will be acceptable to the Court.'* " [101] "Prior to the adoption of the revised plan," he pointed out, the school system transported about 18,000 pupils per day in about 216 buses. The drafters of the revised plan estimated that it "would require at a minimum, with use of staggered school openings, 157 additional buses to transport approximately 16,000 additional pupils." [102] The board's "understanding that it was *required* to achieve a fixed 'racial balance' that reflected the total composition of the school district" was "disturbing" and "suggests the possibility that there may be some misreading of the opinion of the Court in the *Swann* case." Chief Justice Burger was unable to determine from the papers before him whether the busing required under the revised plan "trespasses the limits on school bus transportation indicated in *Swann*," but it would be a "patent violation of *Swann*" if, "to take an extreme example," a plan should require the busing of some students for "*three* hours daily or that some were compelled to travel three hours daily when school facilities were available at a lesser distance. . . . The burdens and hardships of travel do not relate to race; excessive travel is as much a hardship on one race as another." The chief justice did not try "to interpret or characterize" the *Swann* holding, but did say that "nothing could be plainer, or so I had thought, than *Swann*'s disapproval of the 71%-29% racial composition found in the *Swann* case as the controlling factor in assignment of pupils, simply because that was the racial composition of the whole school system." [103]

A few days after this opinion was written, the apparently unprecedented action was taken of mailing it to every federal court of appeals judge and district judge in the country; each copy was marked "For the personal attention of the Judge." Court officials "had no comment on whether Chief Justice Burger had requested the unusual mailing." [104] In sum, it was surely one of the strangest performances in the history of the Court.

Chief Justice Burger, one may speculate, agreed to join the majority in *Swann* and *Davis* so that he could, as chief justice, assign the opinions to himself. He apparently believed that, despite the decision he was required to reach, he would be able to establish meaningful limits on the balancing requirement.

His predecessors on the Court were no doubt delighted, as the busing requirement would thereby be issued under the imprimatur of the new, "conservative" chief justice. His joining the majority would also, apparently, ensure, with Justice Blackmun's concurrence, that there would be no dissent and that the defeat of hopes for a change in the Court's direction would be complete. The lower-court decisions in _Winston-Salem/Forsyth_, however, made clear that any such strategy by Chief Justice Burger had not succeeded. He, evidently, then sought to nullify on his own the busing requirement that he in _Swann_ and _Davis_ had greatly assisted the Court in imposing. [105]

Several months later Chief Justice Burger took another unusual action, which was regarded at the time as bearing on the busing question. On March 27, 1972, the Court denied a petition for certiorari to review a court of appeals decision restraining construction of the Three Sisters Bridge in the District of Columbia. The chief justice, concurring "solely out of considerations of timing," raised the question "whether the Court of Appeals has, for a second time, unjustifiably frustrated the efforts of the executive branch to comply with the will of Congress as rather clearly expressed in §23 of the Federal-Aid Highway Act of 1968, 82 Stat. 827." He then volunteered the opinion that "in these circumstances Congress may, of course, take any further legislative action it deems necessary to make unmistakably clear its intentions with respect to the Three Sisters Bridge project, even to the point of limiting or prohibiting judicial review of its directives." [106] The last phrase—"even to the point of limiting or prohibiting judicial review of its directives"—was interpreted by some in Congress and elsewhere as supporting the constitutionality of measures then pending in Congress that would have limited or prohibited judicial review of proposed legislation restricting the authority of federal courts to order busing. [107] Before his opinion was published in the official reports, however, Chief Justice Burger modified it by adding the words "in this respect" at the end of the phrase, thereby apparently confining his views on the power of Congress to the matter involved in that case. [108]

The Application of *Swann* and *Davis*

Despite Chief Justice Burger's apparent misgivings, the result of *Swann* and *Davis* was, of course, still another round of litigation throughout the South. School districts that had gerrymandered zones and paired and clustered schools but that had not adopted split zoning and busing in order to improve racial balance found themselves in court still again.[109] School districts that had no busing facilities and had never bused students were ordered to acquire such facilities and begin. The argument by the Bessemer, Alabama, school board "that it lacks 'the facilities, the buses, personnel or the knowhow to bus' is," the Fifth Circuit said, "of no avail." There was no need, the court said in a case involving Greenwood, Mississippi, even to consider evidence on the ability of a district to provide free transportation, for "it is the responsibility of school officials to take whatever remedial steps are necessary to disestablish the dual school system, including the provision of free bus transportation to students required to attend schools outside their neighborhoods." Richmond County, Georgia, was told that "such platitudes" as that busing would "irreparably harm 'quality education'" could not be permitted "to perpetuate a dual school system."[110]

The fact that an order for further integration in a system that had already become 79 percent black would "probably result in an all-black student body, where nothing in the way of desegregation is accomplished and where neither the white students nor black students are benefited," was, the Fifth Circuit held, no valid objection to it. The district court had erred in refusing to adopt an HEW plan that "would effectively desegregate the schools though it may cause complete resegregation by resulting in a 100% black school system." Nor was it permissible to attempt to retain white students in a school system by simply closing the predominantly black schools and redistributing the black students. Closings must not be "racially motivated," despite the fact that the whole balancing requirement is racially motivated. Instead of closing two all black schools in a separate all black municipality, the Macon County, Georgia, school board was required to assign whites to them, although, in its opinion, it "would not effect the racial balance [desired] and would do more toward resegregating the races according to color than ever before." "A greater degree of desegregation" was ordered in another decision involving Greenwood, Mississippi, despite the fact that the number of whites in the system had decreased by over 50 percent since the litigation began and despite the fact, as Judge Coleman stated in dissent, that "past experience inexorably teaches that this Order will lead inevitably not to further desegregation but to further depletion in attendance and an even higher ratio of black students only. The public school system in Greenwood will be further weakened, with no corresponding advantages to be reaped from it."[111]

Jacksonville, Florida, however, exceptionally fortunate in the panel of the Fifth Circuit its case happened to come before, was permitted to close five formerly all black schools for such "non-racial reasons" as that one was "in the midst of the hard narcotics area of the city" and "incidences of vandalism and intrusion are such that teachers and children are locked in their rooms for safety. School patrolmen in the halls and on the grounds have proven insufficient deterrents to prevent assaults on teachers and students."[112]

In the Fourth Circuit it was recognized, in theory, that "the expense of busing" may "be so unreasonably burdensome as to warrant denial of the relief." But busing that required an initial expenditure of $3,000,000 for buses and an annual operating cost of $600,000 was found not unreasonable in a district with a "school budget of over 35 million dollars." That busing by the school district might make the city's privately owned transportation system "unprofitable and lead to its discontinuance, with resulting inconvenience to the entire community" did not justify "denial of the constitutional right . . . of the students." In another case the court approved a busing plan requiring travel time "varying from a minimum of forty minutes and a maximum of one hour, each way."[113]

To many courts, and especially the Fifth Circuit, the effect of *Swann* and *Davis*, despite Chief Justice Burger's attempts to state limits, was to remove all bonds of reason and restraint in ordering "desegregation" and to require the mixing of, or the attempt to mix, black and white students regardless of costs and consequences. It was almost as if the weakening of public support for public schools and the increase of racial separation in schools and cities had become, not only the inevitable concomitant of what the federal courts required, but, in the blindness of unrestrained tyranny, the objective.

8 | *Defining the School District: Divisions and Consolidations*

The pursuit of racially balanced school systems, on the basis of no stated defensible principle, is an endless quest. The question of whether further measures should be required must continue to arise and can only be answered on an essentially *ad hoc* basis. *Swann* and *Davis* showed that the requirement of racially balanced schools in formerly segregated school systems was virtually absolute: to the extent possible each school was to have a student body and faculty with the same racial proportions as in the school system as a whole. The objective, apparently, was to give each school as high a proportion of whites as possible and, in particular, to eliminate or drastically reduce the number of predominantly black schools. The Court of Appeals for the Fifth Circuit quickly established that not only schools but classrooms were to be racially balanced. The testing and ability grouping of pupils were prohibited, even in an "admittedly desegregated school" when, as is almost always the case, they "tended to perpetuate segregated [racially imbalanced] classrooms." That court also held that "new teachers may not be hired merely because their qualification . . . exceed [sic] those of the displaced former teachers. If the former teachers are minimally qualified for the jobs they are to receive them." Even where the displacement of present teachers is not involved, the standard teacher qualification test (the National Teachers Examination) cannot be used in hiring new teachers when its use excludes a disproportionate number of black applicants. Over the vigorous dissent of Judge Clark, the court upheld a school board's refusal to renew the contract of white teachers who had enrolled their children in a private school when the children were needed to "desegregate" the public schools.[1] The most important questions, however, that would necessarily arise soon after *Swann* were whether—or perhaps more realistically, when and how—the racial balance requirement would be extended outside the South and whether school districts would be permitted or required to alter their boundaries when a different ratio of blacks to whites in the school population would result.

The Splitting of School Districts

The question concerning the alteration of school boundaries came to the Court first, in a relatively mild form, in *Wright* v. *Council of City of Emporia* and *United States* v. *Scotland Neck City Board of Education*, decided in 1972.[2] Involved was, not the formidable question of whether independent school districts should be required to consolidate to create a system with a larger proportion of whites, but the much less difficult question of whether a school district should be prohibited from splitting if a split would leave one of the parts with a larger proportion of blacks. The cases, with Justices Lewis Powell and William Rehnquist now sitting, produced, nonetheless, the first serious division in the Court on the issue of race and the schools.

Emporia

Until 1967, the city of Emporia was politically and geographically a part of Greensville County, Virginia, and its schools were part of the county school system. The system had been operating since 1965 under a freedom-of-choice plan adopted by the school board after the commencement of segregation litigation and approved by the district court in 1966. In 1967, for reasons apparently related to tax revenues and unrelated to race, and pursuant to long-standing state procedures, Emporia obtained a designation from the state as "a city of the second class."[3] This made it politically independent of the county in all respects and obligated it, under Virginia law, to make its own provision for free public education. It then entered into a contract with the county whereby the county continued to administer Emporia's schools as before; Emporia shared in the cost but not in making policy decisions.

After the *Green* decision, the plaintiffs in the original segregation suit petitioned the district court, which had retained jurisdiction, for "further relief." In 1969 the court issued an order requiring that the schools be "paired" (more accurately, "clustered") so that all children at each grade level would be assigned to the same school; the result would be perfect racial balance in each school. Emporia thereupon sought to terminate its contractual arrangement with the county and to take over the operation of its own schools. It argued that the school budget proposed by the county did not keep pace with inflation or provide the additional funds that would be required to cover the cost of county-wide busing and that direct local control would enable it to raise taxes to provide what the district court found to be "a superior quality educational program."[4] At the time, the school system had 3,759 children, of whom 66 percent were black and 34 percent were white. A separate school system in Emporia would have 1,123 children, 52 percent black and 48 percent white, and the county school system would be left 72 percent black and 28 percent white. Each school in each system would be racially balanced according to the racial composition of the particular system. Upon objection by the plaintiffs, the district court enjoined the separation on the ground that it would reduce the proportion of whites in the county schools and increase it in the city schools.[5] The Court of Appeals for the Fourth Circuit, *en banc*, reversed this decision, finding that Emporia had sound educational reasons for the separation and that it would have only a minimal racial impact on the county schools: it would cause an increase of only 6 percentage points, from 66 percent to 72 percent, in the black student population.[6] The Supreme Court, in an opinion by Justice Stewart, with Chief Justice Burger and Justices Blackmun, Powell, and Rehnquist dissenting, reversed the Fourth Circuit and reinstated the district court's injunction.

Given *Swann* and *Davis*, the question of prohibiting the establishment of a separate school district where the effect would be to leave some schools with a larger number of blacks would not seem a difficult one. The difficulty was to prohibit the separation on the basis of the "disestablishment" rationale of

Green to which the Court was determined to cling and without admitting that it was simply racial balance or making the schools as white as possible that was required. Emporia was constitutionally prohibited from establishing its own school system the Court held, but not, the Court three times insisted, because the resulting "disparity of the racial balance of the city and county schools of itself violates the Constitution," [7] but only because of the constitutional necessity of "dismantling the dual system." [8] And "racial balance," the Court also insisted, "is not required in remedying a dual system." [9]

If, however, racial balance is not constitutionally required, even if only to "dismantle the dual system," why was Emporia constitutionally prohibited from establishing its own school system? The Court explained:

There is more to this case than the disparity in racial percentages reflected by the figures supplied by the school board. In the first place, the District Court found that if Emporia were allowed to withdraw from the existing system, it "may be anticipated that the proportion of whites in county schools may drop as those who can register in private academies," . . . while some whites might return to the city schools from the private schools in which they had previously enrolled. Thus, in the judgment of the District Court, the statistical breakdown of the 1969-1970 enrollment figures between city residents and county residents did not reflect what the situation would have been had Emporia established its own school system.

This is only to say, however, that the racial imbalance between the two systems might be greater than at first appeared and that the possibility of such greater imbalance *is* ground for prohibiting the division, even though the smaller imbalance would not be. "Racial balance is not required," it seems, provided the racial imbalance is very small. Furthermore, consideration of the fact that whites "may be anticipated" to leave a predominantly black system seems inconsistent with *Monroe* unless this reality may be taken into account to find a plan constitutionally inadequate but not to find it constitutionally adequate. Finally, it is doubtful that a significant number of whites "who can" are, in the words of the dissent, "more likely to withdraw their children from public schools that are 72% Negro than from those that are 66% Negro. At most, any such

difference would be marginal, and in fact it seems highly
improbable that there would be any difference at all." It is
also doubtful "that families from the city who had previously
withdrawn their children from the public schools due to impending
desegregation, would return their children to public schools having
more Negro than white pupils." [10] Why, in any event, the
possibility that "some whites might return" to schools 52 percent
black but not to schools 66 percent black (which, contrary
to the Court's statement, the district court had not found)
should be a source of concern is far from clear.

"Second," the Court said, "the significance of any racial
disparity in this case is enhanced by the fact that the two
formerly all-white schools are located within Emporia, while all
the schools located in the surrounding county were formerly
all-Negro. The record further reflects that the school buildings
in Emporia are better equipped and are located on better
sites than are those in the county." "But," the dissenters
correctly responded, "the District Court made no such finding
of fact, and the record does not support the Court's suggestion
on this point. Admittedly, some dissatisfaction was expressed
with the sites of the elementary schools in the county, and
only the city elementary school has an auditorium," but the
three elementary schools in the county were more modern
than any city school building and "the county and city high
school buildings are identical in every respect." A "fair reading
of the entire record" showed that any differences between
the city and county schools "are *de minimis.*" [11]

Finally, the Court stated:

The timing of Emporia's action is a third factor that was properly
taken into account by the District Court in assessing the effect
of the action upon children remaining in the county schools. . . . The
message of this action, coming when it did, cannot have escaped
the Negro children in the county. As we noted in *Brown I:* "To
separate [Negro school children] from others of similar age and
qualifications solely because of their race generates a feeling of inferiority
as to their status in the community that may affect their hearts and
minds in a way unlikely ever to be undone." . . . We think that,
under the circumstances, the District Court could rationally have
concluded that the same adverse psychological effect was likely to

result from Emporia's withdrawal of its children from the Greensville County system.

Whether or not the district judge "could rationally have concluded" that Emporia's separation would have "the same adverse psychological effect" as the segregation held unconstitutional in *Brown*, the fact is that he did not. Or, as the dissent put it, "here, again, the Court seeks to justify the District Court's discretionary action by reliance on a factor never considered by that court. More important, it surpasses the bounds of reason to equate the psychological impact of creating adjoining unitary school systems, both having Negro majorities, with the feeling of inferiority referred to in *Brown I* as engendered by a segregated school system."[12] Furthermore, the dissenters might have added, if *Brown*'s supposed psychological findings are to be treated as a basis of that decision after all, it would seem that evidence gathered in the years since *Brown* on the question of the educational effects of school segregation should be considered.

On the other hand, the Court found Emporia's claim that separation was "necessary to achieve 'quality education,' for city residents," open to question, and that such education cannot, in any event, be "purchased only at the price of a substantial adverse effect upon the viability of the county system." Emporia's desire for local control of its school, was, however, a "more weighty consideration." "Direct control over decisions vitally affecting the education of one's children is a need that is strongly felt in our society, and since 1967 the citizens of Emporia have had little of that control." But Emporia had found its "arrangement with the county both feasible and practical" until 1969, and, the district "court felt," the "desire of city leaders" should "make itself felt despite the absence of any formal control by the city over the system's budget and operation."[13]

Finally, as in *Swann*, the Court held out hope for the future. The decision "does not have the effect of locking Emporia into its present circumstance for all time," for "as already noted," the Court did not hold that "the disparity in racial balance between the city and county schools resulting from the separate systems would, absent any other consideration, be unacceptable." A separate city system may not have "such an adverse effect [as the Court found in this case] upon the students remaining in the county" system "once the unitary system has been established and accepted." [14] One might imagine, apparently, that the establishment of a separate system at a later time would, although it caused the same "disparity in racial balance," be likely to be perceived by blacks in the county as serving Emporia's legitimate educational needs.

Chief Justice Burger, joined by Justice Blackmun and the newly appointed Justices Powell and Rehnquist, issued a long and vigorous dissent. After his *Swann* and *Davis* opinions, however, the unavoidable impression is that after swallowing the camel he strained at the gnat. The Court's decision, he found, "far exceeds the contemplation" of *Brown* I—which is beyond dispute—and of "all succeeding cases, including *Swann*"—which is not. If the separation of Emporia was permitted, "the assignment of children to schools would depend solely on their residence" and "would in no sense depend on race. Such a geographic assignment pattern is prima facie consistent with the Equal Protection Clause." *Green*, it is true, required more than "ostensibly neutral attendance zones or district lines" "where a school system has been operated on a segregated basis in the past" and no such lines "existed before," but here both systems would meet the *Green* requirement of "schools neither Negro nor white, 'but just schools.' " The county and city schools would not have the same racial ratios, "but the elimination of such disparities is not the mission of desegregation." It cannot be said that "racial balance is the norm to be sought," that "a plan providing more consistent racial ratios is somehow more unitary than one which tolerates a lack of racial balance" or that "a plan providing uniform racial balance is more effective or constitutionally preferred." [15]

Although, Chief Justice Burger said, "the Court disavows a 'racial balancing' approach," the "additional factors" relied on are "so negligible as to suggest that racial imbalance itself may be what the Court finds most unacceptable." The separate systems would be nothing "less than fully unitary and nonracial" and "all vestiges of the discriminatory system would be removed. That is all the Constitution commands." "If local authorities devise a plan that will effectively eliminate segregation in the schools, a district court must accept such a plan unless there are strong reasons why a different plan is to be preferred." To be concerned with a "two percent, four percent, or six percent difference in racial composition" is to give "controlling weight to sociological theories, not constitutional doctrine." On the other hand, local control is "vital to continued public support of the schools" as well as "of overriding importance from an educational standpoint," and Emporia's purpose was to establish a system with adequate financial support. As to the Court's statement that the prohibition need not be permanent, the chief justice found it "difficult to understand" how the "passage of time will substantially alter the situation." [16]

Chief Justice Burger's dissent effectively demonstrated that the Court's opinion will not bear critical examination either of its theory or on the basis of the facts. It is unfortunate, however, that he did not similarly examine his own far more important opinions in *Swann* and *Davis*, which, if anything, can bear such examination even less. It is even more unfortunate that the chief justice's objections to a constitutional requirement of racial balance did not find expression before he, in those two cases, gave approval to such a requirement in an even clearer and more extreme form. If, as he now said, racial balance is not "the norm to be sought" or "even constitutionally preferred," *Swann's* "presumption against schools that are substantially disproportionate in their racial composition" and *Davis'* requirement of "every effort to achieve the greatest possible degree of actual desegregation" are inexplicable and incomprehensible.

Scotland Neck

Scotland Neck apparently presented a simpler problem than *Emporia*. The city of Scotland Neck, in Halifax County, North Carolina, had been an independent school district prior to 1936, at which time its school system was merged with that of the county. In 1965 the county school board adopted a freedom-of-choice plan for the formerly segregated district. In 1968, pursuant to an agreement with the Department of Justice, the board took further steps, under an interim plan, to increase integration. It later refused, however, to implement a pairing plan, and the Justice Department filed suit in July 1969. In the 1968-1969 school year, the district had 10,655 students, 77 percent of whom were black, 22 percent white, and 1 percent American Indian. [17]

Beginning in 1963, Scotland Neck took steps to re-establish itself as an independent school district. The necessary legislation was defeated in the North Carolina legislature in 1965 but passed in March 1969. Scotland Neck's purpose, the lower courts found, was to obtain local control of its schools, to increase school expenditures by means of local property taxes, and to "prevent anticipated white fleeing of the public schools." [18] Separation and an increase in property taxes for school purposes were approved by a popular referendum. The separate school district would have had a school population of 695—57 percent white and 43 percent black.

The government's suit asked that the authorizing legislation be declared unconstitutional and that the separation be enjoined. The district court so ordered, finding that the separation "would create a refuge for white students and would interfere with the desegregation of the Halifax County school system." The Fourth Circuit, sitting *en banc*, reversed the district court's decision, finding, as in *Emporia*, that the separation would have only a minimal racial impact on the county schools—raising the proportion of blacks by 3 percentage points from 77 percent to 80—and that it was justified as a measure to increase the quality of education. The fact that the separation was also motivated by "the laudable desire to stem an impending flow of white students from the public schools," while it could not justify unconstitutional action, did not invalidate action otherwise constitutional. [19]

The Supreme Court reversed the Fourth Circuit, finding the district court's determination that the authorizing legislation "was enacted with the effect of creating a refuge for white students of the Halifax County School system" was "the only proper inference to be drawn from the facts of this litigation." In reaching this conclusion, the Court focused on the effects of the separation, not on the county system as a whole, but on a limited portion of the county, designated as District I under the interim plan, where the separation, the Court said, would have had its "major impact." The separation of Scotland Neck would raise the percentage of blacks in the remaining schools of this limited area from 78 percent to 89 percent, and "the traditional racial identities of the schools in the area would be maintained." In this case, unlike *Emporia*, nothing "more" was necessary. The "disparity in the racial composition of the Scotland Neck schools and the schools remaining in District I of the Halifax County system would be 'substantial' by any standard of measurement."[20] Therefore, it seems, the law is that racial balance is not required but "substantial" racial imbalance is forbidden.

As for the argument that the separation "was necessary to avoid 'white flight' by Scotland Neck residents into private schools that would follow complete dismantling of the dual school system," the Court noted that "the system had undergone a loss of students since the unitary school plan took effect" (the percentage of blacks in the system had grown from 77 percent in 1968 to 85 percent in 1970) but found the fact to be of no consequence: "But while this development may be cause for deep concern to the respondents, it cannot, as the Court of Appeals recognized, be accepted as a reason for achieving anything less than complete uprooting of the dual public school system. See *Monroe*."[21]

Despite his strong protest in *Emporia* against a requirement of racial balance and his insistence on the need to maintain public support for the public schools, Chief Justice Burger agreed that the Fourth Circuit must here be reversed. His concurring opinion, in which he was again joined by Justice Blackmun and —more disappointing, because it was their first vote for a requirement of racial balance—by Justices Powell and Rehnquist, agreed that the separation of Scotland Neck "would preclude meaningful desegregation in the southeastern portion of Halifax County," that "further [school population] shifts could reasonably be anticipated," and that "in a very real sense, the children residing in this relatively small area would continue to attend 'Negro schools' and 'white schools.' The effect of the withdrawal would thus be dramatically different from the effect which could be anticipated in *Emporia*." Furthermore, "Scotland Neck's action cannot be seen as the fulfillment of its destiny as an independent governmental entity. . . . The movement toward the creation of a separate school system in Scotland Neck was prompted solely by the likelihood of desegregation in the county." Finally, the separation "was substantially motivated by the desire to create a predominantly white system more acceptable to the white parents of Scotland Neck." [22]

Chief Justice Burger's statement that the movement to create a separate school system—which began in 1963— was "prompted solely" by a desire to avoid integration is contrary to the finding of the lower courts and far from self-evident. Perhaps a system 43 percent black can be usefully described as "predominantly white," but it provides no "refuge" from integration. That it may be "more acceptable" to some than a still blacker system should not of itself be an argument against it. The fact is that it is not possible to separate racial and nonracial "motivation" for an action by a city that has both racial and nonracial consequences. Actions explicable only in terms of race must be treated as racially discriminatory, but here the nonracial justifications could easily have been found adequate, as they were by the able and experienced Judges Craven and Haynsworth, among others, on the Fourth Circuit. The fact that the separation probably offered the only hope—though probably not a strong one—of maintaining a viable racially mixed school system in the area should not have been totally irrelevant.

The Consolidation of School Districts: *Richmond*

School Board of City of Richmond, Virginia v. *State Board of Education of Virginia*[23] (1973) presented, in a sense, the obverse of *Emporia* and *Scotland Neck*. The question now was not whether a school district may split if one of the new districts would be left with a higher proportion of blacks, but whether separate districts may be required to consolidate to create a new district with a lower proportion of blacks. In 1954 the segregated Richmond school system was 56.5 percent white and 43.5 percent black. Segregation litigation began in Richmond in 1961, and by 1969 the system had become 70.5 percent black. The percentage was reduced to 64.2 percent in 1970, in spite of the protest of some blacks, by the annexation to the city of certain almost completely white areas, but it rose again to 69 percent by 1971.[24]

In 1971, the district court, in accordance with *Swann*, ordered a racial-balance plan that would have eliminated the "racial identifiability of each facility to the extent feasible within the City of Richmond." At this point, city officials, in an effort to prevent the school system and the city from becoming virtually all black, moved to have the city system consolidated with the school systems of the two surrounding counties, each of which was about 91 percent white. The district court so ordered. This unification would have created a school district embracing over 750 square miles and 100,000 pupils, of whom about 66 percent were white and 34 percent black. Students were to be selected by a lottery system for transportation out of their neighborhoods so that no school would be more than 40 percent black. On appeal by the two county school boards and the state board of education, the Court of Appeals for the Fourth Circuit, *en banc*, reversed the district court; one judge dissented.[25]

The Fourth Circuit dealt with, and severely limited the meaning of, *Swann* in much the same way that the Sixth Circuit in *Northcross* had dealt with, and limited the meaning of, *Green*. By the simple expedient of looking at the rationale of *Swann*—what the Court had said—rather than at the result reached on the basis of the facts—what the Court had done—the Fourth Circuit had no difficulty in showing that consolidation of the school districts was not required. The wide difference in results depending on whether a court takes the one approach or the other may be illustrated by two cases decided by another court of appeals at about the same time as *Richmond*. In one the court, by comparing in parallel columns the facts of *Swann* with those of the case before it, conclusively proved that racial balance by busing was required in Nashville. In the other, decided a few months later, a different panel of the same court, by confining itself to "the principles enunciated by the Supreme Court in *Swann*" and by finding it "unnecessary to discuss further the facts of the case" before it, was able to uphold a district court's refusal to order busing in Memphis. The dissenting judge, however, who had been a member of the panel in the Nashville case, again compared the facts of the case before him with those of *Swann* in detail and easily showed that busing was also required in Memphis.[26]

The question in *Richmond,* the Fourth Circuit stated, with Judge Craven writing the opinion, was whether a federal district judge may "compel one of the States of the Union to restructure its internal government for the purpose of achieving racial balance" in the schools. Clearly not, it found, for, according to *Swann*, there is no constitutional requirement of racial balance for its own sake but merely of dismantling dual systems. Richmond had already "done all it can do [including busing] to disestablish to the maximum extent possible the formerly state-imposed dual school system within its municipal boundary." Richmond and the two surrounding counties had each once had a dual system, and each was, therefore, required to, and did, "dismantle" it, but there had never been a single area-wide dual system or "joint interaction between any two of the units involved (or by higher State officers) for the purpose of keeping one unit relatively white by confining blacks to another." In the words of the Department of Justice, adopted by the court, "This is not primarily a case about segregation required by law, because state law has never required segregation as between Richmond and the neighboring school systems."[27]

On the basis of the *Green-Swann* rationale for requiring racial balance, the decision is clearly correct; there can be no need to disestablish a dual system that never existed. A lower court is clearly justified in taking the Supreme Court at its word, even though, as in *Swann*, the facts of the Supreme Court case in which that word was given clearly show that it was not in that case followed. Indeed, as Chief Justice Burger had remonstrated in *Winston-Salem,* it is examination of the facts of *Swann* and comparison of them with the facts of other cases that is objectionable.

The Fourth Circuit also found that requiring consolidation of the three school systems would involve "practicalities of budgeting and finance that boggle the mind" and that "the only 'educational' reason offered" by "school experts" for the consolidation was "the egalitarian concept that it is good for children of diverse economic, racial and social background to associate together more than would be possible within the Richmond school district."[28] True enough, but the same could have been said, of course, about the measures approved or required by the Supreme Court in, at least, *Swann*, *Alexander*, and *Carter*. Beginning with *Griffin*'s requirement that Prince Edward County, Virginia, raise taxes and operate a school system, the Court had simply refused to permit "practicalities" to stand in its way. "Practicalities," the Court had made clear, are to be left to school boards; they must obey court orders as best they can, and the people of the area must live as best they can with the consequences.

Certiorari was granted, but the Court was unable to reach a decision; Justice Powell, from Richmond, did not participate, and the remaining justices divided equally. The Fourth Circuit's decision was therefore affirmed, and, as is usual in such cases, the vote of individual justices was not announced and no opinions were written.[29] There was little doubt, nonetheless, that the result was a victory for the opponents of busing. That at least one justice not appointed by President Nixon had voted not to compel interdistrict busing was a clear indication that a limit on busing had finally been found. Indeed, if the "desegregation" rationale of *Green* and *Swann* was now to be taken seriously, compulsory integration was at an end.

Any limit on the requirement of school racial balance must be gratefully received by those concerned with preserving our schools and our cities. It is well that metropolitan Richmond was spared, at least for the moment, further unjustified upheaval, but it is regrettable that it was spared, while other places are not, on grounds essentially arbitrary. The schools of Mecklenburg County, North Carolina (550 square miles, with 84,000 pupils, 29 percent black) and of Mobile County, Alabama (1248 square miles, 73,500 pupils, 42 percent black), must be racially balanced, but the schools of metropolitan Richmond (750 square miles, 100,000 pupils, 34 percent black) need not, because they were not previously organized in a single school district. Charlotte, North Carolina, had made a serious mistake indeed, it now appeared, when in 1961 it consolidated its school system with that of the surrounding county. In an essentially lawless system of government, such as government by the Supreme Court, the most serious consequences can turn on the merest chance.

The practicality or desirability of compelling racially balanced schools in an area cannot rationally depend solely or most importantly on whether the schools of the area were previously organized into one school district or into several. The size of the area, the number of pupils involved, the racial composition, and many other factors will often be far more important determinants of necessary costs and expected gains. It is far from clear, for example, that the practicalities favor compulsory racial balance in single-district Mobile County rather than in much smaller multi-district metropolitan Richmond. The larger proportion of blacks in Mobile County—to consider another factor—would seem to make any hope for stable, meaningful integration there even more doubtful than in metropolitan Richmond.[30] On a reasoned assessment of likely gains and losses, court-imposed school racial balance is justified in neither place. The effect of *Richmond* is to use *Swann*'s untenable rationale to limit *Swann*'s unjustifiable requirement. Metropolitan Richmond was permitted to escape the requirement, but this was small solace to Charlotte and Mobile and, as the Court's next decision was to show, to Denver.

9 | *"Only Common Sense":*
Busing Spreads North and West

The widespread expectation that *Richmond* signaled a general halt by the Supreme Court in its pursuit of racially balanced schools proved short-lived. In *Richmond,* the Fourth Circuit showed that the Supreme Court's "remedy" rationale for compulsory integration—the Court's assertion that integration was not required as such, everywhere and for its own sake, but only to "desegregate," to "disestablish the dual system" of separate racial assignment that had been prohibited in *Brown*—could be used to limit the applicability of the requirement. There obviously could be no need to "desegregate," the Fourth Circuit found, a school system that had never been segregated, and there had never been a system comprising Richmond and two adjacent counties. This logical limitation of the integration requirement to its purported purpose and basis was not to be repeated, however, to prevent extension of the requirement outside the South.

Although integration was purportedly required by *Green* and *Swann* only to "disestablish the dual system" in the context of alleged long-continuing southern defiance, in 1973 the Supreme Court, in *Keyes* v. *School District No. One, Denver, Colorado,*[1] imposed compulsory integration on an area that had never required, but had prohibited, assignment to separate schools according to race and that, indeed, had been in advance of even the Supreme Court in favoring integration. As the Court's remedy rationale for compulsory integration had never provided a tenable basis for requiring integration in the South, it provided no limit to imposing the requirement elsewhere. In fact, the Court, by granting only a partial review of the case, was able to limit the issues before it so that the need to consider the inapplicability of that rationale, and, therefore, the requirement, to a northern city with an exemplary racial history was largely or completely avoided. In brief, a district judge initially ruled that integration was required in a part of Denver on grounds other than the Supreme Court's obviously inapplicable remedy rationale, and the Supreme Court then in effect simply extended the ruling to all of Denver without considering or accepting and by misstating the basis on which that ruling had been made. Denver, even more than Charlotte-Mecklenburg, was subjected to a kind of shell game and found to have lost.

The utter arbitrariness of the "law" thus established is further and perhaps most clearly shown by the fact that the Court in *Spencer* v. *Kugler,* just one year earlier and with only Justice Douglas dissenting, had affirmed, *per curiam,* the ruling of a different district court that integration was not required in New Jersey.[2] What accounts for these opposite results in the make-believe world of constitutional law is not that Denver "segregated" more than New Jersey but that, on the contrary, Denver voluntarily undertook to increase integration and then terminated one of its efforts to do so. An even more important distinguishing factor is that New Jersey was fortunate[3] and Denver most unfortunate in the lower-court judges their cases happened to come before.

Denver: The Wages of Virtue

Denver, like most major cities outside the South, has experienced a rapid growth in its black population since World War II. The number of blacks in the city roughly doubled between 1940 and 1950 and again between 1950 and 1960 and has since continued to grow. With a black population initially very small and still not relatively large, at the time the suit began, Denver had a history unusually free of racial problems and had, like all of Colorado, been a leader in combating racial discrimination. Not only was separation according to race never required in the Denver schools, but it was from the beginning explicitly prohibited by the Colorado constitution.[4] Colorado enacted a law prohibiting racial discrimination in public accommodations in 1895, extended the prohibition in 1917, created an antidiscrimination commission in 1957, and prohibited racial discrimination in housing in 1959.[5]

Far from insulating Denver from a charge of unconstitutional segregation and the need for "remedial" action, however, the city's leadership in racial matters was to prove the source of its constitutional difficulties.

In 1969, when the *Keyes* litigation began, the Denver public school system consisted of 119 schools with 96,580 pupils.[6] The litigation was initially concerned primarily with a group of eight schools (six elementary, one junior high, and one senior high) in an area of northeast Denver known as Park Hill. In the early 1940s, Denver's small black population was concentrated in an area (referred to as the "core" area) just northeast of central Denver; the schools of the core area were, of course, largely black. With the rapid growth of the black population, the area of black residential concentration expanded steadily eastward. By 1960 it had reached Colorado Boulevard, a six-lane north–south thoroughfare on the western edge of Park Hill, and thereafter continued into Park Hill. As a result the Park Hill schools, too, became increasingly black.[7]

The immediate cause of the litigation was, ironically, the extraordinary commitment of the Denver school board to racially balanced schools. In early 1969, two years before *Swann*, the board voluntarily—not because of threatened litigation or HEW pressure —adopted a series of three resolutions designed to improve racial balance in the Park Hill schools by means of satellite zoning and busing.[8] This step, too radical for the people of Denver, as events were to show, was the culmination of a series of steps taken by the board, beginning in 1962, to further integration.

In 1962, six years before *Green*, the board abandoned its official policy of racial neutrality by rejecting a proposal to build a school in an area in the path of black residential expansion, because the school would open, or soon become, predominantly black. At the same time, the board appointed a Special Study Committee on Equality of Educational Opportunity—with a racially and ethnically selected membership—to "study and report on the present status of educational opportunity in the Denver Public Schools, with attention to racial and ethnic factors." In 1964, the committee submitted a report "generally endors[ing] the application of the neighborhood school concept,"[9] but nonetheless recommending, among other things, that the board "consider racial, ethnic, and socio-economic factors in establishing boundaries and locating new schools in order to create heterogeneous school communities."[10] The board promptly adopted a resolution to that effect.[11] School racial discrimination had indeed come to Denver, despite *Brown* and the Colorado constitution, but only such racial discrimination as the Supreme Court was later to approve and require. In 1967, a second similar committee rcommended that no new schools be built in northeast Denver, the area of increasing black residential concentration. This recommendation, too, was adopted by the board, and no additional schools were built in that area.[12]

Race having now been firmly established as a proper basis for school board decisions, the board rapidly accelerated its efforts to achieve a racially balanced system. In May 1968, still before *Green*, a majority of the board adopted a resolution "recogniz[ing] that the continuation of neighborhood schools has resulted in the concentration of some minority racial and ethnic groups in some schools" and directing the superintendent of schools to submit "a comprehensive plan for the integration of the Denver public schools."[13] Acting pursuant to proposals submitted by the superintendent, the board, in a final demonstration of the strength of its commitment to racial balance, adopted in January, March, and April 1969 three resolutions requiring that certain of the Park Hill schools be integrated by busing students.[14] Satellite, or noncontiguous, attendance zones were created. Blacks would be bused out of the Park Hill area to predominantly white schools and whites from other areas would be bused in.

Furthering integration by the placement of schools and drawing of attendance boundaries was one thing, but the imposing of integration by racial busing another, and the people of Denver, predictably, would not have it.[15] In May 1969, before the busing resolutions could be implemented, a school board election was held in which the resolutions became the central issue. The two board members up for re-election who had supported the resolutions were replaced by members pledged to rescind them. In June 1969 the resolutions were rescinded by a majority of the new board. Even this new majority, however, did not return to a policy of racial neutrality. The May 1968 resolution calling for integrated schools was endorsed but was to be implemented by means other than involuntary busing. The superintendent of schools was directed to continue the development of proposals and to take various other steps toward "furthering the integration of the schools." Efforts to improve racial balance, including voluntary majority-to-minority transfer (transfer from a school having a majority of one's race to a school having a minority) with free transportation, were to continue.[16] Only involuntary busing was defeated.

Under the unique system of American government, however, a victory at the polls remains a victory only so long as it is not disapproved by the courts—a function performed in some other systems by the military. Opponents of the rescission immediately brought suit in the name of school children, alleging that it violated their constitutional rights and asking, in effect, that the resolutions be implemented despite their having been rescinded. Plaintiffs also alleged, as a second and separate basis for legal relief, that the entire Denver school system was unconstitutionally segregated, not only in regard to blacks and whites, but also in regard to blacks, "Hispanos," and "Anglos," because the separation of these groups that existed in the schools resulted from the board's use of neighborhood assignment and from other board actions.[17]

The District Court

The district judge issued four opinions in the case. It will simplify discussion to identify them at the start. The first, in July 1969, on plaintiffs' motion for a preliminary injunction, found that the predominantly black Park Hill schools were unconstitutionally segregated and in effect ordered that the rescinded resolutions be implemented. On appeal by the board, the Court of Appeals for the Tenth Circuit vacated the judge's order and remanded the case for more specific findings and for consideration of the 1964 Civil Rights Act's "limitation on the power of the Federal Courts to achieve racial balance by transportation of children from one school to another." In a second opinion, in August 1969, the district judge again granted a preliminary injunction, stating his findings of fact at greater length and concluding that the 1964 act was inapplicable.[18] In his third opinion, in March 1970, the judge again found, on plaintiffs' first claim, that the Park Hill schools were unconstitutionally segregated, and he made his injunction a permanent one. On plaintiffs' second claim, he found that Denver's other schools were not unconstitutionally segregated, but he nonetheless ordered that they be "desegregated"—racially and ethnically balanced—on the ground that the concentration of blacks and "Hispanos" constituted an unconstitutional denial of "equal educational opportunity." The judge's fourth opinion, in May 1970, decreed the steps to be taken by the board.[19] All four opinions fully reflected and, if possible, added to the confusion inherent in the law of race and the schools since *Green.*

The Rescission and the Park Hill Schools

In his first opinion on plaintiffs' motion for a preliminary injunction, the district judge, in the tradition of *Green,* began his discussion of "the applicable law" by purporting to enforce *Brown*'s prohibition of segregation. To him, however, "segregation" no longer meant assignment to separate schools according to race, as in *Brown,* but no more than racial separation, concentration, or imbalance.[20] Taken literally, this meaning would have been enough, of course, to find unconstitutionality in regard to the Park Hill schools, since there was no dispute about the fact that those schools were predominantly black. Although the district judge did not proceed to this conclusion directly, his use of "segregation" made it easy to reach by lending apparent strength to other arguments and findings.

The judge purported, at times, to recognize the distinction— required by the Tenth Circuit decisions up to that time [21] and even, in theory, by *Green*—between unconstitutional *"de jure* segregation" and constitutionally permissible racial separation or so-called *de facto* segregation. As was to be expected, however, of one whose definition of "segregation" obliterated the distinction and who explicitly doubted its continuing validity, the judge had no difficulty in concluding that any need there might be to find *"de jure* segregation" could easily be met. For him, the simple fact that the busing resolutions had been rescinded converted the racial concentration in the Park Hill schools from permissible "*de facto* segregation" to unconstitutional "*de jure* segregation" because "there can be no gainsaying the purpose and effect of the action as one designed to segregate." [22] Although the rescission was without "malicious or odious intent," it was enough for finding unconstitutionality that the rescission "was action which was taken with knowledge of the consequences" and, therefore, "unquestionably wilful." The result, of course, was not to meet the supposed requirement of finding "*de jure* segregation" but to eliminate it.

The term "*de jure* segregation" is meaningful, distinguishable from "*de facto* segregation" (permissible racial separation) only if it is understood to signify racial separation caused by official racial discrimination—explicit, as was involved in *Brown*, or, at the least, found on the basis of acts not reasonably explicable except as racial discrimination. According to the district judge's interpretation, unconstitutional "*de jure* segregation" can be found wherever racial separation or imbalance, however caused, exists. It can be found, for example, in the assignment of children to neighborhood schools when, as almost always, racial imbalance will result. It can be found, indeed, in the use of any method of assignment which does not maximize racial balance. Unconstitutionality, then, turns not on racial discrimination in order to separate the races but on the absence of racial discrimination in order to mix them. To use "*de jure* segregation" in this way is simply to state, even more misleadingly, the result implicit in the judge's use of "segregation": that all racial separation or imbalance is constitutionally prohibited.

Again, however, the judge did not apply his usage, this time of "*de jure* segregation," as its logic would require, simply to hold all racial imbalance unconstitutional. Rescission of the resolutions converted racial imbalance in the Park Hill schools to "*de jure* segregation," but the fact that the resolutions had been limited to Park Hill schools did not convert the racial imbalance that existed in other Denver schools to "*de jure* segregation." The result, according to the judge's reasoning, is that racial imbalance is not constitutionally prohibited as such after all, but is prohibited when steps to correct it are first adopted and then rejected. The fault apparently lies in unrealized good intentions. In this upside-down world, every previous effort by the board to further integration became evidence of unconstitutional segregation. Thus, the 1962 incident in which the board favored integration by rejecting a proposal, apparently otherwise justified, to build a school in a black neighborhood was to the district judge a damning one. To him it seemed bad enough that the proposal had been made and worse that it was rejected "after much debate." The fact that "during the entire decade [of the 1960s] there was regular debate" in Denver on efforts to further integration was an additional point against the board. The board's appointment of two committees that, as was to be expected, "strongly recommended measures which would avoid or remedy" school racial separation showed, not the board's good faith, but that the board had been "warned . . . concerning the segregation trends." The board's adoption of integration as an official policy in 1964, before any such constitutional requirement was suggested, and its decision in 1968 to build no more schools in the black northeastern part of the city did not help, if they did not hurt, the board. Although the rescinded resolutions had originally been adopted only because of the board's exceptional commitment to integration, their rescission was, according to the judge's theory, the "climactic and culminative act of the Board" "officially to reject the integration effort and to restore and perpetuate segregation in the area."[23]

The judge was able, unfortunately, to find a Supreme Court decision lending some support to his looking-glass theory that the termination of voluntary efforts to correct racial imbalance makes that imbalance unconstitutional. *Reitman* v. *Mulkey*, decided in 1967, was, he believed, based on that theory and required his conclusion: "We find and conclude then that *Mulkey* not only supports our position, it is a compelling authority in support of the conclusion which we have reached. It is so closely analogous that we would be remiss if we failed to follow it." *Reitman* presented the following situation: California had enacted legislation prohibiting racial discrimination in the sale or rental of housing. It thereafter adopted by popular referendum an amendment to the state constitution creating a property owner's right to refuse to sell or rent "in his absolute discretion," thereby invalidating and precluding such antidiscrimination legislation. The California Supreme Court, which at the time rivaled the United States Supreme Court in willingness to intervene in the political process, found the amendment violative of the federal Constitution. The United States Supreme Court affirmed, five to four, for reasons that are far from clear, but relying heavily on supposed findings by the state court that the amendment "would involve the State in private racial discrimination to an unconstitutional degree."[24]

Whatever might be said for *Reitman*, the Denver situation was easily distinguishable from it on several grounds. Apart from the fact that *Reitman* was not a school case, it involved not a mere repeal of legislation but a constitutional amendment precluding, throughout the state and fairly permanently, all government efforts to limit racial discrimination in housing; the invalidated constitutional amendment would have permitted, not—like the rescinded resolutions—required, racial discrimination; and there was no question in the Denver case of merely affirming a state court's factual findings. On the other hand and more realistically, it must be admitted that Supreme Court decisions, especially with regard to race, may be considered more important for their "message" than for their specific holdings or supposed rationales. A federal district judge attuned to, and sympathetic with, Supreme Court developments relating to race can hardly be faulted for concluding that means of distinguishing cases furthering integration are not to be sought. The ultimate conclusion of the district judge in *Keyes*, though not its basis, was, in the event, to be not only upheld but extended by the Court. A decision, like *Reitman*, difficult to explain in terms of a principled rationale, is for that reason all the more capable of wide application.[25]

The district judge's theory that the Park Hill schools were unconstitutionally segregated because of the board's unsuccessful attempt to integrate them was, nevertheless, too obviously paradoxical for adoption by the Tenth Circuit and the Supreme Court, neither of which relied on the rescission or mentioned

Reitman. Instead, however, of rejecting the judge's finding of unconstitutionality, those courts held against Denver on the very different theory that the district judge had found *"de jure* segregation" in Park Hill apart from the rescission. They simply ignored the facts that the very notion of *"de jure* segregation" was meaningless or unacceptable to the district judge, that he explicitly denied finding such segregation apart from the rescission, and that it could not have been properly found, in any event, on the facts of the case. The judge's actual findings must be examined in some detail in order to understand the basis on which Denver was condemned and to illustrate the type of "factual" issue on which all "desegregation" cases outside the South are likely to turn. If Denver could be condemned, there can be no doubt that busing to achieve racial balance may be required in any area with a substantial black population as long as the matter is in the hands of the courts.

By far the most important of the district judge's supposed findings of *"de jure* segregation," the only one specifically referred to by the Supreme Court, related to the construction of a single elementary school, one of some hundred construction projects undertaken by the board in a twenty-year period at a cost of over $100,000,000. In 1958 the board made the decision, seemingly innocent and routine enough at the time, to build the Barrett elementary school on a site long owned by the school district one or two blocks west of Colorado Boulevard in northeast Denver. When the school opened two years later with Colorado Boulevard as its eastern attendance-zone boundary, the rapid growth of the black population in the area in the interim had resulted in a student body that was 89.6 percent black. The district judge's findings as to Barrett in his first opinion were that

Barrett was opened in a segregated area in 1960; that it was located with conscious knowledge that it would be a segregated school; that it has remained segregated to the present date; and that the school would have been desegregated under Resolution 1531. At the time Barrett was built Stedman School, in a predominantly white area, and located a few blocks east of Barrett, was operating at approximately 20 percent over capacity. Yet Barrett was built as a relatively small school and was not utilized to relieve the conditions at Stedman.

The judge's second opinion spelled out this finding in nine paragraphs and concluded, in language virtually identical with that he had earlier used to condemn the rescission:

> The action by the Board with respect to the creation of Barrett school was taken with knowledge of the consequences, and these consequences were not merely possible, they were substantially certain. Under such conditions we find that the Board acted purposefully to create and maintain segregation at Barrett.[26]

To find that the board "purposefully" built a neighborhood school in a predominantly black area is, of course, not to find that the board discriminated racially and that, therefore, the school was "*de jure* segregated." If nonracial factors indicated that the school was needed where it was built—and no persuasive evidence to the contrary appears in the record—the only proper conclusion is that the board had not discriminated racially.

At the full trial the following year, the board argued that race played no part in the Barrett decision: A school was needed west of Colorado Boulevard owing to an expanding school-age population in the area; the district had owned the Barrett site since 1949; Colorado Boulevard was used as a boundary because it was a six-lane thoroughfare dangerous for elementary students to cross; and Barrett (with a capacity of 450) was not larger because it was not meant to relieve (and no one school could have relieved) overcrowding east as well as west of Colorado Boulevard. The judge now found that these "factors failed to provide a basis for inferring that a justifiably rational purpose existed for the action taken with respect to Barrett." "First," he said, "the District owned other sites east of Colorado Boulevard," whose use would have resulted in better-integrated schools. Barrett, however, was intended to serve an area *west* of Colorado Boulevard. The board apparently owned, not "other sites," but only *one* unused site east of Colorado Boulevard, and use of that site would, of course, have necessitated requiring children to cross the boulevard. In addition, that site was considered too close to the Stedman elementary school and too far from the area Barrett was meant to serve.[27]

"Second," the judge said, "the fact that in 1960 many elementary school subdistricts included areas on both sides of busy thoroughfares indicates that safety was not a primary factor in setting school boundaries." The fact, however, apparently was that of twelve elementary schools near Colorado Boulevard, only two had attendance zones crossing it. One was built in 1920 and one in 1930, before a comparable traffic hazard existed. An elevated crossing was later built near one of the schools after two pupils were killed.[28]

"Third," the judge continued, "because of Barrett's small size and the location of its subdistrict boundaries, Barrett relieved overcrowding only at the two predominantly Negro elementary schools west of Colorado Boulevard" and not at "overcrowded Anglo Stedman" east of the boulevard. The board had argued, however, that there was a limit to what one school could do, and that by the time Barrett was opened the first two blocks east of Colorado Boulevard already contained more blacks than whites. Moving the school population of that area from Stedman to Barrett would have made Stedman all or nearly all white without significantly affecting the racial balance at Barrett. Any thought of preserving Stedman as a white school in the face of the rapid black population growth could not, in any event, have been seen as other than plainly futile. Stedman, which had been 4 percent black in 1960, was 50 to 65 percent black in 1962 and 87.4 percent in 1963 (and 94.62 percent in 1968).[29]

"Finally," the judge concluded with regard to Barrett, the board could not "claim that it was uninformed as to the racial consequences of its decisions," because "a large portion of the Negro community opposed" the building of Barrett.[30] But that, most clearly, is not to find racial discrimination and, therefore, "*de jure* segregation," but to fault the board for not overcoming all obstacles to greater integration.

The remainder of the district judge's supposed findings of

"*de jure* segregation" relate to a few attendance-zone boundary changes and the use of "mobile" classrooms in the Park Hill area during the 1960s.[31] They need not be reviewed in detail. Each, again, relies on and is merely supplementary to the judge's ruling on the rescission. Although differing judgments are always possible where many conflicting considerations are involved, the few challenged boundary changes, of the many made in the period, and the use of mobile classrooms seem entirely explicable as racially neutral adjustments designed to relieve overcrowding in an area of a rapidly increasing school-age population.[32] In any event, the district judge's objection and finding was, again, not that the board discriminated racially in order to bring about the existing racial imbalance in the schools but that the board should have discriminated even more than it did in order to prevent or correct the imbalance. Again, he found, not "*de jure* segregation," but, at most, insufficient efforts to integrate. And according to the judge's *Reitman* theory, the board's voluntary efforts to improve racial balance made the lack of additional efforts all the more reprehensible.[33]

The district judge left no doubt that his findings as to the Park Hill schools were supplemental to and entirely dependent upon his finding that the rescission was unconstitutional. He refused to find that any racially imbalanced school not affected by the rescission was "*de jure* segregated" and he found unconstitutionality in connection with all schools—those in Park Hill—that were affected. He explicitly relied on the rescission in his findings as to each Park Hill school and he relied on nothing else in his findings as to some of them. Indeed, the judge explicitly said that he had not found racial discrimination—and, therefore, had no basis for finding "*de jure* segregation"—in Park Hill except in connection with the rescission. Explaining his refusal to find "*de jure* segregation" in the core area schools after supposedly finding it in Park Hill, the judge stated that his findings as to the Park Hill schools were made only "as they relate to the purpose for the rescission."[34]

Furthermore, the facts found by the district judge as to the Park Hill schools would not support a meaningful finding of "*de jure* segregation"—racial separation caused by racial discrimination by the board—even if such a finding had been made. The panel of the Tenth Circuit that reviewed the district judge's first two opinions (on the preliminary injunction) found:

> The record before us at the time of our order showed that Colorado has no, and never has had, any state imposed school or residential segregation. No discrimination in school transfers was either shown or claimed. No gerrymandering was shown or claimed. The district court's findings of de jure segregation, or a dual system, were confined to a small number of schools and were based on the failure or refusal of the School Board to anticipate population migration and to adjust school attendance districts to alleviate the imbalance resulting from such population shifts.[35]

The Supreme Court did not later find otherwise; it avoided all consideration of the question by simply denying the board's petition for review and then proceeding on the assumption that the district judge, despite what he said in his opinions, had found racial discrimination to separate the races by the board and, therefore, "*de jure* segregation."[36]

Finally, even if it could be found that the prerescission board racially discriminated to separate the races, despite its history of efforts to further integration, the board actions referred to in the district judge's findings concerning Park Hill were obviously of infinitesimal effect in comparison with the effect of the rapid and overwhelming movement of black population into Park Hill. If Barrett, to take the prime example, was sized, sited, and zoned to preserve the predominantly white status of Stedman, as plaintiffs charged, this action was, as already noted, singularly ineffective. Indeed, if building Barrett had any effect on Stedman, which it apparently did not, it was to delay Stedman's becoming a nearly all black school. Given the expansion of the black population in Park Hill, predominantly black neighborhood schools were inevitable, and it is simply not credible that any action charged to the board significantly contributed to that result. Again, the district judge explicitly stated that he did not find otherwise. The challenged acts of the board in Park Hill were, he said, "probative on the issue of the segregative purpose" of the rescission, although they themselves "may not be a substantial factor contributing to present segregation."[37]

The Core Area Schools

The plaintiffs' second claim was that the entire Denver school system was unconstitutionally segregated and unconstitutionally denied the plaintiffs equal educational opportunity. The district judge purported to reject the plaintiffs' primary contention that assignment to neighborhood schools is itself unconstitutional if it results in racially or ethnically concentrated schools. The judge also rejected the plaintiffs' contention that six such schools in the core area were "*de jure* segregated" schools because of boundary changes beginning in 1952 and because of the location of one school built in 1953. The judge found the "evidentiary as well as the legal approach" to these schools to be "quite different" from that used with regard to Park Hill schools. The major difference to the judge was, of course, that "we do not here have legislative action similar to the rescission." It apparently did not occur to the judge that the challenged boundary and school location decisions constituted "legislative action" fully as much as did the rescission.[38] Although the plaintiffs' claims of racial discrimination by the board were at least as plausible as those made regarding the Park Hill schools, the judge now declared: "It is to be emphasized here that the Board has not refused to admit any student at any time because of racial or ethnic origin. It simply requires everyone to go to his neighborhood school unless it is necessary to bus him to relieve overcrowding." He concluded: "The complained of acts are remote in time and do not loom large when assessing fault or cause. The impact of the housing patterns and neighborhood population movement stand out as the actual culprits."[39]

The judge's finding that there was no "*de jure* segregation" outside of the Park Hill schools that were affected by the rescission was, however, of very limited benefit to Denver. A constitutional violation was nonetheless found in connection with the other racially or ethnically imbalanced schools. Switching now to the approach of the district court in *Swann*, the judge found that a concentration of blacks or "Hispanos" in a school produces an inferior school and therefore unconstitutionally denies "equal educational opportunity."[40] The inferiority of such schools was shown, the plaintiffs contended, by the lower average scholastic achievement and higher dropout rates of black and "Hispano" students and by the fact that such schools had fewer experienced teachers and a higher rate of teacher turnover.[41] The plaintiffs also alleged that schools in black and "Hispano" areas were older and had smaller sites than in "Anglo" areas.[42] The judge recognized that factors cited by the school board, such as "home and community environment, socioeconomic status of the family, and the educational background of the parents" were "relevant," but found: "We must conclude that segregation, regardless of its cause, is a major factor producing inferior schools and unequal educational opportunity."[43] This "unequal educational opportunity" the judge held to be constitutionally prohibited. Since, however, it was not caused by "*de jure* segregation," the remedy, he thought, could be less drastic and more gradual (with "all deliberate speed"?) than that required in Park Hill. Half of the elementary schools designated as "concentrated" had to be "desegregated" by the following school year and the remaining half by the year after that. A school would be considered "desegregated" for this purpose if it had "an Anglo composition in excess of 50%." It was "probably not con-stitutionally required" that the "minority student population in each of these schools [be] apportioned equally between Negro and Hispano children," but the "desirability" of this was "apparent." The judge ordered other relief with regard to the junior and senior high schools involved. The board was to institute a program of voluntary majority-to-minority (integration-increasing) student transfers on a space-must-be-made-available basis and with free transportation to be provided. The board was also to institute a revised educational program, including, "at a minimum," "extended school years," classes in "Negro and Hispano culture and history," and "Spanish language training."[44]

Perhaps nothing emerges more clearly from consideration of the district judge's opinions in this case than the fact of the almost totally unrestrained freedom of choice district judges possess in "desegregation" litigation. If this one judge had found—as he should have and as the federal judges in New

Jersey did find in *Spencer* v. *Kugler*—that the racial imbalance in the schools was not the result of racial discrimination by school officials, the travail of Denver would have been at an end. Never in our history has the fate of so many people so importantly depended on the whim of a single, unelected, lifetime official. It was not by law but by the antithesis of law that busing for racial balance was brought to Denver, as it had been brought to Charlotte and would soon be brought to Detroit.

The Court of Appeals

The Court of Appeals for the Tenth Circuit affirmed the district judge's decision on the plaintiffs' first claim, concerning the Park Hill schools, and reversed on plaintiffs' second, concerning Denver's other racially imbalanced schools. The affirmance did not, however, accept the essential basis of the district judge's decision. The court found it "unnecessary" to decide whether the rescission was "an act of de jure segregation in and of itself."[45] The court had earlier recognized, in reviewing the grant of the preliminary injunction, that the district judge had not found any "state imposed school or residential segregation" but had faulted the board only for failure to make greater efforts to counteract the population shifts in Park Hill—in fact, for terminating such an effort.[46] Now, however, a completely different panel of the court, though reviewing essentially the same findings of the district judge, determined that the district judge had made meaningful findings of "*de jure* segregation" and that these findings were not "clearly erroneous," as is required for reversal.[47]

The different conclusions reached by the two panels cannot, it seems from the later opinion, be fully explained by the fact that different judges were involved. As is perhaps inevitable when the Supreme Court says one thing and obviously means another, the court, which had limited experience in "desegregation" matters, was hardly less confused than the district judge.[48] It seemed concerned to find meaningful "*de jure* segregation"—such as is "intentionally created and maintained through gerrymandering, building selection and student transfers"—but unable to determine how to distinguish unconstitutional segregation from permissible racial separation. On the one hand, the court stated that the board's duty was to use nothing "less than absolutely neutral criteria" in making its decisions and reiterated that "the rule of the Circuit is that neighborhood school plans, when impartially maintained and administered, do not violate constitutional rights even though the result of such plans is racial imbalance." On the other hand, it quoted the district judge's finding that the construction of the Barrett school was action "taken with knowledge of the consequences"[49]—as if the fact of such knowledge established something other than racial neutrality and as if the judge's finding constituted a meaningful finding of "*de jure* segregation."

Similarly, although the court did not rely on the rescission, it apparently found significance in such statements by the district judge as that "the action of the board in rescinding" the resolutions was "wilful as to its effect" on a particular school. According to this panel of the Tenth Circuit, the issue of "*de jure* segregation" turned on "segregative intent," and it determined that the district judge had found such an intent, apart from his reliance on the rescission, in, for example, the construction of Barrett, and that such a finding was supported by evidence. The board's "stated purpose" in constructing Barrett— to relieve "overcrowded conditions at nearby schools"—was, the court of appeals declared, "belied" by the fact that the Barrett building was not big enough to relieve overcrowding at Stedman, east of Colorado Boulevard. The use of Colorado Boulevard as a boundary for the Barrett attendance zone was not "a valid exercise of board discretion," the court found, because "the board admits that other elementary school attendance areas are intersected by major traffic thoroughfares and that in at least one instance an elevated crossing was built to facilitate pupil safety. Thus, it was not an immutable boundary which absolutely precluded the extension of attendance lines."[50] There are, of course, few "immutable boundaries" and little is "absolutely precluded," but to find racial discrimination or "segregative intent" on this basis is not to find that the board did not comply with the court's purported requirement that the board use "absolutely neutral criteria" when its decisions have racial effects. The fact that the district judge stated that he did *not* find the construction of Barrett or any other board action except the rescission a "substantial factor contributing to present segregation" was simply ignored. The court, it seemed, had not, as to the issue of the Park Hill schools, read the opinion it was purportedly reviewing.

Turning to the plaintiffs' second claim, the court also affirmed, as not "clearly erroneous," the district judge's finding that the racially or ethnically imbalanced schools outside Park Hill were not "*de jure*" segregated." It reversed, however, the district judge's conclusion that the existence of these schools constituted an unconstitutional denial of equal educational opportunity. Despite its affirmance of the district judge's decision as to Park Hill, the court now recognized that this was not a case "dealing with a school district which was segregated by unlawful state action" and that "it would be incongruous to require the Denver School Board to prove the non-existence of a secret, illicit, segregatory intent." The district judge's conclusion, the court also recognized, amounted to holding Denver's neighborhood-school policy unconstitutional, despite the district judge's denial that he so held. The court rejected the district judge's theory that integration is required to improve black and "Hispano" academic performance. "Pupil dropout rates and low scholastic achievement" occur, it found, in "even a completely integrated setting." While these constitute a "very serious educational and social ill," the court expressed the "firm conviction" that it was "without power" to correct them.[51]

The Supreme Court

The Supreme Court denied the board's petition for certiorari and let the Tenth Circuit's decision as to the Park Hill schools stand. It granted certiorari to the plaintiffs, however, on their second claim—that schools outside of Park Hill were also unconstitutionally segregated—reversed the Tenth Circuit, and remanded that claim to the district court for further proceedings. The district judge was virtually instructed to hold for the plaintiffs again on their second claim and to order "all-out desegregation."[52] He was to do it this time, however, not on the basis of his theory that equal educational opportunity had been denied, but by finding that the core city schools were also "*de jure* segregated." He could do this, the Court said, on the basis of his supposed finding that the Park Hill schools were "*de jure* segregated." Justice Brennan wrote the opinion of the Court. Chief Justice Burger concurred in the result without writing an opinion. Justice Douglas wrote a short concurring opinion. Justice Powell wrote a long opinion concurring in part and dissenting in part, and Justice Rehnquist a short dissenting opinion. Justice White did not participate.

Justice Brennan's Opinion for the Court

Justice Brennan, repeatedly invoking the name of "common sense," wrote an opinion that strains logic and credulity to an extent rarely equaled even in "desegregation" cases. He began with "a word . . . about the district court's method of defining a segregated school." He found that the district judge erred in finding that "Negroes and Hispanos should not be placed in the same category to establish the segregated character of a school." "Hispanos," Justice Brennan found, "constitute an identifiable class for purposes of the Fourteenth Amendment." He found "much evidence that in the Southwest Hispanos and Negroes have a great many things in common."[53] The point of all this may not be immediately clear. Members of every racial or ethnic group undoubtedly "constitute an identifiable class for purposes of the Fourteenth Amendment" and are protected from discrimination against them as members of such a group. Equation of any group with blacks is not necessary for this protection.[54] The point, of course, was not to show that "Hispanos" are protected from ethnic discrimination, but to make them, under the new meaning of "desegregation" developed in relation to blacks, eligible for ethnic discrimination. An actual prohibition of racial or ethnic discrimination, with which the Court still purported to be concerned, would make it senseless to speak, as Justice Brennan later did, of proving "all of the essential elements of *de jure* segregation."[55] Assignment of a child to a school on the basis of his race or ethnic group would be the only "essential element," and the racial or ethnic composition of that school would be irrelevant. The result of the Court's finding that "Hispanos" were an "identifiable group" for the purpose of determining the "segregated character of a school" was to go a long way—actually, in the context of the whole decision, all the way—to establishing that blacks must be placed in schools not merely predominantly white but predominantly "Anglo" and that "Hispanos" must be treated similarly.

Justice Brennan then turned to "the only other question" requiring decision: whether the lower courts "applied an incorrect legal standard" in finding no "*de jure* segregation" in the core city schools.[56] He found that they did. Justice Brennan now openly used "segregated" to mean little, if anything, more than racially imbalanced.

The segregated character of the core city schools could not be and is not denied. Petitioners' proof showed that at the time of trial 22 of the schools in the core city area were less than 30% in Anglo enrollment and 11 of the schools were less than 10% Anglo. Petitioners also introduced substantial evidence demonstrating the existence of a disproportionate racial and ethnic composition of faculty and staff at these schools.[57]

Indeed, although he repeatedly spoke of "state-imposed segregation," or "*de jure* segregation,"[58] as if to distinguish it from mere "segregation," it appeared, at other times, that even with these qualifications nothing more than racial imbalance was required for unconstitutionality. "*De jure* segregation" was defined as "a current condition of segregation resulting from intentional state action." This definition is sufficient, of course, to invalidate all school racial imbalance, since assignment to neighborhood schools is undeniably "intentional state action"—that is, action by government officials. Justice Brennan found that the district judge erred in two respects in considering the constitutionality of the racially imbalanced core city schools. Having supposedly found "*de jure* segregation" in Park Hill, the district judge, first, should have considered whether—and he could have found that—this caused the "segregated character of the core city schools," and even if he did not so find, he, second, should have presumed that the core city "segregation" was "not adventitious" but the result of the "segregative design" found in Park Hill.[59] On the basis either of such a finding or of this presumption, the core city "segregation" could be found to be itself "*de jure*."

As to the first approach, "it is only common sense," Justice Brennan said, that where "state-imposed segregation" is found "as to a substantial portion of the school system," a court can "predicate on that fact a finding that the entire school system is a dual system." And the Park Hill schools were not "an insubstantial or trivial fragment of the school system." "On the contrary, respondent School Board was found guilty of following a deliberate segregation policy at schools attended, in 1969, by 37.69% of Denver's total Negro school population, including one-fourth of the Negro elementary pupils, over two-thirds of the Negro junior high pupils, and over two-fifths of the Negro high school pupils."[60] Because "it is obvious that a practice of concentrating Negroes in certain schools . . . has the reciprocal effect of keeping other nearby schools predominantly white" and "may have a profound reciprocal effect on the racial composition of residential neighborhoods," "common sense dictates the conclusion that racially inspired school board actions have an impact beyond the particular schools that are the subjects of those actions."[61]

This was "not to say, of course, that there can never be a case in which the geographical structure of or the natural boundaries within a school district may have the effect of dividing the district into separate identifiable and unrelated units. Such a determination is essentially a question of fact to be resolved by the trial court in the first instance, but such cases must be rare." Lest Denver take too much hope from this, however, Justice Brennan went on to "observe that on the record now before us there is indication" that Denver's was not one of the rare cases. The district judge had found a "high degree of interrelationship" among the schools in the Park Hill area, and there was "cogent evidence"—although the district judge did not find any—"that the ultimate effect of the Board's actions was not limited to that area." Although,

Justice Brennan noted, the core area and Park Hill "are separated by Colorado Boulevard, a six-lane highway," "at least two elementary schools, Teller and Steck, have attendance zones which cross the Boulevard." The district judge's finding as to Barrett "suggests that Colorado Boulevard is not to be regarded as the type of barrier that of itself could confine the impact of the board's actions to an identifiable area of the school district, perhaps because a major highway is generally not such an effective buffer between adjoining areas."[62]

Whatever the validity of Justice Brennan's reasoning in general, it would seem inapplicable to the case that was before him. The core city schools were black or nearly black long before the Park Hill schools began to change from white to black. It is difficult to understand how the board actions that supposedly caused the "segregation" in Park Hill could have caused or contributed to the earlier "segregated condition of the core city schools"—in fact, the district judge had not found that those actions had caused even the "segregation" in Park Hill.

As if this first instruction to the district judge was not enough to ensure the plaintiffs' success on their second claim, Justice Brennan went on to show a second means of finding unconstitutionality in regard to the core city schools. Those schools could be found "*de jure* segregated" "even if it is determined that different areas of the school district should be viewed independently of each other." The district judge erred in requiring the plaintiffs "to prove all of the essential elements of *de jure* segregation" in regard to the core city schools. It was necessary to "emphasize that the differentiating factor between *de jure* segregation and so-called *de facto* segregation . . . is *purpose* or *intent* to segregate." The district judge "proceeded on the premise that the finding as to the Park Hill schools was irrelevant to the consideration of the rest of the district." But, Justice Brennan said, "we hold that a finding of intentionally segregative school board actions in a meaningful portion of a school system, as in this case, creates a presumption that other segregated schooling within the system is not adventitious." Thus, where "a pattern of intentional segregation has been established in the past," "the existence of subsequent or other segregated schooling within the same system justifies a rule imposing on the school authorities the burden of proving that this segregated schooling is not also the result of intentionally segregative acts."[63]

Again, the applicability of this reasoning to the present case, whatever its validity otherwise, is unclear. The board actions regarding the core city schools that were challenged by the plaintiffs took place almost entirely in the 1950s, while those challenged regarding Park Hill took place almost entirely in the 1960s. There could be no question on remand, therefore, of showing "segregative intent" in connection with "subsequent . . . segregated schooling" on the basis that "a pattern of intentional segregation had been established in the past." The need would be to show "segregative intent" in acts of the 1950s by showing such intent in acts of the 1960s. The relevance of Justice Brennan's reasoning to the case before him must, therefore, lie in the words "or other" which he inserted between the words "subsequent" and "segregated schooling."[64]

To rebut the presumption against them, "it is not enough, of course, that the school authorities rely upon some allegedly logical, racially neutral explanation for their actions." They must, instead, show that "segregative intent was not among the factors that motivated their actions." And "any degree" of such intent is enough for condemnation. But the task of rebutting this presumption, like the task of showing parts of a school district to be separable, is not to be thought impossible: "This is not to say, however, that the prima facie case may not be met by evidence supporting a finding that a lesser degree of segregated schooling in the core city area would not have resulted even if the board had not acted as it did." That is—canceling out the negatives—the board can disprove "segregative intent" by showing that it did all it could to improve racial balance. But that is something the board will not be able to do if racial imbalance exists. The result, of course, is not to prohibit "*de jure* segregation" or "segregative intent" but simply racial imbalance itself and to answer in the negative the question that the court purported to leave open about the constitutionality of racially imbalanced neighborhood schools.[65]

Justice Brennan continued to insist, however, that the Court was not requiring racially balanced schools as such but requiring only that "present segregation" resulting from "past segregative acts" be remedied. The board, therefore, had one further line of defense. It could show that "its past segregative acts did not create or contribute to the current segregated condition of the core city schools." But this defense, too, is not likely to succeed, for it is "clear" "that a connection between past segregative acts and present segregation may be present even when not apparent and that close examination is required before concluding that the connection does not exist."[66] It is clear indeed. To repeat: the board's "past segregative acts" in Park Hill—which the district judge did not find had caused or contributed to the "segregated condition" even in Park Hill—occurred after the "segregated condition of the core city schools" had developed. If this does not show that those acts did not cause the "segregated condition of the core city schools," it is difficult to see how it can be shown.

Chief Justice Burger, despite his insistence in *Swann* that the Court was concerned only with "dismantling the dual system," concurred separately "in the result"—that is, in the disposition of the case but not for the reasons given in the Court's opinion. Denver's school system, apparently, was "dual" enough and the actions ordered by the Court justifiable as a "dismantling." Because he wrote no opinion, however, the basis of his agreement with the result and of his disagreement with the Court's opinion does not appear. Justice Douglas purported to "join the opinion of the Court," thereby supposedly giving it the status of a majority (five-justice) opinion of the full Court. To him, however, Justice Brennan's herculean efforts were irrelevant. Douglas was of the view that "there is no constitutional difference between *de jure* and *de facto* segregation." He believed that "when a State forces, aids, or abets, or helps create a racial 'neighborhood,' it is a travesty of justice to treat that neighborhood as sacrosanct in the sense that its creation is free from the taint of state action."[67] He did not find it necessary, however, to show how this or other statements in his brief opinion applied to the facts of the present case.

Justice Powell's Concurrence and Dissent

Justice Powell, concurring in part and dissenting in part, submitted a long and potentially important opinion, worth careful attention. He made a strong but only partially successful effort to introduce an element of reality to "desegregation" law. He began, as one must for this purpose, by recognizing that *Green* cannot be made to follow from the "limited constitutional rationale" of *Brown* or be justified as an enforcement of *Brown*'s prohibition of school segregation. As the result of *Green*, *Brown* was "transformed into the present constitutional doctrine" of "affirmative duty." Any "doubt as to whether the affirmative-duty concept would flower into a new constitutional principle of general application was laid to rest" by *Swann*.[68]

The "affirmative duty" requirement cannot be justified as a requirement of "desegregation," Justice Powell continued, because school districts have been required to "alleviate conditions which in large part did *not* result from historic, state-imposed *de jure* segregation." The "familiar root cause of segregated schools in *all* the biracial metropolitan areas of our country is essentially the same: one of segregated residential and migratory patterns."[69] Justice Powell quoted the findings of Karl Taeuber that "a high degree of residential segregation based on race is a universal characteristic of American cities" and that it exists "regardless of the character of local laws and policies." The "remedial obligations of *Swann*," therefore, "extend far beyond the elimination of the out-growths of the state-imposed segregation outlawed in *Brown*"; specifically, "compulsory student transportation went well beyond the mere remedying of that portion of school segregation for which former state segregation laws were ever responsible." Use of the "*de jure/de facto* distinction" as the basis for a constitutional requirement of integration can, therefore, no longer "be justified on a principled basis" and should be abandoned.[70]

Justice Powell then showed that the Court's newly announced

standard of "segregative intent" to establish "*de jure* segregation" was of no help. He quoted the Court's statement in *Emporia* that "an inquiry into the 'dominant' motivation of school authorities is as irrelevant as it is fruitless," and continued:

The Court has never made clear what suffices to establish the requisite "segregative intent" for an initial constitutional violation. Even if it were possible to clarify this question, wide and unpredictable differences of opinion among judges would be inevitable when dealing with an issue as slippery as "intent" or "purpose," especially when related to hundreds of decisions made by school authorities under varying conditions over many years. . . . Every act of a school board and school administration, and indeed every failure to act where affirmative action is indicated, must now be subject to scrutiny. The most routine decisions with respect to the operation of schools, made almost daily, can affect in varying degrees the [racial make-up of schools]. . . . These decisions include action or nonaction with respect to school building construction and location; . . . the drawing or gerrymandering of student attendance zones; the extent to which a neighborhood policy is enforced; the recruitment, promotion and assignment of faculty and supervisory personnel; policies with respect to transfers from one school to another; whether, and to what extent, special schools will be provided . . . ; the determination of curriculum, including whether there will be "tracks" . . . and the routing of students into these tracks; and even decisions as to social, recreational, and athletic policies.[71]

The concern of the law, here as elsewhere, is presumably with the objective consequences of actions, not with mental states. When an action, such as the use of neighborhood assignment in a racially imbalanced neighborhood, has both desired and undesired consequences, a value judgment as to gains and losses is unavoidably involved. To purport to test the legality of the action by "intent" is only to make the basis of that judgment obscure, as Justice Brennan's opinion and the opinions of the Tenth Circuit and the district court well illustrate.

Justice Powell would not, however, abandon completely some constitutional requirement of school racial integration and return to a simple prohibition of racial discrimination. Such a requirement should, he contended, be retained, but the "constitutional right which is being enforced" should be redefined. *Brown* II's identification of "the 'fundamental principle' enunciated in *Brown I* as being the unconstitutionality of 'racial discrimination in public education' " and requirement of "admission to public schools as soon as practicable on a nondiscriminatory basis" he found "ambiguous." He would substitute therefor "the right, derived from the Equal Protection Clause, to expect that once the State has assumed responsibility for education, local school boards will operate *integrated school systems* within their respective districts."[72]

An "integrated school system" was not, for Justice Powell, merely one with a "total absence of any laws, regulations, or policies supportive of the 'legalized' segregation condemned in *Brown*":

A system would be integrated in accord with constitutional standards if the responsible authorities had taken appropriate steps to (i) integrate faculties and administration; (ii) scrupulously assure equality of facilities, instruction, and curriculum opportunities throughout the district; (iii) utilize their authority to draw attendance zones to promote integration; and (iv) locate new schools, close old ones, and determine the size and grade categories with this same objective in mind. Where school authorities decide to undertake the transportation of students, this also must be with integrative opportunities in mind.[73]

Justice Powell's attempt to justify the requirement of integration he would thus impose shows that, despite his insistence on realism, he was unable or unwilling to abandon the confusion and pretenses of *Green*. In an integrated system, he said, "all citizens and pupils may justifiably be confident that racial discrimination is neither practiced nor tolerated." Such a system "provides the best assurance of meeting the constitutional requirement that racial discrimination, subtle or otherwise, will find no place in the decisions of public school officials."[74] Compulsory integration, however, *requires* that racial discrimination be practiced and made a basis of decision by school officials. One may argue, of course, that the use of racial discrimination to further integration should be constitutionally distinguished from the use of racial discrimination to separate the races, but it is hardly a return to candor and clarity to argue as if that distinction was not being made and, like the Court, to require the use of racial discrimination to increase racial mixing under cover of a general prohibition of all racial discrimination.

Justice Powell's argument here, which he did not further articulate, was apparently that racial discrimination to integrate should be required as a prophylactic measure, to assure that there is no racial discrimination to separate the races. This argument would be at least the beginning of a rationale for compulsory integration, though not one likely to persuade anyone not committed to compulsory integration on other grounds.[75] Important as such assurance is, the argument fails to consider whether it might not be adequately obtained today by means less destructive of principle, less costly in other values, and less likely—for reasons later stated by Justice Powell in opposing extensive busing—to be self-defeating. Justice Powell, it may be noted, wisely refrained from mentioning the theory relied on by the district judge: that integration is necessary to improve black or "Hispano" academic performance.

Justice Powell's basic justification, however, for his own requirement of integration was as follows:

School board decisions obviously are not the sole cause of segregated school conditions. But if, after such detailed and complete public supervision, substantial school segregation still persists, the presumption is strong that the school board, by its acts or omissions, is in some part responsible. Where state action and supervision are so pervasive and where, after years of such action, segregated schools continue to exist within the district to a substantial degree, this Court is justified in finding a prima facie case of a constitutional violation. The burden then must fall on the school board to demonstrate it is operating an "integrated school system."[76]

Thus, Justice Powell offered what is in essence a "remedial" rationale for compulsory integration little different from that which he had earlier in his opinion shown to be baseless. Integration is not to be required, as the need to give assurance of the absence of "racial discrimination" might indicate, wherever a certain degree of racial imbalance exists, but only where school authorities may be found "responsible" for such imbalance. In place of the Court's search for "segregative intent," Justice Powell would substitute a search for board responsibility aided by a strong "presumption" that such responsibility indeed exists.

The "detailed and complete public supervision" of public schools by school authorities, relied on by Justice Powell, cannot, of

course, distinguish constitutional from unconstitutional "segregation," for such supervision everywhere exists. The existence of such
supervision is, however, of no relevance to the question of whether
greater integration than that resulting from a prohibition of
racial discrimination should be required by the Court. Its apparent
relevance, if any, is only to precisely the type of "legalism rooted
in history"—that is, the supposed applicability of the Fourteenth
Amendment to only "state [official] action"—that Justice Powell
earlier deplored in rejecting the "*de facto/de jure* distinction."[77] No
presumptions are necessary to show that neighborhood assignment
will almost always result in racially imbalanced schools or that
neighborhood assignment is adopted as the result of a conscious
decision by a school board. But Justice Powell purported not to
rely simply on these facts, for to do so would be to make neighborhood assignment almost everywhere unconstitutional and openly to
require integration for its own sake. The purpose of Justice
Powell's presumption is to make the existence of racially imbalanced
schools the basis for finding racial discrimination by a school
board so that compulsory integration can be justified as a remedy
for a constitutional violation. This reasoning flies in the face,
however, of the intractable fact, otherwise the fulcrum of his
opinion, that school racial imbalance ordinarily cannot be attributed to past or present racial discrimination by school authorities.

The fallacy of Justice Powell's reasoning on this point is illustrated
by his attempt to analogize school racial imbalance to racial
exclusion in jury selection. He points out that the Court had stated:

"Circumstances or chance may well dictate that no persons in a certain
class will serve on a particular jury during some particular period. But
it taxes our credulity to say that *mere chance* resulted in there being no
members of this class among the over six thousand jurors called in the
past 25 years. *The result bespeaks discrimination, whether or not it was a
conscious decision on the part of any individual jury commissioner.*"[78]

The attempted analogy does not support but undermines
Justice Powell's argument. No one contends that racially imbalanced
schools are the result of "mere chance"; they are plainly the result
of neighborhood assignment in racially imbalanced neighborhoods.
Their existence in such neighborhoods "taxes [no] credulity" and
"bespeaks," not a board's racial discrimination, but its failure to

discriminate racially. Again, one may argue that school boards should be required to discriminate racially in order to integrate and attempt to justify the requirement on its own merits. But Justice Powell was no more willing than the Court to undertake that unappealing argument and no less willing to cloak a requirement of integration as a corrective for racial imbalance resulting from racial discrimination by school boards in the past. Justice Powell's only real contribution to this issue is that he, elsewhere in his opinion, showed that a requirement of integration *cannot* be so justified. Nor was Justice Powell's argument helped by his quotation of Judge Wisdom's portentous but baseless statement that "when the figures [showing school racial imbalance] speak so eloquently, a *prima facie* case of discrimination is established." [79] Given the existence of racially imbalanced neighborhoods, racially imbalanced schools speak of nothing but neighborhood assignment.

Justice Powell, quoting the Court of Appeals for the Fifth Circuit, also argued:

" 'The Negro children [in racially imbalanced schools in the North and West] would receive little comfort from the assertion that the racial make-up of their school system does not violate their constitutional rights because they were born into a de facto society, while the exact same racial make-up of the school system in the 17 Southern and border states violates the constitutional rights of their counterparts, or even their blood brothers, because they were born into a de jure society. All children everywhere in the nation are protected by the Constitution, and treatment which violates their constitutional rights in one area of the country, also violates such constitutional rights in another area.' " [80]

The existence of racially imbalanced schools outside the South indeed shows that compulsory integration cannot be justified in the South as "desegregation"—the ending or remedying of unconstitutional segregation; it does not show, however, that compulsory integration can be justified anywhere or that compulsory integration should, as Justice Powell argued, be extended. "Negro children" and everyone else undoubtedly can derive a great deal of "comfort" from knowing that they may not be dealt with on the basis of race. It is indeed "essential," as Justice Powell further argued, "that no racial minority feel demeaned or discriminated against," [81] but this goal can probably best be achieved by in fact prohibiting all racial discrimination. A black child, for example, may "receive little comfort from" being told that he may not attend school in his neighborhood because that school already has enough blacks. Little may be as demeaning to him as the insistence that he receive the "advantages" of transportation to a distant school that has more whites.

Justice Powell also quoted an assertion by Senator Abraham Ribicoff that the distinction between the "legally supported *de jure* segregation of the South" and the "residential segregation in the North" was a "hard distinction for black children in the totally segregated schools in the North to understand." [82] The difficulty, however, lies not in understanding the Court's prohibition of segregation but in understanding the Court's attempt to justify compulsory integration as a "remedy" for segregation in the past and thereby to distinguish racially imbalanced schools in the South from racially imbalanced schools in the North; illogical and baseless distinctions are always difficult to understand. The difference between segregated schools (*"de jure* segregation") and racially imbalanced schools resulting from racially imbalanced neighborhoods (*"de facto* segregation") is not at all difficult to understand, except, apparently, for some judges and other initiates in constitutional law. Nathan Glazer, who is not a lawyer, has found it quite easy to understand:

The distinction was meaningful when the Supreme Court handed down *Brown* and is meaningful today. In the *de facto* situation, to begin with, not all schools are 100 percent segregated. Indeed, none may be. A child's observation alone may demonstrate that there are many opportunities to attend integrated schools. The family may have an opportunity to move, the city may have open enrollment, it may have a voluntary city-to-suburb busing program. The child may conclude that if one's parents wished, one could attend another school, or that one could if one lived in another neighborhood—not all are inaccessible economically or because of discrimination—or could conclude that the presence of a few whites indicated that the school was not segregated.

. . . . .

Perception is not only based on reality, a reality which to me makes the *de facto* segregated school a very different thing from the *de jure* segregated school. Perception can turn the lovely campuses of the West Coast into "jails" which confine young people, and can turn those incarcerated by courts for any crime into political prisoners. If we feel a perception is wrong, one of our duties is to try to correct it, rather than to assume that the perception of being a victim must alone dictate the action to be taken. False perceptions are to be responded to sympathetically, but not as if they were true.[83]

Justice Powell's basis for finding a requirement of integration is no less fictitious than the Court's use of "segregative intent" and would avoid none of his objections to it. Unconstitutionality requiring "remedy" would be as widespread as under the Court's approach, and the "remedy" required would be as uncertain. Because Justice Powell's "prima facie case of a constitutional violation" requires only the existence of "segregated school conditions" (racially imbalanced schools) and "detailed and complete public supervision," there would ordinarily be nothing for a defendant school board to rebut. It would be no defense for the board to show complete racial neutrality in all of its decisions, for the board is deemed "in some part responsible" for existing racial imbalance, and that imbalance "bespeaks discrimination" too "eloquently" to be outspoken. The board must show that it has an "integrated school system" in accordance with Justice Powell's definition—that it has, among other things, "taken appropriate steps" to "utilize [its] authority" to "draw attendance zones," "locate new schools, close old ones and determine the size and grade categories," in order to promote integration. These are precisely the sorts of things that Denver did do beginning in 1962, but Denver apparently did not do enough. Very few, if any, school boards will be able to show a greater commitment to integration. Many boards believed, on the basis of *Brown*, that they did *not* have the "authority" to discriminate racially for any purpose; many or all would have, in any event, found racial discrimination in order to integrate unjustifiable and inconsistent with continued public support. Justice Powell's "presumption" seems, therefore, not merely "strong" but conclusive.

Justice Powell's approach, no less than the Court's, would subject virtually every school board action or inaction to judicial scrutiny while providing no ascertainable standard. A board using neighborhood assignment, as nearly all not undertaking "desegregation" do, must show, for example, that attendance-zone boundaries were "drawn to integrate, to the extent practicable, the school's student body." "This does not imply," Justice Powell said, that decisions "must be made to the detriment of all neutral, nonracial considerations," but it clearly does require that decisions be made to the detriment of some such considerations. The question is how to determine with regard to each board decision whether further integration was "practicable" or whether nonracial considerations could be permitted to prevail. No meaningful standard is or can be provided. How wide and dangerous a highway, for example, must elementary school children be required to cross in order that a school system may achieve a given degree of improvement in racial balance? May the "risk [of] setting in motion unpredictable and unmanageable social consequences," which Justice Powell would consider in connection with busing, also be considered here? An answer is hardly possible in any given set of circumstances except on the basis of almost purely personal judgment, and "wide and unpredictable differences of opinion among judges" will be no less "inevitable" than in applying the Court's test of "segregative intent."

Although Justice Powell's approach would result in a finding of unconstitutionality as readily as, and with no more justification than, the Court's, he parted with the Court on the question of the "remedy" to be required. The significance of his opinion lies in the fact that he would largely confine the "remedy" to requiring boards to do the things listed in his definition of an "integrated school system." Specifically and most importantly, he strongly disagreed with the Court on the requirement of busing: "To the extent that *Swann* may be thought to *require* large-scale or long-distance transportation of students in our metropolitan school districts, I record my profound misgivings. Nothing in our Constitution commands or encourages any such court-compelled disruption of public education." School boards are obliged "to promote desegregation," but there must be a "more balanced evaluation" of that obligation "with other educational and societal interests a community may legitimately assert." Foremost among these is the interest in maintaining neighborhood schools.

The neighborhood school does provide greater ease of parental and student access and convenience, as well as greater economy of public administration. These are obvious and distinct advantages, but the legitimacy of the neighborhood concept rests on more basic grounds.

Neighborhood school systems, neutrally administered, reflect the deeply felt desire of citizens for a sense of community in their public education. Public schools have been a traditional source of strength to our Nation, and that strength may derive in part from the identification of many schools with the personal features of the surrounding neighborhood. . . . This Court should be wary of compelling in the name of constitutional law what may seem to many a dissolution in the traditional, more personal fabric of their public schools.[84]

The interest in sending one's children to neighborhood schools appears, indeed, to have the status of a constitutional right. The Court had previously recognized "the right to educate one's children as one chooses." [85] This right cannot "be confined solely to a parent's choice to send a child to public or private school. Most parents cannot afford the luxury of a private education for their children, and the dual obligation of private tuitions and public taxes. Those who may for numerous reasons seek public education for their children should not be forced to forfeit all interest or voice in the school their child attends. . . . The interest of the parent in the enhanced parent-school and parent-child communication allowed by the neighborhood unit ought not to be suppressed by force of law." [86]

The "rights and interests of children affected by a desegregation program" must also be considered.

Any child, white or black, who is compelled to leave his neighborhood and spend significant time each day being transported to a distant school suffers an impairment of his liberty and his privacy. Not long ago, James B. Conant wrote that "[a]t the elementary school level the issue seems clear. To send young children day after day to distant schools by bus seems out of the question." A community may well conclude that the portion of a child's day spent on a bus might be used more creatively in a classroom, playground, or some other extracurricular school activity. Decisions such as these, affecting the quality of a child's daily life, should not lightly be held constitutionally errant.[87]

"Broader considerations" further demonstrate that a "remedial requirement of extensive student transportation solely to further integration" is not justifiable.

[First], any such requirement is certain to fall disproportionately on the school districts of our country, depending on their degree of urbanization, financial resources, and their racial composition. Some districts with little or no biracial population will experience little or no educational disruption, while others, notably in large, biracial metropolitan areas, must at considerable expense undertake extensive transportation to achieve the type of integration frequently being ordered by district courts. At a time when public education generally is suffering serious financial malnutrition, the economic burdens of such transportation can be severe, requiring both initial capital outlays and annual operating costs in the millions of dollars.[88]

Second, "the remedy exceeds that which may be necessary to redress the constitutional evil," since the "fundamental problem" is "residential segregation": "It is, indeed, a novel application of equitable power—not to mention a dubious extension of constitutional doctrine—to require so much greater a degree of forced school integration than would have resulted from purely natural and neutral nonstate causes." Third, "compulsory transportation of students carries a further infirmity as a constitutional remedy" because "the full burden of the affirmative remedial action is borne by children and parents who did not participate in any constitutional violation."[89]

Finally and most significantly, Justice Powell would have extricated the Court from the ostrich-like position that "constitutional principles" preclude consideration of reality. The Court must recognize, he argued, that its insistence on busing "risk[s] setting in motion unpredictable and unmanageable social consequences." It may "hasten an exodus to private schools, leaving public school systems the preserve of the disadvantaged of both races"; it may give "impetus" to "the movement from inner city to suburb, and the further geographical separation of the races"; and it may "cause deterioration of community and parental support of the public schools." The problem of "desegregation," "especially since it has focused on the 'busing issue,' has profoundly disquieted the public wherever extensive transportation has been ordered."[90]

"As a minimum," Justice Powell concluded, the "Court should not require school boards to engage in unnecessary transportation away from their neighborhoods of elementary age children." And even as to secondary school students "it would ultimately be wisest, where there is no absence of good faith, to permit affected communities to decide this delicate issue of student transportation on their own."[91]

In short, Justice Powell would have retained a requirement of school racial mixing but would have attempted to keep it within what he saw as more reasonable and acceptable bounds. His failure simply to return to *Brown* can be explained, even if not justified, by recognition that insistence on strict neutrality in dealing with race is not necessarily the complete answer to all school racial questions. School boards must and do, as Justice Powell said, make and refuse to make innumerable decisions that have a foreseeable impact on school racial composition. This impact cannot reasonably be ignored but must be evaluated either positively or negatively. In most places increased integration has undoubtedly been evaluated negatively by most whites and, to the extent they could escape housing discrimination and were economically able to move from poor predominantly black areas, by blacks as well. School boards, not sharing the Court's elevated position and freedom from elections, have been properly concerned with maintaining necessary public support for public school systems and unable to see the value of furthering an "integration" likely to lead to greater racial separation. Justice Powell would in effect have reversed this situation by requiring that greater integration now be considered a factor of positive value but not of so great a value that it would completely outweigh the value of neighborhood schools and thereby raise the "busing issue" and create a "profoundly disquieted . . . public."

The difficulties in Justice Powell's approach, however, are the same as in any imposition of integration as a constitutional requirement. Chief among these, as discussed above in connection with *Green*, are that the extremely valuable principle prohibiting racial discrimination by government officials is seriously undermined and that no meaningful principle is substituted in its place. One may believe that if all review of school board decisions was in Justice Powell's hands a way would be found for public school systems to be preserved while integration is encouraged, but review is, as a practical matter, very largely in the hands of lower-court judges such as those who initially decided *Swann*, *Richmond*, and the present case. If, in accordance with Justice Powell's approach, every school district is to be made, in the words of Justice Rehnquist, "a candidate for what is in practice a federal receivership,"[92] many of these judges must be among the least suitable receivers.

Even the most competent judges, cognizant of the limits of their knowledge and power, cannot properly deal with the real problems presented by an unprincipled integration requirement. It is hardly conceivable, for example, that a judge could properly find further integration "impracticable" where the white population has ready financial or geographical means of escape but "practicable" where it does not. Even if it is possible to agree on nothing else relating to resolution of these problems, it should be possible to agree that they cannot properly be resolved by judges. As James Coleman, one of the nation's leading authorities on questions of education and race, has said, "Courts are the very worst of all possible instruments for carrying out a very sensitive activity like integrating schools."[93] Nathan Glazer, another eminent authority, has written:

When one reads cases such as those in Indianapolis, Detroit, and elsewhere, the mind reels with the complexity of numerous school-zoning and construction decisions. Briefs, hearing transcripts, exhibits run to thousands of pages. And at least one conclusion that this reader comes to is that no judge can or ought to have to make decisions on such issues, and the chances are that whatever decision he makes will be based on inadequately analyzed information.[94]

While a requirement of racial neutrality and prohibition of racial discrimination do not solve all racial problems, they may solve all that can or should be solved by courts as a matter of constitutional law. Whatever justification the Court's attempt to do more may once have had is surely much lessened by the substantial increase in the legal protection, and continuing increase in the political influence, of blacks.

Justice Rehnquist's Dissent

Only Justice Rehnquist, dissenting in a short opinion, completely rejected the idea that compulsory integration in some way follows from *Brown*. He would have returned to a simple prohibition of racial discrimination.

The drastic extension of *Brown* which *Green* represented was barely, if at all, explicated in the latter opinion. To require that a genuinely "dual" system be disestablished, in the sense that the assignment of a child to a particular school is not made to depend on his race, is one thing. To require that school boards affirmatively undertake to achieve racial mixing in schools where such mixing is not achieved in sufficient degree by neutrally drawn boundary lines is quite obviously something else.[95]

Separation of the races as a result of racial discrimination in performing such functions as drawing attendance zones and locating schools is, of course, constitutionally prohibited as much as is the "statutorily required segregation" involved in *Brown*. "It certainly would not reflect normal English usage," however, "to describe" an entire school district such as Denver's "as 'segregated' " on the basis of an instance of such discrimination and thereby make it "a candidate for what is in practice a federal receivership." The district judge, "thoroughly sympathetic to plaintiffs' claims," found no "segregative intent" as to the core area schools; this finding applied proper legal standards and was affirmed by the court of appeals.[96] The court of appeals' denial of relief on the claim under review should, therefore, have been affirmed by the Supreme Court.

The District Court's Decision after Remand of the Case by the Supreme Court

On the remand of the case, the district judge showed little concern with, and less understanding of, Justice Brennan's subtleties and refinements. As he understood the Court's decision, "a new standard was pronounced governing the *de facto–de jure* concepts" and that new standard made irrelevant the fact that he had found—as he here repeated—that "the segregated schools" of Park Hill "became so as a result of neighborhood patterns rather than state action" (racially discriminatory action taken by the school board). "The Supreme Court," he stated, "reexamined the facts and approved the conclusion that conduct [in Park Hill] during the 1960's constituted *de jure* segregation."[97] The district judge's interpretation of the Supreme Court's opinion was wrong in almost every regard except in realizing the decision he was expected to reach. Justice Brennan had purported to announce no "new standard," but to suggest ways of finding that the "segregated schools" outside Park Hill *were* the result of racially discriminatory "state action." The Court had refused to grant review of the lower courts' decisions regarding Park Hill and, therefore, had not "reexamined the facts," or purported to reexamine the facts, regarding Park Hill. Instead of approving the district judge's conclusion that the Park Hill schools were segregated "as a result of neighborhood patterns," Justice Brennan purported to believe that the district judge had found a "deliberate policy of racial segregation" in regard to those schools—exactly the opposite of what the judge now reiterated he had in fact found. Denver continued to be whipsawed by courts that agreed on almost nothing except that a constitutional violation requiring racial balance was to be found. That a constitutional violation was to be found by the district judge could not be doubted. Subtleties aside, "the Supreme Court's viewpoint," the judge correctly perceived, "is that the Denver school system is a dual system. There can be no doubt as to its view of the case in the absence of new and cogent evidence." It was certainly "the Supreme Court's viewpoint" that the *district judge* should find that Denver had a "dual system"; the judge, therefore, erred only technically in apparently thinking that the Supreme Court had already made that finding itself. He was, in any event, entirely willing to, and did, corroborate that supposed finding by the Supreme Court despite his own finding that the racially imbalanced schools in Denver were not the result of racial discrimination by the board. "New and cogent evidence" showing that Denver did not have a dual system was simply not possible. The board attempted to show that "segregated conditions in individual schools outside the Park Hill area are wholly the product of external factors such as demographic trends and housing patterns"—which is what the judge himself had found. The board was unable to show, however, that these "segregated conditions" were "in no way the product of any [of its] acts or omissions"—the board, there was no denying, had operated a school system in Denver, and some of these schools were racially or ethnically imbalanced.[98] No more was required by the judge's standard for finding a constitutional violation, and he was, therefore, "not persuaded" by the board's showing.

Hearings were held the following year, 1974, on the proper "remedy" for Denver's constitutional violations. By this time, the schools were well on their way to having a majority of blacks and "Hispanos."[99] To the judge, this indicated the "scope and magnitude of the problem," but it provided no basis for abandoning the quest for racially balanced schools; the board would simply have to use those "Anglos" who were still available. He rejected a board plan that would have provided an "Anglo" student body of no less than 25 percent or more than 75 percent of each school. He stated:

> For elementary schools the court has considered desirable a 40% minimum percentage of Anglo students, and it has considered the permissible maximum range to extend to 70% Anglo population. In the secondary schools the minimum figure that has been used is somewhat higher, and it has been considered desirable to have 50-60% Anglos in some instances.

He decided, however, that "in some of the schools which have a preponderant Chicano population it has seemed to the court more desirable to pursue bilingual and bicultural programs than to change the numbers." For "Chicanos," therefore, he ordered the board to adopt an extensive plan prepared by the "Congress of Hispanic Educators."[100]

Dissatisfied with both the plaintiffs' and the board's plan regarding blacks and "Anglos," the judge called upon John Finger of Charlotte-Mecklenburg fame. Finger was able to devise a plan meeting the judge's requirements by using satellite zoning and a system that the judge found "more refined than school pairing," whereby students would spend each day partly in a "home school" and partly in an "integrated setting." The judge explained:

> Thus, in the segregated school one-half of the students in a class are transported to an Anglo or majority school and simultaneously one-half of the Anglo or majority students are transported to the minority school. The student spends a major portion of each day at the receiving school, but he commences his school day at the home school and he completes his school day at that school.[101]

The judge saw many advantages in this arrangement, including that it both "exposes the pupils to an integrated setting during the heart of the school period" and "gives the student an identifiable local neighborhood school to maintain as an anchor."[102] Finger informed the judge that "there will be considerable opposition from the citizens of Denver," for although "most citizens really believe in the American ideal of equality and equal opportunity, . . . that ideal gets in conflict with the desire to provide for one's children" and "few people want to pay a price at the expense of their children." Finger, however, reassured the judge:

> Despite the widespread opposition to busing, there is no evidence that it hurts anybody. The facts are that many children enjoy it. Others

view it as just a thing one does like driving to work in one's car. One just does it. Some children don't like it, but that usually is because the bus is unsupervised and the children are teased or assaulted.[103]

On appeal by all parties, the Tenth Circuit affirmed the district judge's decision except as to his "part-time pairing plan" and his adoption of the Hispanic Educators' Plan. The court recognized that the Finger plan would impose a "heavy burden" on children bused from the core area to "extreme southern portions of the city," but it noted: "The Finger Plan requires provision of extra buses to pick up stragglers, transportation for students between home and school necessitated by emergencies, and transportation for parents wishing to attend PTA and other activities at school." The court rejected part-time pairing and required full-time integration because "although we acknowledge such neighborhood contact to be important, we cannot place it above the constitutional rights of children to attend desegregated schools." Similarly, it rejected the Hispanic Educators' Plan because "bilingual education . . . is not a substitute for desegregation." Furthermore, that plan would have required "an overhaul of the system's entire approach to education of minorities." For example, it required "early childhood education (beginning at age three) and adult education for minorities, and provision of adequate clothing for poor minority school children." The court also disapproved the judge's order, apparently unrelated to "desegregation," that two high schools be consolidated "into a campus complex." As to this, it found that the district "court appears to have acted solely according to its own notions of good educational policy unrelated to the demands of the Constitution." It approved, however, the district judge's order that "as a goal, . . . the District . . . achieve ratios of Hispano and black personnel to Anglo that 'reflect more truly' the ratios of Hispano and black students to Anglo students in the District."[104]

As of December 1974, "white enrollment in Denver had decreased nearly 30 percent since 1970." The system lost 17,000 students since integration was first ordered by the judge in 1969 and "some 7,200 students, most of them white" in 1974 alone. The people of Denver, unlike those of South Boston, mounted few protest demonstrations; instead, the "whites," an independent researcher reported, "will just quietly disappear in two to three years." The people of Colorado did take the step, however, in November 1974, of adopting an amendment to the Colorado constitution to remove Denver's power to annex suburban land. It was through this power that Denver had "avoided the shrinking tax base and declining population that has spelled doom for other core cities and their school systems." The busing program and the loss of this power will, Denver's planning director stated, "turn the tide and make Denver a ghettoized city."[105]

Perhaps the most noteworthy and surely the most disappointing aspect of *Keyes* is that the appointment of four justices of the Supreme Court by a president who made opposition to busing a major part of his program for domestic peace resulted, in so extreme a case, in but one unequivocal dissent. If, as is often alleged, "the Court follows the election returns," it does not, it seems, follow them closely enough to make its policy-making consistent with the continuation of a workable democracy. President Franklin Roosevelt did ultimately succeed in stopping the Court's invalidation of his New Deal,[106] but that was a conservative Court, seeking to impede basic social change. The Court since *Brown* has become the nation's principal engine of change. The superiority of its policy-making over policy-making by elected representatives has, therefore, been so long and so loudly proclaimed by many of our most articulate and influential citizens that the power of the Court is now much more difficult to overcome. [107]

10 | The Result of Two Decades of Judicial Policy-Making: Busing to Achieve Racial Balance though the Whites Have Left

The Supreme Court's decision in *Milliken* v. *Bradley*,[1] the Detroit case, provides a fitting conclusion to the unhappy story of the Supreme Court's decisions on race and the schools since *Brown*. The decision, unsurprising and anticlimactic after *Richmond* and *Keyes*, is unsatisfactory from almost any point of view. As expected, Justice Powell's vote provided a majority—Justices Douglas, Brennan, White, and Marshall dissented—for the decision that had been affirmed by an equally divided court in *Richmond:* "Desegregation" would, as its logic—the undoing of segregation—requires, be confined to the school district found to have been previously segregated; there is no constitutional requirement that districts be consolidated to make all schools predominantly white. On the other hand, supposed lower-court findings of "*de jure* segregation" were, as in *Keyes*, permitted to stand, although Detroit had never had explicit racial assignment and had early taken voluntary steps to further integration in spite of massive black population growth: "Desegregation" could, despite its logic, be required in a northern school district not in fact shown to have ever been segregated. It is good that some limit on the busing requirement was found, but the overall result—compulsory busing to achieve racial balance within the confines of a school system with a majority of blacks— can be the product only of an irrational system of lawmaking. The decision is perhaps principally significant because of the simple fact that, for the first time since before *Gaines* (1938), the Court, in a signed opinion, rejected the position of the NAACP in a decision on race and the schools.

Detroit: Denver Writ Large

On the question of *"de jure* segregation" in Detroit, without which the question of the appropriate "remedy" would not have arisen, *Milliken* is little more than a replay of *Keyes,* except that the fact that Detroit had a majority-black school system made the attribution of majority-black schools to *"de jure* segregation" in the past even more preposterous than in Denver. In 1970, when the litigation began, Detroit, the nation's fifth largest city, had a population of about 1,500,000 and a public school population of about 290,000 in 319 schools. The black proportion of the total population had increased from 9.2 percent in 1940 to 16.2 percent in 1950, 28.9 percent in 1960 and 43.9 percent in 1970. In the words of the district judge in 1971, "Detroit today is principally a conglomerate of poor black and white plus the aged. Of the aged, 80 percent are white." The Detroit public schools, which were 45.8 percent black in 1961, had a majority (51.3 percent) of blacks in 1963 and were 63.8 percent black in 1970.[2] The percentage of black pupils has since continued to increase: to 64.9 percent in 1971, 67.3 percent in 1972, and 69.8 percent in 1973.[3]

Detroit shared with Denver the paradoxical experience of being charged with unconstitutional segregation as the result of an unsuccessful voluntary attempt to increase integration. Michigan, like Colorado, had been a leader in efforts to promote racial equality. Racial discrimination in the public schools was prohibited by statute in 1867 and thereafter by the Michigan constitution.[4] Michigan enacted a Fair Employment Practices Act in 1955 and established a Civil Rights Commission in 1964. At the time of the suit, the state board of education had "recently established an Equal Educational Opportunities section having responsibility to identify racially imbalanced school districts and develop desegregation plans." In 1966, two years before *Green,* the state board of education and the Michigan Civil Rights Commission adopted a "Joint Policy Statement on Equality of Educational Opportunity" that said: "Local school boards must consider the factor of racial balance along with other educational considerations in making decisions about selection of new school sites [and] expansion of present facilities. . . . Each of these situations presents an opportunity for integration." The state board issued a

"School Plant Planning Handbook" that declared: "Care in site locations must be taken if a serious transportation problem exists or if housing patterns in an area would result in a school largely segregated on racial, ethnic, or socio-economic lines."[5]

The Detroit board of education, too, had early been active in efforts to promote integration. The district judge found that for some time prior to 1970 it had "followed a most advanced and exemplary course in adopting and carrying out what is called the 'balanced staff concept'—which seeks to balance faculties in each school with respect to race, sex, and experience, with primary emphasis on race." The Detroit board had adopted "affirmative policies designed to achieve racial balance in instructional staff" and in the school administration, with the result that between 1960 and 1970 the proportion of black teachers in the system increased from 23.3 percent to 42.1, and of black administrators from 4.5 percent to 37.8. By 1970, Detroit employed "black teachers in a greater percentage than the percentage of adult black persons in the City of Detroit" and had a "higher proportion of black administrators than any city in the country." In 1970 "the board held open 240 positions in schools with less than 25% black, rejecting white applicants for these positions until qualified black applicants could be found and assigned." "In many other instances and in many other respects," the district judge found, the Detroit board had "undertaken to lessen the impact of the forces of segregation and attempted to advance the cause of integration."[6]

As in Denver, however, the board's commitment to integration finally led it to adopt a plan to improve school racial balance by busing, and, thereby, to go too far for community acceptance. On April 7, 1970, the board adopted a plan that would have changed the attendance zones of twelve of Detroit's twenty-one high schools so as "to effect a more balanced ratio of Negro and white students at the senior high level." The plan was to be implemented during a three-year period beginning in September 1970. In July 1970, however, Michigan enacted a statute known as Act 48, that, in effect, abrogated the April 7 plan and substituted for it a policy of voluntary open enrollment for all schools, with priority to be granted, in case of overcrowding, on the basis of residential proximity. Detroit voters then initiated a recall election that was held in August 1970, and the four board members who had voted for the board's plan (two had opposed it and one did not vote) were removed from office and replaced by members appointed by the governor.[7] The reconstituted board then rescinded the plan.[8] But again, as in Denver, the voters had acted too late.[9]

A federal district court action challenging the constitutionality of Act 48 was promptly instituted in the name of the Detroit branch of the NAACP and individual school children and their parents. Named as defendants were the governor and the attorney general of Michigan, the state board of education, the state superintendent of public instruction, the Detroit board of education, individual members of the Detroit board, and the Detroit superintendent of schools. The plaintiffs sought to enjoin the effectuation of Act 48 and, in effect, to require the implementation of the April 7 plan. The complaint also alleged that the Detroit school system was unconstitutionally segregated and demanded a plan eliminating the "racial identity of every school in the system."[10]

A motion by the plaintiffs for a preliminary injunction against effectuation of Act 48 was denied by the district judge, and the plaintiffs appealed to the Court of Appeals for the Sixth Circuit. The court of appeals recognized that according to its prior decisions a "unitary non-racial school system had no constitutional obligation to bus white and Negro children away from districts of their residences in order that racial complexion be balanced in each" of the system's schools. The Detroit school system had not yet been found to be anything but unitary and nonracial, but the court, citing the decision of the district judge in *Keyes*, nonetheless held Act 48 to be unconstitutional. "In the present case," it explained, "the Detroit Board of Education in the exercise of its discretion took affirmative steps on its own initiative to effect an improved racial balance in twelve senior high schools. This action was thwarted, or at least delayed, by an act of the State Legislature." Although the court did not explicitly mention it, the rescission of the April 7 plan by the Detroit board was, presumably, unconstitutional for the same or a similar reason. Again, a proposal to integrate that was not constitutionally required could not, once it was voluntarily adopted, constitutionally be rejected. The district judge's denial of a preliminary injunction was affirmed, however, on the ground that it did not constitute an abuse of discretion, since no "*de jure* segregation" had yet been found. The case was remanded for trial with a direction to the district judge "to give no effect to . . . Act 48, because of its unconstitutionality."[11]

On remand, however, the plaintiffs again moved for an injunction to require implementation of the April 7 plan. This time the motion was on the ground that implementation was required "in order to remedy the deprivation of constitutional rights wrought by the unconstitutional statute."[12] Although the trial had not yet begun and no finding of "*de jure* segregation" had been made, the district judge ordered the board to submit a plan providing for "no less pupil integration" than would have resulted from the April 7 plan.[13] The board then submitted, and the district judge, in December 1970, ordered it to adopt, a "magnet school plan" (some schools to be "designed to attract children because of [their] superior curriculum") to be implemented at the beginning of the next school year, in September 1971. The plaintiffs again appealed to the Sixth Circuit, seeking a summary reversal of the district judge's failure to order "immediate implementation of the April 7 Plan." The court, however, denied further relief and again remanded the case for trial.[14]

The District Court

The Constitutional Violation

Some "desegregation" having already been ordered, a trial of the constitutionality of Detroit's school system was finally held, and unconstitutionality was duly found. Despite his finding that the Detroit board had used the "most advanced and exemplary" hiring practices and had in many other respects "attempted to advance the cause of integration," the district judge concluded that "both the State of Michigan and the Detroit Board of Education have committed acts which have been causal factors in the segregated condition of the public schools of the city of Detroit."[15] Again as in *Keyes,* the judge's standard for finding a "segregated condition" made this conclusion both inevitable and meaningless and in fact no more than a simple condemnation of majority-black schools whatever their cause. The judge's statement would have been equally true, given his use of "segregated condition," if Michigan and Detroit had done no more than simply provide a public school system for Detroit with its majority-black school population.

The judge made clear that he saw the finding of "*de jure* segregation" as merely a foolish game the Supreme Court required him to play as a preliminary to ordering further racial mixing. "As we assay the principles essential to a finding of de jure segregation," began his discussion of the law, officials "must have taken some action or actions with a purpose of segregation," and "this action or these actions must have created or aggravated segregation in the schools in question." In his view, however, he candidly stated, it was "unfortunate that we cannot deal with public school segregation on a no-fault basis, for if racial segregation in our public schools is an evil, then it should make no difference whether we classify it de jure or de facto. Our objective, logically, it seems to us, should be to remedy a condition which we believe needs correction."[16] Or, as he expressed this view at another point in the litigation: "We must bear in mind that the task we are called upon to perform is a social one, which society has been unable to accomplish. In reality, our courts are called upon, in these school cases, to attain a social goal, through the educational system by using law as a lever."[17] It is not surprising, therefore, that the judge had difficulty in adhering, even verbally, to the supposed requirement of finding "actions with a purpose of segregation" that caused the existing "segregation." In fact it was "not necessary," he concluded, citing the Denver district judge's first opinion in *Keyes,* that there be a finding of "any evil intent or motive." "Motive, ill-will and bad faith" had, he thought, "long ago been rejected as a requirement" for finding "*de jure* segregation." The law as he understood it was simply that "the affirmative obligation of the defendant board has been and is to adopt and implement pupil assignment practices and policies that compensate for and avoid incorporation into the school system the effects of residential racial segregation." Therefore, "a school board may not, consistent with the Fourteenth Amendment, maintain segregated elementary schools" ("segregated" meaning, as in "residential racial segregation," merely "majority-black").

The judge recognized that "blacks, like ethnic groups in the past, have tended to separate from the larger group and associate together. The ghetto is at once both a place of confinement and of refuge." This voluntary association did not, however, make the resulting majority-black neighborhood schools any less "segregated." It meant only that the "black components" of the community must share in the "fault or blame" for the "condition which we believe needs correction." And there was, he found, "enough blame for everyone to share." Nathan Glazer commented on this:

> We would all agree with [the judge] that the ghetto must not be a place of confinement and that everything possible must be done to make it as easy for blacks to live where they wish as it is for anyone else. But why should it be the duty or the right of the federal government and the federal judiciary to destroy the ghetto as a place of refuge if that is what some blacks want? [The judge] is trying to read into the Constitution the crude Americanizing and homogenizing which is certainly one part of the American experience, but which is just as certainly not the main way we in this country have responded to the facts of a multi-ethnic society. The doctrines to which [the judge] lends his authority would deny not only to blacks, but to any other group, a right of refuge which is quite properly theirs in a multi-ethnic society built on democratic and pluralist principles.[18]

There is no reason to doubt that intensive investigation of all aspects of the operation of a large, racially mixed school system during a period of twenty years will produce at least some evidence of racial discrimination in almost every case, and no reason to think that the Detroit system was an exception. Whether or not, however, meaningful findings of racial discrimination could have been made on the basis of the record, the judge's findings clearly cannot be accepted as constituting such findings; even more clearly, the racial composition of Detroit's schools cannot be attributed to whatever racial discrimination might have been found. Having better observed what the Supreme Court had done since *Green* than what it had said, the judge, as already noted, concluded that the absence of racial discrimination to integrate was constitutional violation enough—that is, that the constitutional requirement was simply to achieve racially balanced (in fact, majority-white) schools and not, as the Supreme Court insisted, to "dismantle the dual system" that had been prohibited in *Brown*. As was true of *Keyes,* therefore, little purpose would be served by attempting to assess in detail the available evidence on the matters involved in the judge's findings. The dubious nature of these findings must be briefly noted, however, if only because of their later use by the dissenting Supreme Court justices and because, after all, they sufficed to require busing for racial balance in Detroit and would, except for one vote in the Supreme Court, have sufficed to require it in a much larger area.

The district judge purported to find constitutional violations by the Detroit board on several grounds.[19] First, the judge found that the board during the 1950s, had "created and maintained optional attendance zones in neighborhoods undergoing racial transition," the "natural, probable, foreseeable and actual effect" of which was "to allow white youngsters to escape 'black' schools." Second, in transporting children to relieve overcrowding, the board had "admittedly bused black pupils past or away from closer white schools with available space to black schools" and "with one exception (necessitated by the burning of a white school)" had "never bused white children to predominantly black schools . . . despite the enormous amount of space available in inner-city schools." Third, the board had "created and altered attendance zones, . . . grade structures and . . . feeder school patterns in a manner which had the natural, probable and actual effect of continuing black and white pupils in racially segregated schools." It was found to have used north–south attendance-zone boundaries despite its "awareness (at least since 1962) that drawing boundary lines in an east–west direction would result in significant integration." The judge noted in connection with this, that "every school which was 90% or more black in 1960, and which is still in use today, remains 90% or more black." Finally, the judge found unconstitutionality in the board's school construction policies. He noted that, of fourteen schools that were opened for use in 1970-1971, "eleven opened over 90% black and one opened less than 10% black." Furthermore, the board had, since 1959, "constructed at least 13 small primary schools with capacities of from 300 to 400 pupils"; this "practice negates opportunities to integrate, 'contains' the black population and perpetuates and compounds school segregation."

It should be obvious that most, if not all, of these findings cannot be considered and hardly purport to be meaningful findings of "*de jure* segregation." To condemn the Detroit board, as the judge repeatedly did, for acts whose "natural, probable and actual" effect is school racial imbalance or separation is not—unless those acts cannot be justified on nonracial grounds—to find racial discrimination and therefore "*de jure* segregation," but to condemn the board for failure to discriminate racially in order to avoid racial imbalance. It is to make racial imbalance itself unconstitutional and, therefore, to obliterate the "*de jure–de facto*" distinction supposedly being applied.[20] In light of the growth and proportion of the black population in Detroit, not racial discrimination but its absence is probably shown, again, by the fact that schools that were 90 percent or more black in 1960 remained so in 1971 and that many new schools opened with a student body over 90 percent black in 1971. On the question of "small primary schools," Nathan Glazer noted:

In Detroit, one charge against the school board, accepted by [the district judge], was that the board built small schools of 300 in order to contain the population and make desegregation more difficult. Paul Goodman and many others would argue that even schools of 300 are probably too large. In [a San Francisco case in which "*de jure* segregation" was found], on the other hand, the argument was that schools were expanded to "contain" the black and white population. The Detroit judge, it seems, would have preferred the large San Francisco schools, and the San Francisco judge would have preferred the small Detroit schools, if one takes their arguments at face value. But one may be allowed to suspect that if the situations had been reversed, they would still both have found "*de jure*" segregation in their respective cities.[21]

The most substantial matter—as a possible basis for finding "*de jure* segregation"—referred to by the district judge was the alleged relieving of overcrowding by busing students from predominantly black schools to other such schools and past predominantly white schools. Because the Detroit board did not seek Supreme Court review of the district judge's findings, the question of "*de jure* segregation" in Detroit was not directly before that Court and its record on the question is very incomplete. The brief of the defendant-petitioner state officials did, however, very concisely dispute each of the district judge's findings regarding the Detroit board. On the alleged busing of blacks past predominantly white schools, that brief argued that "during the decade of the 1960's, the vast majority of transportation to relieve overcrowding was from sending schools with a higher percentage of black students to receiving schools with a lower percentage of black students, thereby increasing integration."[22] A detailed statistical compilation available in the Supreme Court record seems to support this statement. It shows that of 250 instances of such transportation from 1961 through 1970, 173 involved transporting blacks to schools with a higher percentage of whites and only 20 involved transporting blacks to schools with a higher percentage of blacks. Data for the years 1964 to 1970 show 117 instances of busing to relieve overcrowding that had the effect of increasing integration and only 5 that did not.[23] If the Detroit school board discriminated racially in order to impede or lessen integration, the fact is not unequivocally apparent from the district judge's findings or the Supreme Court record.

The district judge supposedly found "*de jure* segregation" in Detroit on the basis of acts of "the State of Michigan" as well as the Detroit board. As he put it, "the State," too, had "committed acts which have been causal factors in the segregated condition" of Detroit's schools.[24] The judge's findings regarding acts by state officials are even more dubious than those regarding the Detroit board, but in any event they were unnecessary for finding a violation of the Fourteenth Amendment. There could be no doubt that, according to Supreme Court decisions, the actions of the Detroit board constituted "state action" for the purposes of the Fourteenth Amendment.[25] It seems, therefore, that the district judge's findings of acts constituting "*de jure* segregation" by "the State" were in anticipation of, and to lay some apparent basis for, the interdistrict "remedy"—not confined to Detroit—that he was later to order.

The district judge found culpability by the "State and its agencies" on three grounds.[26] First was "their general responsibility for and supervision of public education" in Michigan, including Detroit. This, of course, was merely a legal conclusion which, even if correct, provided no basis for finding "*de jure* segregation" in Detroit or elsewhere. As a matter of fact, neither the district judge's opinion nor the affirming opinion of the court of appeals, which contains a much more detailed review of the evidence, cited evidence that any state-level official required, encouraged, or was even aware of any of the acts allegedly constituting "*de jure* segregation" by the Detroit board.

The district judge also found culpability on the part of the state in that

the State refused, until this session of the legislature, to provide authorization or funds for the transportation of pupils within Detroit regardless of their poverty or distance from the school to which they were assigned, while providing in many neighboring, mostly white, suburban districts the full range of state supported transportation. This and other financial limitations, such as those on bonding and the working of the state aid formula whereby suburban districts were able to make far larger per pupil expenditures despite less tax effort, have created and perpetuated systematic educational inequalities.

Again, this statement clearly does not support a finding of racial discrimination by state officials. The unequal allocation of transportation funds to urban and rural or suburban areas was plainly justifiable on nonracial grounds. A different district judge in Michigan held in another "desegregation" case:

It is an urban-rural classification distinction based upon known differences usually characteristic of urban and rural areas: absence of pupil transportation, sidewalks, lesser density of student population and generally longer distances. It is in no part related to racial difference.

The exercise of legislative discretion in this regard is as valid as is that which sees the Grand Rapids School District receive annually over $1,000,000 in compensatory aid money under Section 3 of the State Aid Act, funds in which the suburban school districts do not participate at all.[27]

Apart from the fact that the Supreme Court has held that financial disparities between school districts do not necessarily constitute unconstitutional "educational inequalities,"[28] the judge's finding that "suburban districts were able to make far larger per pupil expenditures despite less tax effort" appears to be simply wrong. Compared with the other eighty-three school districts in the three-county surrounding area, Detroit was apparently *above* average in per pupil expenditure and *below* average in "tax effort."[29]

Finally, the judge found "the State" culpable because it had "acted through Act 48 to impede, delay and minimize racial integration in Detroit schools." The effect of the act, he said, was to abrogate the April 7 "desegregation plan," and the act's "criterion [sic] of free choice (open enrollment) and neighborhood schools (nearest school priority acceptance) . . . had as their purpose and effect the maintenance of segregation." Act 48, it seems, was, if possible, even more potently unconstitutional than the rescission in *Keyes*: Not only did it convert permissible racial imbalance to unconstitutional "*de jure*" segregation," but it provided a basis for requiring more integration than would have obtained if it had never been passed and the April 7 plan had been implemented.

Even if it is possible to believe that the judge found or could have found racial discrimination in the cited acts of the Detroit board and "the State," it is not possible to believe that those acts caused or significantly contributed to the racial composition of Detroit's schools in 1970. Detroit's schools in 1970 were necessarily in a "segregated condition"— that is, majority-black—because a majority of the school population of Detroit was black, and that, in turn, was because of the movement of blacks into, and of whites out of, Detroit during and since the Second World War. It was not contended that the actions charged to the Detroit board or "the State" were responsible for or accelerated that movement. On the contrary, to the extent, if any, that those acts had the effect of preserving some majority-white schools, as alleged by the plaintiffs, they probably served to delay the inevitable metamorphosis of the school system into one that was overwhelmingly black.[30] Indeed, the judge did not find that those acts caused the "segregated condition" of the Detroit schools. He stated:

While it would be unfair to charge the present defendants with what other governmental officers or agencies have done, it can be said that the actions or the failure to act by the responsible school authorities, both city and state, were linked to that of these other governmental units. . . . Perhaps the most that can be said is that all of them, including the school authorities, are, in part, responsible for the segregated condition which exists.[31]

To find that the defendants were, "in part, responsible for the segregated condition which exists"—"perhaps the most that can be said"—because of their "actions or failure to act" is to find only that they failed to prevent that condition: The defendants could not have prevented majority-black schools in Detroit except by requiring the interdistrict busing that the judge later required. In effect, interdistrict busing was found to be constitutionally required because the defendants unconstitutionally failed to require it.

The "Remedy"

Having thus found that the Detroit school system was *"de jure* segregated," the judge turned to the question of the necessary "remedy." Since—and further demonstrating that—he in fact saw no need for such a finding, however, he allowed it to play no part in determining the appropriate "remedy." The judge, in effect, dropped all pretense of remedying the *"de jure* segregation" he had supposedly found and directly undertook to correct "the condition which we believe needs correction." That "condition," the existence of majority-black schools, obviously could not be "corrected" by limiting remedial measures to the confines of a majority-black school system. As he asked, rhetorically, several times during the trial, "How do you desegregate a black city, or a black school system?"[32]

At a post-trial conference on the question of relief, the judge announced that he "entertain[ed] serious reservations about a plan of integration, which encompasses no more than the public schools of the City of Detroit. It appears to us that perhaps only a plan which embraces all or some of the greater Detroit metropolitan area can hope to succeed in giving our children the kind of education they are entitled to constitutionally." He thereupon ordered the Detroit board to submit a "desegregation plan" limited to Detroit, but at the same time ordered the state defendants to submit a "metropolitan plan" encompassing all or some of the eighty-five independent school districts (none of which had been made parties to the litigation) in the three-county area surrounding Detroit.[33] This area, including Detroit, covered 1,952 square miles and was approximately—as the Supreme Court was to note—"the size of the State of Delaware (2,057 square miles), more than half again the size of the State of Rhode Island (1,214 square miles) and almost 30 times the size of the District of Columbia (67 square miles)." The area contained over four million people, almost half the population of Michigan, and had a total public school enrollment of about one million children.[34]

In early February 1972, forty-three of the school districts in the three-county area (combined to form only four parties) moved for permission to intervene. This motion was not granted by the judge until March 15, and then only with extremely restricted conditions. The intervening districts were not "permitted to assert any claim or defense" or "reopen any question or issue" that the judge had previously decided; to "initiate discovery proceedings, except by permission of the court"; to "file counterclaims or cross-complaints"; or to seek the joinder or dismissal of parties if it would cause delay. They were permitted to intervene "for two principal purposes: (a) To advise the court, by brief, of the legal propriety or impropriety of considering a metropolitan plan; (b) to review any plan or plans for the desegregation of the so-called larger Detroit Metropolitan area, and submitting objections, modifications or alternatives to it or them, and in accordance with the requirements of the United States Constitution and the prior orders of this court."[35] The intervening districts were also bound to adhere to the hearing schedule that the judge had previously established. This schedule required that briefs on the question of an interdistrict plan be submitted by March 22, allowing the intervenors only seven days to prepare them. Two days thereafter, March 24, the judge ruled that a metropolitan plan could properly be considered should a Detroit-only plan be found "inadequate." On March 28, before the intervenors had an opportunity to present oral arguments or evidence, he ruled that a metropolitan plan would be required.[36]

In finding a metropolitan plan necessary, the judge rejected two Detroit-only plans submitted by the Detroit board, on the ground that they did "not promise to effect significant desegregation."[37] He found that such a plan submitted by the plaintiffs, requiring the "transportation of 82,000 pupils" and the "acquisition of some 900 vehicles," would "accomplish more desegregation" than either of the board's plans, but it, too, was rejected. "The racial composition of the student body [of Detroit] is such" the judge said, "that the plan's implementation would clearly make the entire Detroit public school system racially identifiable as Black." Furthermore, the plaintiffs' plan would "not lend itself as a building block for a metropolitan plan," would "leave many of [Detroit's] schools 75 to 90 per cent Black," and "would change a school system which is now Black and White to one that would be perceived as Black, thereby increasing the flight of Whites from the city and the system, thereby increasing the Black student population." The judge, therefore, found the conclusion "inescapable that relief of segregation in the public schools of the City of Detroit cannot be accomplished within the corporate geographical limits of the city." "Desegregation," it appeared, now required not only racially balanced schools—that each school in a school system have the same proportion of blacks and whites as in the whole system—but majority-white schools, and even in a majority-black school district, though this meant capturing whites in other districts.

The parties then submitted a number of plans encompassing all or some of the eighty-five districts, in addition to Detroit, in the three-county area. In June 1972, after extensive hearings, the judge rejected all of these plans and ordered the parties to set up a panel, with the members he named, to formulate a new plan for "maximum actual desegregation" in accordance with the findings and conclusions he set forth in a lengthy opinion. "It should be noted," he stated at the outset, that "the court has taken no proofs with respect to the establishment of the boundaries of the 86 public school districts in the counties of Wayne, Oakland and Macomb, nor on the issue of whether, with the exclusion of the city of Detroit school district, such school districts have committed acts of de jure segregation." He nonetheless determined, adopting the plaintiffs' proposal, that fifty-three independent school districts should be added to Detroit to form the relevant "desegregation area." This area was to be divided into fifteen smaller areas, each containing a portion of Detroit, and in each of these pupils were to be reassigned "so as to achieve the greatest degree of actual desegregation to the end that, upon implementation, no school, grade or classroom be substantially disproportionate to the overall pupil racial composition."[38]

The fifty-four-district "desegregation area" had a school population of about 780,000 children, 25.3 percent of whom were black. A plan submitted by the state board of education, encompassing thirty-six districts with about 550,000 pupils, 36 percent of whom were black, was rejected on the ground that it "would result in some schools being substantially disproportionate in their racial composition to the tri-county area."[39] Why the racial composition of this tricounty area provided the standard for the racial balance necessary to undo the "*de jure* segregation" supposedly found in Detroit alone was not explained. The irrelevance to the district judge of the "remedy-desegregation" rationale for requiring racial mixing was perhaps most clearly demonstrated by the fact that two of the school districts he included in his "desegregation area" had a higher proportion of black pupils in their schools than did Detroit. Four additional districts that were included had a higher proportion of blacks than there would have been in the "desegregation area" if they had not been included.[40] The inclusion of these districts could not, therefore, contribute to removing the "racial identifiability" of Detroit's predominantly black schools, but made the proportion of blacks in the area greater than it would otherwise have been. Their inclusion can only be explained on the ground that the judge undertook to eliminate predominantly black schools wherever he found them, regardless of whether or not they had been found to be "*de jure* segregated."

The "practicalities of budgeting and finance that boggled

the mind," referred to by the Fourth Circuit in *Richmond*, where the merger of only three independent school districts was involved, did not, according to the district judge in Detroit, merit even initial consideration. All questions of "governance, finance, and administrative arrangements" involved in the integration of fifty-four independent school districts he simply deferred for decisions at a "subsequent hearing." He thought it "sufficient to note" at this stage that "overlaying some broad educational authority over the area" might later prove necessary. He also noted that there had been "no showing that the existing school district boundaries are rationally related to any legitimate purpose" and found that "the particular welter of existing boundaries for 86 school districts" in the three-county area was "not necessary to the promotion of any compelling state interest." He was "of the view that the shifts in faculty, staff, resources and equipment and the exchanges of pupils necessary to accomplish maximum actual desegregation may be made, at least on an interim basis, by contractual agreements or otherwise among and between the existing school districts."[41]

The judge did, however, consider the problems of pupil reassignment and transportation in the fifty-four-district area and found that no undue burden would be involved. There were "various methods of pupil assignment to accomplish desegregation" that could be used, including "pairing, grouping, and clustering of schools; various strip, skip, island, and non-contiguous zoning; various lotteries based on combinations of present school assignment, geographic location, name or birthday." The "judicious use of these techniques," combined with "reasonable staggering of school hours and maximizing use of existing transportation facilities," could "lead to maximum actual desegregation with a minimum of additional transportation." The transportation would be a "two-way process with both black and white pupils sharing the responsibility for transportation requirements at all grade levels." The judge believed that the transportation requirements were so obviously reasonable, if not indeed beneficial, that objection to them could be regarded as evidence of racism. "Within appropriate time limits" busing "is a considerably safer, more reliable, healthful and efficient means of getting children to school than either car pools or walking, and this is especially true for younger children." Car pools are "many, many times more dangerous than riding on the school bus." "In Michigan and the tri-county area, pupils often spend upwards of one hour, and up to one and one half hours, one-way on the bus ride to school each day. . . . Such transportation of school children is a long-standing, sound practice in elementary and secondary education in this state and throughout the country." "For school authorities or private citizens to now object to such transportation practices" would, therefore, raise "the inference not of hostility to pupil transportation but rather racially motivated hostility to the desegregated school at the end of the ride."[42]

The judge found "general agreement among the experts" that, "but for 'political' considerations," kindergarten children should also be bused. Not being one to be stopped by " 'political' considerations," he concluded: "Transportation of kindergarten children for upwards of 45 minutes, one-way, does not appear unreasonable, harmful, or unsafe in any way. In the absence of some compelling justification, which does not yet appear, kindergarten children should be included in the final plan of desegregation."[43]

The judge estimated that the contemplated plan would require transporting "approximately 40%, or 310,000, of the 780,000 children within the desegregation area." Noting that "in the recent past more than 300,000 pupils in the tri-county area regularly rode to school on some type of bus," he found that "any increase in the number of pupils to be transported" under the contemplated plan "should be minimal."[44] He failed to take into account, in making this comparison, that thirty-three of the eighty-six districts in the three-county area—generally those that were the most distant from Detroit and the least populous, and, therefore, that accounted for much of the existing busing—were not included in the "desegregation area." He also failed to note that some of the busing already going on for reasons other than "desegregation" would presumably have to continue.

The judge also found that "the actual cost of transportation for a two-way plan of desegregation should be no greater than fifty to sixty dollars per pupil transported, comparable to the present cost per pupil through the state." He did not state that, with 310,000 children to be transported, the annual operating cost would be from $15,500,000 to $18,600,000. Regarding the number of buses that would be required, the judge noted: "In the tri-county area in the recent past there were approximately 1,800 buses (and another 100 smaller vans) used for the transportation of pupils. Assuming a rough average of 50 pupils per bus carrying three loads of students per day, this transportation fleet may prove sufficient to carry some 270,000 pupils." He also observed that "various public transit authorities now transport an additional 60,000 pupils on their regular public runs," but was uncertain about "whether these public transit facilities may be fully utilized in a plan of desegregation." He concluded that "additional transportation facilities, at least to the number of 350 buses, will have to be purchased."[45] This number, he failed to state, would, at an estimate of $10,000 per bus,[46] require an initial expenditure of $3,500,000. The judge's overall conclusion about the effect of the transportation requirements on the feasibility of multidistrict "desegregation" was: "For all the reasons stated heretofore—including time, distance, and transportation factors—desegregation within the area described is physically easier and more practicable and feasible, than desegregation efforts limited to the corporate geographic limits of the city of Detroit."[47] This remarkable statement is not otherwise explained, but it is apparently based, at least in part, on the fact that expanding the relevant area beyond Detroit would make more buses at once available. In relying on the total number of buses available in the three-county area, however, the judge again failed to note that many of the school districts in that area were not included in his "desegregation area." According to his apparent reasoning, however, their inclusion might have made a metropolitan plan even more feasible.

In his opinion on constitutional violations, the district judge indicated that he had found nothing objectionable and much to commend in the Detroit board's racial practices with regard to faculty and staff, and he had, of course, taken no evidence about any other district. He nonetheless now found, without stating a basis, that there had been "systematic and substantial under-employment of black administrators and teachers in the tri-county area." He therefore ordered the adoption of "an affirmative program for black employment" and the making of "every effort . . . to hire and promote, and to increase such on-going efforts as there may be to hire and promote additional black faculty and staff." "In the context of the evidence in this case," he said, without citing that evidence, "it is appropriate to require assignment of no less than 10% black faculty and staff at each school, and where there is more than one building administrator, every effort should be made to assign a bi-racial administrative team."[48]

Although no additional evidence had been taken on constitutional violations, the judge apparently now discovered still another, and perhaps the most surprising, basis for finding a violation. This was the past "school construction practices throughout the metropolitan area." The suburban school districts had apparently violated the Constitution by building their own schools rather than sending their children to schools in Detroit. During a twenty-year period, from 1950 to 1969, the judge found, many schools had been built "in school districts which were less than 2% black in their pupil racial composition in the 1970-71 school year." Despite his finding, at an earlier point in his opinion, that "relative to suburban districts Detroit public schools, as a whole, are considerably over-capacity," he found, at this point, that "there were vacant seats throughout the city to which students could have been assigned at lesser cost" than the cost of building suburban schools. Therefore, he concluded, the "construction of new schools designed to service particular areas of racial concentration," which "schools opened as and have continued to be racially identifiable," was "in violation of the Fourteenth Amendment." It was not possible, the judge found, to measure the "precise effect of this massive [suburban] school construction on the racial composition of Detroit area public schools," but "it is clear . . . that the effect has been substantial," for "it is obvious that the white families who left the city schools would not be as likely to leave in the absence of [suburban] schools, not to mention white schools, to attract, or at least serve, their children." The judge ordered that thereafter "needed new school capacity" in the "desegregation area" "should be added on a priority basis in the city of Detroit."[49]

Finally, the judge ruled on several "additional factors" found to be "essential to implementation and operation of an effective plan of desegregation." Apparently considering them too simple and obvious to require discussion, the judge settled by fiat some of the most difficult and controversial issues of educational and social policy. For example, he prohibited the use of "tracking, whether so labeled or by any test, which has racial effects." He required "in-service training for faculty and staff for multi-ethnic studies and human relations." "Curriculum content, and all curriculum materials and student codes" were to "reflect the diversity of ethnic and cultural backgrounds of the children [who would be] now in the schools." Each school was to ensure that "conduct standards respect the diversity of students from differing ethnic backgrounds." "The entire grading, reporting, counseling, and testing program" was to be "reviewed in light of desegregated schools compared to traditional schools." Classes were not to be "substantially disproportionate in their racial composition from the relevant school or grade mix" unless "necessary to promote a compelling educational objective." The schools were to "create bi-racial committees, employ black counselors, and require bi-racial and non-discriminatory extra-curricular activities."[50]

The judge found it unnecessary to consider the availability of funds for the program he contemplated except to say that "funds must either be raised or reallocated" and that "the relatively small amounts of money required . . . can be found." Any "different rule" than this, he said, "would be a cruel mockery of constitutional law" and "would constitute a gigantic hypocrisy." "After all"—according to his view of our federal system—"schooling is . . . the most important task of government left to the states by the Constitution."[51]

The district judge's decision to require busing across fifty-four school districts and an area of several million people in order to create predominantly white schools, made with little warrant or justification other than the strength of one man's will, was to be essentially approved by six judges of a court of appeals and four justices of the Supreme Court. But for one vote in the Supreme Court, the decision would be what "the Constitution requires," and Detroit, the state of Michigan, and the nation would now be attempting to live somehow with the consequences. The American experiment in government by the people according to law has surely never before reached so precarious a state.

The Court of Appeals

The defendants appealed to the Court of Appeals for the Sixth Circuit. The Detroit board, however, in effect shifted to the plaintiffs' side of the case on the issue of the "remedy" and supported the requirement of a metropolitan plan if the district judge's finding of "*de jure* segregation" in Detroit should be upheld. The Detroit board, as reconstituted after the recall election, was apparently more willing to have blacks bused out of Detroit and whites bused in than to bus for racial balance within Detroit. Judge Paul Weick, dissenting in the court of appeals, noted:

It is obvious that the Detroit Board was motivated by its concern that a 63.8%-black and a 37.2%-white quota was too heavily weighted with black pupils, and that it owed a constitutional duty to dilute that quota and to distribute the black-pupil population of Detroit into the other three counties and fifty-two additional school districts, in order to effectuate a quota of about 25%-black and 75%-white children in each school.[52]

The court of appeals, first sitting as a three-judge panel and then *en banc*, approved, by a vote of 6 to 3, virtually all that the district judge had said and done on the issues of "*de jure* segregation" in Detroit and the need for a metropolitan plan. It reversed only the district judge's ruling on the particulars of the metropolitan plan because, it held, all affected school districts were necessary parties to the litigation and should have been given an opportunity to be heard. The opportunity to be afforded the suburban districts, however, would have amounted to little more than an opportunity to be heard after the case had been decided against them, for the district judge was not "required to receive any additional evidence" relating to his basic decisions that the court had affirmed.[53] The court issued a lengthy opinion but, because it simply adopted the approach and reasoning of the district judge, it contains almost no serious discussion or useful analysis of the facts and issues involved. Indeed, it consists in large part of extensive quotations that almost completely reproduce the district judge's opinions and of strings of citations of other cases, as if the issues were to be drowned in a plethora of words.

The court's affirmance of the district judge's finding of *"de jure* segregation" added nothing to its validity. According to the court's reasoning, as according to the district judge's, such a finding was the inevitable result of a showing that racially imbalanced or predominantly black schools existed and it was, therefore, meaningless except as a simple condemnation of such schools. It was enough, the court said, quoting the district judge, that "the natural and actual effect" of the Detroit board's "acts and failures to act" was "the creation and perpetuation of school segregation." By this test, *"de jure* segregation" could be and was found in, for example, the construction of neighborhood schools in racially imbalanced neighborhoods. The court devoted two pages of its opinion to demonstrating the undisputed and unsurprising fact that from 1967 to 1970 many schools in Detroit opened with a student body that was over 90 percent black, and some with one that was predominantly white. It then quoted and adopted the conclusion of the plaintiffs' "desegregation expert" who had testified: "My opinion is that construction practices were followed in such a way as to increase segregation. I say this because of the large number of schools that were opened that were either all black or all white or with a disproportionate number of one race or the other upon opening."[54]

Turning to "the constitutional violations found to have been committed by the State of Michigan," the court upheld the district judge on five grounds.[55] First, the Detroit board, the court said, was an "instrumentality" of the state board of education and of the legislature, and its "segregative actions and inactions" were, therefore, "the actions of an agency of the State of Michigan." Since, however, the Detroit board is itself an "agency of the State" for the purposes of the Fourteenth Amendment, the attribution of its "actions and inactions" to another state agency adds nothing to a finding of unconstitutionality.

Second was the enactment of Act 48 by "the State Legislature," which the court had earlier held to be unconstitutional. "While this statute has since been invalidated by the judgment of this court," the court now said, "its contribution to preventing desegregation and to continuing and increasing segregation of the Detroit school system cannot be overlooked." How the statute, invalidated before it was implemented, could possibly have had these effects the court did not find necessary to explain.

Third:

The clearest example of direct State participation in encouraging the segregated condition of Detroit public schools . . . is that of school construction in Detroit and the surrounding suburban areas. Until 1962 the State Board of Education had direct statutory control over site planning for new school construction. During that time, as was pointed out above, the State approved school construction which fostered segregation throughout the Detroit Metropolitan area. . . . Since 1962 the State Board has continued to be involved in approval of school construction plans.

The court's earlier discussion of school construction, however, was of necessity confined to construction in Detroit, since no evidence had been taken regarding any other area. This did not prevent the court from now citing that discussion as supporting conclusions about construction in "the surrounding suburban areas" and "segregation throughout the Detroit Metropolitan area." Furthermore, according to the court's own statement, "the State Board of Education had direct statutory control over site planning for new school construction" only "until 1962." All or nearly all of the construction earlier discussed by the court or by the district judge took place after 1962—indeed, after 1967 and mostly in 1969 and 1970. Moreover, the accuracy of the court's statement about state control over school sites is extremely questionable, to say the least, even in relation to the period before 1962. The only basis cited by the court (earlier in its opinion) for its statement about state responsibility for the building of schools was a Michigan statute dealing with fire, health, and safety requirements in school construction and authorizing the state superintendent of public instruction (not the state board of education) to review construction plans and specifications. Until 1962, when the statute was amended, the superintendent was authorized to consider, presumably in relation to health and safety, "the adequacy and location of the site." The statute never spoke of "site planning"; the authority to "locate, acquire, purchase or lease" school sites was, by another statute, given to the local school districts.[56] The construction-requirements statute, both before and after its amendment, expressly applied to private as well as public school construction. According to the court's reasoning, state officials had "direct statutory control over site planning" for private schools, too, before 1962, and a constitutional violation by "the State" might have been found because of the location of such schools.

The court's statement that the state board of education "continued to be involved in approval of school construction plans" after 1962 is true, to the extent of the authority granted by the amended statute (except that the court should have referred to the state superintendent instead of the board). No constitutional violation was found, however, in building construction as such, but only in siting; after 1962 the statutes relied on did not even mention siting. The relevance of the court's statement to what it was attempting to show is therefore not apparent. There was no evidence that the defendant state superintendent or, for that matter, any prior holder of the office ever engaged in racial discrimination in the exercise of such statutory authority as he had before or after 1962. State education officials, it should be noted, did not collect data on the racial make-up of school districts until 1966. Hence it seems that the court's "clearest example" of racial discrimination and constitutional violation by "the State" was in fact no example of such at all.

Fourth, the court found a constitutional violation by "the State" in its allocation of funds: "During the critical years covered by this record the School District of Detroit was denied any allo-

cation of State funds for pupil transportation, although such funds
were made generally available for students who lived over a mile and
a half from their assigned schools in rural Michigan."[57] The
court did not explain, any more than had the district judge,
how racial discrimination was shown by the fact that special
transportation funds were provided for rural but not for urban
school districts, especially since other funds were provided only
for urban districts.

Finally, the court held that a constitutional violation by "the
State" could be found on a basis not mentioned in the opinions
of the district judge. It appeared that in the late 1950s—"back
in '57, '58,"—the Detroit board voluntarily agreed to accept, on
a lease arrangement (with costs paid by the sending district),
high school students from an adjacent predominantly black school
district (Carver) that "did not have a place for adequate high
school facilities." These students were bused past a Detroit high
school to a more distant one that was, apparently, predominantly
black. The Detroit school superintendent had testified, but the
court did not note, that the reason was "simply that [the nearer
school] was much more crowded."[58] The court saw in this
episode a constitutional violation by both the Detroit school
board and the state board of education. In the part of its opinion
discussing the Detroit board, the court stated:

> The record indicates that in at least one instance Detroit served
> a suburban school district by contracting with it to educate its black
> high school students in a Detroit high school which was overwhelmingly
> black by transporting them away from nearby suburban white high
> schools and past Detroit high schools which were predominantly white.
> The District Judge found on this score that for years black children in
> the Carver School District were assigned to black schools in the inner
> city because no white suburban district (or white school in the city)
> would take the children.

The court did not in this instance cite the portion of the record to
which it referred, and the alleged finding by the district judge does
not appear in any of his opinions, which make no mention of the
episode. As the Supreme Court was later to note, "There is nothing
in the record supporting the Court of Appeals' supposition that suburban white schools refused to accept the Carver students." The court

of appeals, it seems, simply wished the much needed facts and finding into being. In the part of its opinion discussing violations by "the State," the court stated that the transportation of Carver students "could not have taken place without the approval, tacit or express, of the State Board of Education."[59] Again, there is nothing in the record to support this statement. There was no evidence that any member, past or present, of the state board (located in Lansing) was aware of the lease arrangement in the 1950s, much less of the particular school assignments and the races of the children involved; race statistics, as has been indicated, were not kept by the state until 1966. The court did not attempt to explain how this episode in the 1950s, even if the district judge had found it to constitute racial discrimination, contributed to the racial make-up of the Detroit school system in 1970.

The court then affirmed the district judge's ruling that a metropolitan plan was constitutionally required. It quoted with approval the judge's conclusion that "relief of segregation in the public schools of the City of Detroit cannot be accomplished within the corporate geographical limits of the city" because "the racial composition of the student body is such" that a Detroit-only plan would "clearly make the entire Detroit public school system racially identifiable as Black." "Any less comprehensive a solution than a metropolitan area plan would," the court said, "result in an all black school system immediately surrounded by practically all white suburban school systems." The court could not "see how such segregation can be any less harmful to the minority students than if the same results were accomplished within one school district."[60] In effect, the court simply held area-wide racial imbalance to be unconstitutional per se. Judge Wallace Kent, dissenting, noted:

> Through the majority's opinion runs the thread which holds it together. That thread is the unwillingness apparent in the minds of the majority to sanction a black school district within a city which it concludes will be surrounded by white suburbs. While the majority does not now state that such a demographic pattern is inherently unconstitutional, nevertheless, I am persuaded that those who subscribe to the majority opinion are convinced, as stated in the slip opinion of the original panel, "big city school systems for blacks surrounded by suburban school systems for whites cannot represent equal protection of the law." While that

statement has been removed from the opinion of the majority, yet the premise upon which the statement was obviously based must necessarily form the foundation for the conclusions reached in the majority opinion.[61]

The court's basis for requiring area-wide racial balance was clearly erroneous according to the reasoning of the Supreme Court in *Green* and *Swann* (also *Keyes,* which, however, had not been decided when the court's opinion was written). Racial balance or the elimination of majority-black schools was constitutionally required, according to those decisions, not because racial imbalance or separation was "harmful to the minority students," but because of the necessity of correcting racial separation resulting from "*de jure* segregation" in the past. According to the court's rationale for requiring majority-white schools—that racial separation, even in different school districts, is "harmful to minority students"—there would have been no need to find "*de jure* segregation" even in Detroit. The court, of course, had not in fact seen such a need.

The Supreme Court
Chief Justice Burger's Majority Opinion

The defendant state officials and the school district intervenors sought and obtained a writ of certiorari from the Supreme Court on the rulings affecting them. The Detroit board, however, apparently content with the overall effect of the lower-court decisions, did not seek a review. The result was that the Court again, as in *Keyes,* did not have the occasion to consider directly the threshold question of whether "*de jure* segregation," requiring the *Swann* "remedies," had properly been found by the lower courts in a school system that had never practiced explicit racial assignment and on a basis that made the finding simply a condemnation of racial imbalance as such. The issue was now referred to by the Court only in a footnote. It was not, the Court said, "presented for review in petitioners' briefs and petitions for writs of certiorari"; the issue, therefore, was not before the Court for full consideration and actual decision. But, the Court continued, "two of the petitioners argue in brief that [the lower court] findings constitute error." The Court then stated that in this situation its Rules of Court, "at a minimum, limit our review of the Detroit violation findings to 'plain error' "— that is, the Court could reverse the lower courts' findings of "*de jure* segregation" in Detroit only, if at all, they were erroneous on their face, beyond doubt and the possibility of reasonable argument. "And," the Court concluded, applying this strict standard, "under our decision last Term in *Keyes* . . . , the findings appear to be correct."[62] In *Keyes,* however, the lower court's findings of "*de jure* segregation" in Denver were not explicitly passed on at all, the Court having denied the Denver school board's petition for review. The Court's reliance on *Keyes* here seems, therefore, something of a bootstrap operation in which an issue of the greatest magnitude—the constitutionality of school racial imbalance or of majority-black schools—was apparently resolved, at least to some extent, without being anywhere expressly considered.

In any event, according to the Court's decision on the metropolitan plan in this very case, the lower courts' findings of "*de jure* segregation" in Detroit should not have survived even a "plain error" test. The lower courts plainly had not distinguished between finding acts of racial discrimination to separate the races in the schools and finding a failure to discriminate racially in order to mix them more completely; the lower courts, therefore, had in effect held that it was racial imbalance itself that was unconstitutional. But mere racial imbalance or separation, the Supreme Court was to hold, in reversing the lower courts' requirement of a metropolitan plan, was an "erroneous standard" for finding unconstitutionality. The findings of "*de jure* segregation" in Detroit should also have been reversed as "plain error" on the additional ground that the acts relied on by the lower courts for those findings— even if those acts could have been found racially discriminatory—plainly were not a "substantial cause" of the racial composition of the Detroit school system at the time of the suit. Only racially discriminatory acts that were a "substantial cause" of existing racial imbalance, the Court held in its decision on the metropolitan plan, could be the basis of a finding of unconstitutionality.[63]

The question of "*de jure* segregation" in Detroit having been disposed of or avoided in a footnote, the only issue for decision was the propriety of the lower courts' requirement of a metropolitan plan. The Fourth Circuit's decision in *Richmond* showed that the reversal of the lower courts on this issue was a matter of simple logic. No more was necessary than for the Court now to recall and, for the first time, take seriously the "desegregation" rationale of *Green* and *Swann*, according to which school racial balance or the elimination of majority-black schools was not required as such but only to "remedy" "*de jure* segregation" and "dismantle the dual system." There obviously could be no constitutional requirement of desegregation for schools not found to have been unconstitutionally segregated. As Chief Justice Burger said, quoting his opinion in *Swann*, the "task is to correct . . . 'the condition that offends the Constitution,'" and "'the nature of the violation determines the scope of the remedy.'"[64] "*De jure* segregation" offends the Constitution and requires "desegregation," but it had been found only in Detroit and there was, therefore, no basis for "desegregation" except in Detroit.[65]

It was easy to show that the lower courts had misunderstood the "desegregation" requirement in ordering a metropolitan plan. The district judge had said, Chief Justice Burger pointed out, that a Detroit-only plan would not "accomplish desegregation" because, given "the racial composition of the student body" of Detroit, such a plan "would clearly make the entire Detroit public school system racially identifiable," "leav[ing] many of its schools 75 to 90 percent Black." Similarly, the court of appeals had said that "any Detroit only segregation plan will lead directly to a single segregated Detroit school district overwhelmingly black in all of its schools, surrounded by a ring of suburbs and suburban school districts overwhelmingly white in composition."

Viewing the record as a whole, it seems clear that the District Court and the Court of Appeals shifted the primary focus from a Detroit remedy to the metropolitan area only because of their conclusion that total desegregation of Detroit would not produce the racial balance which they perceived as desirable. Both courts proceeded on an assumption that the Detroit schools could not be truly desegregated—in their view of what constituted desegregation—unless the racial composition of the student body of each school substantially reflected the racial composition of the population of the metropolitan area as a whole.[66]

At this point, however, Chief Justice Burger put his argument in an unnecessarily complex and vulnerable form. The district judge, he said, had required a plan pursuant to which *"no school, grade or classroom* [would be] substantially disproportionate to the overall pupil racial composition" of the metropolitan area. But, the chief justice continued, quoting his opinion in *Swann*, there was no "substantive constitutional right" to "any particular degree of racial balance or mixing." The "clear import of this language," he concluded, was that "desegregation, in the sense of dismantling a dual school system, does not require any particular racial balance in each 'school, grade or classroom.' "[67]

There could be no doubt that the lower courts had in fact condemned racial imbalance or majority-black schools as such, but Chief Justice Burger's apparent desire to use his language in *Swann*—that there was no requirement of "any particular degree of racial balance"—served only to weaken his showing that the lower courts had erred. For, as Justice Marshall pointed out in his dissent, "the use of racial ratios in this case in no way differed from that in *Swann*." If what the district judge in *Swann* required was not "any particular degree of racial balance," as the chief justice had said in *Swann*, then neither was what the district judge required here. Chief Justice Burger should simply have said, in accordance with the "desegregation" rationale for the requirement of racial balance that he otherwise strictly adhered to in his opinion, that *no* degree at all of racial balance was constitutionally required in an area that was not *"de jure* segregated." No "particular degree" of racial balance was required, the passage quoted from *Swann* purported to show, even in an area that *was "de jure* segregated." The chief justice did say this more clearly and directly in a footnote further discussing *Swann. Swann,* he said, held that the "continued existence of some schools that are all or predominantly of one race" in a formerly dual system obligates school authorities to show that "school assignments are genuinely nondiscriminatory." This, he pointed out, "is a very different matter from equating racial imbalance with a constitutional violation calling for a remedy." To the same effect was his reply, in a later footnote, to the "suggestion in the dissent of Mr. Justice Marshall that schools which have a majority of Negro students are not 'desegregated.' " On the contrary, Chief Justice Burger cogently responded, the Court had in prior cases approved "desegregation plans" providing for school systems in which the percentage of black students would be 57 *(Green)*, 66 *(Emporia)*, and 77 *(Scotland Neck)*. It is true that the districts with which those cases were concerned did not have white students in surrounding districts who might have been captured as the result of an order creating a larger school district, but surely the constitutionality of a school system cannot depend on whether or not whites are available in nearby districts: "Constitutional principles applicable in school desegregation cases cannot vary in accordance with the size or population dispersal of the particular city, county, or school district as compared with neighboring areas."[68]

The Court emphatically rejected the district judge's "conclusion that school district lines are no more than arbitrary lines on a map drawn 'for political convenience.'" This "notion," it said, "is contrary to the history of public education in our country. No single tradition in public education is more deeply rooted than local control over the operation of schools; local autonomy has long been thought essential both to the maintenance of community concern and support for public schools and to quality of the educational process." "The Michigan educational structure," as was evident in many Michigan statutes cited by the Court, "provides for a large measure of local control." The "extent to which the interdistrict remedy approved by the two courts could disrupt and alter the structure of public education in Michigan" was obvious:

The metropolitan remedy would require, in effect, consolidation of 54 independent school districts historically administered as separate units into a vast new super school district. . . . Entirely apart from the logistical and other serious problems attending large-scale transportation of students, the consolidation would give rise to an array of other problems in financing and operating this new school system. Some of the more obvious questions would be: What would be the status and authority of the present popularly elected school boards? Would the children of Detroit be within the jurisdiction and operating control of a school board elected by the parents and residents of other districts? What board or boards would levy taxes for school operations in these 54 districts constituting the consolidated metropolitan area? What provisions would be made for financing? Would the validity of long-term bonds be jeopardized unless approved by all of the component districts as well as the State? What body would determine that portion of the curricula now left to the discretion of local school boards? Who would establish attendance zones, purchase school equipment, locate and construct new schools, and indeed attend to all the myriad day-to-day decisions that are necessary to school operations affecting potentially more than three quarters of a million pupils?

Furthermore, "the scope of the interdistrict remedy" would require that the district court "become first, a *de facto* 'legislative authority' to resolve these complex questions, and then the 'school superintendent' for the entire area. This is a task which few, if any, judges are qualified to perform and one which would deprive the people of control of schools through their elected representatives."[69]

Though each of the matters mentioned by the Court is undoubtedly of great importance, they were all, according to the "desegregation" rationale for the requirement of racial balance, irrelevant to the present case. Since "*de jure* segregation" had been found only in Detroit, a metropolitan plan would not have been constitutionally required even if it had presented no administrative problems. The Court did not doubt that, despite their importance, "school district lines and the present laws with respect to local control are not sacrosanct" and that "boundary lines may be bridged where there has been a constitutional violation calling for interdistrict relief." But no such violation had been found in this case. "The controlling principle consistently expounded in our holdings is," the Court said, "that the scope of the remedy is determined by the nature and extent of the constitutional violation." Therefore, a cross-district (metropolitan) remedy cannot be required unless "there has been a constitutional violation within one district that produces a significant segregative effect in another district. Specifically, it must be shown that racially discriminatory acts of the state or local school districts, or of a single school district have been a substantial cause of interdistrict segregation." "Without an interdistrict violation and interdistrict effect, there is no constitutional wrong calling for an interdistrict remedy." The record in the case, "voluminous as it is, contains evidence of *de jure* segregated conditions only in the Detroit schools"; there was "no showing of significant violation" by any other district and "no evidence of any interdistrict violation or effect." The metropolitan plan was, therefore, "a wholly impermissible remedy based on a standard not hinted at in *Brown I* and *II* or any holding of this Court."[70]

The Court's rejection of the metropolitan plan applied the theory of *Green*, *Swann*, and *Keyes* that school racial mixing is not constitutionally required for its own sake but is required only to the extent necessary to "desegregate" a segregated system, to "remedy" the segregation held unconstitutional in *Brown*. The Court concluded its discussion of the applicable law with the most specific statement of this requirement that it had ever made: "But the remedy is necessarily designed, as all remedies are, to restore the victims of discriminatory conduct to the position they would have occupied in the absence of such conduct."[71] If taken seriously, this statement would obviate the need for most if not all further "desegregation" in the nation and would certainly have obviated the need in Detroit. It would not have been possible to show and, regardless of who had the burden of proof, hardly possible to believe that the creation in Detroit of schools that were 70 percent black and 30 percent white would restore "victims of discriminatory conduct" by school authorities "to the position they would have occupied in the absence of such conduct."

The Court concluded its opinion by showing that the constitutional violations found to have been committed by state-level agencies did not, contrary to the argument of the dissenters, provide a basis for an interdistrict remedy. Even assuming, for the purpose of argument, it said, that such violations were properly found, there was no showing, except for the Carver School District, that they had any racial effect outside Detroit. The Court demonstrated this by reviewing each of the five grounds for "State" liability relied on by the court of appeals.[72]

First, even assuming that "the State" could be held "derivatively responsible for the Detroit Board's violations," "it does not follow that an interdistrict remedy is constitutionally justified or required." There was no showing that any "activity . . . had a cross-district effect," that any school district boundaries "were established for the purpose of creating, maintaining, or perpetuating segregation of races," or that any of the districts except Detroit had "ever maintained or operated anything but unitary school systems."

"Where the schools of only one district have been affected," the Court reiterated, "there is no constitutional power in the courts to decree relief balancing the racial composition of that district's schools with those of the surrounding districts."[73]

Second, the sending of high school students, in the late 1950s, from the "Carver School District, a predominantly Negro suburban district" to "a predominantly Negro school in Detroit" "may have had a segregative effect on the school populations of the two districts involved," but this would not justify a remedy involving fifty-two other districts. Third, the state's enactment of Act 48 "had the effect of rescinding Detroit's voluntary desegregation plan" of April 7, but that plan "affected only 12 of 21 Detroit high schools and had no causal connection with the distribution of pupils by race between Detroit and the other school districts within the tricounty area." Fourth, the court of appeals' finding that the state board of education's control of school site selection until 1962 "fostered segregation throughout the Detroit Metropolitan area" was without support in the record: "There was no evidence suggesting that the State's activities with respect to either school construction or site acquisition within Detroit affected the racial composition of the school population outside Detroit or, conversely, that the State's school construction and site acquisition activities within the outlying districts affected the racial composition of the schools within Detroit." Finally, there was no indication in the record or in the lower-court opinions that the state's provision of certain financial aid only to students outside Detroit "might have affected the racial character of any of the State's school districts."[74]

The lower courts' requirement of a metropolitan plan was, therefore, "based upon an erroneous standard" and had to be reversed. The case was remanded to the district court for the "prompt formulation of a decree directed to eliminating the segregation found to exist in Detroit city schools."[75]

Given the momentum of the Court's prior decisions, this outcome was, no doubt, the best that could have been expected by busing opponents. Actually finding and applying a limit on compulsory racial integration was, in view of all the circumstances, a great achievement; not all evils can be undone in a day. It is necessary to reiterate, nonetheless, that the Court's requirement of a Detroit-only plan can no more than the lower courts' requirement of a metropolitan plan be supported as a remedy for "*de jure* segregation." At issue, therefore, is simply the point at which reality shall be permitted to intrude. The Court found this point to be where forcing further racial mixing would require crossing previously existing, racially neutral school district boundaries. Some recognition of reality is better than none, but the overall result of the Court's decision is not otherwise justifiable. A constitutional requirement hardly explicable except on the basis of a belief that blacks should go to predominantly white schools was applied to a system where that was not possible and where the effect will almost certainly be to make the schools even more predominantly black. Busing to achieve racial balance must take place throughout the nation's fifth largest city even though it serves no useful purpose according to any assumptions.

Justice Stewart's Concurrence

Justice Stewart joined in the opinion of the Court, but thought it "appropriate, in view of some of the extravagant language of the dissenting opinions, to state briefly [his] understanding of what it is that the Court decides today." His opinion closely followed that of the Court. He stated somewhat more strongly and clearly than did the Court that the finding of a constitutional violation in Detroit was "accepted by the Court today." The case, he said, therefore did not present "questions of substantive constitutional law," but only a question of remedy. In requiring a metropolitan plan because a Detroit-only plan would leave Detroit's schools predominantly black, the lower "courts were in error for the simple reason that the remedy they thought necessary was not commensurate with the constitutional violation found." Like the Court, Justice Stewart explicitly recognized that an interdistrict remedy may be "proper, or even necessary," if a violation involving more than one district is found.

[But] since the mere fact of different racial compositions in contiguous districts does not itself imply or constitute a violation of the Equal Protection Clause in the absence of a showing that such disparity was imposed, fostered, or encouraged by the State or its political subdivisions, it follows that no interdistrict violation was shown in this case. The formulation of an interdistrict remedy was thus simply not responsive to the factual record before the District Court and was an abuse of that court's equitable powers. [76]

The principal purpose of Justice Stewart's opinion was, apparently, to respond to the assertion in Justice Marshall's dissenting opinion that "the most essential finding [made by the district court]was that Negro children in Detroit had been confined by intentional acts of segregation to a growing core of Negro schools surrounded by a receding ring of white schools." "This conclusion," Justice Stewart countered, "is simply not substantiated by the record presented in this case." There was no showing that the "segregative acts" found in Detroit produced "an increase in the number of Negro students *in the city as a whole*." The "essential fact" was that Detroit had a "predominantly Negro school population," and "that accounts for the 'growing core of Negro schools,' a 'core' that has grown to include virtually the entire city." "The Constitution," he continued, "simply does not allow federal courts to attempt to change that situation unless and until it is shown that the State, or its political subdivisions, have contributed to cause the situation to exist." Since no such showing was made, "it follows that the situation over which my dissenting Brothers express concern cannot serve as the predicate for the remedy adopted by the District Court and approved by the Court of Appeals." [77]

Justice Douglas' Dissent

Justice Douglas filed a brief dissenting opinion. "The Court of Appeals," he said, "has acted responsibly and we should affirm its judgment." "Metropolitan treatment of metropolitan problems is commonplace," and there would be no doubt about Michigan's constitutional authority "if this were a sewage problem or a water problem" and "it sought a metropolitan remedy." True enough, no doubt, but no question of Michigan's constitutional authority was involved in this case, and Michigan sought only the reversal of federal court orders. Justice Douglas then distinguished *Richmond* from this case on the ground that in Virginia "local school boards had 'exclusive jurisdiction' of the problem" while "education in Michigan is a state project." [78] Leaving aside the question of accuracy, the relevance of this statement, too, is unclear, since it is doubtful that a state's allocation of authority over education can or should control its constitutional obligations. One may doubt that Justice Douglas found the Virginia arrangement a stumbling block when the *Richmond* case was before him.

Justice Douglas thought that the Court's decision was a "dramatic retreat," not only from *Brown,* but also from *Plessy.* In 1973 the Court had held, in *San Antonio Independent School District* v. *Rodriguez,* that a state is not constitutionally required to equalize the differing expenditures per pupil that occur in different school districts as the result of local school financing. "Today's decision," the justice said, "given *Rodriguez,* means that there is no violation of the Equal Protection Clause though the schools are segregated by race and though the Black schools are not only 'separate' but 'inferior.' "

Finally, Justice Douglas reiterated the opinion he expressed in *Keyes:* "There is so far as the school cases go no constitutional difference between *de facto* and *de jure* segregation. Each school board performs state action for Fourteenth Amendment purposes when it draws the lines that confine it to a given area, when it builds schools at particular sites, or when it allocates students." That is, it would seem, racial separation or imbalance among schools is unconstitutional as such, since every school board does the things referred to. And racial separation is unconstitutional even if, as in the present case, the schools are in different school districts. On the latter point, the justice was explicit: "Given the State's control over the educational system in Michigan, the fact that the black schools are in one district and the white schools in another is not controlling—either constitutionally or equitably." Whatever its practical difficulties, this constitutional position would at least be comprehensible. It is not, however, a position that Justice Douglas was willing to take openly and unambiguously, for he immediately went on to state that "the issue is not whether there should be racial balance." He also thought it "conceivable that ghettos develop on their own without any hint of state action" but found—without stating his basis and despite the fact that no evidence had been taken on the question—that "Michigan by one device or another has over the years created black school districts and white school districts." The issue, therefore, he stated, was "whether the State's use of various devices that end up with black schools and white schools brought the Equal Protection Clause into effect."[79] The net effect was to reduce the discussion to little more than gibberish: to seem to condemn racial imbalance ("*de facto* segregation") but to deny doing so, and to seem to require a showing of racial discrimination but to find it in the fact that racial imbalance existed.

The Dissenting Opinions of Justices White and Marshall

Justices White and Marshall filed long dissenting opinions; each justice joined in the opinion of the other, and Justices Douglas and Brennan joined in both. The opinions are essentially similar. Their central vitiating defect is that, like Justice Douglas' opinion, they are inexplicable except as a simple condemnation of racially imbalanced or, more specifically, predominantly black schools, yet, much more so than Douglas' opinion, they resolutely purport to accept and apply the "desegregation" rationale of *Green, Swann, Keyes,* and the present Court: that racially balanced or majority-white schools are not constitutionally required as such but only to remedy "*de jure* segregation." They would have required metropolitan "desegregation," but they did not attempt to refute, but simply attempted to evade, the basic premise of the Court's decision: that "desegregation" cannot be required or justified for schools—those outside Detroit—that had not been found to be "*de jure* segregated." The result is that the opinions seem little more than exercises in ambiguity and word play, heavily seasoned with indignant charges of intellectual and other shortcomings on the part of the Court.

Both White's and Marshall's opinions rely heavily on overstatements of the nature and extent of the constitutional violation found in Detroit by the district judge—as if findings of true and substantial segregation in Detroit would somehow justify "desegregation" outside Detroit. Justice White repeatedly asserted that, for example, the district judge found "unquestioned violations of the equal protection rights of Detroit Negroes by the Detroit School Board and the State of Michigan," "deliberate acts of segregation," and "thinly disguised, pervasive acts of segregation." Justice Marshall was even more emphatic, insisting, for example, that "the constitutional violation found here was not some *de facto* racial imbalance, but rather the purposeful, intentional, massive, *de jure* segregation of the Detroit city schools," that the record showed "widespread and pervasive racial segregation," and that the case must be considered "in the context of a community which historically had a school system marked by rigid *de jure* segregation."[80] The racial policies of Detroit and Michigan were, one might conclude from these opinions, hardly distinguishable from those of pre-*Brown* Mississippi. Unlike the district judge, the dissenting justices did not consider that fairness required them to note that the Detroit board had voluntarily adopted "affirmative policies designed to achieve racial balance in instructional staff" and had "in many other instances and in many other respects, undertaken to lessen the impact of the forces of segregation and attempted to advance the cause of integration." "Nowhere," Justice Marshall said, "did the District Court indicate that racial imbalance" between school districts or between Detroit schools was itself unconstitutional, although neither the district judge's opinions nor his orders—for example, his inclusion of predominantly black school districts in the "desegregation area"—can be understood except as indicating just that. It escaped the notice of the dissenting justices, apparently, that the distinction between *"de jure"* and *"de facto"* segregation that they purported to accept and apply had not in fact been applied but obliterated by the lower courts which had found the basis of a constitutional violation in, for example, the fact that many schools had opened predominantly black. The district judge's findings of constitutional violations by the Detroit board may have been "unquestioned," as Justice White said, in that the board did not seek a review, but they were nonetheless obviously very questionable. If regarded, as the dissenting justices purported to regard them, as meaningful findings of official racial discrimination that was a significant cause of the racial situation in Detroit's schools, they were simply incredible.

The dissenters' characterization of the district judge's findings is not only seriously misleading but, at least in part, plainly inaccurate. For example, Justice Marshall, referring to the alleged transportation of black high school students from the Carver school district past a predominantly white Detroit school, stated: "Certainly the District Court's finding that the State Board of

Education had knowledge of this action and had given its tacit or express approval was not clearly erroneous."[81] The fact, however, was that the district judge made no such finding, and could not have made it on the basis of anything in the record. The "finding" was an original—and unauthorized—contribution by the court of appeals.

Justice White's dissenting opinion rests primarily, if not entirely, on persistent misstatement of the basis of the Court's decision. "The core of my disagreement" with the Court's judgment and opinion, he began, "is that deliberate acts of segregation and their consequences will go unremedied, . . . because an effective remedy would cause what the Court considers to be undue administrative inconvenience to the State." This statement is repeated in various forms throughout the opinion. "The Court," he charged, "fashions out of whole cloth an arbitrary rule that remedies for constitutional violations occurring in a single Michigan school district must stop at the district line. . . . Otherwise, it seems, there would be too much disruption of the Michigan scheme for managing its educational system, too much confusion and too much administrative burden." He was "surprised that the Court" would claim to know better than the lower courts "whether an interdistrict remedy for equal protection violations practiced by the State of Michigan would involve undue difficulties for the State in the management of its public schools." He insisted that "the District Court's remedial power does not cease at the school district line." After several more such statements, he ended by again accusing the Court of placing an "arbitrary limitation on the equitable power of federal district courts, based on the invisible borders of local school districts."[82]

The Court, of course, had made clear that it had not rejected a metropolitan plan on the ground that it would cause "undue administrative inconvenience," "too much disruption," or "undue difficulties for the State" or that the "remedial power" of the district court "cease[d] at the school district line." It explicitly recognized that "school district lines . . . are not sacrosanct" and "may be bridged where there has been a constitutional violation calling for interdistrict relief." It explicitly based its decision on the ground that no such violation had been shown in the present case, that the record "contains evidence of *de jure* segregated conditions only in the Detroit schools."

Justice White was "even more mystified how the Court" could, by rejecting a metropolitan plan, "ignore the legal reality that the constitutional violations, even if occurring locally, were committed by governmental entities for which the State is responsible and that it is the State that must respond to the command of the Fourteenth Amendment." Again, White apparently failed to read what the Court had said. The Court twice stated that it was willing to and did assume that "agencies having statewide authority participated in maintaining the dual school system found to exist in Detroit." Specifically answering the dissenters, it stated that "it is not on this point that we part company," for, even assuming "state responsibility," a metropolitan plan could not be justified as a remedy for a violation that had been found only in Detroit. Justice White did not argue that a metropolitan plan did *not* have to be justified as a remedy for the violation found, that the Constitution should be held to require majority-white schools for their own sake. He insisted throughout his opinion that he, too, was concerned only with remedying the violation found; he agreed that the only requirement was to "desegregate," to "correct the constitutional violations herein found," to "eradicate completely the resulting dual system."[83] He did not, however, attempt to explain how a metropolitan plan could be justified on that basis. His dissent, therefore, simply failed to respond—as the Court repeatedly pointed out—to the reasoning on which the Court's decision was actually based.

Justice White did argue that a metropolitan plan would be "a much more effective desegregation plan" than one confined to Detroit, because even "if 'racial balance' were achieved in every school in [Detroit], each school would be approximately 64% Negro. A remedy confined to the district could achieve no more desegregation."[84] But this is not to justify a metropolitan plan as "desegregation"—as a remedy for the constitutional violation found—but simply to require the elimination of predominantly black schools regardless of the extent of that violation. The argument rests on no more than a change in the meaning of

"segregation" while moving from the premise to the conclusion—
that is, while moving from the violation, "*de jure* segregation,"
to the remedy, "desegregation." The "segregation" prohibited
is "*de jure*," includes racial discrimination as an essential element,
but the "segregation" to be undone is simply the existence
of predominantly black schools. The district judge, seeing that this
was not "logically" defensible, would have abandoned the "desegregation" rationale and openly prohibited predominantly black schools
(the "condition which we believe needs correction"). The dissenters
kept the rationale and abandoned logic.

Justice White's reasoning would have reduced the need to find
a constitutional violation as the basis for requiring racial balance
(in fact, in this case, the elimination of predominantly black
schools) to at most a preliminary formality which, once complied
with, would have no bearing on the extent of the racial
balance required except that the requirement would continue
to be labeled, for tactical reasons, as a "remedy" for the violation.
And he made clear, by adopting the reasoning of the lower courts
on the requirement of finding a constitutional violation, that for
him that formality would present no serious difficulty. He agreed,
for example, that "*de jure* segregation" in Detroit was properly found
by the lower courts on the basis of the passage of Act 48,[85] despite
the fact that, apart from all else, that act had never been put into
effect.

Although he purported to accept the remedy ("desegregation")
rationale for compulsory racial mixing, Justice White did balk at
the Court's most explicit formulation of the rationale, for that
formulation deprived it of much of its useful ambiguity. He was
"wholly unpersuaded by the Court's assertion that 'the remedy
is necessarily designed, as all remedies are, to restore the victims
of discriminatory conduct to the position they would have occupied
in the absence of such conduct.' " "In the first place," he stated,
"under this premise the Court's judgment is itself infirm." If "the
Detroit school system [had] not followed an official policy of
segregation throughout the 1950's and 1960's," he explained, "there
would have been no, or at least not as many, recognizable Negro
schools and no, or at least not as many, white schools, but 'just
schools,' and neither Negroes nor whites would have suffered from

the effects of segregated education, with all its shortcomings."
A Detroit-only plan, therefore, would not "restore to the Negro
community, stigmatized as it was by the dual school system, what
it would have enjoyed over all or most of this period" because
such a plan would "leave many of the schools almost totally
black." Apart from the fact that the Detroit board never had "an
official policy of segregation," Justice White simply ignored the
additional fact that the obvious and overwhelming cause of
"Negro schools" in Detroit was the great growth of the black
population and the decline of the white population. "Moreover,"
he continued, "when a State has engaged in acts of official
segregation over a lengthy period of time, as in the case before
us, it is unrealistic to suppose that the children who were victims
of the State's unconstitutional conduct could now be provided
the benefits of which they were wrongfully deprived." It is
unrealistic indeed, but both that fact and White's prior argument
show that a requirement of racial mixing cannot be justified as a
remedy for the violation supposedly found in Detroit *even* if the
requirement is confined to Detroit; they do not show that the
requirement can be justified as a remedy for that violation if
the requirement is applied to a wider area. Justice White
avoided this conclusion with the statement—again turning on the use
of "segregation" in two different senses—that these arguments
provide the "reasons that the Court has consistently followed the
course of requiring the effects of past official segregation to be
eliminated 'root and branch' by imposing, in the present, the duty to
provide a remedy which will achieve 'the greatest possible degree of
actual desegregation, taking into account the practicalities of the
situation,' "[86] The reasoning seems to be that the Court's very
inability to justify compulsory integration in Detroit as a remedy
for the violation found in Detroit warrants the Court's imposing compulsory integration outside Detroit and calling it a remedy for that
violation. Today's students in a fifty-four-district area must be
assigned to schools on a racial basis because other students in
Detroit were, supposedly, so assigned in the past, and that fact
cannot now be changed.

Justice Marshall's separate dissenting opinion added little to
Justice White's except—to use Justice Stewart's words—"ex-

travagant language." The Court's rejection of a metropolitan plan, Justice Marshall said, constituted an "emasculation of our constitutional guarantee of equal protection of the laws," made a "solemn mockery" of *Brown* I, and was, he feared, "more a reflection of a perceived mood that we have gone far enough in enforcing the Constitution's guarantee of equal justice than . . . the product of neutral principles of law."[87]

In most of his opinion Justice Marshall, too, seemed obtusely unable to grasp the basis of the Court's decision, that a metropolitan plan was improper because the violation to be remedied had occurred only in Detroit. He persisted in asserting, for example, that "this Court holds that the District Court was powerless to require the State to remedy its constitutional violation in any meaningful fashion." Similarly, he stated: "Nowhere in the Court's opinion does the majority confront, let alone respond to, the District Court's conclusion that a remedy limited to the city of Detroit would not effectively desegregate the Detroit city schools."[88] The Court, however, had not found that the district judge was "powerless" to remedy the violation found but that a metropolitan plan would go beyond the violation found. The Court had directly responded to the district judge's conclusion that a Detroit-only plan would be ineffective by finding that he had applied an erroneous standard and that Detroit's schools would be "effectively desegregated" by a Detroit-only plan despite the fact that they would remain predominantly black.

Justice Marshall found "totally inaccurate" the Court's view that the district judge, in ordering a metropolitan plan, "was 'equating racial imbalance with a constitutional violation calling for a remedy.'" The Court, Marshall charged, had "conjured up a largely fictional account of what the District Court was attempting to accomplish" and had done "a great disservice to the District Judge" by accusing him of "some unprincipled attempt to impose his own philosophy of racial balance on the entire Detroit metropolitan area." On the contrary, the justice said, "the District Court determined that interdistrict relief was necessary and appropriate only because it found that the condition of segregation within the Detroit school district could not be cured with a Detroit-only remedy."[89] Apart from the fact that the district judge left little doubt that he was imposing his "philosophy of racial balance" and that his decisions—for example, requiring the incorporation of predominantly black school districts in the "desegregation area"—cannot be otherwise explained, Justice Marshall's indignation was again based on no more than his failure to recognize that the Court rejected a metropolitan plan because such a plan could *not* validly be described or justified as "relief," a "cure," or a "remedy" for a constitutional violation not found to exist or have effects outside Detroit. The difficulty, as with all the dissenting opinions, arose from the combination of an unwillingness openly to abandon the "remedy-desegregation" rationale for the racial balance requirement and an unwillingness to accept its limitations, from a desire to require racial balance for its own sake and to avoid having to justify that requirement.

Justice Marshall next undertook to show that "the State itself," as distinguished from the Detroit board of education, "had committed acts of *"de jure* segregation,"" and he adopted each of the grounds relied on for this purpose by the court of appeals. In the course of this effort, it was Justice Marshall, it seems, who "conjured up a largely fictional account" of what the district judge had done. He said:

The record amply supports the District Court's findings that the State of Michigan, through state officers and state agencies, had engaged in purposeful acts which created or aggravated segregation in the Detroit schools. The State Board of Education, for example, prior to 1962, exercised its authority to supervise local school site selection in a manner which contributed to segregation. 484 F. 2d, 215, 238 (CA6 1973). Furthermore, the State's continuing authority, after 1962, to approve school building construction plans had intertwined the State with site selection decisions of the Detroit Board of Education which had the purpose and effect of maintaining segregation.[90]

The district court did not, however, make the findings Justice Marshall here attributed to it.[91] He cited only the court of appeals, and his statement that the state board "exercised its authority to supervise local school site selection in a manner which contributed to segregation" seems to go beyond what can be found even in that court's opinion.[92] Futhermore, the record would not support the quoted paragraph's suggestion of racial discrimination by the state board even if such a finding had been made.[93]

Justice Marshall also asserted that the practice of "*de jure* seg-regation" by state officials had been properly found by the lower courts by reason of the passage of Act 48 and by reason of the "dis-criminatory restrictions placed by the State on the use of transportation within Detroit."[94] There is no basis in the record or in common sense, however, on which either of these legislative actions can be said to be acts of racial discrimination responsible for the racial situation in Detroit, as a finding of "*de jure* segregation" requires. For example, Act 48 had never been put in effect, and transporta-tion aid for rural areas does not establish racial discrimination.

Finally, Justice Marshall stated:

Also significant was the State's involvement during the 1950's in the transportation of Negro high school students from the Carver school district past a closer white high school in the Oak Park district to a more distant Negro high school in the Detroit district. Certainly the Dis-trict Court's finding that the State Board of Education had knowledge of this action and had given its tacit or express approval was not clearly erroneous. Given the comprehensive statutory powers of the State Board of Education over contractual arrangements between school districts in the enrollment of students on a nonresident tuition basis, including certification of the number of pupils involved in the transfer and the amount of tuition charged, over the review of transportation routes and distances, and over the disbursement of transportation funds, the State Board inevitably knew and understood the significance of this discrimina-tory act.[95]

Again, however, the fact is that the district court had not made the finding here attributed to it; this was the "finding" only of the court of appeals. Furthermore, Justice Marshall's conclusion that the "State Board inevitably knew and understood the signif-icance of this discriminatory act" is not supported by anything in the record or by the statutes he cited in footnotes. Those statutes show only that local school districts were required to report to the state board the number of nonresident students in the district and the amount of tuition charged and that the state superintendent of schools (not the state board) was authorized to supervise trans-portation routes and equipment and travel distances (nothing appears regarding "the disbursement of transportation funds").[96] If for no other reason than that racial statistics were not kept by the state until much later, Marshall's conclusion that the state board must have at least knowingly acquiesced in racial discrimination is totally baseless.

Justice Marshall then argued that, in addition to these "acts of purposeful segregation" by state officials, "the State was responsible for the many intentional acts of segregation committed by the Detroit Board." He found that "under Michigan law 'a school district is an agency of the State government'" and that "racial discrimination by the school district, an agency of the State, is therefore racial discrimination by the State itself, forbidden by the Fourteenth Amendment."[97] The relevance of this argument is obscure. There was not the slightest question that a school district is "an agency of the State" for the purposes of the Fourteenth Amendment, regardless of the district's status under state law. Indeed, the relevance of this entire section of Justice Marshall's opinion, including his argument that racial discrimination "by the State itself" could be found, is not apparent, since the Court had expressly assumed all that he set out to prove. The Court's holding, to which his argument did not respond, was that state participation in, or responsibility for, the *"de jure* segregation" found in Detroit would not change the fact that it was found only in Detroit.

Perhaps the purpose of this argument by Justice Marshall was to suggest an analogy between Michigan in this case and Denver in *Keyes* and, thereby, to find support in *Keyes* for requiring a metropolitan plan. He had earlier argued, quoting *Keyes*, that "what we confront here is 'a systematic program of segregation affecting a substantial portion of the students, schools . . . and facilities within the school system'" and that this, "under our decision in *Keyes*, forms 'a predicate for a finding of the existence of a dual school system' . . . and justifies 'all-out desegregation,'"[98] Perhaps Justice Marshall did not explicitly bring his argument to the suggested conclusion because a decision on the basis of *Keyes* would probably not have been of much help. *Keyes* itself, after all, purported to rest on the "desegregation" rationale for requiring racial balance, and the Court had remanded that case for factual hearings on the question of the city-wide racial effects, if any, of the *"de jure* segregation" the district judge had supposedly found in Park Hill. Application of *Keyes* to the present case would, therefore, have resulted, at most, in a remand for a hearing on the question of "*de jure* segregation" outside Detroit. But even according to the Court's present decision, permitting an interdistrict remedy where an interdistrict violation is found, the plaintiffs were not precluded from proceeding on the basis of *Keyes*, although the Court's new-found realism about the "desegregation" rationale—insisting that the racial balance requirement was applicable only to imbalance substantially caused by "*de jure* segregation"—indicated, perhaps, that the plaintiffs would be unlikely to succeed.

Justice Marshall then came to the heart of his opinion, under-taking to explain why a metropolitan plan was required. The need, he said, was to "cure Detroit's condition of segregation," and this meant, according to *Green*, that "Negro students are not only entitled to neutral nondiscriminatory treatment in the future," but—he quoted *Emporia*—to "a school system in which all vestiges of enforced racial segregation have been eliminated."[99] With this statement, however, the Court did not disagree; according to the Detroit-only plan it ordered, black students would not "only" receive "neutral nondiscriminatory treatment" but would, as re-quired by *Green*, receive racially discriminatory treatment—assign-ment to schools on the basis of race—in order that a maximum of integration might be achieved in Detroit where the "enforced racial segregation" to be "cured" had been found.

Justice Marshall's opinion illustrates even better than Justice White's that their central argument turns on using "segregation" in two different senses. Thus, Justice Marshall argued:

> We held in *Swann* that where *de jure* segregation is shown, school authorities must make "every effort to achieve the greatest possible degree of actual desegregation." . . . If these words have any meaning at all, surely it is that school authorities must, to the extent possible, take all practicable steps to ensure that Negro and white children in fact go to school together. This is, in the final analysis, what desegregation of the public schools is all about.[100]

According to *Green* and *Swann*, a requirement of racial mixing is indeed "what desegregation of the public schools is all about," but the requirement remains nonetheless, at least in theory, a requirement of "desegregation" or—to eliminate ambiguity and make Justice Marshall's conclusion consistent with his premise—a requirement of "de-*de jure* segregation." The need to undo *"de jure* segregation," was the only justification ever offered by the Court for the requirement of racial mixing, and Marshall was still not prepared to offer any other.

Similarly, Justice Marshall heatedly objected to the Court's reliance on "the accepted principle that 'the nature of the violation determines the scope of the remedy.' " He found that the Court's approach was not only "hopelessly simplistic, but more important, the Court reads these words in a manner which perverts their obvious meaning."

The nature of a violation determines the scope of the remedy simply because the function of any remedy is to cure the violation to which it is addressed. In school segregation cases, as in other equitable causes, a remedy which effectively cures the violation is what is required. . . . No more is necessary, but we can tolerate no less. To read this principle as barring a district court from imposing the only effective remedy for past segregation and remitting the Court to a patently ineffective alternative is, in my view, to turn a simple common sense rule into a cruel and meaningless paradox. Ironically, by ruling out an interdistrict remedy, the only relief which promises to cure segregation in the Detroit public schools, the majority flouts the very principle on which it purports to rely.[101]

Justice Marshall had indeed created a "meaningless paradox," but only because the "segregation" (racial imbalance or separation or predominantly black schools) he would have "cured" was not the "segregation" (*"de jure"*) that, "under the segregation cases," required a cure.

Justice Marshall attempted to meet the Court on the actual ground of its decision at only one point in his opinion, arguing, very briefly, that a metropolitan plan could be justified as a remedy for the violation found. To do this, he had to assert that a constitutional violation had been found outside Detroit, and he apparently did so assert. "The most essential finding" of the district judge, he stated, "was that Negro children in Detroit had been confined by intentional acts of segregation to a growing core of Negro schools surrounded by a receding ring of white schools." Marshall did not, however, point out where the "finding" appeared in the district judge's opinions. Other statements in Justice Marshall's opinion were equally without support, but this one was important enough to require refutation. It apparently brought forth Justice Stewart's separate concurring opinion in which he pointed out, quite accurately, that Marshall's "conclusion is simply not substantiated by the record presented in this case."[102]

Justice Marshall responded to Justice Stewart by adding a footnote, claiming that Stewart had misunderstood him. Marshall did not mean, he said, that "the state or its political subdivisions have been responsible for the increasing percentage of Negro students in Detroit. . . . Whether state action is responsible for the growth of the core of all-Negro schools in Detroit is, in my view, quite irrelevant." The "growing core" statement was made, it now appeared, only because Marshall thought it had something to do with the need "to formulate an appropriate remedy," and this need, he said, should not be "confused" with the finding of a "substantive constitutional violation."[103] Thus limited, however, Justice Marshall's "growing core" statement added nothing to his argument for a metropolitan "remedy." Marshall simply conceded that he had not discovered a basis for finding official responsibility for the metropolitan area racial imbalance and, therefore, for finding *"de jure* segregation" outside Detroit. This concession completely removed the basis for the arguments Marshall had built on his "growing core" assertion, but he did not let that fact cause him to remove those arguments from his opinion. For example, he retained the argument:

Nor can it be said that the State is free from any responsibility for the disparity between the racial makeup of Detroit and its surrounding suburbs. The State's creation, through *de jure* acts of segregation, of a growing core of all-Negro schools inevitably acted as a magnet to attract Negroes to the areas served by such schools and to deter them from settling either in other areas of the city or in the suburbs. By the same token, the growing core of all-Negro schools inevitably helped drive whites to other areas of the city or to the suburbs.[104]

The argument that official responsibility could be found for the metropolitan racial disparity was, it seems, simply too important for Justice Marshall to abandon despite the concession he was forced to make to Justice Stewart that there was no basis for finding such responsibility. Having denied that he meant to use his "growing core" statement to establish a constitutional violation outside Detroit, Marshall nonetheless continued so to use it.

Similarly, Justice Marshall argued that a metropolitan plan was required because "racially identifiable schools are one of the primary vestiges of state-imposed segregation which an effective desegregation decree must attempt to eliminate." Detroit's schools would remain "racially identifiable" under a Detroit-only plan because the Detroit school system was majority-black. But that system had not been found majority-black, as Justice Marshall had in effect conceded to Justice Stewart, because of "state-imposed segregation." Justice Marshall, therefore, could not consistently with that concession argue that making those schools majority-white by a metropolitan plan could be justified as removal of one of the "vestiges of state-imposed segregation."[105]

Whatever the purpose of Justice Marshall's "growing core" argument, the assumptions he based it on are neither unquestionable nor supported by evidence. If it is a fact that "all-Negro schools inevitably acted as a magnet to attract Negroes" to their areas, the fact would seem to militate against seeking to have such schools eliminated. No firmer basis is apparent for the assumption that the acts charged to "the State" or the Detroit board of education "helped drive whites to other areas of the city or to the suburbs." It is far more likely that if the alleged attempts to preserve majority-white schools in Detroit had any effect, it was to keep whites in the areas of those schools and in the city.

Justice Marshall further argued:

> The State must also bear part of the blame for the white flight to the suburbs which would be forthcoming from a Detroit-only decree and would render such a remedy ineffective. Having created a system where whites and Negroes were intentionally kept apart so that they could not become accustomed to learning together, the State is responsible for the fact that many whites will react to the dismantling of that segregated system by attempting to flee to the suburbs.[106]

The assumption here is that greater experience with racially mixed schools would have made whites more likely to accept compulsory racial balance in a system that was 64 percent (by 1973, 70 percent) black—a proposition that is neither self-evident nor readily demonstrable.

In the final section of his opinion, Justice Marshall found that the "web of problems" foreseen by the Court in ordering a fifty-four-district plan was "constructed of the flimsiest of threads." First, he said, "the practicality of a final metropolitan plan is simply not before us at the present time," and he saw "no basis whatever for assuming that the District Court will inevitably be forced to assume the role of legislature or school superintendent." Indeed, he noted, the district judge had explicitly stated that his "task is to enforce constitutional rights not to act as a schoolmaster." Although Justice Powell "may have retreated," in *Keyes*, from the "guidelines set forth in *Swann*" regarding "the propriety of transportation of students to achieve desegregation," Justice Marshall refused to do so. The transportation requirements of the metropolitan plan contemplated by the district judge would, Marshall found, be "fully consistent with these guidelines" as to the number of children to be transported (310,000) and the time ("a ceiling of 40 minutes one way") and distances involved ("the average statewide bus trip is 8½ miles one way" and some "students already travel for one and a quarter hours or more each way"). As to cost, surprisingly, "a metropolitan plan would actually be more sensible than a Detroit-only remedy" because "the tri-county area . . . already has an inventory of 1,800 buses, many of which are now under-utilized," and, therefore, fewer buses would have to be purchased initially. This ignored, however, that not all of the tricounty area was included in the metropolitan plan. More important, according to this logic a plan including all of Michigan might have been "more sensible" still. "Some disruption, of course," Justice Marshall conceded, "is the inevitable product of any desegregation decree," but "desegregation is not and was never expected to be an easy task."[107]

If the dissenting opinions are less than scrupulous in their use of facts and logic, it must be said on the dissenters' behalf that the Court had never before allowed such scruples to hamper its pursuit of the goal of greater racial integration.

To the dissenters, still pursuing that goal, it must have seemed that the rules of the game had suddenly been changed—and surely everyone must have known by now that the Court's continuing to speak of "desegregation," "remedy," or "dismantling the dual system" was only a game and that the requirement in fact was simply the maximum dispersal of blacks. Moreover, the fact that the Court permitted busing in Detroit indicated that it was even now being only selectively scrupulous. The decision, Justice Marshall charged, is "more a reflection of a perceived public mood . . . than it is the product of neutral principles of law."[108] Except for the greater number of people who would be affected, what the dissenters wanted to do to metropolitan Detroit was, after all, no less justifiable or more outrageous than what the Court had no difficulty, just the year before, in doing to Denver. If facts and logic were still to be taken lightly, as in approving a Detroit-only plan, why should they not be taken lightly in the cause of greater integration rather than in making Detroit's schools still blacker more quickly? It is no credit to the dissenters, however, that, seeing where their "desegregation" rationale for compulsory integration had finally led, they were still unwilling to argue openly that the constitutional requirement should be simply the creation of majority-white schools and thus that there should either be busing in the Detroit metropolitan area or no busing at all, not busing only in predominantly black Detroit. They might well have been able to find a majority in favor of the second—the only defensible—alternative. Rather than simply adandoning the foolish "desegregation" game begun in *Green*, however, both the majority and the dissenters preferred to permit self-defeating racial busing in Detroit.

This completes the story of how the Constitution came to require racially balanced schools and the busing necessary to achieve such schools. A prohibition of segregation, justifiable as a condemnation of all racial discrimination by government, became a requirement of integration, mandating racial discrimination by government. Because a requirement of integration could not be justified as such, it was never openly admitted but was presented as a continued insistence on the elimination of all racial discrimination. This untenable rationale for an indefensible requirement—the real purpose of which was to create majority-white schools—led to the almost totally irrational result of busing to achieve racial balance in a major city with a school system already predominantly black. This was done to avoid the result—which would have quickly proved equally irrational—of requiring the busing of children throughout fifty-four school districts. Unless the national objective has become to foster the creation of black cities under black control—an objective favored by some black leaders—an American variant of South Africa's *bantustan* policy, the consequences of twenty years of Supreme Court policy-making on race and the schools must be seen as disastrous.

One must believe that a requirement so obviously self-defeating and so unwanted cannot long persist, but while the matter remains in the hands of the courts confidence is not possible. It would require an almost superhuman effort for the Supreme Court—whose members are all too human—simply to hold that it had made a terrible mistake and caused so much hardship and disruption needlessly and that, therefore, the compulsory integration requirement is no more. It would be possible for the Court to find in all cases hereafter that the racial separation now existing in the schools is not the result of segregation in the past and therefore to conclude, in accordance with *Milliken*, that "desegregation" is not "constitutionally justified or required." The Court's post-*Milliken* failure to preclude even interdistrict busing[109] indicates, however, that this is not likely to happen soon, and many lower courts will, in any event, not quickly be convinced that the time for busing is over.[110] The courts are in a sense even more firmly enmeshed than the rest of the nation in the web they have so wrongfully and foolishly spun. Our elected representatives, now long accustomed to leaving the resolution of difficult problems to the courts, must at some point accept the fact that where the courts are themselves the cause of the problem this means of escape from responsibility is not available.

11 | Effects of the Supreme Court's Attempt to Compel School Racial Integration: A Self-Defeating Requirement

This analysis has attempted to recount and explain in detail how the country has been brought to its present position, increasingly recognized as intolerable, on race and the schools—from prohibition of racial discrimination separating the races in the schools, quickly extended to prohibition of all segregation, to a requirement of racial discrimination in order to increase school racial mixing beyond that resulting from the prohibition of segregation. The Supreme Court's decision in *Brown* to prohibit segregation was, it has been argued, justifiable on the principle that all racial discrimination by government is an evil, or, more specifically, that no person should be disadvantaged by government because of his race. Reasoned objection to *Brown* was hardly possible except on the ground of the danger inherent in having a decision of such magnitude made by an institution so far removed from popular control; the seriousness of that danger has been fully demonstrated by subsequent events. If it is granted that the Court should have decided the question, it must be recognized that a decision again upholding segregation would have given new vigor to forces almost everywhere in retreat and would have served only to delay their eventual defeat. A decision refusing to prohibit segregation would not have required segregation, but, because of the almost universal failure to distinguish between the Court's permitting and the Court's requiring or recommending a policy, the practical effect of such refusal would not have been simply to leave the question where it was. Probably an inevitable, and certainly one of the most unfortunate, consequences of the Court's power to invalidate as unconstitutional the policy judgments of other institutions of government is that a decision declining to invalidate comes to be seen, not as merely leaving the matter to the electoral process, but as a certification of the wisdom and morality of the policy judgment involved. The Court's "imprimatur of constitutionality upon a piece of legislation is likely to enshrine it as the recommended solution of a difficult question of public policy."[1]

It has also been argued that the very principle that best and most easily justifies *Brown*'s prohibition of segregation—that all racial discrimination by government is prohibited—presented perhaps the greatest obstacle to justification of the Court's decisions, beginning with *Green*, that require racial discrimination to increase racial mixing. The difficulty was so great that the Court has never openly admitted the new requirement or attempted to justify compulsory integration on its own merits. The Court has, instead, attempted to disguise its new requirement as a continuation and enforcement of the old prohibition. This impossible task has required it to resort to methods—unfair and inaccurate statements of fact, patently fallacious reasoning, and perversion of the 1964 Civil Rights Act—that would be considered scandalous in any other institution or official of American government.

Analysis of the Court's methods of decision-making in any area of constitutional law may be considered incomplete, however—little more than an academic exercise—without some consideration of the "ultimate results" of the decisions reached. Good enough "results," it can be argued, will justify, or at least cause to be soon forgotten or forgiven, any defects or improprieties in the means by which these results were achieved. In the words of the late Alexander Bickel:

Professors in New England—and elsewhere, to be sure—parse the glories of the Warren Court, criticize its syllogisms, reduce its purported logic to absurd consequences, disprove its factual assertions, answer the unavoidable questions it managed to leave unasked, and most often conclude by regretting its failures of method, while either welcoming its results or professing detachment from them. Historians a generation or two hence, however—other professors in New England—may barely note, and care little about, method, logic, or intellectual coherence, and may assess results in hindsight—only results, and by their own future lights.

Past historians have so dealt with the Court, as do many—outside the profession, most—contemporary observers, and one sensed that this was what the Justices of the Warren Court expected, and that they were content to take their chances. They relied on events for vindication more than on the method of reason for contemporary validation.[2]

It is difficult for one cognizant of the limited possibility of principled decision-making—"general propositions," as Holmes said, "do not decide concrete cases"[3]—and skeptical of absolutes to quarrel with the standard of "only results," except to insist—as is the function of ethics and of the ideal of law—that "results" be not too narrowly conceived. Indeed, the distinction between methods and results is to some extent a false one; principle, honesty, and logic are not mere matters of taste or form. The use of improper methods in reaching a decision has its own results that detract from any good to be achieved, and the use of proper methods lends some assurance that the good results desired will in fact be achieved and, if achieved, will come to be seen as good. In no other area of constitutional law has the Court so consistently and so clearly "relied on events for vindication more than on the method of reason for contemporary validation." In no area is such vindication more unlikely to be forthcoming. On the contrary, it appears that it is particularly according to the standard of "only results," however narrowly conceived, that the Court's compulsory integration decisions will most clearly be seen as mistaken.

The most unfortunate result of the Court's integration requirement may well prove, if it has not already proved, to be simply that it has, in this multiracial and multiethnic society, reintroduced race as a permissible, and made it for the first time a sometimes constitutionally required, basis of government action. One of the problems caused by this new constitutional policy was illustrated, but not resolved, in a case brought to the Court in 1974, *DeFunis* v. *Odegaard*.[4] The University of Washington Law School denied admission to the plaintiff, a white of Jewish ancestry, while granting admission, pursuant to a "minority admissions program," to persons of lesser academic qualifications whose "dominant" racial or ethnic origin was "Black, Chicano, American-Indian or Filipino." A lower Washington state court, relying on *Brown*, held this to be unconstitutional racial discrimination and ordered that the plaintiff be admitted to the school; the Washington Supreme Court, relying on *Green* and *Swann*, reversed this decision.[5] The United States Supreme Court granted certiorari, but then dismissed the case without deciding the constitutional question, finding that it had become moot by reason of the plaintiff's admission to the school. Only Justice Douglas, dissenting from the dismissal, dealt with the merits, and he found that the open use of racial discrimination by state officials was unconstitutional. The difficulty, however, of reconciling this view with the Court's integration decisions is indicated by Justice Douglas' attempt to do so :

In [*Swann*], 402 U.S. 1, 16, we stated that as a matter of educational policy school authorities could, within their broad discretion, prescribe that each school within their district have a prescribed ratio of Negro to white students reflecting the proportion for the district as a whole, in order to disestablish a dual school system. But there is a crucial difference between the policy suggested in *Swann* and that under consideration here: the *Swann* policy would impinge on no person's constitutional rights, because no one would be excluded from a public school and no one has a right to attend a segregated public school.[6]

Justice Douglas' suggested distinctions are clearly invalid. First, the Court in *Swann*, at the page he cited, was not speaking of the need "to disestablish a dual school system," but explicitly approving the voluntary use of racial assignment by school boards in order to achieve racial balance, "absent the finding of a constitutional violation." Where the need "to disestablish a dual school system" is involved, racial assignment is not merely permissible but mandatory. Second, reliance on the "crucial difference" seen by Douglas would mean approval of a return to "separate but equal" schools; racial exclusion from a particular public school "would impinge on no person's constitutional rights," provided that an alternative public school was made available.

A decision is most clearly mistaken, however, according to the criterion of "only results" if it not only fails to bring about the result desired but is self-defeating. The Court's integration requirement is self-defeating for two reasons. First, instead of increasing actual racial mixing in the schools beyond that resulting from the prohibition of segregation and, more particularly, instead of eliminating or reducing the number of majority-black schools, the requirement tends to increase racial separation not only in the schools but elsewhere. Second, the requirement has created a political issue of such overwhelming importance to many that it threatens to distort the political process and give rise to forces sufficient not only to eliminate the requirement but to halt or set back progress toward racial equality.

A constitutional requirement less promising than school racial integration, balance, or majority-white schools is difficult to imagine. All relevant factors seem to combine to militate against its success. In brief, its disadvantages are great, immediate, and personal, its advantages remote and elusive at best. Most important, means of frustrating achievement of the objective of the requirement are widely available.

The Costs of Abandoning Neighborhood Schools

The problem of compulsory school racial integration is in essence that it seeks to overcome the fact of residential racial concentration. If the races were evenly distributed residentially, the problem would not arise. To achieve a greater degree of school than of residential racial integration requires that children be assigned to schools according to their race instead of according to the neighborhoods in which they live. The disadvantages of abandoning or substantially departing from neighborhood assignment, however—even disregarding all questions of principle involved in racial assignment—are overwhelming.

To require a child to attend a school not the nearest to

his home is to require him to spend an additional portion of his life in traveling to and from school and, usually, in being transported—a portion that he and his parents would almost invariably prefer he spend otherwise. The requirement must therefore be recognized as a substantial infringement of individual freedom by government and as having the aspect of using people as pawns. As Justice Powell said in *Keyes*, "Any child, white or black, who is compelled to leave his neighborhood and spend significant time each day being transported to a distant school suffers an impairment of his liberty and his privacy."[7] The eminent sociologist and educational authority Nathan Glazer has written:

In busing to distant schools, white children were in effect being conscripted to create an environment which, it had been decided, was required to provide equality of educational opportunity for black children. It was perhaps one thing to do this when the whites in question were the children or grandchildren of those who had deprived black children of their freedom in the past. But when a district judge in San Francisco ruled that not only white children but Chinese children and Spanish-speaking children must be conscripted to create an environment which, he believed, would provide equality of educational opportunity for black children, there was good reason for wondering whether "equal protection of the laws" was once again being violated, this time from the other side.

. . . . .

Constitutional law often moves through strange and circuitous paths, but perhaps the strangest yet has been the one whereby, beginning with an effort to expand freedom—no Negro child shall be excluded from any public school because of his race—the law has ended up with as drastic a restriction of freedom as we have seen in this country in recent years.[8]

Though it is usually mentioned in constitutional law only to be deprecated, there is also and inevitably the question of money. To increase the travel distance between home and school is to increase the cost of transportation, whether it is publicly or privately borne, and the costs can be great. As Justice Powell stated, "At a time when public education generally is suffering serious financial malnutrition, the economic burdens of such transportation can be severe, requiring both initial capital outlays and annual operating costs in the millions of dollars."[9]

The costs of busing and the consequences of measures taken to minimize these costs have been reiterated in depressing detail by school officials from throughout the country in a seemingly endless and fruitless series of congressional hearings.[10] In Nashville, Tennessee, for example, "pupil eligibility for transportation was extended from 1¼ to 1½ miles minimum distance; the high school day was shortened from 7 hours to 6 hours, 141 school openings were staggered to begin at 20-minute intervals from 7 a.m. to 10 a.m.; and transportation is no longer available for field trips and special fine arts performances." Nonetheless, "estimated costs of additional equipment, operation and maintenance are: $1,418,100 for 87 84-passenger buses, at $16,300 each; $177,000 for maintenance equipment; $700,000 for operation costs for 1 year; $1,350,000 for maintenance facilities and land area for these facilities to take care of some 300 large buses and 65 small buses; and $56,000 for the installation of safety loading zones at 42 schools." The early opening and late closing for different schools meant in the winter that some children "may be on the street as much as 1 hour before sunrise" and that "those elementary children on late shifts who live 1½ miles or less from schools will be walking home in darkness." In Tampa, Florida, the board closed some schools "as early as 12 noon and others as late as 5 p.m." in an effort to limit the number of buses needed to comply with a court order, but the system still "owed $1 million for school buses with no funds to pay for them other than to decrease expenditures for other items in our education budget in the years ahead." "Nearing the end of the third year of court-ordered, racial balance busing," the Kalamazoo, Michigan, school system had "lost twenty percent of [its] school population and spent in excess of $4,000,000 in implementing the court order." The Dallas superintendent of schools testified that "the time invested in desegregation by staff members adds up to $3 million in salaries" and that in an eight-month period he "had invested approximately two-thirds of [his] work in the desegregation process."[11] Compulsory integration has also typically meant the closing of otherwise usable school facilities, either in compliance with HEW or court orders or to minimize busing. The losses resulting from this alone have run to hundreds of millions of dollars.[12]

Even the largest sums can be minimized by comparing them with still larger amounts, as the courts have frequently done, but what may appear insignificant to a judge—who may half-believe the rhetoric of absolute constitutional rights—can appear to taxpayers and school boards an intolerable additional burden. Sometimes—constitutional rhetoric notwithstanding—additional funds are not available, and the additional transportation and other expenses of compulsory integration cannot be borne or can be met only by a substantial reduction in the quality or number of educational programs and services.

Substantial as they may be to those who must bear them, costs in time and money are not the only, or always the most important, disadvantages of abandoning neighborhood schools. Students lose the comfort and security of familiar surroundings, of closeness to home, and of the presence of siblings and neighborhood friends. The need to conform to bus schedules seriously interferes with participation in school-centered activities before and after the usual school hours. Of utmost importance to many parents is the "strongly felt" need, referred to in *Emporia*, for "direct control over decisions vitally affecting the education of one's children."[13] The abandonment of neighborhood schools tends to limit parental participation in, and supervision of, the operation of the school system and lessens the importance of the school as a center of community concern and cohesion. As Glazer has stated:

Clearly this is one way of reducing the influence of people over their own environment and their own fate. I believe indeed that the worst effect of the current crisis is that people already reduced to frustration by their inability to affect a complex society and a government moving in ways many of them find incomprehensible and undesirable, must now see one of the last areas of local influence taken from them in order to achieve a single goal, that of racial balance.[14]

Justice Powell made a similar point in *Keyes*:

Neighborhood school systems, neutrally administered, reflect the deeply felt desire of citizens for a sense of community in their public education. Public schools have been a traditional source of strength to our Nation, and that strength may derive in part from the identification of many schools with the personal features of the surrounding neighborhood. Community support, interest, and dedication to public schools may well run higher with a neighborhood attendance pattern: distance may encourage disinterest. . . . This Court should be wary of compelling in the name of constitutional law what may seem to many a dissolution in the traditional, more personal fabric of their public schools.[15]

Glazer's criticism of the abandonment of neighborhood schools and Powell's appraisal of their value seem far more realistic than the Court's grudging concession, in *Swann*, that "all things being equal . . . it might well be desirable to assign pupils to schools nearest their home." Nor is the value shown to be less or the loss shown to be justified in a particular case by pointing out, as the Court did in *Swann*, that school busing is common.[16]

The tangible and intangible values of neighborhood schools are substantial and legitimate grounds for opposition to compulsory integration, and surely sufficient grounds for many who would otherwise prefer increased integration. There is little doubt, however, that much of the strength and intensity of the opposition to compulsory integration derives from the fact that increased integration is often not preferred but is seen as itself objectionable. Proponents of compulsory integration would characterize such opposition as racism,[17] but the opposition would probably be very little less today if all differences in color should somehow disappear overnight while the individuals involved and all other circumstances remained the same.[18] Differences in economic status and cultural background and in standards of behavior would remain. Because blacks, despite great recent advances, are still disproportionately poorer than whites,[19] compulsory school racial integration typically amounts to compulsory class integration. It may, of course, be favored by some for this very reason, but it is also intensely resisted by many for the same reason.

Resistance to class integration cannot, as easily as racism, be dismissed as indefensible. There is much in the American ideal that looks to a classless society, but also much that recognizes the desire to attain and enjoy economic and cultural advantage as legitimate, or even as essential to progress. Realism, unhappily, demands a recognition that compulsory school integration asks of many that a significant portion of this advantage be given up, and that it asks it as to a peculiarly sensitive area, the welfare of one's children.

Perhaps the greatest value of an official policy of racial neutrality is that it makes the consideration of racial differences largely or completely irrelevant and, indeed, almost inherently improper and offensive. A system of law focusing on the individual has little need to consider the general characteristics of the race or social class to which the individual might be assigned, and anyone who would dwell on these matters in a discussion of legal policy has the burden of justifying his doing so. But compulsory school racial integration is an official policy of racism and makes consideration of these matters relevant and unavoidable; once they are considered, overwhelming grounds for opposition become apparent. The brutal fact—the very fact, indeed, that is the basis of the drive for compulsory integration—is that there is an enormous difference in the academic performance of the average white and the average black child at the same age or grade level.

At least in America, the average white child scores about 15 points higher on standardized tests than the average black child. This disparity is apparent among first graders, and it persists throughout school and college. In terms of mental ages or grade levels, blacks fall further and further behind whites. The average black 6 year old is 1 year behind the average white 6 year old. By the time he is 12, the average black child is scoring at the same level as the average white 10 year old. The average black 18 year old has scores comparable to a white 14 or 15 year old.

These differences are quite consistent on both IQ and achievement tests. Some studies report racial differences of less than 15 points, while others report more, but virtually none report anything like equal performance.[20]

Compulsory integration of blacks and whites of the same age or grade level almost invariably means, therefore, the lowering of a school's academic standards, potential, and educational results in proportion to the increase in the percentage of blacks— especially where, as is the rule in school systems operating under court order, ability grouping in separate classrooms is also constitutionally prohibited because of its inevitable "segregative effect."[21]

Perhaps even more important than the effect of compulsory integration on a school's academic potential is its effect on the maintenance of discipline and on sheer physical safety. Whatever the cause or causes, the fact is that conditions in many of our public schools today, especially in larger cities, are almost unbelievably bad and growing worse. A 1975 preliminary report of a Senate subcommittee investigating the matter states:

It is alarmingly apparent that student misbehavior and conflict within our school system is no longer limited to a fist fight between individual students or an occasional general disruption resulting from a specific incident. Instead our schools are experiencing serious crimes of a felonious nature including brutal assaults on teachers and students, as well as rapes, extortions, burglaries, thefts, and an unprecedented wave of wanton destruction and vandalism. Moreover our preliminary study of the situation has produced compelling evidence that this level of violence and vandalism is reaching crisis proportions which seriously threaten the ability of our educational system to carry out its primary function.

. . . . .

Data from an earlier survey of large urban school districts conducted by the Subcommittee showed that assaults on teachers in those systems increased 612 percent between 1964 and 1968. In Chicago alone the number of such assaults went from 135 to 1,065 in that same period.

. . . . .

The NEA [National Educational Association] estimates that in the 1972-73 school year alone 69,000 teachers were physically attacked by students and 155,000 teachers had their personal property maliciously damaged. Another study found that 75,000 teachers are injured badly enough each year to require medical attention.

. . . . .

Although the level of violence, directed against teachers revealed by these statistics, is indeed alarming, the principal victims of the rising tide of crime in our schools are not the teachers, but the students.[22]

There is little doubt that compulsory integration is a contributing cause of school disruption and violence. In 1970 the *New York Times* conducted surveys of the situation both nationally and in New York City. Under the heading "Racial Strife Undermines Schools in City and Nation" it reported that, nationally, "racial polarization, disruptions and growing racial tensions that sometimes explode into violence are plaguing school administrators in virtually every part of the country where schools have substantial Negro enrollments." About New York City, it reported:

Racial fears and resentment are steadily eroding relations between white teachers and administrators and black students in many, possibly most, high schools here.

In a few schools, this erosion has gone so far as to create conditions of paralyzing anarchy in which large police detachments have been deemed necessary to keep classrooms functioning and put down sporadic outbursts of violence by rebellious students.

. . . . .

A respected Brooklyn principal, who didn't want to be quoted by name, talked not of small minorities but uncontrollable masses. "What can you do," he asked, "when you have 1,000 blacks in your school, all programmed for special behavior and violence?"

. . . . .

In the furor over whether it is the schools that are failing to teach blacks and other nonwhites or the students themselves who are failing to learn there is one undisputed fact—that the results are catastrophic.[23]

James Coleman, principal author of the famous Coleman Report, *Equality of Educational Opportunity* (1966), stated in 1975:

Disorder clearly comes from lower-class schools. For example, many observations of ghetto-school classrooms describe an enormous degree of disorder in those classrooms. It is very hard to blame any white parents, or any black parents for that matter, who would like to see their children out of that classroom, given the degree of disorder and the degree to which schools as they're presently constituted have failed to control lower-class black children. So I think it's quite understandable for families not to want to send their children to schools where 90 per cent of the time is spent not on instruction but on discipline.[24]

Perhaps most destructive of any hope for acceptance of compulsory integration is the notorious fact that many who most strongly favor it for the children of others find reasons not to favor it for their own and that, therefore, in practice it is imposed only on the lower economic classes. Glazer has forcefully stated:

A second issue that would seem to have some constitutional bearing is whether those who are to provide the children for a minority black environment are being conscripted only on the basis of income. The prosperous and the rich can avail themselves of private schooling, or they can "flee" to the suburbs. And if the Richmond and Detroit [district court] rulings should be sustained, making it impossible to "escape" by going to the suburbs, the class character of the decisions would become even more pronounced. For while many working-class and lower-middle class people can afford to live in suburbs, very few can afford the costs of private education.

Some observers have pointed out that leading advocates of transportation for integration—journalists, political figures, and judges—themselves send their children to private schools which escape the consequences of these legal decisions. But even without being *ad hominem*, one may raise a moral question: if the judges who are imposing such decisions, the lawyers who argue for them (including brilliant young lawyers from the best law schools employed by federal poverty funds to do the arguing), would not themselves send their children to the schools their decisions bring into being, how can they insist that others poorer and less mobile than they are do so? Clearly those not subject to a certain condition are insisting that others submit themselves to it, which offends the basic rule of morality in both the Jewish and Christian traditions. I assume there must be a place for this rule in the Constitution.[25]

It is hardly surprising that the intensity of resistance to compulsory integration is matched by the intensity of resentment.[26]

The Doubtful Benefits of Compulsory Integration

The real and unequal sacrifices demanded by compulsory school racial integration make opposition difficult to overcome at best. Hope might nonetheless be entertained if it could be shown, or at least with some basis promised, that some great social gain would result. When, as in the case of the Supreme Court, political power is remote from popular control, unpopular measures may be successfully imposed if their results cause opposition to diminish before it can be made effective. Few social gains would be more significant, would better justify drastic and initially unpopular measures, than a solution, or a substantial contribution to a solution, of the nation's race or race-related problems. It does not appear, however, that compulsory integration has achieved or promises to achieve a solution. It appears, on the contrary, that the Court's attempt to compel integration is more likely to exacerbate than to ameliorate America's racial problems.

Although the Court has never offered more than its obviously fictional "desegregation" rationale for compulsory integration, there can be no doubt that the basic impetus is the claim, or hope, that it will somehow serve to close the enormous gap that has been shown to exist between the academic performance of blacks and whites.[27] This is presumably to be accomplished by raising the academic performance of blacks, but lowering the performance of whites would undoubtedly also be acceptable to some of compulsory integration's proponents.[28] A further but related claim is that racial mixing in school may lead to greater interracial understanding and acceptance among school children. Neither their intrinsic plausibility nor available scholarly studies, however, support these claims or hopes sufficiently to make it likely that opposition to compulsory integration will decrease with experience.

There is no reason to believe that the mixing of races in a school or classroom is in itself an aid to academic achievement. The claim of beneficial effects on black academic performance is based instead on the mixing of cultural and economic classes that is usually involved.[29] Thus the mixing of classes is not merely an incidental effect of the race-mixing requirement but its aim; the requirement continues to be stated in racial terms only for the purposes of constitutional law. The principal contentions are that class-mixing may improve black academic performance by raising black academic aspirations or academic self-esteem or by ensuring that blacks obtain a proportionate allocation of school resources. These contentions have been the subject of intensive empirical investigations. There appears to be general and growing agreement that the claim of improved black academic performance as a result of compulsory integration is dubious and that compulsory integration is not likely to be justified on that basis.

One important discussion indicates the nature of the arguments and considerations involved. Sociologist David J. Armor specifically addressed himself to *"assessing the effects of induced school integration via busing,* and not necessarily the effects of integration brought about by the voluntary actions of individual families that moved into integrated neighborhoods."[30] On the basis of a review of the major empirical studies of the matter, Armor concluded: "None of the studies were able to demonstrate conclusively that integration has had an effect on academic achievement as measured by standardized tests." None showed significant black improvement, and in one case "a follow-up done three years later showed that the integrated black students were even further behind the white students than before the integration project began." Furthermore, another study showed a drop in the grade-point average, as distinguished from achievement test scores, of bused black secondary school students. Armor found this result unsurprising: "Since black students of the same age are, on average, behind white students in all parts of the country with respect to academic achievement, we should expect their grades to fall when they are taken from the competition in an all-black school to the competition in a predominantly white school."[31]

The argument that schooling together with whites will raise black educational aspirations is based on the assumption that such aspirations are generally low. It appears, however, as Armor noted, that "black students actually have higher aspirations than white students at similar levels of achievement," and that the effect of forced integration may be to lower aspirations. The principal study reviewed by Armor found "a significant decline for the bused students, from 74% wanting a college degree in 1968 to 60% by May 1970." "At the very least," he stated, "we can conclude that the bused students do not improve their aspirations for college. The same is true for occupational aspirations." "Some educators have hypothesized that integration has a *positive* effect in lowering aspirations to more realistic levels; of course, others would argue that any lowering of aspirations is undesirable."[32]

The principal study showed that busing also had an adverse

effect on black "academic self-concept"—measured by asking students "to rate how bright they were in comparison to their classmates." "Again," Armor stated, "this finding makes sense if we recall that the academic performance of the bused students falls considerably when they move from the black community to the white suburbs. In rating their intellectual ability, the bused students may simply be reflecting the harder competition in suburban schools." Two other studies, using a related concept of "self-esteem" found that "integration does not seem to affect the self-esteem measures in any clearly consistent or significant way."[33]

A leading student of these issues, with a long-term personal "commitment to integration," Nancy St. John, "reviewed more than 120 studies of the relation of school racial composition and the achievement, attitudes, or behavior of children." She concluded in 1975:

As implemented to date, desegregation has not rapidly closed the black-white gap in academic achievement, though it has rarely lowered and sometimes raised the scores of black children. Improvement has been more often reported in the early grades, in arithmetic, and in schools over 50% white, but even here the gains have usually been mixed, intermittent, or non-significant. White achievement has been unaffected in schools that remained majority white but significantly lower in majority black schools.

Biracial schooling is apparently not detrimental to the academic performance of black children, but it may have negative effects on their self-esteem. It is not merely academic self-concept in the face of higher standards that is threatened, but also general self-concept. In addition, desegregation apparently lowers educational and vocational aspirations. It is possible, however, to interpret a reduction of unrealistically high aspirations as an overall gain. Moreover, there is some evidence that in the long run desegregation may encourage the aspiration, self-esteem, and sense of environmental control of black youth.[34]

The available studies were also reviewed by Christopher Jencks and seven other educational experts highly sympathetic to the cause of racial equality. They reported that of the busing studies surveyed, "some show inconsistent gains. Some show no difference. Very few show (or at least report) losses." They concluded, "The case for or against desegregation should not be argued in terms of academic achievement."[35]

The argument that racial mixing is necessary to ensure an equal distribution of educational resources is also difficult to support. A vitiating fallacy, all else apart, of the "separate but equal" doctrine was the fact that black schools were very rarely equal to white schools in physical facilities and personnel and, as a practical matter, often could not be made so. Equality is practicable, however, once segregation is prohibited and blacks have obtained an effective political voice.[36] Because of special federal grants and other reasons, school districts, today, often spend more per student in predominantly black than in predominantly white schools. Indeed, one of the prime ironies of compulsory integration is that it can result in a lessening of expenditures for black students.[37]

It appeared as early as 1966 that the general assumption that predominantly black schools were inferior was largely incorrect. The most important source of data on the subject of schools and race is the so-called Coleman Report of 1966, entitled *Equality of Educational Opportunity*, the result of a massive study conducted for the United States Office of Education pursuant to the 1964 Civil Rights Act. As Frederick Mosteller and Daniel Moynihan have stated, "the findings on equality of facilities were quite unexpected."

For those school facilities measured by [the Coleman Report], while there are reported differences in those available to the majority as against the minority groups, they are surprisingly small differences. And while on balance the differences favor the majority, it is by no means the case that they consistently do so. Obviously this was disconcerting. No one then thought the result would be even close, not the investigators for the Office of Education, nor the authors of this chapter.[38]

The Coleman Report further found that such differences as did exist had very little relationship to academic achievement. Mosteller and Moynihan stated: "The pathbreaking quality of [the report] had to do with its analysis of the relation of variation in school facilities to variation in levels of academic achievement. It reported so little relation as to make it almost possible to say there was none."[39] Inferior facilities resulting from racial discrimination cannot be justified, of course, regardless of their extent and regardless of their effect. But neither can compulsory integration be justified as necessary to remove such inequalities as may exist. As Frank Goodman has said, "A judicial decree requiring equal division of all educational inputs might or might not be easily enforced; but it is hard to believe the difficulties would surpass those presented by massive, community resented, desegregation."[40]

Because little can be confidently claimed for compulsory racial integration as a means of improving black academic achievement, its supporters have increasingly relied on a claim that it will serve to increase interracial understanding and acceptance among school children. This claim may be an even clearer example of the wish fathering the thought. The situation in schools operating under integration orders is often known only to the children attending those schools and their parents. The school officials involved are often virtually enjoined from publicizing race-related incidents; to do so is to risk a judicial finding of an insufficiently cooperative attitude or inadequate enthusiasm for integration and to risk subjection to further court-imposed restrictions.[41] It is notorious that even the otherwise most ardent advocates of free speech often find it of limited value where racial questions are concerned.

School racial integration achieved by involuntary busing may mean, in practice, that, for example, halls, lunchrooms, washrooms, and playgrounds must be more strictly monitored and sometimes closed, that maintaining discipline becomes a paramount concern, and that a word or a touch can occasion a racial incident.[42] Children who have brought lunch or other money to school may encounter children who have not and demands for contribution; the situation has resulted where "the white kids were really paying tuition to come to school each day. And the black kids were collecting. It's called extortion."[43] Where all or most members of a different race are also of a different economic and cultural background, the immature are not likely to distinguish between race and background. All attempts to teach children the irrelevance of race in determining individual worth—probably futile, in any event, where the children are being bused past or away from their neighborhood schools because of their race—can be quickly undone. Racial antipathy and animosity are more likely than increased understanding and acceptance to be the result.[44] Armor has pointed out:

One of the central sociological hypotheses in the integration policy model is that integration should reduce racial stereotypes, increase tolerance, and generally improve race relations. Needless to say, we were quite surprised when our data failed to verify this axiom. Our surprise was increased substantially when we discovered that, in fact, the converse appears to be true. The data suggest that, under the circumstances obtaining in these studies, integration heightens racial identity and consciousness, enhances ideologies that promote racial segregation, and reduces opportunities for actual contact between the races.[45]

Black students who have been bused, the principal study reviewed by Armor indicated, are "*more* in favor of attending *non-white* schools" than those who have not been bused and "much more likely to support the idea of black power." Furthermore, Armor stated:

The changes do not appear to be in ideology alone. From 1969 to 1970 the bused students reported less friendliness from whites, more free time spent with members of their own race, more incidents of prejudice, and less frequent dating with white students. . . . In other words, the longer the contact with whites, the fewer the kinds of interracial experiences that might lead to a general improvement in racial tolerance.

The apparent effects on white students were similar:

Those students who had direct classroom contact with bused black students showed *less* support for the busing program than those without direct contact. In fact, the kind of students who were generally the most supportive—the middle-class, high-achieving students— showed the largest decline in support as a result of contact with bused black students. This finding is based on cross-sectional data and does not indicate a change over time, but it is suggestive of the possibility that a general polarization has occurred for both racial groups.

"The main point we are making," Armor said, "is that the integration policy model predicts that integration should cause these sentiments [favoring integration] to *increase*, while the evidence shows they actually *decrease*, leaving the bused students *more opposed* to integration than the non-bused students. Only further research can determine whether this trend will continue until the majority of bused students shifts to a general anti-integration ideology."[46]

Armor's overall conclusion was that "massive mandatory busing for purposes of improving student achievement and interracial harmony is not effective and should not be adopted at this time."[47]

Compulsory Integration Is Self-Defeating

Because the losses resulting from compulsory integration are real, substantial, and immediate and the possible gains elusive at best, it is strongly opposed by an overwhelming majority of the American people, as public opinion polls and referenda have repeatedly shown.[48] More important, opposition increases in extent and intensity as the threat of compulsory integration moves closer to home,[49] as events in Boston dramatically demonstrated and as is most convincingly demonstrated by the accelerated exodus of the middle class from school systems subject to the requirement. It is rightly opposed by many black civil rights leaders and organizations on the ground that it "stigmatizes Blacks by placing a premium on their dispersal." The National Black Convention held in Gary, Indiana, in March 1972 and attended by over ten thousand blacks overwhelmingly adopted a resolution condemning compulsory integration as a "bankrupt, suicidal method of desegregating schools based on the false notion that Black children are unable to learn unless they are in the same setting with white children."[50]

The opposition of the elected branches of government to compulsory integration is also clear. It was made explicit in several provisions of the 1964 Civil Rights Act. The Court's effective nullification of these provisions in Swann quickly led to a continuing flood of proposals for additional legislation and constitutional amendments prohibiting or restricting racial busing.[51] In March 1972, President Nixon proposed legislation that would have severely limited the power of federal courts to require busing. His recommendations were adopted by the House in August 1972, but defeated in the Senate by a filibuster, the historic weapon of opponents of civil rights.[52] Congress was able to enact only a weak "compromise" which, as might have been expected, proved totally ineffective. In the Education Amendments of 1972, Congress provided that federal funds were not to be used for transportation or the purchase of transportation equipment "to overcome racial imbalance" or "to carry out a plan of desegregation" except "on the express written voluntary request" of local school officials[53] and that federal district court orders requiring transportation "for the purposes of achieving a balance among students with respect to race, sex, religion, or socioeconomic status" were to be stayed pending appeals.[54]

President Nixon signed the 1972 act despite his belief that stronger measures were necessary, warning that "the relief it provides is illusory."[55] He was quickly proved correct. In denying a motion based on the act for a stay, pending appeal, of a district court busing order, Justice Powell explained that the district court had ordered busing not to achieve "racial balance" but only "desegregation" and that, therefore, the legislation did not apply.[56] As a consequence, the act, like the limitations contained in the 1964 Civil Rights Act, had no more effect than if it had never been passed. President Nixon continued to make opposition to racial busing a major element of his domestic program, promising in his campaign for re-election that he would work for further legislation, and, if necessary, a constitutional amendment. It is generally agreed by political analysts that this position played an important part in his subsequent overwhelming re-election.

A Court decision is not shown to be ineffective or self-defeating in terms of the Court's immediate objective, however, by a showing that it is opposed by the American people or their elected representatives or that it does not seem justified by its effects. For better or worse, the Court has become, especially since *Brown*, an important wielder of independent political power, and its decisions carry strong inducements to compliance. Compliance ordinarily results because, in part, of quasi-theological beliefs, held by all sections of the political spectrum, regarding the nature of the Constitution and of the Supreme Court as its expositor.[57] Compliance also results because of the simple facts that it is ordinarily difficult to avoid, that only a limited number of causes can be successfully mounted, and that life must somehow go on despite disappointments, frustrations, and the mistakes of rulers. The Court, it seems easy for many to forget, is not limited, like moralists and philosophers, to persuasion but has, as Little Rock can attest, a strong call on the government's monopoly of legalized physical force. This is not to say, of course, that the Court's power is absolute, but neither does that fact establish, as many of the Court's defenders have argued, that its power is reconcilable with democracy.[58] All power is limited; democracy is a matter of degree, and the degree of the Court's insulation from popular control and, therefore, its power to work its will despite popular opposition is very great.[59] Nothing better illustrates this, indeed, than the fact that it decided to require busing and that two presidential election victories and four Supreme Court appointments by an opponent of busing have not sufficed to prevent busing from taking place.

The Court's decision to compel school racial integration is ineffective and self-defeating and, therefore, mistaken according to any standard, not because it is opposed by the American people, but because means to frustrate the achievement of its apparent objective—the creation of majority-white schools—are available to many of the individuals involved. Many Court decisions not approved by the American people are effective nonetheless. The Court's decision prohibiting or severely restricting capital punishment, for example, is opposed by a large majority, but capital punishment has ceased throughout the nation.[60] Such decisions may contribute to a feeling that control of government has been lost and to the much lamented apathy toward elections—there being less and less for those who are elected to decide—but they have little direct and immediate effect on the daily life of the average person and, more important, there is little he can do, in any event, to prevent their effectuation. The Court's attempt to compel school racial integration, in contrast, is unique in the seriousness of its direct and immediate impact on the lives of millions of people and in that individual escape, although often at great cost, is legally possible.

At present, compulsory integration can be avoided for one's children by two methods: removing them from public to private schools or moving the family's residence, or the children's residence, to an area the buses have not yet reached. Freedom to comply with compulsory education requirements by the use of other means than public school systems is, by virtue of a Supreme Court decision in an earlier era of judicial activism, a constitutional right.[61] That decision can, of course, be overruled, but it is currently enjoying a vigorous revival.[62] Private schools can, probably should, and no doubt will be prohibited from practicing racial discrimination,[63] but because of their tuition charges and locations, the prohibition would not significantly diminish their attractiveness as a means of avoiding compulsory integration.

Escape from compulsory integration or its most objectionable effects is even more generally available by moving from school districts with a high percentage of blacks. This means of escape can be made increasingly onerous, in effect limited to those of a higher economic status, by requiring the consolidation of school districts over ever wider areas, ignoring city, county, and even state lines. It is unlikely, however, that even this process would succeed before limitations would have to be recognized by even the most determined of judges or, as the Court may have realized in deciding *Milliken*, before Congress would finally be moved to effective action.

Families can move across school district and municipal boundaries far faster than integration plans can. Fathers can commute longer distances than school children can be bused. Sites for schools can be "strategically chosen" (although sometimes so much controversy attends site selection that school districts simply stop building new schools), but by the time the school is built, the white exodus is well under way, and shortly after it opens, the new school is as segregated as the one it was built to replace. Much the same is likely to prove true of the attempt to outflank parents with large-scale "educational parks." To keep up with the volatile white families, the buildings of the grand new park would have to be a fleet of house trailers.[64]

Most, if not all, claims that gains may result from racially integrated schools turn on the assumption that such schools will be at least majority-white, and some assume the schools will be at least 70 percent white. Neither goal is achievable, however, within the confines of many of our major cities where school systems are already majority-black. The trend toward increasingly black urban school systems is nationwide.[65] This trend is due to many factors, including a continuing movement of blacks from rural to urban areas and a higher black than white birth rate, but there can be little doubt that compulsory integration serves to accelerate it. James Coleman has concluded from a study of the available statistics for the period 1968 to 1973 that in the nation's twenty largest cities, "it seems to be an issue of how long before the segregating actions ["white flight"] completely overcome the results of the integration, leading to a system that is more segregated than was the case before."[66] The benefits of racially integrated schools may be debatable, but the error of seeking to compel integration where it cannot meaningfully be achieved and where greater racial separation results is not.

Impact on School Systems, Cities, and the Political Process

That compulsory integration often operates to create more rather than fewer majority-black schools is not, unfortunately, its most serious defect. Insofar as it drives the middle and upper classes, white and black, from public school systems, it deprives those systems of important if not essential sources of leadership and support, and thereby weakens what is undoubtedly our best hope for the achievement of educational and social equality.

When white parents withdraw their children from the central city, more is lost than students alone. With them go a significant source of tax revenue and, most important, community leadership in programs for good public education. The parents who typically provide this leadership campaign for bond issues support good teachers and new programs and generally exercise their influence in ways that will benefit all children in the schools. But they do this because they live in the community and because *their* children will benefit, too. . . . When these groups finally decide that community schools are "past redemption" and withdraw their support, they provide a situation that is well and truly past redemption.

There is more than a loss of leadership. All over the nation, communities that for decades have passed every proposed school bond issue are now defeating them, and new dissatisfactions triggered by integration campaigns are probably partly responsible.[67]

To the extent that compulsory integration drives the middle class from our cities, it accelerates urban deterioration and makes for racial separation not only in schools but generally. The Supreme Court may, from its Olympian pinnacle, continue to insist that the actual effects of compulsory integration are irrelevant, but a system that would survive on the face of the earth must at some point take reality into account.

Another reality to be taken into account in appraising the Supreme Court's integration requirement is its effect on the political process. Democracy, as Churchill has said, has little to commend it except its alternatives. One of these is government by unelected lifetime judges, a major disadvantage of which is that judgments found to be mistaken are extremely difficult to alter. Because the changing of the Court's membership and, therefore, of its policies is not subject to direct electoral control but can be influenced—subject to the fortuities of longevity and, ever more rarely, resignation—only by votes for candidates for other offices, particularly the presidency, the Court's policies can have a serious impact on the workability of democracy. The Court's integration requirement has introduced into the political process an issue that could not otherwise have arisen on the national level or in most state or local jurisdictions and that, given its effects, should not have arisen. Having arisen, it is often of such importance to the daily lives of so many that it overwhelms all other issues.[68] The issue of participation in Asian wars, for example, can seem remote in comparison. The effect is to complicate further and to limit electoral choice, to make necessary for many the choice of candidates who would not otherwise be preferred, and grossly to distort the process of representative government.

The Supreme Court provides for those whose policies it favors a tempting shortcut to success, an apparent means of avoiding the onerous burden of attempting to gain popular approval and consent. Those who succeed in the Court despite popular opposition must not be surprised, however, when they are elsewhere defeated. A looming danger in the Court's mis-guided effort to further racial equality by means of compulsory integration is that the opposition it arouses will prove sufficient to preclude effective steps toward equality that might otherwise be taken. Unless quickly corrected, this mistake may prove, like other mistakes made by the Court in the past on racial questions,[69] to be itself the greatest obstacle to a solution of the nation's racial problems.

Notes

Chapter 1. Introduction

1. "Busing—the Arrogance of Power," *Wall Street Journal*, July 25, 1975, p. 4; "The Schism in Black America," *Public Interest*, No. 27 (Spring 1972), 5. See also political columnist Joseph Kraft: "Unmitigated disaster seems at first glance the right verdict to pronounce in marking the 20th anniversary of the Supreme Court decision against school segregation" (Austin [Texas] *American-Statesman*, May 22, 1974, p. 4).

2. Speech, May 3, 1907, as quoted in William Lockhart, Yale Kamisar, and Jesse Choper, *Constitutional Law* (3d ed.; St. Paul, 1970), 7.

3. 347 U.S. 483.

4. As is shown, in part, by the fact that the decision was urged by the federal executive branch as well as by the American Jewish Congress, the American Civil Liberties Union, the American Federation of Teachers, the Congress of Industrial Organizations, and the American Veterans Committee, each of which filed a brief *amicus curiae*. See also Richard Bardolph, "Reviving Hopes: 1938–1954," in *The Civil Rights Record: Black Americans and the Law* (New York, 1970), Part V. Important state civil rights legislation was passed in the 1938 to 1954 period (*ibid.*, 250-59), and national political platforms opposed racial discrimination ever more strongly (*ibid.*, 243-50). Racial discrimination in defense industries and racial segregation in the armed services were prohibited by executive orders in 1941 and 1948, respectively (*ibid.*, 300-308). "This era saw also . . . the end of lynching; the leveling of barriers in professional sports; a sharp increase in the number of [blacks] appointed and elected federal, state, city, county, and local governmental officials. . . . By the middle 1950's every major church body in America had condemned racial discrimination and intolerance in principle. Hundreds of tax-supported municipal and semi-official agencies were working to promote racial peace and friendship. . . . By 1954, in short, racism was fast losing its intellectual respectability" (*ibid.*, 233-34). See also Harvey Wish, "A Historian Looks at School Segregation," *W. Res. L. Rev.* 16 (1965) 569-70; Alfred Kelly, "The School Desegregation Case," in *Quarrels*

That Have Shaped the Constitution, John Garraty, ed. (New York, 1964) 246-49 (referring to "the Negro's new nationalized political power, his enhanced economic position, and the vast improvement in ideological climate in the country" by the early 1940s).

5. See, e.g., *Hammer* v. *Dagenhart,* 247 U.S. 251 (1918), and *Bailey* v. *Drexel Furniture Co.,* 259 U.S. 20 (1922), invalidating federal laws limiting child labor; and *Carter* v. *Carter Coal Co.,* 298 U.S. 238 (1936), and *United States* v. *Butler,* 297 U.S. 1 (1936), invalidating basic New Deal measures. The latter cases are discussed in Robert Jackson, *The Struggle for Judicial Supremacy* (New York, 1941).

6. Justice, later Chief Justice, Harlan F. Stone, "The Common Law in the United States," *Harv. L. Rev.* 50 (1936) 7, 25. What, however, if it is the Court that imbibes? Nothing, history seems to show, is more intoxicating than unrestrained power.

7. *The Supreme Court and the Idea of Progress* (New York, 1970), 7-8 (citations omitted); *Roe* v. *Wade,* 410 U.S. 113 (1973); *Furman* v. *Georgia,* 408 U.S. 238 (1972).

8. *Green* v. *County School Board of New Kent County,* 391 U.S. 430 (1968).

9. *Swann* v. *Charlotte-Mecklenburg Board of Education,* 402 U.S. 1 (1971).

10. *Milliken* v. *Bradley,* 418 U.S. 717 (1974).

11. Max Friedman, *Roosevelt and Frankfurter* (Boston, 1967), 383.

Chapter 2. *The First Revolution: The Supreme Court Prohibits Racial Segregation*

1. Robert Leflar and Wylie Davis, "Segregation in the Public Schools—1953," *Harv. L. Rev.* 67 (1954) 377, 378-79, n. 3.

2. "There was more to this carefully stage-managed selection of cases for review than meets the naked eye. [Each of the four state cases—from Kansas, Virginia, South Carolina, and Delaware—and the District case represented a different situation.] The NAACP had touched all bases" (Loren Miller, *The Petitioners* [New York, 1967], 344).

3. 347 U.S. 483 (1954); 347 U.S. 497 (1954).

4. See Robert McKay, " 'With All Deliberate Speed': A Study of School Desegregation," *N.Y.U.L. Rev.* 31 (1956) 991, 998: "Any evaluation of the success of that decision, then, requires an analysis of whether the Supreme Court, with or without the assistance of Congress and the President, can make the decision 'stick.' "

5. 42 U.S.C., sects. 1971, 2000 a–h (1970); Public Law No. 88-352, 78 Stat. 241 (July 2, 1964).

6. " 'I think that lawyers and judges too often fail to recognize that *the decision consists in what is done, not what is said by the court in doing it,'* said Judge Cuthbert W. Pound recently. 'Every opinion is to be read with regard to the facts in the case and the question actually decided. . . .' . . . Precedents are to be construed *'as meaning what they ought to mean, rather than what the Judge who writes the opinion says about their meaning.* . . . A bad reason may be given for a good decision.' " (Jerome Frank, *Law and the Modern Mind* [New York, 1930], 126n).

7. Nina Totenberg, "Behind the Marble, Beneath the Robes," *New York Times Magazine*, March 16, 1975, 66.

8. 347 U.S. 489.

9. See, "Southern Declaration on Integration," March 12, 1956, signed by nineteen senators and seventy-seven representatives of the Congress, in *The Struggle for Racial Equality*, ed. Henry Commager (New York, 1967), 55. "Every one of the twenty-six states that had any substantial racial differences among its people either approved the operation of segregated schools already in existence or subsequently established such schools by action of the same law-making body which considered the Fourteenth Amendment" (*ibid.*, 56). Leflar and Davis concluded that even "in the post-Civil War period of ardor for equality" those who "wanted to do away with separate schools for Negroes thought that they had to do it by legislation, which is the way they in fact tried to do it" (385-86). Alexander Bickel, "The Original Understanding and the Segregation Decision," *Harv. L. Rev.* 69 (1955) 58 states: "The obvious conclusion to which the evidence, thus summarized, easily leads is that section 1 of the fourteenth amendment . . . as originally understood, was meant to apply neither to jury service, nor suffrage, nor antimiscegenation statutes, nor segregation." The eminent constitutional historian Alfred H. Kelly, who served as an NAACP consultant in *Brown*, was able to bring himself to argue, however, that the purpose of the amendment as to school segregation was unclear. He later explained that he was faced with "the deadly opposition between my professional integrity . . . and my wishes and hopes with respect to a contemporary question of values, of ideals, of policy, of partisanship, and of political objectives. . . . The problem we faced was not the historian's discovery of the truth" but "the formulation of an adequate gloss on the fateful events of 1866 sufficient to convince the Court that we had something of a historical case. . . . It is not that we were engaged in formulating lies; there was nothing as crude and naive as that. But we were using facts, emphasizing facts, bearing down on facts, sliding off facts, quietly ignoring facts, and above all interpreting facts in a way to do what [NAACP counsel, now justice] Marshall said we had to do—'get by those boys down there' " (quoted in William Harbaugh, *Lawyer's Lawyer: The Life of John W. Davis* [New York, 1973], 510).

10. 347 U.S. 490.

11. 83 U.S. (16 Wallace) 36, 67-72 (1873).

12. 100 U.S. 303, 307-308 (1890); quoted in 347 U.S. 490, n. 5. The Court also cited *Virginia* v. *Rives*, 100 U.S. 313, 318 (1880) and *Ex parte Virginia*, 100 U.S. 339, 344-45 (1880). In *Rives*, the Court had stated that the object of the Fourteenth Amendment "was to place the colored race, in respect of civil rights, upon a level with whites," to make "the rights and responsibilities, civil and criminal, of the two races exactly the same." *Ex parte Virginia* stated that the purpose of the Thirteenth and Fourteenth Amendments "was to raise the colored race . . . into perfect equality of civil rights with all other persons within the

jurisdiction of the States. They were intended to take away all possibility of oppression by law because of race or color."

13. See Charles Black, "The Lawfulness of the Segregation Decisions," *Yale L. J.* 69 (1960) 421.

14. 163 U.S. 537 (1896). The Court had earlier held unconstitutional, as a burden on interstate commerce, a Louisiana law from the Reconstruction period prohibiting racial discrimination in public transportation, *Hall* v. *DeCuir,* 95 U.S. 485 (1877).

15. 163 U.S. 540, 551, 544-45, 550-51. Many of the cases cited by the Court were decided before the adoption of the Fourteenth Amendment and, indeed, before the Civil War. The Court relied particularly on, and closely followed the reasoning of, the then leading case, *Roberts* v. *City of Boston,* 59 Mass. (5 Cush.) 198 (1850).

16. 347 U.S. 497, 500 (1954): "In view of our decision that the Constitution prohibits the States from maintaining racially segregated public schools, it would be unthinkable that the same Constitution would impose a lesser duty on the Federal Government."

17. 163 U.S. 559.

18. 175 U.S. 528 (1899). See Harold Horowitz and Kenneth Karst, *Law, Lawyers and Social Change* (Indianapolis, 1969), 153-54. The former high school for blacks had been converted into additional primary school facilities for blacks. The board of education explained that "it would be unwise and unconscionable to keep up a high school for sixty pupils and turn away three hundred little negroes who are asking to be taught their alphabet and to read and write" (*ibid.,* 533). The Court said that blacks could obtain a high school education in available private schools at no greater cost than in the former public high school for blacks (*ibid.,* 544).

19. See Alan Westin, "John Marshall Harlan and the Constitutional Rights of Negroes: The Transformation of a Southerner," *Yale L. J.* 66 (1957) 637, 663, which notes that in his 1871 campaign for the Kentucky governorship, Harlan had stated that "in the public schools it was obviously 'right and proper' to keep 'whites and blacks separate.' "

20. 211 U.S. 45 (1908). The statute also made it unlawful to attend an integrated school. However, private schools could maintain separate branches for each race provided they were "not less than twenty-five miles distant" (*ibid.,* 59). Justice Harlan again dissented, finding that the statute constituted "an arbitrary invasion of the rights of liberty and property," but adding: "Of course what I have said has no reference to regulations prescribed for public schools, established at the pleasure of the state and maintained at the public expense" (*ibid.,* 67, 69). Justices Oliver Wendell Holmes and William Moody concurred in the Court's decision but not in its opinion. Justice William Day also dissented.

21. 275 U.S. 78 (1927), 80, 85-86, 87, 86.

22. See Jack Greenberg, *Race Relations and American Law* (New York, 1959), 35-39. In 1939 the NAACP Legal Defense and Educational Fund

was incorporated to "aid and direct litigation in the civil rights field" (*ibid.*, 37). Lawyers for the NAACP and the Fund have "presented" every school segregation case decided by the Supreme Court beginning with *Gaines* (*ibid.*, 401-402).

23. 305 U.S. 337 (1938).

24. *Ibid.*, 342, 349.

25. *Ibid.*, 351. Thereafter, "the plaintiff disappeared and no one pressed for [desegregation of the law school]. Subsequently the state erected a colored law school" (Greenberg, 40).

26. 332 U.S 631 (1948).

27. *Fisher* v. *Hurst*, 333 U.S 147, 150 (1948).

28. 339 U.S. 629 (1950), 631, 634.

29. 339 U.S. 637 (1950), 640, 641, 642. The Court also stated: "It may be argued that appellant will be in no better position when these restrictions are removed, for he may still be set apart by his fellow students. This we think irrelevant. There is a vast difference—a Constitutional difference—between restrictions imposed by the state which prohibit the intellectual commingling of students, and the refusal of individuals to commingle where the state presents no such bar." The Court, unfortunately, was unable to see this difference some years later when, as will be seen, it in effect found racial segregation and racial separation equally unconstitutional.

30. 347 U.S. 491, 494.

31. *Ibid.*, 494 and n. 11.

32. See Edmond Cahn, "Jurisprudence," *N.Y.U.L. Rev.* 30 (1955) 150; Morroe Berger, "Desegregation, Law, and Social Science," *Commentary* 23 (1957) 471, 475. See also Herbert Garfinkel, "Social Science Evidence and the School Segregation Cases," *J. Politics* 21 (1959) 37; Ernest Van den Haag, "Social Science Testimony in the Desegregation Cases—A Reply to Professor Kenneth Clark," *Villanova Law Review* 6 (1960) 69; and A. James Gregor, "The Law, Social Science and School Segregation: An Assessment," *W. Res. L. Rev.* 14 (1963) 621.

33. Reprinted, "The Effects of Segregation and the Consequences of Desegregation: A Social Science Statement," *Minnesota Law Review* 37 (1953) 427.

34. Quoted in Cahn, 162-63, Van den Haag, 77.

35. "The Problem of Kenneth Clark," *Commentary* 58 (Nov. 1974) 40.

36. David Cohen, "Segregation, Desegregation, and *Brown*," *Society*, Nov.-Dec. 1974, 39. See below, Ch. 11.

37. See *Stell* v. *Savannah-Chatham City Board of Education*, 220 F. Supp. 667 (S.D. Ga. 1963), reversed, 333 F. 2d 55 (5th Cir.), certiorari denied, 379 U.S. 933 (1964); *Evers* v. *Jackson Municipal School District*, 232 F. Supp. 241 (S.D. Miss. 1964), affirmed, 357 F. 2d 653 (5th Cir., 1966). See *Armstrong* v. *Board of Education*, 333 F. 2d 47, 51 (5th Cir., 1964): "Insofar as the opinions of experts in the fields of psychology and anthropology, in deposition, book and pamphlet form, may constitute

an attack upon the major premise [that separate educational facilities are inherently unequal], they are rejected out of hand."

38. 347 U.S. 497 (1954).

39. "No person shall . . . be deprived of life, liberty, or property without due process of law."

40. 347 U.S. 499, quoting from *Gibson* v. *Mississippi,* 162 U.S. 565, 591 (1896). The Court found it "unthinkable that the same Constitution would impose a lesser duty on the Federal Government" than *Brown* found it imposed on the states, *(ibid.,* 500).Of course, the "same Constitution" does not apply to the states and the federal government; the U.S. Constitution explicitly imposes different limitations on each.

41. *Florida* ex rel. *Hawkins* v. *Board of Control of Florida,* 347 U.S. 971 (1954) (state law school); *Tureaud* v. *Board of Supervisors of Louisiana State University and Agricultural and Mechanical College* (state university), *ibid.;* *Muir* v. *Louisville Park Theatrical Association* (state park), *ibid.*

42. *Mayor of Baltimore* v. *Dawson,* 350 U.S. 877 (1955) (public beaches and bath houses); *Holmes* v. *Atlanta,* 350 U.S. 879 (1955) (municipal golf courses); *Gayle* v. *Browder,* 352 U.S. 903 (1956) (buses).

43. See Herbert Wechsler, "Toward Neutral Principles of Constitutional Law," *Harv. L. Rev.* 73 (1959) 1, 33: "In the context of a charge that segregation *with equal facilities* is a denial of equality, is there not a point in *Plessy* in the statement that if 'enforced separation stamps the colored race with a badge of inferiority' it is solely because its members choose 'to put that construction upon it'?"

44. See Leflar and Davis, 392–404; John Kaplan, "Segregation Litigation and the Schools—Part II: The General Northern Problem," *Northwestern University Law Review* 58 (1963) 157, 162-65. "With the benefit of hindsight, the doctrine of *Plessy* v. *Ferguson* might be counted wrong on another, more pragmatic, ground. It is fair to say that, at least as applied to public education, the separate but equal doctrine in practice had turned out to be a failure. The Negro schools, which were undeniably separate, were generally by no means equal in their most obvious physical characteristics, let alone in more subtle matter such as their quality of education. For instance, in 1950, some 54 years after *Plessy* v. *Ferguson,* Mississippi, which had almost equal numbers of white and Negro students, had half again as many teachers in the white schools. Moreover, the widespread belief that from the 1940's on, the Southern states had moved with great energy and rapidity to ease the obvious inequalities in its schools, seems to be refuted by statistics" (Kaplan, 162-63 [citations omitted]).

45. In addition to Black, Cahn, and Kaplan, see Louis Pollak, "Racial Discrimination and Judicial Integrity: a Reply to Professor Wechsler," *Pennsylvania Law Review* 108 (1959) 1; and Ira Heyman, "The Chief Justice, Racial Segregation, and the Friendly Critics," *Calif. L. Rev.* 49 (1961) 104. But see Owen Fiss, "Racial Imbalance in the Public Schools: The Constitutional Concepts, "*Harv. L. Rev.* 78 (1965) 564. A

decade after *Brown*, Fiss announced that, properly understood, it had been "decided on the basis of the equal-educational-opportunity principle" (594), which, he argued, may require that schools be racially balanced. *Brown*, that is, had not been based on the principle that all racial discrimination by government is prohibited but may, indeed, require racial discrimination by government to increase school racial mixing. One may, of course, distinguish the use of racial discrimination to separate the races from the use of racial discrimination to mix them and attempt to justify the latter while condemning the former. One may not, however, as Fiss and later the Court attempted, justify compulsory integration by merely citing *Brown.* On the contrary, the attempt requires that the force of the principle—all governmental racial discrimination is prohibited—that best and most easily justifies *Brown*—whatever "meaning" can be cabalistically found in *Brown*—be overcome.

46. 347 U.S. 483, Brief for Appellants on Reargument, 15; Leon Friedman, ed., *Argument* (New York, 1969) 47, 402.

Chapter 3. *"With All Deliberate Speed": A Time for Caution*

1. *Brown* v. *Board of Education of Topeka*, 349 U.S. 294, 300-301 (1955).

2. *Ibid.*, 300.

3. Robert McKay, " 'With All Deliberate Speed': A Study of School Desegregation," *N.Y.U.L. Rev.* 31 (1956) 991 (citations omitted).

4. Louis Lusky, "The Stereotype: Hard Core of Racism," *Buffalo Law Review* 13 (1963) 459.

5. 349 U.S. 298, n. 2.

6. James Vander Zanden, *Race Relations in Transition* (New York, 1965), 88.

7. Vander Zanden found that "long drawn-out and complicated policies [of desegregation] appear to maximize confusion and resistance" and "to provide opponents of the plan with an opportunity to regard the issue as essentially open and debatable" (*ibid.*, 76). See also Charles Black, "Paths to Desegregation"(1957), in *The Occasions of Justice* (New York, 1963), 144. Cf. *History of the Supreme Court of the United States*, Vol. VI, Charles Fairman, *Reconstruction and Reunion, 1864–88*, Part I (New York, 1971), 350: Following the Civil War, southern leaders argued regarding the question of granting black male suffrage, "We cannot be expected to cut off our own heads, but we are willing that you should order them cut off. . . . If you want our state reconstructed on the basis of universal suffrage say so, order it done, prescribe the manner in which it shall be done, and then we can do it. But for us to volunteer action in that direction would be to excite a storm against ourselves."

8. Alexander Bickel, "The Decade of School Desegregation: Progress and Prospects," *Colum. L. Rev.* 64 (1964) 193-203.

9. See Louis Lusky, "Racial Discrimination and the Federal Law: A Problem in Nullification," *Colum L. Rev.* 63 (1963) 1172, n. 37; and J. W. Peltason, *Fifty-eight Lonely Men* (New York, 1961).

10. Lusky, "Racial Discrimination," 1172, n. 37.

11. Lusky, "The Stereotype," 457-58.

12. See below, Ch.6.

13. In addition to cases cited in Chapter 2, nn. 41 and 42, see *New Orleans City Park Improvement Association* v. *Detiege,* 358 U.S. 54 (1958) (public parks and golf courses); *State Athletic Commission* v. *Dorsey,* 359 U.S. 533 (1959) (athletic contests); *Turner* v. *Memphis,* 369 U.S. 350 (1962) (airport restaurant); *Johnson* v. *Virginia,* 373 U.S. 61 (1963) (courtroom seating); *Schiro* v. *Bynum,* 375 U.S. 395 (1964) (municipal auditorium).

14. 358 U.S. 1 (1958); 358 U.S. 101 (1958). Developments in the lower courts and elsewhere up to 1957 are described in Robert McKay, " 'With All Deliberate Speed': Legislative Reaction and Judicial Development, 1956-1957," *Va. L. Rev.* 43 (1957) 1205, and Don Shoemaker, ed., *With All Deliberate Speed* (New York, 1957).

15. See McKay, 991; and Daniel Meador, "The Constitution and the Assignment of Pupils to Public Schools," *Va. L. Rev.* 45 (1959) 517.

16. *Briggs* v. *Elliott,* 132 F. Supp. 776, 777 (E.D.S.C. 1955). This view was quickly affirmed by the courts of appeals for the Fifth and the Fourth Circuits, the courts with jurisdiction over the states of the deep South (the Fifth Circuit consists of Texas, Louisiana, Mississippi, Alabama, Georgia, and Florida; the Fourth includes South Carolina, North Carolina, and Virginia). See *Avery* v. *Wichita Falls Independent School District,* 241 F. 2d 230 (5th Cir.), certiorari denied, 353 U.S. 938 (1957) (quoting *Briggs* v. *Elliott* with approval); and *School Board of the City of Charlottesville, Virginia* v. *Allen,* 240 F. 2d 59, 62 (4th Cir., 1956), certiorari denied, 353 U.S. 911 (1957) (the Supreme Court did "not compel the mixing of the races in the public schools. . . . Consequently, compliance with the ruling may well not necessitate such extensive changes in the school system as some anticipate"). In *Rippy* v. *Borders,* 250 F. 2d 690, 692 (1957), the Fifth Circuit reversed a district court decision because it prohibited a school district not only from requiring but from *"permitting segregation of the races"* (italics in the original).

17. *Carson* v. *Warlick,* 238 F. 2d 724 (4th Cir., 1956), certiorari denied, 353 U.S. 910 (1957). See also *Carson* v. *Board of Education,* 227 F. 2d 789 (4th Cir., 1955), an earlier opinion in the same case. Racial assignment, combined with the "remedy" provided by a pupil placement law, was upheld as constituting the ending of segregation as late as 1959 (*Covington* v. *Edwards,* 264 F. 2d 780 [4th Cir., 1959]). See also *Holt* v. *Raleigh City Board of Education,* 265 F. 2d 95 (4th Cir.), certiorari denied, 361 U.S. 818 (1959).

18. 358 U.S. 8, 15, 7.

19. The situation at the time is indicated by the fact that the Court felt it useful to insist that *Brown* would not be overruled. *Brown,* it stated, had been unanimously decided only after "the most serious consideration," and the three new justices who had come to the

Court since *Brown* "are at one with the Justices still on the Court who participated in that basic decision as to its correctness, and that decision is now unanimously reaffirmed" (*ibid.,*19). Also, the opinion, for the first and only time in the Court's history, was signed by (that is, issued under the names of) all of the justices.

20. 358 U.S. 101 (1958).

21. Ala. Code, Title LII, sect. 61 (4) (1960).

22. *Ibid.,* sect. 61 (8).

23. Except that, according to counsel for the plaintiffs, "one Negro child was placed in a school designated as a White school but he was removed three weeks hence because of community pressure and ill will generated by the pressure" (*Shuttlesworth* v. *Birmingham Board of Education,* 162 F. Supp. 372, 382, n. 11 [N.D. Ala. 1958]).

24. *Ibid.,* 384 (italics in the original). The court found that the plaintiffs had not shown the act to be "utterly void in toto," and it could not say that the act "will not be properly and constitutionally administered" (*ibid.,* 382). Cf. the earlier decisions in *Bush* v. *Orleans Parish School Board,* 138 F. Supp. 337 (E.D. La. 1956), affirmed, 242 F. 2d 156 (5th Cir.), certiorari denied, 354 U.S. 921 (1957), and *Adkins* v. *School Board of City of Newport News,* 148 F. Supp. 430 (E.D. Va. 1957), affirmed, 246 F. 2d 325 (4th Cir.), 355 U.S. 855 (1957), holding unconstitutional, respectively, the pupil placement laws of Louisiana and Virginia.

25. 358 U.S. 101 (1958).

26. Meador, 542-43.

27. *Education: United States Commission on Civil Rights Report,* Book II (Washington, D.C., 1961), 8.

28. *McNeese* v. *Board of Education,* 373 U.S. 668 (1963), made clear that the exhaustion of administrative remedies could no longer be required. See *Green* v. *School Board of City of Roanoke,* 304 F. 2d 118 (4th Cir., 1962); *Bush* v. *Orleans Parish School Board,* 308 F. 2d 491 (5th Cir., 1962); and *Northcross* v. *Board of Education of City of Memphis, Tennessee,* 302 F. 2d 818 (6th Cir., 1962). But see *Calhoun* v. *Latimer,* 321 F. 2d 302 (5th Cir., 1963), approving a pupil placement plan under which desegregation was not to reach all grades until 1970. The Supreme Court granted certiorari, but instead of reversing outright, remanded the case to the district court for further consideration in light of certain modifications of the plan that had been adopted in the interim and in light of intervening decisions indicating that greater speed might be required (377 U.S. 263 [1964]).

29. 373 U.S. 683 (1963), 687, 688, 687, 689.

30. *Ibid.,* 689. A week earlier, in *Watson* v. *City of Memphis,* 373 U.S. 526, 530 (1963), involving racial segregation in the use of public parks and recreational facilities, the Court had said: "Given the extended time which has elapsed, it is far from clear that the mandate of the second *Brown* decision requiring that desegregation proceed with 'all deliberate speed' would today be fully satisfied by types of plans or programs

for desegregation of public educational facilities which eight years ago
might have been deemed sufficient."

31. 377 U.S. 218 (1964), 221.

32. *Ibid.,* 233, 234.

33. Prince Edward County thereafter appropriated money for the
reopening of public schools. The Fourth Circuit then enjoined the
county from making tuition grants to private schools even though the
public schools were open (*Griffin* v. *County School Board of Prince Edward
County,* 339 F. 2d 486 [1964]). The result of all this by 1968 was that
all but 8 of the 1,600 pupils in the county public schools were black;
1,200 whites attended privately supported schools; and 200 whites, unable
to afford tuition payments, attended no school (Harold Horowitz and
Kenneth Karst, *Law, Lawyers and Social Change* [Indianapolis, 1969], 273,
citing Jacoby, "Prince Edward County: Back Where They Started,"
Washington *Post,* March 24, 1968, Potomac section, p. 22).

34. *The Supreme Court and the Idea of Progress* (New York, 1970), 175.

35. *Bradley* v. *School Board of the City of Richmond, Virginia,* 382 U.S.
103, 105 (1965); *Rogers* v. *Paul,* 382 U.S. 198, 199 (1965).

36. *Rogers* v. *Paul,* 200.

37. E.g., *Kemp* v. *Beasley,* 352 F. 2d 14 (8th Cir., 1965) (complete
desegregation by the 1967-1968 school year).

38. 396 U.S. 19, 20 (1969).

39. Bickel, "The Decade of School Desegregation," p. 214.

Chapter 4. *The First Revolution Succeeds—and Brings a Call for a New Crusade*

1. 42 U.S.C., sects. 1971, 2000 a–h (1970); Public Law No. 88-352,
78 Stat. 241.

2. 42 U.S.C., sect. 2000 c–6 (1974), 78 Stat. 248; sect. 2000c (b) (1974),
78 Stat. 246; sect. 2000c-6(A) (1974), 78 Stat. 248; sect. 2000c-9
(1974), 78 Stat. 249.

3. 42 U.S.C., sect. 2000d (1974), 78 Stat. 252; sect. 2000d-1; sect.
2000d-2 (1974), 78 Stat. 253.

4. U.S. Commission on Civil Rights, *Survey of School Desegregation in
the Southern and Border States, 1965-66* (Washington, D.C., 1966), 2;
20 U.S.C., sect. 241a, 79 Stat. 27 (1965). As stated in the *Survey of School
Desegregation.* (2): "With funds of such magnitude at stake, most school
systems would be placed at a serious disadvantage by termination of
Federal assistance."

5. 110 *Cong. Rec.* 1518, 6539, 6545, 6552, 6560 (1964).

6. *Ibid.,* 12714.

7. *Ibid.,* 12715.

8. 324 F. 2d 209, 213 (7th Cir., 1963), quoting from *Brown* v. *Board of
Education,* 139 F. Supp. 468, 470 (1955), and the district court opinion
in *Bell,* 213 F. Supp. 819, 829 (N.D. Ind. 1963).

9. 110 *Cong. Rec.* 12715 (1964).

10. *Ibid.,* 12715-16.

11. *Ibid.,* 12716-17.

12. *Ibid.,* 12717.

13. "Policies and Guidelines for School Desegregation," *Hearings before the Committee on Rules, House of Representatives, on H. Res. 826,* 89th Cong., 2d sess. (1966), part 2, 89-90.

14. 45 C.F.R. 80 (1964). The Office of Education acted through a section first called the Office of Equal Opportunity and later the Equal Educational Opportunity Program.

15. "General Statement of Policies under Title VI of the Civil Rights Act of 1964 Respecting Desegregation of Elementary and Secondary Schools." This first edition was never published in the Federal Register, as are official government regulations. It is printed as an appendix to *Price* v. *Denison Independent School District Board of Education,* 348 F. 2d 1010, 1015 (5th Cir., 1965).

16. This alternative was somewhat obscured, however, by an additional requirement of assurance that there did not "remain any other practices characteristic of dual or segregated school systems."

17. E.g., *Bradley* v. *School Board of City of Richmond, Virginia,* 345 F. 2d 310 (4th Cir., 1965) *(en banc)*; *Lockett* v. *Board of Education of Muscogee/County School District,* 342 F. 2d 225 (5th Cir., 1965); *Kemp* v. *Beasley,* 352 F. 2d 14 (8th Cir., 1965).

18. *Singleton* v. *Jackson Municipal Separate School District,* 348 F. 2d 729 (5th Cir., 1965); *ibid.,* 355 F. 2d 865 (5th Cir., 1966). To adopt a more lenient requirement in passing on the constitutionality of a plan would, the court said, encourage litigation, because compliance with a court decree was accepted by the guidelines as compliance with the act.

19. 42 U.S.C. Ch. 20A (1970); 71 Stat. 634.

20. U.S. Commission on Civil Rights, *Survey of School Desegregation.*

21. "Is Busing Necessary?" *Commentary,* 53 (March 1972) 39.

22. U.S. Commission on Civil Rights, *Survey of School Desegregation,* 29.

23. *Ibid.,* 53, 54.

24. 45 C.F.R., sect. 181 (1967).

25. *Ibid.,* sect. 181.11; sect. 181.33(b); sect. 181.12.

26. *Ibid.,* sect. 181.54(c), (d); sect. 181.54 (d); sect. 181.54(f)(1).

27. "Policies and Guidelines for School Desegregation," 30–34.

28. 372 F. 2d 836 (1966), affirmed *en banc,* 380 F. 2d 385 (5th Cir., 1967), certiorari denied, 389 U.S. 840 (1967), 372 F. 2d 851, 849.

29. *Ibid.,* 848; 846, n. 5; 855.

30. *Ibid.,* at 846, n. 5; 845-46; 846-47, n. 5.

31. *The Spirit of Liberty,* ed. I. Dillard (3d ed.; New York, 1960), 131. Throughout its opinion, the court employed standards of advocacy that would be questionable for a professed advocate. For example, the court quoted extensively from a district court opinion—*Barksdale* v. *Springfield School Committee,* 237 F. Supp. 543 (D. Mass. 1965)—that, it said, could not "accept the view in *Bell* [v. *School City of Gary, Indiana;* see n. 8, above]

that only forced segregation is" unconstitutional. It then stated that "on appeal, the First Circuit accepted the district court's finding of fact though vacating the district court's order and dismissing the complaint" (372 F. 2d 874-75). In fact, however, the First Circuit in that case had cited *Bell* with approval and expressly disapproved of the district court's view on the question of constitutionality (348 F. 2d 261, 264 [1965]).

32. 372 F. 2d, 861, 849.

33. As Senator Humphrey put it: "If anyone can be against that, he can be against Mother's Day. How can anyone justify discrimination in the use of Federal funds and Federal programs?" (110 *Cong. Rec.* 6543 [1964]).

34. 372 F. 2d 878.

35. See 110 *Cong. Rec.* 1598 (1964).

36. *Ibid.,* 2280. Congressman Celler, chairman of the House Judiciary Committee and floor manager of the bill, stated, "The amendment offered by the gentleman from Florida is acceptable"; it was thereupon adopted by the House (*ibid.*).

37. Senator John Pastore of Rhode Island had defended Title VI against the accusation of regionalism by declaring that all rules and regulations pursuant to it "must be national. They must apply to all fifty states. We could not draw one rule to apply to the State of Mississippi, another rule to apply to the State of Alabama, and another rule to apply to the State of Rhode Island. There must be only one rule, to apply to every state" (110 *Cong. Rec.* 7059 [1964]).

38. 372 F. 2d 881.

39. See above, pp. 49, 51.

40. 213 F. Supp. 822.

41. 372 F. 2d 910, 906.

42. *United States* v. *Jefferson County Board of Education,* 380 F. 2d 385, 389 (1967).

43. " 'In the South,' as the Civil Rights Commission has pointed out, the Negro 'has struggled to get into the neighborhood school. In the North, he is fighting to get out of it' " (*ibid.,* 389, n. 1).

44. *Ibid.,* 389, 390.

45. *Ibid.,* 397, 404, 405.

46. *Ibid.,* 406, 407, 409.

47. *Ibid.,* 412, 414.

48. *Ibid.,* 418.

49. *Ibid.,* 419-20.

50. *Ibid.,* 421.

51. *Caddo Parish School Board* v. *United States,* 389 U.S. 840 (1967).

52. *Bowman* v. *County School Board of Charles City County, Virginia,* 382 F. 2d 326, 327 (4th Cir., 1967) (*en banc*) ("Compulsory assignments to achieve a greater inter-mixture of the races" are not required); *Green* v. *County School Board of New Kent County, Virginia,* 382 F. 2d 338 (4th Cir., 1967) (companion to *Bowman*), reversed, 391 U.S. 430 (1968);

Monroe v. *Board of Commissioners, City of Jackson, Tennessee,* 380 F. 2d 955, 958 (6th Cir., 1969) ("To apply a disparate rule" to the South "would be in the nature of imposing a judicial Bill of Attainder"); *Mapp* v. *Board of Education of City of Chattanooga, Tennessee,* 373 F. 2d 75, 78 (6th Cir., 1967) (There is no "constitutional duty to balance the races in the school system in conformity with some mathematical formula"); *Raney* v. *Board of Education of Gould School District,* 381 F. 2d 252 (8th Cir., 1967), reversed, 391 U.S. 443 (1968). But cf. *Kemp* v. *Beasley,* 352 F. 2d 14 (8th Cir., 1965), 389 F. 2d 178 (1968), and *Board of Education of Oklahoma City Public Schools* v. *Dowell,* 375 F. 2d 158 (10th Cir., 1967).

Chapter 5. The Second Revolution: The Supreme Court Requires School Racial Integration in the South

1. 391 U.S. 430 (1968).
2. A brief history of Virginia's initial response to *Brown* is given in *NAACP* v. *Patty,* 159 F. Supp. 503 (E.D. Va., 1958).
3. 391 U.S. 430 (1968), Record, 53a–61a.
4. 391 U.S. 430 (1968), Brief for Petitioners, 8.
5. *Bowman* v. *County School Board of Charles City County, Virginia,* 382 F. 2d 327, 328 (1967), which was made the basis for the disposition of *Green* (*ibid.,* 338), a companion case. Two judges dissented in both cases, favoring the approach of the Fifth Circuit in *United States* v. *Jefferson County Board of Education.* In a revealing commentary on the influences operating on judges, they pointed out: "A recent article in the Virginia Law Review declares the Fifth Circuit to be 'at once the most prolific and the most progressive court in the nation on the subject of school desegregation'" (*Bowman,* 331, n. 6). James Dunn, author of the encomium, was the legal advisor to the Equal Educational Opportunities Program, U.S. Office of Education. He was also of the opinion that "racial balance in the legal sense is a singularly northern concept which has no application in the South" ("Title VI, the Guidelines and School Segregation in the South," *Va. L. Rev.* 53 [1967] 78).
6. 391 U.S. 433, n. 2; 432.
7. *Ibid.,* 435.
8. *Ibid.,* 435–36.
9. E.g., *Brown* I was "fourteen years ago" (*ibid.,* 435); it was now "thirteen years after *Brown II*" (437) (see below, p. 72).
10. *Ibid.,* 437–39.
11. *Ibid.,* 441.
12. *Ibid.,* 439, 442.
13. 391 U.S. 443 (1968).
14. 381 F. 2d 252, 256 (1967).
15. 391 U.S., 447–48.
16. 391 U.S. 450 (1958).
17. 380 F. 2d 955 (1967), 958.
18. 391 U.S. 458, 459.

19. *Ibid.* See below, pp. 81–82.

20. See *Moses* v. *Washington Parish School Board*, 276 F. Supp. 834, 851-52 (E.D. La. 1967). The district judge's opinion in this case is also noteworthy for its exceptionally clear and thoughtful statement of reasons for rejecting the argument—adopted in *Green*—that a constitutional requirement of integration can be found in *Brown*. The judge pointed out the confusion resulting from use of the term "desegregation plan," after the time for delay in ending segregation had ended, and of the terms "*de facto*" and "*de jure* segregation": "The term '*de jure* segregation' means simply 'segregation' in the traditional sense" (*ibid.*, 840). He rejected the argument that "educational opportunities of Negro students are unequal, can never be equal, unless they are placed in classes with white students" (843). "No one could dispute" that *Brown* was "directed solely at *de jure* segregation—segregation imposed by the State." He concluded, "Those who wish to rule *de facto* segregation unconstitutional must come to reasonable, logical and proper legal conclusions of their own to support this position" (840-41).

21. See Christopher Jencks *et al.*, *Inequality* (New York, 1972), 40: "In principle, we believe that an ideal pupil assignment system should give every student an opportunity to attend any public school he (or his parents) find appealing. Indeed, we would go so far as to *define* a 'public' school as one that is open to any student who wants to attend. All other schools, regardless of formal control or financing, are to some degree 'private.'"

22. For example, Title II of the 1964 Civil Rights Act, prohibiting racial discrimination in places of public accommodation, exempts a landlord who rents no more than five rooms in a place he occupies as his residence (42 U.S.C. sect. 2000a(b)(1) (1974). See *Springfield School Committee* v. *Barksdale*, 348 F. 2d 261, 264, n. 7 (1st Cir., 1965): Geographic school assignment may "in fact serve to foster ethnic similarities and prejudice. However, all furtherance of security and mutual interests does not fall into negative categories." See also *Moose Lodge No. 107* v. *Irvis*, 407 U.S. 163 (1972) (permitting racial discrimination by a private club.)

23. The Court also quoted the "views of the United States Commission on Civil Rights, which we neither adopt nor refuse to adopt" (391 U.S. 440–41, n. 5): The Commission found that "freedom of choice plans . . . have tended to perpetuate racially identifiable schools in the Southern and border States" because many blacks were deterred from choosing formerly white schools by "fear of retaliation and hostility from the white community," "threats of violence and economic reprisal by white persons," "harassment by white classmates," improper influence by public officials, and "poverty." "Some Negro parents are embarrassed to permit their children to attend such schools without suitable clothing." Finall "improvements in facilities and equipment . . . have been instituted all-Negro schools in some school districts in a manner that tends discourage Negroes from selecting white schools."

24. *Civil Rights Cases*, 109 U.S. 3, 25 (1883).

25. The 1965 Voting Rights Act, 42 U.S.C. sects. 1971, 1972–1973p. (1970), 79 Stat. 437, required drastic but effective measures to prevent denial of the right to vote on grounds of race. The 1968 Civil Rights Act, Title VIII (Fair Housing), 42 U.S.C., sects. 3601 ff (1970), 82 Stat. 81, prohibited racial discrimination in the sale or rental of most housing.

26. The court in *Moses* (847) prohibited freedom of choice and required geographic assignment basically on this ground. The court explicitly rejected "the theory that 'free-choice' has not 'worked' to integrate the school system and that a different method must therefore be tried." Plaintiffs in *Green* cited and quoted from *Moses* on the unworkability of free-choice plans. (Brief for Petitioners, 19-20, 391 U.S. 430 [1968]). Defendants did not argue for the *Moses* approach because for their objective—retention of freedom of choice—it went too far; the Court did not adopt the *Moses* approach because for the Court's objective—compulsory integration—it did not go far enough.

27. E.g., mandatory statement of choice in writing upon entering school or a school of the next level or at the end or beginning of each school year. Such procedural protections had been worked out in detail by the courts and 1966 guidelines prior to *Green*.

28. U.S. Commission on Civil Rights, *Racial Isolation in the Public Schools* (Washington, D.C., 1967), 199.

29. See above, Ch. 3, n. 33. A dissenting opinion in *Jefferson County*, 380 F. 2d 416, n. 6, pointed out that the result of "desegregation" in Taliaferro County, Georgia, was the conversion of a school system with 600 blacks and 200 whites in 1965 to one with 527 blacks and no whites in 1967.

30. The school board's brief in *Raney* stated that in the Lynwood School District of Jefferson County, Arkansas, adjacent to Gould, "62 white children enrolled with over 300 Negro students during 1966-67" under freedom of choice, but that following consolidation of the district's two schools (one school for all children in grades 1 through 4 and one for grades 5 through 8) in 1968, all but two whites left the system. The brief also stated that under freedom of choice in Gould, "every white child in the district is attending an integrated school where Negro students exceed 20% of the student body" (Brief for Respondents, 63-64).

31. To the Civil Rights Commission, ironically, the fact that freedom of choice may lead to "improvements in facilities and equipment . . . in all-Negro schools" is an additional reason to condemn it. See above, n. 23.

32. Jencks *et al.*, 40-41.

33. 391 U.S. 459.

34. 391 U.S. 450 (1968), Brief for Respondents, 54.

35. 391 U.S. 459.

36. *Terminiello* v. *Chicago*, 337 U.S. 1, 37 (1949) (dissenting opinion): "There is danger that, if the Court does not temper its doctrinaire logic

with a little practical wisdom, it will convert the constitutional Bill of Rights into a suicide pact."

37. See above, in Ch. 4, "The 1964 Civil Rights Act."

38. See Harold Horowitz, "The Misleading Search for 'State Action' under the Fourteenth Amendment," *Southern California Law Review* 30 (1957) 208; Charles Black, " 'State Action,' Equal Protection, and California's Proposition 14," *Harv. L. Rev.* 81 (1967) 69; and Owen Fiss, "Racial Imbalance in the Public Schools: The Constitutional Concepts," *Harv. L. Rev.* 78 (1965) 564.

39. See Karl Taeuber, "Residential Segregation," *Scientific American* 213 (Aug. 1965) 14: "A high degree of residential segregation based on race is a universal characteristic of American cities. This segregation is found in the cities of the North and West as well as of the South; in large cities with hundreds of thousands of Negro residents as well as those with only a few thousand, and in cities that are progressive in their employment practices and civil rights policies as well as those that are not."

40. See the excellent discussion in Frank Goodman, "De Facto School Segregation: A Constitutional and Empirical Analysis," *Calif. L. Rev.* 60 (1972) 275.

41. See 118 *Cong. Rec.* 564 (1972). HEW estimated that in 1971, 43.9 percent of black public school pupils attended majority-white schools in the eleven states of the deep South, while only 27.8 percent did so in the North and West.

42. See A. James Gregor, "The Law, Social Science, and School Segregation: An Assessment," *Wes. Reserve L. Rev.* 14 (1963) 635: Desegregation requires that white children "be exposed to members of a group possessed, whatever the ultimate cause, of a higher index of delinquency, immorality, and communicable disease as well as a lower index of academic performance. . . . Real differences between the two racial groups exist as a concrete fact."

43. "All rights," Justice Holmes pointed out, "tend to declare themselves absolute to their logical extreme. Yet all in fact are limited by the neighborhood of principles of policy which are other than those on which the particular right is founded, and which become strong enough to hold their own when a certain point is reached" (*Hudson County Water Company* v. *McCarter*, 209 U.S. 349, 355 [1908]).

44. John Kaplan, "Segregation Litigation and the Schools,—Part II: The General Northern Problem," *Northwestern University Law Review* 58 (1963) 188. Kaplan pointed out that to require racial classifications to increase integration "is a much more drastic step than merely allowing" them (*ibid.*, n. 75). Some of the extremely difficult problems caused by merely allowing official racial discrimination to increase integration or to give preference to blacks are excellently discussed by Boris Bittker, in "The Case of the Checker-board Ordinance: An Experiment in Race Relations," *Yale L.J.* 71 (1962) 1387. But see Paul Freund, *On Law*

and Justice (Cambridge, Mass., 1968), 44-47.

45. Kaplan, 183.

46. *History of the Supreme Court of the United States,* Vol. VI, Charles Fairman, *Reconstruction and Reunion, 1864–88,* Part I (New York, 1971), 1258, referring to the Court's decision in *Jones* v. *Mayer,* 392 U.S. 409 (1968), that the Civil Rights Act of 1866 was meant to prohibit racial discrimination by private individuals. Rarely has a Court decision received so informed and capable an analysis or has the impropriety of the Court's performance in reaching a decision been so fully documented. Fairman concluded that the Court "appears to have had no feeling for the truth of history" and "allowed itself to believe impossible things" (*ibid.*).

47. The American Jewish Congress also filed an *amicus* brief urging reversal of the courts of appeals' decisions. Nothing better indicates, perhaps, the "spirit of the times" than that a return to racial classification should be supported by spokesmen for a group with so much to lose. It was not long before Jewish spokesmen were among the strongest opponents of racial classification, as almost any issue of *Commentary,* published by the American Jewish Committee, will indicate; see Nathan Glazer and Milton Himmelfarb, "McGovern and the Jews: A Debate," *Commentary* 54 (Sept. 1972) 43; and Norman Podhoretz, "Is It Good for the Jews?" *Commentary* 53 (Feb. 1972) 7. In *De Funis* v. *Odegaard,* 416 U.S. 312 (1974), the American Jewish Congress and the Anti-Defamation League of B'nai B'rith filed briefs urging the Court to hold racial discrimination "in favor" of blacks and other "minorities" (not including Jews) unconstitutional.

Chapter 6. *Caution Turns to Wrath: Racial Integration "at Once"*

1. 395 U.S. 225 (1969), 232.

2. *Montgomery County Board of Education* v. *Carr,* 400 F. 2d 1, 8 (5th Cir., 1968) (italics in the original). The decision was by Judge Walter Gewin, a dissenter in *Jefferson County,* joined by a district judge sitting by designation. Judge Thorneberry dissented (402 F. 2d 784).

3. 395 U.S. 230 (1969).

4. *Ibid.,* 228, 235.

5. *Ibid.,* 236.

6. 396 U.S. 19 (1969), 20.

7. *United States* v. *Hinds County School Board,* 417 F. 2d 852 (1969), certiorari denied, 396 U.S. 1032 (1970).

8. See *Alexander* v. *Holmes County Board of Education,* 396 U.S. 1218 (Hugo Black, circuit justice).

9. *Ibid.,* 1222.

10. 396 U.S. 20.

11. *Singleton* v. *Jackson Municipal Separate School District,* 419 F. 2d 1211, 1216, 1217, n. 1, certiorari denied, 396 U.S. 1032 (1969).

12. 396 U.S. 290, 291 (1970).

13. 396 U.S. 291, 292, 293.

14. *Ibid.*, 293-94. See Judge John Brown's summary of these events in *United States* v. *Texas Education Agency*, 467 F. 2d 848, 891 (5th Cir., 1972) (dissenting opinion): In *Alexander*, the Fifth Circuit was "summarily reversed" for granting "a modest request delivered safehand by air courier by the Secretary of HEW to the Chief Judge at his home for a 60-day extension of the effective date of a plan for some 20 Mississippi school districts." On remand, the court, "in recognition of the late time in the school year, . . . again thought that there was a reasonable basis for a postponement of pupil assignment until the next September at the commencement of the next school year. With the ink scarcely dry on our order, we were told again in positive terms [in *Carter*] to get on with the business—the business we had tried so hard to prosecute since 1957!"

15. *Singleton* v. *Jackson Municipal Separate School District*, 425 F. 2d 1211 (5th Cir., 1970), 1217-24.

16. 397 U.S. 232 (1970).

17. *Northcross* v. *Board of Education of the Memphis, Tennessee, City Schools*, 420 F. 2d 546, 548 (1970).

18. *Ibid.*

19. 397 U.S. 235.

20. *Ibid.*, 237. Among the problems were "Whether, as a constitutional matter, any particular racial balance must be achieved in the schools; to what extent school districts and zones may or must be altered as a constitutional matter; and to what extent transportation may or must be provided to achieve the ends sought by prior holdings of the Court."

21. See the dissenting opinion of Judge Martin Van Oosterhaut in *Clark* v. *Board of Education of Little Rock School District*, 426 F. 2d 1035, 1046 (8th Cir., 1970), certiorari denied, 402 U.S. 952 (1971), relying on Chief Justice Burger's opinion for the view that racial balance was not required.

22. See Judge Clark's dissenting opinion in *Singleton*, 425 F. 2d 1221: "Certainly the court doesn't make today's decree because it got mad at the school district litigants when they were found to be circumstanced as they are. It's also implausible that the hasty action, taken without any real semblance of the usual briefing and argument, could be predicated on a feeling 'We have these people on the run—don't let them catch their breath.' "

23. 397 U.S. 237.

24. *Singleton*, 425 F. 2d 1219-20 (dissenting opinion) (bracketed insertion by Judge Clark).

25. See *Adams* v. *Matthews*, 403 F. 2d 181 (5th Cir., 1968) (forty-four cases); *Hall* v. *St. Helena Parish School Board*, 417 F. 2d 801 (5th Cir.), certiorari denied, 396 U.S. 904 (1969) (thirty-eight cases); *United States* v. *Hinds County School Board*, 417 F. 2d 852 (5th Cir.), certiorari denied, 396 U.S. 1032 (1969) (twenty-five cases).

26. See Judge Clark's dissenting opinion in *Singleton,* 425 F. 2d 1218, 1220: "If our remedy is unreasoned and so abrupt that the non-Negro community exercises its freedom and withdraws its participation and support for a public school or a public school system, then in the end we have remedied nothing in that school or district. This is not specious speculation. It is happening at this very moment in districts before us today. . . . One thing is sure—what we do here today has the greatest possible potential for creation of all-black school systems within many of the counties and parishes before us." Judges J. Braxton Craven, Clement Haynsworth, and Albert Bryan, dissenting and concurring, in *Brunson v. Board of Trustees of School District No. 1 of Clarendon County, South Carolina,* 429 F. 2d 820, 821-22 (4th Cir., 1970), stated: "Constitutional principles may not be allowed to yield to community opposition" but "judges in fashioning remedies cannot successfully ignore reality." "The extreme remedy proposed by HEW and approved by this court threatens to swallow up, rather than vindicate, the constitutional mandate for integrated schools in" a district with a "ten to one ratio of black to white students." "In 1969, 110 white students fled the public school system" to a private school, "leaving only 256 white students in the public schools." It appears "that approximately 100 more white students" will leave in 1970. This suggests "that some degree of moderation in selecting a remedy" may accomplish more integration than will an "unyielding fidelity to the arithmetic of race. It will be ironic, and contrary to the spirit of *Brown* . . . , if the result of application of the *Brown* constitutional principle in this case is simply to accomplish an all-black school system."

27. *Singleton,* 419 F. 2d 1211 (1969).

28. *Adams* v. *Matthews,* 188.

29. A district court judge, sitting by designation, was the third member. The full Fifth Circuit bench at this time consisted of fifteen judges in "regular service" and four "senior judges" (semiretired). Except when the court sat *en banc,* results in "desegregation" cases, given the uncertainty of the *Green* requirement, varied widely, depending on particular (three-judge) panels.

30. *Ellis* v. *Board of Public Instruction of Orange County, Florida,* 423 F. 2d 203 (5th Cir., 1970). The various modifications ordered by the court in the plan approved by the district court reduced the number of all black schools in the system (18 percent black) from eleven, with 51 percent of the blacks, to three, with 16 percent. Most of the schools thereby "desegregated," however, had only a very small number of whites. The court's geographic requirement was so strict that traffic conditions had to be ignored in drawing zone boundaries where the effect was to assign an additional 53 whites to a school with 404 blacks and 48 other whites.

31. *Mannings* v. *Board of Public Instruction of Hillsborough County, Florida,* 427 F. 2d 874 (5th Cir., 1970). Pairing consists of treating two

schools as a unit and assigning all of the students involved to one school for some grades (e.g., 1 to 4) and to the other school for the remaining grades (e.g., 5 to 8). The court found that such pairing did not require "departing from neighborhood school concepts" (*ibid.*, 877) and was "singularly distinguishable from the grouping of several schools, located in other than a neighborhood area, into one group for assignment purposes in order to manipulate racial balances through inordinate transportation requirements" (*ibid.*, 877, n. 2). The court-ordered plan reduced the number of all black schools in the system (19 percent black) from nineteen, with 60 percent of the blacks, to eight, with 21 percent. Again, however, many of the newly "desegregated" schools remained very largely black.

32. *Davis* v. *Board of School Commissioners of Mobile County*, 430 F. 2d 883 (5th Cir., 1970), reversed 402 U.S. 33 (1971) (the number of all black schools was reduced from nineteen with 60 percent of the blacks to eight with 23 percent); *Wright* v. *Board of Public Education of Alachua County*, 431 F. 2d 1200 (5th Cir., 1970).

33. E.g., *Andrews* v. *City of Monroe*, 425 F. 2d 1017 (5th Cir., 1970); *Bradley* v. *Board of Public Instruction of Pinellas County, Florida*, 431 F. 2d 1377 (5th Cir., 1970), certiorari denied, 402 U.S. 943 (1971); *Allen* v. *Board of Public Instruction of Broward County, Florida*, 432 F. 2d 362 (5th Cir., 1970); *Valley* v. *Rapides Parish School Board*, 434 F. 2d 144 (5th Cir., 1970); *Ross* v. *Eckels*, 434 F. 2d 1140 (5th Cir., 1970); *Pate* v. *Dade County School Board*, 434 F. 2d 1151 (5th Cir., 1970). Clustering is similar to pairing, except that more than two schools are involved. In *Andrews* the board was required to close a school valued at two million dollars. In *Allen* the closing of schools in black neighborhoods was required despite protests by blacks. In *Singleton*, 432 F. 2d 927, the Fifth Circuit reversed the district court's acceptance of a plan prepared by a biracial committee (six blacks named by plaintiffs and six whites named by the school board) because the plan left too great a percentage of blacks in all black schools in the majority-black Jackson, Mississippi, school system. The court, however, expressed the "confident hope that a constitutional unitary system will be established" after one more district court hearing.

34. *Andrews*, 1021; *Bradley*, 1381.

35. See *Bradley*, 1380 (14.2 percent of the blacks were left in all black schools); *Ross*, 1140, 1148 (fifteen all black or nearly all black schools remained); *Pate*, 1151, 1154 (24 percent of the blacks were left in all black or nearly all black schools).

Chapter 7. "*And Even Bizarre*": The Supreme Court Requires Busing to Achieve School Racial Balance in the South

1. 402 U.S. 1 (1971); 402 U.S. 33 (1971).

2. The district was formed in 1961 by the consolidation of formerly independent county and city school districts "upon economic and ad-

ministrative grounds not connected with questions of segregation" (*Swann* v. *Charlotte-Mecklenburg Board of Education*, 300 F. Supp. 1358, 1362 [W.D.N.C. 1969]). As it turned out, "questions of segregation" made the consolidation extremely unwise, but, of course, no one could have foreseen in 1961 that cross-district racial busing would become a constitutional requirement.

3. Record, 298a, 402 U.S. 1 (1971).

4. *Shuttlesworth* v. *Birmingham Board of Education*. See above, in Ch. 3, "A Decade of Hesitation by the Court."

5. *Swann*, 300 F. Supp. 1362.

6. The plan provided for voluntary minority-to-majority transfer, which, after *Goss*, was made general and nonracial. In the 1965 school year, 91 blacks exercised their option to transfer from the predominantly white schools to which they had been geographically assigned to predominantly black schools, and 262 blacks chose to transfer to predominantly white schools. "Most, but not quite all," of 396 whites geographically assigned to predominantly black schools chose to transfer to predominantly white schools (*Swann* v. *Charlotte-Mecklenburg Board of Education*, 369 F. 2d 29, 30-31 [4th Cir., 1966]).

7. *Swann* v. *Charlotte-Mecklenburg Board of Education*, 243 F. Supp. 667 (W.D.N.C. 1965), affirmed, 369 F. 2d 29 (4th Cir., 1966). In 1965, District (later Circuit) Judge Craven, upholding the operation of the system, expressed the "hope" that "with the implementation of the 1964 Civil Rights Act the incidence of such cases will diminish." Affirming, the Fourth Circuit reiterated its prior holdings: "There is no constitutional requirement that [the board] act with the conscious purpose of achieving the maximum mixture of races in the school population. The Constitution permits the Board to consider natural geographic boundaries, accessibility of particular schools and many other factors which are unrelated to race. So long as the boundaries are not drawn for the purpose of maintaining racial segregation, the School Board is under no constitutional requirement that it effectively and completely counteract all of the effects of segregated housing patterns " (369 F. 2d. 32).

8. 300 F. Supp. 1372. The judge's reported opinions in the case are at 300 F. Supp. 1358 (April 23, 1969); *ibid.*, 1381 (June 20); 306 F. Supp. 1291 (Aug. 15); *ibid.*, 1299 (Nov. 7, and supplementary opinion of Dec. 1).

9. "1. The use of federal funds for special aid to the disadvantaged . . . 2. Use of mobile classrooms . . . 3. The quality of the school buildings and equipment . . . 4. Coaching of athletics . . . 5. Parent-Teacher Association contributions and activities . . . 6. School fees . . . 7. School lunches . . . 8. Library books . . . 9. Elective courses . . . 10. Individual evaluation of students . . . 11. Gerrymandering . . ." (300 F. Supp. 1366-67).

10. "The system of assigning pupils by 'neighborhoods,' with 'freedom of choice' for both pupils and faculty, superimposed on an urban population pattern where Negro residents have become concentrated almost entirely in one quadrant of a city of 270,000, is racially discriminatory.

This discrimination discourages initiative and makes quality education impossible" (*ibid.,* 1360).

11. *Ibid.,* 1372, 1360.

12. *Ibid.;* 306 F. Supp. 1297.

13. "At least in America, the average white child scores about 15 points higher on standardized tests than the average black child. This disparity is apparent among first graders, and it persists throughout school and college" (Christopher Jencks *et al., Inequality* [New York, 1972], 81).

14. 306 F. Supp. 1297 (italics in the original); 300 F. Supp. 1369. If true, this would, of course, be a strong argument against integration and for segregation in majority-black school systems. "The experts [also] agreed that if children are underprivileged and undercultured, their school performance will be generally low. One . . . said that socio-economic-cultural background is the sole major determinant of school performance" (300 F. Supp. 1368-69).

15. 306 F. Supp. 1297.

16. See Frederick Mosteller and Daniel Moynihan, "A Pathbreaking Report," in *On Equality of Educational Opportunity,* Mosteller and Moynihan, eds. (New York, 1972) 3; and Jencks *et al.,* 97-106. See below, in Ch. 11, "The Doubtful Benefits of Compulsory Integration."

17. 300 F. Supp. 1371. "It would tend to eliminate shopping around for schools; . . . it would make all schools equally 'desirable' or 'undesirable' depending on the point of view; it would equalize the benefits and burdens of desegregation over the whole county; . . . it would get the Board out of the business of lawsuits and real estate zoning and leave it in the education business; and it would be a tremendous step toward the stability of real estate values in the community and the progress of education of children" (*ibid.*).

18. Record, 823(a); 300 F. Supp. 1372, 1369, 1370.

19. As of March 21, 1970, the judge had issued orders covering "more than one hundred pages. The motions and exhibits and pleadings and evidence number thousands of pages, and the evidence is several feet thick" (Record, 1221a). His solution for all problems, however, was quick, easy, and always the same: "With all due deference to the complexities of this school system, which have already been fully noted in previous opinions, the Board and the community must still observe the Constitution" (306 F. Supp. 1305). "Black community leaders" complained that closing majority-black schools and busing blacks to distant majority-white schools was "an affront to the dignity and pride of the black citizens," but "despite their undoubted importance, pride and dignity should not control over the Constitution and should not outweigh the prospects for quality education of children" (*ibid.,* 1296). "The school closing issue has provoked strident protests from black citizens and others. . . . A correspondent who signs Puzzled inquires: 'If the whites don't want it and the blacks don't want it, why do we have to have it?' The answer is the Constitution of the United States" (*ibid.,* 1293).

20. 306 F. Supp. 1312. The board was ordered to provide Finger with working space at its headquarters, pay "all of his fees and expenses," and provide him with all needed "professional, technical and other assistance," including stenographic, drafting, computer and communications services (*ibid.*, 1313-14).

21. Record, 744a–46a.

22. The judge had earlier stated in this regard: "The fact that other communities might be more backward in observing the Constitution than Mecklenburg would hardly seem to support the denial of constitutional rights to Mecklenburg citizens" (306 F. Supp. 1305).

23. Record, 323a, 691a, 744a–46a.

24. Record, 937a–38a.

25. Record, 835a–37a.

26. 300 F. Supp. 1361 (italics in the original); Record, 819a.

27. "Thus a 60-passenger bus (the average size) can if necessary transport 75 children" (Record, 1216a).

28. Record, 1217a–19a, 431 F. 2d 138. The court helpfully pointed out that the system would have to pay only half of the operating cost of additional transportation, since North Carolina provided funds to local systems for pupil transportation. North Carolina, however, not having contemplated that its school transportation subsidies would be expended for racial busing, immediately enacted legislation prohibiting such use. This the Supreme Court found unconstitutional (*North Carolina State Board of Education* v. *Swann*, 402 U.S. 43 [1971]).

29. Record, 1198a. The judge did not share the board's concern that "a plan that generates unnecessary transportation costs and occasions unnecessary burdens and inconveniences for parents and children alike would jeopardize the public support which provides the tax and bond money upon which our schools are totally dependent for financing the already high cost of education" (Record, 732a).

30. Record, 1218a, 1201a, 1218a–19a, 1219a.

31. Record, 821a.

32. Record, 823a, 824a.

33. *Swann* v. *Charlotte-Mecklenburg Board of Education*, 431 F. 2d 138 (1970), 155.

34. In the Fifth Circuit, "166 appeals in school desegregation cases were heard between December 2, 1969, and September 24, 1970" (*Swann* v. *Charlotte-Mecklenburg Board of Education*, 402 U.S. 14, n. 5 [1971]).

35. 431 F. 2d 138, 156. It may also be worth noting that the briefs prepared for the board were, as is usually the case, not equal in quality to those of the lawyers for the NAACP Legal Defense Fund, full-time professionals in constitutional law relating to race. Plaintiffs also had the advantage in the court of appeals and the Supreme Court of briefs prepared by the National Education Association, another continuing participant in litigation on race and the schools, always or nearly always in support of the plaintiffs.

36. 431 F. 2d 141-42, citing *Shelley* v. *Kramer,* 334 U.S. 1 (1948).

37. Quoted in Nathan Glazer, "Is Busing Necessary?" *Commentary* 53 (March 1972) 41. Glazer noted that, indeed, one of the antibusing measures "had been offered by Michigan Congressmen, long-time supporters of desegregation, because what had been decreed for Charlotte, North Carolina, Mobile, Alabama, and endless other Southern cities was now on the way to becoming law in Detroit and its suburbs." Unfortunately, Congressman Edwards proved mistaken; busing did come to Michigan, but it did not stop in Alabama.

38. 431 F. 2d 142, 143.

39. *Ibid.,* 142, 144, 145. A "reasonable estimate" of the distance these blacks would be bused was twelve or thirteen miles each way (*ibid.,* 145, n. 5).

40. *Ibid.* The court was "favorably impressed" by the suggestion of the United States, appearing as *amicus curiae,* that "alternate plans, particularly for the elementary schools" should be considered. The United States, now (1970) under a new administration, was no longer taking the most extreme integrationist position. It was, however, apparently still unable or unwilling to argue simply that the Constitution would be more than fully satisfied with acceptance of the board's plan.

41. *Ibid.,* 152.

42. *Swann* v. *Charlotte-Mecklenburg Board of Education,* 399 U.S. 926 (1970). At the same time, the Court reinstated the district court's order pending review.

43. *Swann* v. *Charlotte-Mecklenburg Board of Education,* 402 U.S. 1, 6 (1970), 28.

44. *Ibid.,* 28.

45. *Ibid.,* 13, 14.

46. *Ibid.,* 16.

47. *Ibid.,* 17. The Court did not quote from section 410: "Nothing in this title shall prohibit classification and assignment for reasons other than race, color, or national origin."

48. *Ibid.,* 16, 17-18.

49. Congress might have had difficulty, in 1964, in recognizing the Court's definition of "de facto segregation." See Senator Humphrey's statement: "The courts would hold that if there were gerrymandering of school districts to provide for segregation, the order of the court to declare such gerrymandering unconstitutional would prevail. That is what we call the de facto school segregation problem." Senator Byrd of West Virginia replied, "Yes" (110 *Cong. Rec.* 12715 [1964]).

50. See above, p. 49.

51. Senator Sam Ervin, who had participated in the *Swann* case, commented: "Section 401(b) . . . says in about as plain words as can be found in the English language that" assignments to schools were to be nonracial. "It could not have found simpler words

to express that concept. Yet, in the *Swann* case the Supreme Court ignored that definition and said in effect that 'desegregation' requires that school boards should take into consideration matters of race . . . in making assignments.

"But then, the Congress decided to take no chances with the courts, so it put in something else that even a judge ought to be able to understand. It not only defined 'desegregation,' affirmatively, but also defined what 'desegregation' is not. The Supreme Court adopted exactly the opposite interpretation of the meaning of the word 'desegregation.' It said, in effect, in the *Swann* case that 'desegregation' shall mean the assignment of students to public schools in order to overcome racial imbalance. . . .

"There is not a word in this whole title that indicates any intention of Congress to regulate 'de facto segregation' that is based upon residence. Yet, the Supreme Court nullified this act of Congress by holding that Congress was a bunch of legislative fools and that Congress had attempted to regulate 'de facto segregation' instead of 'de jure segregation.' " (*Busing of School Children, Hearings before the Subcommittee on Constitutional Rights of the Committee on the Judiciary, United States Senate,* 93d Cong., 2d sess. [1974], 42-43).

52. 402 U.S. 20, 21.

53. See S. Sidney Ulmer, "Earl Warren and the Brown Decision," *J. Politics* 33 (1971) 699, quoting Justice Felix Frankfurter's statement "It is not fair to say that the South has always denied the Negroes this Constitutional right [not to be assigned racially to separate schools]. It was not a constitutional right till May 17/54" when *Brown* was decided.

54. Record, 1219a.

55. 402 U.S. 22.

56. *Ibid.*

57. *Ibid.,* 23-25.

58. *Ibid.,* 24. Two sentences later, the Court again referred to the "Total failure" of the school board.

59. The closest the district judge seems to have come to such a "finding" is his reference to "the majority of the School Board, who, at last reckoning, still did not appear to accept the court's order as representing the law of the land" (Record, 819a).

60. 431 F. 2d 154, n. 9.

61. 402 U.S. 25-26. The Charlotte-Mecklenburg school system had, the court of appeals pointed out (431 F. 2d 142), closed 7 schools and reassigned the pupils primarily to increase racial mixing, "drastically gerrymandered school zones to promote desegregation," and submitted the above described plan. In these circumstances, the relevance of the need to "determine that school assignments are not part of state-enforced segregation" does not appear.

62. 402 U.S. 26.

63. *Ibid.*
64. *Ibid.,* 27-28.
65. *Ibid.*
66. *Ibid.,* 29, 30.
67. *Ibid.,* 30, n. 12. "Additionally, it should be noted that North Carolina requires provision of transportation for all students who are assigned to schools more than one and one-half miles from their homes," *(ibid.).* One may doubt that the result would have been different if North Carolina had not so provided. As already noted, the North Carolina statute prohibiting the use of public funds to provide busing for racial balance was held unconstitutional in a companion case, *North Carolina State Board of Education* v. *Swann.*
68. 402 U.S. 30-31.
69. *Ibid.,* 28.
70. *Ibid.,* 31. "Remedial judicial authority does not put judges automatically in the shoes of school authorities whose powers are plenary. Judicial authority enters only when local authority defaults" *(ibid.,* 16).
71. *Ibid.,* 31-32.
72. *Ibid.,* 13, 22-23.
73. *Keyes* v. *School District No. One, Denver, Colorado,* 413 U.S. 189 (1973); see Ch. 9, below.
74. Judge Clark dissenting, in *Ross* v. *Eckels,* 434 F. 2d 1140, 1149-50 (5th Cir., 1970).
75. 362 F. Supp. 1223, 1228 (1973); "The movement of children from one place to another within the community and the movement of children into the community are not within the control of the school board. The *assignment* of those children to particular schools *is* within the total control of the school board" (328 F. Supp. 1346, 1349 [1971]). "The Board [must] adopt and implement a continuing program, computerized or otherwise, of assigning pupils and teachers during the school year as well as at the start of each year for the conscious purpose of maintaining each school and each faculty in a condition of desegregation" (334 F. Supp. 623, 631 [1971]). The board must take steps "to maintain racial stability" (362 F. Supp. 1223, 1232 [1973]). The latest of the judge's continuing series of decisions and orders in this case is in 379 F. Supp. 1102 (1974).
76. *Calhoun* v. *Cook,* 332 F. Supp. 804, 805-08 (N.D. Ga. 1971). The court then refused to order further steps to produce racial balance, but that, it must be noted, was far from the end of the "annual agony of Atlanta." The court's refusal to order further "desegregation" and dismissal of the suit was vacated by the Fifth Circuit, and the court was ordered to consider a plan submitted by plaintiffs (451 F. 2d 583 [1971]). The court's rejection of this plan was also vacated the following year (469 F. 2d 1067 [1972]), and the court's acceptance of a plan (362 F. Supp. 1249) was vacated the year after that (487 F. 2d 680 [1973]). The case received national attention in 1973—by which time the school system

had become 79 percent black—because the Atlanta branch of the NAACP reached an agreement with the Atlanta school board to refrain from insisting on further busing in return for the promise by the board to appoint a black superintendent and make the school administrative staff at least 50 percent black. The arrangement could not be carried out, however, because of the disapproval of the national office of the NAACP, which promptly suspended the local branch. See "N.A.A.C.P. Scores Atlanta Branch," *New York Times*, March 9, 1973, p. 74. In October 1975, Judge Clark stated for the Fifth Circuit that "every judicial design for achieving racial desegregation in this system has failed. A totally segregated system which contained 115,000 pupils in 1958 has mutated to a substantially segregated system serving only 80,000 students today. A system with a 70% white pupil majority when the litigation began has now become a district in which more than 85% of the students are black." Therefore, the NAACP's request for further "desegregation" measures in Atlanta was denied. The agony of Atlanta, however, was far from over; a new suit had been begun "to combine or consolidate the Atlanta school system with the public educational facilities in neighboring communities" (522 F. 2d 717, 718, 719).

77. "Busing Plan Ends in Coast Suburb," *New York Times,* May 11, 1975, 26.

78. *Spangler* v. *Pasadena City Board of Education,* 519 F. 2d 430 (9th Cir., 1975).

79. 402 U.S. 33 (1971), 28.

80. *Ibid.,* 34. Mobile County was larger, indeed, than the state of Rhode Island.

81. Brief for the Board of School Commissioners of Mobile County, 6, n. 1.

82. *Davis* v. *Board of School Commissioners of Mobile County,* 430 F. 2d 883, 885, n. 1 (5th Cir., 1970), 888. The court also noted the desirability of "maintaining the neighborhood school concept" (*ibid.,* 886), which, however, was very loosely interpreted in order to increase integration. For example, some elementary school students were assigned to a school as much as seven miles away from their homes rather than to a school within a mile and a half (Brief for Respondent, 52).

83. Record, 714a.

84. 402 U.S. 35.

85. It could be argued that even the earlier plan did not merit this criticism. The full sentence, written by Judge Thorneberry, quoted in part by the Court, is: "It is apparent that the District Court relied wholly upon and gave literal interpretation to the directive in our decision of March 12, 1968, . . . that new attendance zones be drawn on a non-racial basis and ignored the unequivocal directive to make a conscious effort in locating attendance zones to desegregate and eliminate past segregation" (414 F. 2d 610). For a lower court to take literally and rely wholly on a higher court's directive is not ordinarily considered a failing. In any event, the directive was not

"unequivocal." The district court had been told that attendance-zone lines must be drawn "on a non-racial basis so that the attendance-area plan will promote desegregation rather than perpetuate segregation" (393 F. 2d 690, 694), which is not quite the same thing as a directive to "eliminate past segregation," which, given *Green's* confusion of terminology, is itself hardly unequivocal.

86. Brief for Respondent, 45.

87. 402 U.S. 36.

88. The Court did not otherwise give the basis of its calculation, but even thus limited, its "about 50%" figure seems much too high. There were some 31,000 blacks in the system (42 percent of 73,500 students). Even if only 15,000—less than half—of these were in the elementary schools and all of the 5,310 students in question were black—as the Court seemed to assume, but as was not the case—the figure would be only about 35 percent.

89. 402 U.S. 36; Record, 708a.

90. 402 U.S. 37.

91. For example, of some 70,000 students assigned to racially mixed schools for the 1969-1970 school year, only 55,314 actually attended (Brief for Respondent, 31).

92. 402 U.S. 37.

93. *Ibid.*

94. As even a sympathetic commentator has concluded, "the Court misrepresented the record" (Lucas Powe, "The Road to *Swann*: Mobile County Crawls to the Bus," *Texas Law Review* 51 (1973) 525.

95. *North Carolina State Board of Education* v. *Swann*, 402 U.S. 43, 45-46: A North Carolina statute forbidding racial assignment and busing to achieve racial balance was invalidated on the ground that it would "obstruct the remedies" granted by the district court in *Swann* v. *Charlotte-Mecklenburg* and "deprive school authorities of the one tool absolutely essential to fulfillment of their constitutional obligation to eliminate existing dual school systems." In *McDaniel* v. *Barresi*, 402 U.S. 39, also decided the same day, the Court reversed the holding of the Supreme Court of Georgia that school assignment on the basis of race violated the Fourteenth Amendment and the 1964 Civil Rights Act. Such assignment, the Court said, will "almost invariably" be required in the "remedial process" (*ibid.*, 41).

96. 404 U.S. 1221 (1971).

97. *Adams* v. *School District Number 5, Orangeburg County, South Carolina*, 444 F. 2d 99, 100, 101, certiorari denied, 404 U.S. 912 (1971).

98. 404 U.S. 1225.

99. *Ibid.*, 1231, 1226, 1222, 1223.

100. *Ibid.*, 1224-25.

101. *Ibid.*, 1225 (Chief Justice Burger's italics).

102. *Ibid.*, In *Swann*, it may be recalled, the Finger plan, approved by the Court, required, according to the district court's estimate (with "discount factors"), the use of 138 additional buses to transport

13,300 additional pupils and, according to the board's estimate, 422 additional buses to transport 19,285 additional pupils.

103. *Ibid.*, 1227, n. 1; 1228.

104. *New York Times*, Sept. 1, 1971, p. 1.

105. For a somewhat different explanation of Chief Justice Burger's performance, see Nina Totenberg, "Behind the Marble, Beneath the Robes," *New York Times Magazine*, March 16, 1975, 15: "Critics of Burger cite his voting behavior in the Court's first big busing case [*Swann*]. . . . The first vote in conference was said to have been 6 to 3 against busing. . . . Then several Justices had second thoughts and switched their votes. Soon the vote was 6 to 3 for busing, with Burger, Blackmun and Black dissenting. Eventually, the three capitulated. . . . And Burger, who had envisioned himself writing the opinion against busing, ended up writing the opinion for it and incorporating much of the language from the drafts of the more liberal Justices.

"Some who know the Chief Justice well contend that he changed his vote for personal and political reasons rather than reasons of legal judgment. At the time, they speculate, Burger did not wish to be a part of a small minority if that stance would cause people to think of him as an automatic supporter of positions favored by then President Nixon. Critics point to other examples of Burger's fighting hard in conference to get a conservative position upheld, only to switch to the other side when he saw he had lost."

106. *Volpe* v. *D.C. Federation of Civic Assns.*; quoted from 92 S. Ct. 1290-91.

107. See Frank Strong, "Three Little Words and What They Didn't Seem to Mean," *American Bar Association Journal* 59 (1973) 29.

108. 405 U.S. 1030, 1031.

109. See *Adams* v. *School District Number 5* (reversing and remanding ten cases).

110. *Brown* v. *Board of Education of City of Bessemer*, 464 F. 2d 382, 384 (1972); *United States* v. *Greenwood Municipal Separate School District*, 460 F. 2d 1205, 1207 (5th Cir., 1972); *Acree* v. *County Board of Education of Richmond County, Georgia*, 458 F. 2d 486, 487-88 (5th Cir., 1972). The Fort Worth school board contended that the busing plan ordered in *Flax* v. *Potts*, 464 F. 2d 865 (5th Cir., 1972), "would require bus trips of up to two hours and twenty minutes and a round trip of up to 70 miles" (*Keyes* v. *School District No. One, Denver, Colorado*, 413 U.S. 189, 238, n. 17 [1973] [concurring and dissenting opinions]).

111. *Lee* v. *Macon County Board of Education*, 465 F. 2d 369, 370 (5th Cir., 1972); *ibid.*, 448 F. 2d 746, 751, n. 8 (5th Cir., 1971); *Russell* v. *Greenwood Municipal Separate School District*, 445 F. 2d 388, 389-90 (5th Cir., 1971).

112. *Mims* v. *Duval County School Board of Education,* 447 F. 2d 1330, 1332 (5th Cir., 1971). In *Boykins* v. *Fairfield Board of Education,* 457 F. 2d 1091 (5th Cir., 1972), an all black school had been "desegregated" by the assignment to it of fifty-seven whites, who thereupon left the system (*ibid.,* 1093, n. 3). On this round of the case, Judge Wisdom found that the school had, therefore, only been "integrated on paper" (*ibid.,* 1095) and ordered further measures.

113. *Brewer* v. *School Board of City of Norfolk, Virginia,* 456 F. 2d 943, 947, n. 6 (4th Cir., 1972); 947; *Thompson* v. *School Board of City of Newport News,* 465 F. 2d 83, 87 (4th Cir., 1972) (*en banc*). See also *Medley* v. *School Board of Danville, Virginia,* 482 F. 2d 1061, 1065 (4th Cir., 1973) (*en banc*), which reversed a district court decision that a busing plan would be hazardous and found the "board's present lack of transportation facilities is not controlling." But see a later decision in *Thompson*—498 F. 2d 195, 196-97 (1974) (*en banc*)—where there was a 4 to 3 affirmance of a district court decision that further busing "was neither 'practical' nor 'feasible.'" In the Sixth Circuit deference was usually shown to the decision of the district judge, but results varied widely according to the particular panel involved. Cf. *Newberg Area Council, Inc.* v. *Board of Education of Jefferson County, Kentucky,* 489 F. 2d. 925 (1973), in which furthei integration was required in already majority-black Louisville, with *Northcross* v. *Board of Education of the Memphis, Tennessee, City Schools,* 489 F. 2d 15 (1973), in which a plan was approved although it left twenty-five schools all or nearly all black, and with *Goss* v. *Board of Education of Knoxville, Tennessee,* 482 F. 2d 1044 (1973) (*en banc*; *semble*). See also cases discussed in Ch. 8, n. 26, below.

Chapter 8. *Defining the School District: Divisions and Consolidations*

1. *Moses* v. *Washington Parish School Board,* 456 F. 2d 1285 (1972) (ability grouping); *Adams* v. *Rankin County Board of Education,* 485 F. 2d 324 (1973) (displacing teachers); *Baker* v. *Columbus Municipal School District,* 462 F. 2d 1112 (1972) (use of National Teachers Examination); *Cook* v. *Hudson,* 511 F. 2d 744 (1975) (teachers' children in private schools).

2. 407 U.S. 451 (1972); 407 U.S. 484 (1972).

3. 407 U.S. 454 (1972). The step was not taken to avoid the county-wide racial-balance requirement that was later imposed. No racial-balance requirement existed in 1967 and, as the Fourth Circuit found, "could not have been anticipated by Emporia, and indeed, was not envisioned by this court" (*Wright* v. *Council of City of Emporia,* 442 F. 2d 570, 572 [1971]).

4. *Wright* v. *County School Board of Greensville County, Virginia,* 309 F. Supp. 671, 674 (1970). Also, Emporia had just been "notified for the first time by counsel that in all probability its contract

with the county for the education of the city children was void under state law" (442 F. 2d 573).

5. 309 F. Supp. 671.

6. *Wright* v. *Council of City of Emporia*, 442 F. 2d 570 (1971). Five judges participated, one of whom dissented.

7. 407 U.S. 459. "We need not and do not hold that this disparity . . . would be a sufficient reason, standing alone, to enjoin the creation of the separate school district" (*ibid.*, 464). "Our holding today does not rest upon a conclusion that the disparity . . . resulting from separate systems would, absent any other considerations, be unacceptable" (*ibid.*, 470).

8. E.g., *ibid.*, 460. "The constitutional violation that formed the predicate for the District Court's action was the enforcement until 1969 of racial segregation in a public school system of which Emporia had always been a part" (*ibid.*, 459). The fact that the school system had operated since 1965 under a plan that was approved by the district court did not, apparently, end the "constitutional violation" as of that time.

9. *Ibid.*, 465. For, the Court pointed out, quoting *Swann*, "desegregation" "does not mean that every school in every community must always reflect the racial composition of the school system as a whole" (*ibid.*, 464). If it is understood that nothing short of this would be a requirement of racial balance and that the rejection of the board's plan in *Swann* was not such a requirement, we may be confident that racial balance has not been and never will be required, for not "every" school will "always" reflect the racial composition of the whole system no matter what the Court requires.

10. *Ibid.*, 464-65, 475. The dissent pointed out that the difference between a school 72 percent black and one 66 percent black was likely to "represent a change in the racial identity of 1.5 students per class on the average" (*ibid.*, 473, n. 1).

11. *Ibid.*, 465, 475-76.

12. *Ibid.*, 465-66, 476. It may be said in the Court's favor, however, that the district judge's failure to reach the conclusion attributed to him by the Court might have been merely an oversight and that he, who later ordered the consolidation of the school systems of Richmond, Virginia, and its surrounding counties, might well have so "concluded" had he but thought of it.

13. *Ibid.*, 467-69. "At the final hearing in the District Court, the respondents presented detailed budgetary proposals and other evidence demonstrating that they contemplate a more diverse and more expensive educational program than that to which the city children had been accustomed in the Greensville County schools" (*ibid.*, 467-68).

14. *Ibid.*, 470.

15. *Ibid.*, 471-74.

16. *Ibid.*, 474, 476-78, 481.

17. *United States* v. *Scotland Neck City Board of Education*, 442 F. 2d 575 (4th Cir., 1971).

18. *Ibid.*, 580.

19. *Ibid.*, 577, 581. The district court opinion is unreported. The Fourth Circuit invalidated, however, a provision adopted by the Scotland Neck board that would have permitted transfers between the city and county schools. Under this provision, 350 whites and 10 blacks opted for transfer from the county to the city, and 44 blacks for transfer from the city to the county. The court found, as, unfortunately, it clearly had to under *Green* and *Monroe*, that this provision "tended toward establishment of a resegregated system" (*ibid.*, 583).

20. 407 U.S. 489–490.

21. *Ibid.*, 491.

22. *Ibid.*, 491–92.

23. 412 U.S. 92 (1973).

24. *Bradley* v. *School Board of City of Richmond, Virginia*, 462 F. 2d 1058, 1074 (4th Cir., 1972) (dissenting opinion). The annexation of predominantly white areas was challenged, unsuccessfully, as unconstitutional on the ground that its purpose was to prevent political control of Richmond by blacks (*Holt* v. *City of Richmond*, 459 F. 2d 1093 [4th Cir., 1972]).

25. 325 F. Supp. 828, 835 (E.D. Va. 1971); 338 F. Supp. 67 (E.D. Va. 1972); 462 F. 2d 1058 (1972).

26. *Kelly* v. *Municipal Board of Education of Nashville, Tennessee*, 463 F. 2d 732 (6th Cir., 1972); *Robinson* v. *Shelby County Board of Education*, 467 F. 2d 1187 (6th Cir., 1972) (Memphis). Thus is the fate of America's cities determined by a kind of roulette. *Kelly* also illustrates the tendency of judges when ordering racial balance to adopt a high moral tone, substituting rhetoric for reason. The concluding section of the opinion, for example, entitled "One America," states: "The Constitution of the United States was written for one nation, 'indivisible.' As it speaks to men's consciences, the Constitution argues against division and apartheid." "In the public domain . . . the Constitution commands. Here the constitutional command is One America" (463 F. 2d 746). Similarly, nothing except the fact that different district judges made the initial decisions appears to explain why busing is required in Chattanooga, Tennessee, but not in Knoxville, Tennessee, is required in Pontiac and Kalamazoo, Michigan, but not in Grand Rapids, Michigan. Nonetheless, the Sixth Circuit affirmed the district judge in each case, and the Supreme Court denied all petitions for certiorari (*Mapp* v. *Board of Education of City of Chattanooga, Tennessee*, 329 F. Supp. 1374 [E.D. Tenn. 1971], affirmed, 477 F. 2d 851 [1973], certiorari denied, 414 U.S. 1022 [1974]; *Goss* v. *Board of Education of Knoxville, Tennessee*, 340 F. Supp. 711 [E.D. Tenn. 1972], affirmed, 482 F. 2d 1044 [1973], certiorari denied, 414 U.S. 1171 (1974); *Davis* v. *School District of City of Pontiac*,

309 F. Supp. 734 [E.D. Mich. 1970], affirmed, 443 F. 2d 573, certiorari denied, 404 U.S. 913 [1971]; *Oliver* v. *Kalamazoo Board of Education*, 368 F. Supp. 143 [W.D. Mich. 1973], affirmed, 508 F. 2d 178 [1974]; *Higgins* v. *Board of Education of City of Grand Rapids*, 508 F. 2d 779 [1974]).

27. 462 F. 2d 1060, 1061, 1065.

28. *Ibid.*, 1068. "Each of the three political subdivisions involved here has a separate tax base and a separate and distinct electorate. The school board of the consolidated district would have to look to three separate governing bodies for approval and support of school budgets" (*ibid.*).

29. 412 U.S. 92 (1972).

30. In *Richmond* the district judge stated: "Current research indicates that . . . there is an optimum racial composition which should be sought in each school. Dr. Pettigrew placed this at from 20 to 40% black occupancy. . . . When the black population in a school rises substantially above 40%, it has been Dr. Pettigrew's experience that white students tend to disappear from the school entirely at a rapid rate, and the Court so finds" (338 F. Supp. 194). Thomas Pettigrew, a Harvard professor of sociology and frequent "expert witness" for plaintiffs in "desegregation" cases, is perhaps the nation's leading academic proponent of school racial balance.

Chapter 9. *"Only Common Sense": Busing Spreads North and West*

1. 413 U.S. 189 (1973).

2. 404 U.S. 1027 (1972).

3. *Spencer* v. *Kugler*, 326 F. Supp. 1235 (N.J., 1971), (three-judge court). No more was necessary for the court to deny relief than to note that the plaintiffs in *Brown* "had been denied admission to schools attended by white children under laws requiring or permitting segregation according to race" (*ibid.*, 1239). Quotation of a few appropriate passages from *Swann* tying that decision to the historic dual system of the South was sufficient to corroborate that there was no constitutional requirement of integration or racial balance as such or that "*de facto* segregation" be eliminated (*ibid.*, 1242).

4. Denver's black population was 7,204 (2.5 percent) in 1930; 7,386 (2.4 percent) in 1940; 15,059 (3.6 percent) in 1950; 30,251 (6.1 percent) in 1960; and 47,011 (9.1 percent) in 1970 (Respondents' Brief, 10). "Nor shall any distinction or classification of pupils be made on account of race or color" in the public schools (Colo. Const., Art. IX, sect. 8).

5. Colo. Rev. Stat., ch. xxv, Art. I, sect. 1, Art. II, sect. 3, Art III; ch. lxix, Art. VII (1963); Respondents' Brief, 16.

6. 413 U.S. 191–92.

7. 303 F. Supp. 279, 282 (D. Colo. 1969).

8. *Ibid.*, 283. Denver constitutes a single school district as well as a city and a county. The school district is governed by a seven-member board, elected to serve staggered six-year terms, which is politically and financially independent of the city and county (Respondents' Brief, 8).

9. Record, 1999a, 2006a, 2008a. The committee found that "the benefits and predictable results [of neighborhood school assignment] outweighed deficiencies when compared with other methods of assigning pupils to schools" (Record, 2008a) and that "the transportation of students . . . involves considerable added costs, inconveniences to pupils and parents, particularly in emergency or illness, inability of the pupil to enter into extra-curricular activities, and difficulty in promoting close contacts with parents" (*ibid.*, 2011a).

10. 445 F. 2d 990, 996 (10th Cir., 1971). The committee made no finding of racial discrimination, and found "every evidence" that the board's rules and procedures governing school boundaries "have been followed carefully and without prejudice in the granting of transfers" (Record, 2009a). It also found, however, "that de facto segregation exists in Denver, especially in regard to Negro citizens" and that "even though the Denver Public Schools have not created this pattern of residential segregation," it "adversely affects equal opportunity" (303 F. Supp. 283, n. 1). The committee "strongly believe[d]," however, that "the effects of segregation" must be minimized "if the principles of the *Declaration of Independence* and the Constitution are to be a reality."

11. Denver Public Schools Policy No. 5100, May 6, 1964, stating in part that neighborhood schools have caused "concentration of some minority racial and ethnic groups in some schools" and that having more "diverse groups in schools is desirable to achieve equality of educational opportunity." But this did "not mean the abandonment of the neighborhood school principle" (Record, 1989a–90a).

12. 303 F. Supp. 283; Respondents' Brief, 40–41. Overcrowding in northeast Denver resulting from this decision was relieved by the transfer of students from the area to two new schools built in southeast Denver (Record, 98a, 103a, 104a).

13. Record, 1991a. The superintendent was to consider, among other things, "the use of transportation and the degree to which transportation should be mandatory or voluntary" (*ibid.*, 1995a).

14. Record, 42a–70a.

15. This does not mean that a majority of Denver's citizens favored any of the board's previous departures from its former policy of racial neutrality. A bond issue proposed by the board to finance the building of large middle schools (grades 4, 5, and 6) to serve a more heterogeneous population was defeated by Denver voters in 1967 (Respondents' Brief, 41).

16. 303 F. Supp. at 284; Resolution 1533, June 9, 1969. The rescinded resolutions were found to be "hastily prepared, inappropriate to accomplish their intended purposes and [to] lack community support" (Record, 2111a).

17. " 'Hispano' is a term used by the Colorado Department of Education to refer to a person of Spanish, Mexican or Cuban heritage" (413 U.S. 195, n.6). In the West it refers primarily to persons of Mexican descent. Those using it, or "Chicano," refer to other nonblacks as "Anglos," a mild pejorative similar to "the Establishment." Thus, one of, for example, Italian, Jewish, or Chinese ancestry may be surprised to learn upon arrival in the West that he is an "Anglo" and, therefore, excluded from significant "minority group" membership. In 1970 the Denver school system had 514,678 pupils, of whom 72.3 percent (371,842) were "Anglo"; 16.8 percent (86,345), "Hispano"; 9.1 percent (47,011), black; and 1.8 percent (9,480), "others" (Respondents' Brief, 10).

18. 303 F. Supp. 279; Record 455a–56a. The board again appealed and the court of appeals, on August 27, 1969, again stayed the injunction (except provisions relating to orders for buses and retention of records) pending a full trial of the issues (Record, 459a). Two days later, four days before the schools were to open, Acting Circuit Justice Brennan vacated the stay on the ground that the court of appeals had not found an abuse of discretion by the district judge (396 U.S. 1215). On September 15, 1969, the court of appeals denied a further motion by the board for a stay, on the ground that the schools had already opened pursuant to the reinstated injunction (Record, 467a).

19. 313 F. Supp. 61; 313 F. Supp. 90.

20. He said, for example, "The migration" of Negroes to certain areas "caused those areas to become substantially Negro and segregated" (303 F. Supp. 282).

21. *Downs* v. *Board of Education*, 336 F. 2d 988 (10th Cir., 1964); *Board of Education of Oklahoma City Public Schools* v. *Dowell*, 375 F. 2d 158 (10th Cir., 1967).

22. 303 F. Supp. 287, 285, 286. "Whether the [Tenth Circuit] would now give broad effect to its holdings that there is ['no affirmative duty to integrate'] is, of course, irrelevant in the present case, but in view of later developments in the law, the question arises as to whether it would say the same thing today since the cases which it cited in support of this proposition have been largely overruled" (*ibid.*, 286-87, n. 8, citing *Jefferson County*). "There is no discernible difference between the *de facto* and *de jure* varieties" (313 F. Supp. 77, n. 20).

23. 303 F. Supp. 283, 285. The judge's initial opinion left little doubt that he held the rescission to be unconstitutional simply because

he strongly favored the rescinded resolutions. The Conclusion of that opinion castigated the rescission as "the precipitate and unstudied action of four members of the Board rescinding and nullifying the school integration plan, which plan had been adopted after almost ten years of debate and study" (*ibid.*, 288).

24. 387 U.S. 369; 313 F. Supp. 68–69; 387 U.S. 371, 378–79.

25. See Charles Black, "Foreword: 'State Action,' Equal Protection and California's Proposition 14, *Harv. L. Rev.* 81 (1967) 69. See also *Lee* v. *Nyquist*, 402 U.S. 935 (1971), affirming without opinion, 318 F. Supp. 710 (W.D.N.Y. 1970), in which a three-judge court held that a statute *prohibiting* racial discrimination in school assignment, including assignment to achieve racial balance, constituted unconstitutional racial discrimination.

26. Respondents' Brief, 24; 303 F. Supp. 285, 290–91.

27. 313 F. Supp. 64–65; Respondents' Brief, 28.

28. 313 F. Supp. 65; Respondents' Brief, 28.

29. 313 F. Supp. 65; Respondents' Brief, 26–29; 445 F. 2d 998.

30. 313 F. Supp. 65.

31. These were, "more properly, self-contained classrooms, installed on concrete foundations with air-conditioning and toilet facilities" (Respondents' Brief, 30).

32. See Respondents' Brief, 31–36.

33. The judge's finding was simply that "the School Board knew the consequences and intended or at least approved the resultant racial concentrations" (313 F. Supp. 65). The judge found the use of mobile classrooms to increase school capacity in black neighborhoods particularly objectionable in light of the board's adoption of Policy No. 5100 in 1964, "which provided that ethnic and racial characteristics of the school population should be considered" in school decisions (303 F. Supp. 285). An example of racial discrimination—though not one justifying the "remedy" ordered—might have been found in the board's assignment of teachers. Although no school had an all black faculty, predominantly black schools had a disproportionately high number of black faculty members. This might, however, have resulted from, for example, the preferences of individual teachers. The court of appeals found that this situation was "not reflective of segregative desires" on the part of the board, because the board "operated on the prevailing educational theory of the day . . . that the image of a successful, well educated Negro at the head of the class provided the best kind of motivation for Negro children and that in turn the Negro teacher had a greater understanding for the Negro pupil's educational and social problems. . . . In response to new educational theories, the Denver public school system has today assigned Negro teachers to schools throughout the system and has reduced the percentages of Negro teachers in the predominantly minority

schools" (445 F. 2d 1007).

34. 313 F. Supp. 69–77; 303 F. Supp. 290–94; 313 F. Supp. 74–75, n. 18.

35. Record, 467a–68a.

36. "The District Court found that . . . the respondent School Board had engaged over almost a decade after 1960 in an unconstitutional policy of deliberate racial segregation with respect to the Park Hill schools" (413 U.S. 192 [1973]). This statement is not only palpably unjust to Denver and the Denver school board, but clearly misleading as to what the district judge had actually found, unless the basis of those findings—the unconstitutionality of the rescission—was noted and accepted, which the Supreme Court did not do.

37. 313 F. Supp. 74–75, n. 18.

38. *Ibid.*, 76–77, 69. The judge's additional distinctions, of doubtful relevance, were that the alleged discriminatory actions occurred "at an earlier date," that "community attitudes were different," and that "the transitions [to racial and ethnic concentration] were much more gradual and less perceptible" than in Park Hill.

39. *Ibid.*, 73, 75. Some of these acts (*ibid.*, 69–73) were less remote in time (e.g., 1962) and would seem to "loom larger" as a possible cause of racial imbalance than, for example, the Barrett decisions (1958 and 1960) that he earlier seemed to find significant.

40. *Ibid.*, 82. The judge found the plaintiffs' contention that blacks and "Hispanos" should be placed "all in one category" in "establishing the segregated character of the school" to be "often an oversimplification" (*ibid.*, 69). He adopted, instead, without giving a basis, the "rule of thumb" that a school is "segregated" when it is "in the general area of 70 to 75 percent" black *or* "Hispano" (*ibid.*, 77–78).

41. *Ibid.*, 77. The Denver Classroom Teachers Association agreement with the board provided that teacher requests for transfer to schools with vacancies would be granted on the basis of seniority. "This policy results in the more experienced teachers at minority schools transferring out of those schools when vacancies are opened at predominantly Anglo schools, with the resulting vacancies being filled by inexperienced teachers" (*ibid.*, 80).

42. The judge, citing no evidence, "would agree that, in most general terms, this disparity exists," but found such disparities not "substantial factors affecting the educational opportunity offered at a given school" (*ibid.*, 80–81).

43. *Ibid.*, 81, 82. The judge regally referred to himself as "we" throughout his opinions. A small suggestion for aiding recognition by district judges of the source of their pronouncements might be that the first person singular be more favored.

44. *Ibid.*, 98, 99.

45. 445 F. 2d 990, 1002 (1971).

46. See above, p. 173.

47. Federal Rules of Civil Procedure, Rule 52.

48. It apparently believed, for example, that the constitutionality of segregation depended upon the circumstances and the justifications offered: "Once plaintiffs prove state imposed segregation, justification for such discrimination must be in terms of positive social interests which are protected or advanced" (445 F. 2d 1006). Perhaps the court, like the earlier panel, believed strongly in the value of not disturbing the school status quo; because of the preliminary injunction, the rescinded resolutions had by this time been implemented for some two years. Perhaps it saw its overall disposition of the case, otherwise favorable to Denver, as something of a compromise; if so, it made the mistake of reckoning without the Supreme Court.

49. *Ibid.*, 999, 1002, 999, 997–98.

50. *Ibid.*, 999, 1000.

51. *Ibid.*, 1006, 1005, 1004, 1005.

52. 413 U.S. 189, 214.

53. *Ibid.*, 195–98. Justice Brennan found this "evidence," not in the record or anything relating specifically to Denver, but in United States Civil Rights Commission reports on "the Southwest." He quoted the "basic finding" of one report: "minority students in the Southwest—Mexican-Americans, Blacks, American Indians—do not obtain the benefits of public education at a rate equal to that of their Anglo classmates" (*ibid.*, 198, n. 8). Quoting the district judge's statement that "one of the things which the Hispano has in common with the Negro is economic and cultural deprivation and discrimination" (*ibid.*, 197–98), Justice Brennan found "agreement that . . . Negroes and Hispanos in Denver suffer identical discrimination in treatment" in comparison with "Anglo students" (*ibid.*, 198). He did not quote the judge's further statement that "the problems applicable to [Hispanos] are often different" from those of blacks (313 F. Supp. 69).

54. The equation may show, however, that slavery, the black codes, Jim Crow laws, and the history of the Fourteenth Amendment are not as significant in explaining the Court's decisions involving blacks as is often thought.

55. 413 U.S. 205.

56. *Ibid.*, 198.

57. *Ibid.*, 206.

58. E.g., *ibid.*, 200, 205.

59. *Ibid.*, 205, 206, 208.

60. *Ibid.*, 200, 199. Justice Brennan arrived at these figures by stating that the "Board was found guilty of intentionally segregative acts of one kind or another" affecting eight Park Hill schools. He recognized that with regard to two of these schools, Cole Junior High and East High, "the conclusion rests on the rescission of the resolutions" (*ibid.*, 199, n. 10). Unless the Court was here adopting the district judge's rescission theory, which the rest of the

opinion seems carefully to avoid, these two schools, at least, should not have been included in the Court's computation. To exclude them would be to exclude one of the two junior high schools and the only senior high school involved and to reduce the number of black students subject to the "deliberate segregation policy" from 5,139 (the basis of the Court's 37.69 percent) to 3,216, or 23.5 percent.

61. *Ibid.*, 201–203.

62. *Ibid.*, 203–205. Justice Brennan asserted: "The District Court did not state this, or indeed any, reason why the Park Hill finding was disregarded when attention was turned to the core city schools—beyond saying that the Park Hill and core city areas were in its view 'different' " (*ibid.*, 204). The district judge had made clear, however, that for him a "distinguishing point" regarding the core city schools "is that we do not here have legislative action similar to the rescission" (313 F. Supp. 69).

63. 413 U.S. 208, 205, 208, 205, 208, 210.

64. Another interesting technique of argument is illustrated by Justice Brennan's statement: "Where school authorities have been found to have practiced purposeful segregation in part of a school system, they may be expected to oppose system-wide desegregation, as did the respondents in this case, on the ground that their purposefully segregative actions were isolated and individual events, thus leaving plaintiffs with the burden of proving otherwise. But at that point where an intentionally segregative policy is practiced in a meaningful or significant segment of a school system, as in this case, the school authorities cannot be heard to argue that plaintiffs have proved only 'isolated and individual' unlawfully segregative actions" (*ibid.*, 208–209). It does not appear from the board's brief, however, that it made the argument here attributed to it. In placing "isolated and individual" in quotation marks, Justice Brennan was apparently quoting only himself. Furthermore, the passage seems to say that by making the supposed argument the board acted just as "may be expected" of a proven segregator.

65. *Ibid.*, 210, 211. "We have no occasion to consider in this case whether a 'neighborhood school policy' of itself will justify racial or ethnic concentrations in the absence of a finding that school authorities have committed acts constituting *de jure* segregation" (*ibid.*, 212).

66. *Ibid.*, 211.

67. *Ibid.*, 214, 216. See also Douglas' dissenting opinion in *Spencer* v. *Kugler*, 404 U.S. 1027 (1972) ("The right to education in the environment of a multi-racial community seems . . . fundamental"); and his opinions as circuit justice in *Guey Heung Lee* v. *Johnson*, 404 U.S. 1215 (1971) (persons of Chinese ancestry, once segregated in California schools, were denied a stay of a federal district court order requiring reassignment from predominantly Chinese-American

neighborhood schools pursuant to a program of "desegregation" of predominantly black schools), and *Gomperts* v. *Chase*, 404 U.S. 1237 (1971).

68. 413 U.S. 220, 221.

69. *Ibid.*, 222–23; 223, n. 9, citing "Residential Segregation," *Scientific American*, 213 (Aug. 1965) 14, and Karl and Alma Taeuber, *Negroes in Cities: Residential Segregation and Neighborhood Change* (Chicago, 1965), 36.

Later in his opinion Justice Powell stated: "There can be little doubt that principal causes of the pervasive school segregation found in the major urban areas of this country, whether in the North, West, or South, are the socio-economic influences which have concentrated our minority citizens in the inner cities while the more mobile white majority disperse to the suburbs" (413 U.S. 236).

70. 413 U.S. 223, 225, 224.

71. *Ibid.*, 231, 233–35.

72. *Ibid.*, 225–26 (Justice Powell's italics).

73. *Ibid.*, 226.

74. *Ibid.*, 226, 227.

75. See Frank Goodman, "De Facto School Segregation: A Constitutional and Empirical Analysis," *California Law Review* 60 (1972) 292–93.

76. 413 U.S. 227–28.

77. *Ibid.*, 218–19.

78. *Ibid.*, 232, quoting *Hernandez* v. *Texas*, 347 U.S. 475, 482 (1954) (Justice Powell's italics).

79. *Ibid.*, 236, quoting *United States* v. *Texas Education Agency*, 467 F. 2d 848, 873 (5th Cir., *en banc*, 1972).

80. 413 U.S. 229–30, quoting *Cisneros* v. *Corpus Christi Independent School District*, 467 F. 2d 142, 148 (5th Cir., *en banc*, 1972), which quoted *United States* v. *Jefferson County Board of Education*, 380 F. 2d 385, 397 (5th Cir., *en banc*, 1967) (dissenting opinion).

81. 413 U.S. 242.

82. *Ibid.*, 219, n. 5.

83. "Is Busing Necessary?" *Commentary*, 53 (March 1972) 46.

84. 413 U.S. 238, 253, 246.

85. *Ibid.*, 247, quoting *Griswold* v. *Connecticut*, 381 U.S. 482 (1965), which referred to *Pierce* v. *Society of Sisters*, 268 U.S. 510 (1925).

86. 413 U.S. 247.

87. *Ibid.*, 247–48.

88. *Ibid.*, 248.

89. *Ibid.*, 249–50.

90. *Ibid.*, 250.

91. *Ibid.*, 251, 252, n. 32.

92. *Ibid.*, 257.

93. "A Scholar Who Inspired It Says Busing Backfired," *National Observer*, June 7, 1975, 18.

94. "Is Busing Necessary?" 47.
95. 413 U.S. 258.
96. *Ibid.*, 256–57, 264–65.
97. 368 F. Supp. 207 (1973), 208.
98. *Ibid.*, 210.
99. As of September 1973, the elementary schools were 54.1 percent "Anglo," the junior high schools 56.6 percent, and the high schools 63.8 percent (380 F. Supp. 674 [1974]).
100. *Ibid.*, 686, 687, 696–701.
101. *Ibid.*, 687. For some reason, the judge "emphasized that this must not be a before lunch or after lunch program. The integrated setting should last through a minimum of one-half of the school period plus the lunch period as well. There can be no compromises on this" (*ibid.*, 690).
102. *Ibid.*
103. *Ibid.*, 705.
104. *Keyes* v. *School District No. 1, Denver, Colorado*, 521 F. 2d 465 (1975).
105. Austin (Texas) *American-Statesman*, Dec. 19, 1974, p. B13 (Associated Press). "A boycott called by the Citizens Association for Neighborhood Schools (CANS) fizzled when fewer than 10 percent observed it" (*ibid.*).
106. One of President Roosevelt's appointments, Justice Black, continued on the court for more than thirty years and another, Justice Douglas, for more than thirty-five.
107. See William Buckley, *Four Reforms* (New York, 1973), 94: "The public—under the tutelage of its moral and intellectual leaders—is being trained, as regards the Supreme Court of the United States . . . to accept its rulings as if rendered ex cathedra, on questions of faith and morals." *"If that is what the Supreme Court says*, the most urbane American lawyers, governors, ministers, and journalists will say—*why that is how it shall be.* It is my point that it is something more than compliance that then results. It is something more akin to what, in religion, they call 'internal assent.' If-that-is-what-the-Supreme-Court-says-that-is-the-way-it-will-be, graduates towards: If that is what the Supreme Court says, that is the way it *ought* to be. The docility becomes religious in character" (*ibid.*, 91).

Chapter 10. *The Result of Two Decades of Judicial Policy-Making: Busing to Achieve Racial Balance though the Whites Have Left*

1. 418 U.S. 717 (1974).
2. *Bradley* v. *Milliken*, 338 F. Supp. 582, 585–86 (E.D. Mich. 1971), 585, 586.
3. 418 U.S. 765, n. 1 (dissenting opinion of Justice White).
4. 418 U.S. 749, n. 23.
5. 338 F. Supp. 594, 588.

6. *Ibid.*, 589–91.

7. *Bradley* v. *Milliken*, 433 F. 2d 897, 898 (6th Cir., 1970), 898–901.

8. *Bradley* v. *Milliken*, 484 F. 2d 215, 219 (6th Cir., 1973).

9. The sequence—adoption of a busing plan by a "liberal" school board, change of board members by voter action, rescission, and a finding of unconstitutionality—has become familiar: e.g., *Brinkman* v. *Gilligan*, 503 F. 2d 684 (6th Cir., 1974); *NAACP, Lansing Branch* v. *Lansing Board of Education*, 485 F. 2d 569 (6th Cir., 1973); *Oliver* v. *Kalamazoo Board of Education*, 368 F. Supp. 143 (W.D. Mich. 1973). Voters in many communities have apparently paid inadequate attention to the make-up of their school boards, undoubtedly considering that any truly objectionable action could always be undone. The federal courts, however, have made this inattention a very costly mistake.

10. 418 U.S. 717 (1974), Record, 1a, 15a.

11. 433 F. 2d 897 (1970), 904, 905.

12. 338 F. Supp. 584.

13. Unreported opinion, quoted in *Bradley* v. *Milliken*, 438 F. 2d 945, 947 (6th Cir., 1971).

14. 438 F. 2d 945 (1971).

15. 338 F. Supp. 592.

16. *Ibid.*

17. Quoted by Judge Paul Weick, dissenting, in 484 F. 2d 260–61. He commented: "This is incredible!"

18. 338 F. Supp. 592, 593, 592; Nathan Glazer, "Is Busing Necessary?" *Commentary* 53 (March 1972) 49.

19. 338 F. Supp. 587-89.

20. See Glazer, p. 43.

21. Glazer, p. 48. The San Francisco case referred to is *Johnson* v. *San Francisco Unified School District*, 339 F. Supp. 1315 (N.D. Cal. 1971).

22. 418 U.S. 717 (1974), Brief for Petitioners, 48.

23. 418 U.S. 717 (1974), Record, Va 169-79.

24. By reason of the Eleventh Amendment, a state is not, in theory, subject to suit without its consent. This amendment has long been effectively nullified, however, by the fiction that a suit against state officials, even for acts committed in their official capacity, is not a suit against the state (*Ex parte Young*, 209 U.S. 123 [1908]). See Charles Wright, *Federal Courts* (2d ed., St. Paul, 1970), 183–86. To avoid the Eleventh Amendment's prohibition, therefore, the judge should have found that the acts in question were the acts of the particular state officials named as parties defendant rather than of "the State of Michigan" as such; even fictions have their demands. That, however, would have presented difficulties, and where "desegregation" is involved even the fiction has been largely ignored.

25. See *Evans* v. *Newton*, 382 U.S. 296 (1966); *Burton* v. *Wilmington Parking Authority*, 365 U.S. 715 (1961); *Pennsylvania* v. *Board of Trusts*, 353 U.S. 230 (1957). The very same act may be both "state action" for

the purposes of the Fourteenth Amendment and not be the action of the state for the purpose of the Eleventh (see n. 24, above). Constitutional law, however, is as little dependent on logic as on constitutional provisions, and this particular riddle is generally ignored. See the dissenting opinion of Judge Weick, 484 F. 2d 271-72.

26. 338 F. Supp. 589.

27. *Higgins* v. *Board of Education of the City of Grand Rapids, Michigan* (W.D. Mich., CA 6386, July 18, 1973, 77–78). In the 1969–1970 school year, Detroit received $1,729,755 under the State Aid Act referred to (418 U.S. 717 [1974], Brief for Petitioners, 31).

28. *San Antonio Independent School District* v. *Rodriguez*, 411 U.S. 1 (1973).

29. 418 U.S. 717 (1974), Brief for Petitioners, 28–29.

30. William Cohen, "Racial Imbalance in the Pasadena Public Schools," *Law and Society Review* 2 (1967) 43–44: "In mid-1953 the local branch of the NAACP demanded" that the Pasadena, California, school board eliminate liberal transfer policies and the use of optional zones, and the board did so. "This application, however, of a more rigid neighborhood school policy led many families to move away from the high Negro attendance areas or enroll their children in private schools.

"The late 1950s saw a rapid increase in the Negro population of the Pasadena School District, with a corresponding increase of racial imbalance in the schools. By 1961 it was clear that not merely one or two but a tier of elementary schools across the western end of the city were, or were becoming, predominantly Negro."

31. 338 F. Supp. 587.

32. Quoted in 418 U.S. 728–29, n. 8.

33. 418 U.S. 717 (1974), Record, 40a, 43a.

34. 418 U.S. 729, n. 10. An appeal by the defendants from the finding of "*de jure* segregation" in Detroit and from the order requiring submission of "desegregation plans" was dismissed by the Sixth Circuit on the ground that the rulings were not final (468 F. 2d 902 [1972]). A petition for certiorari to the Supreme Court was denied (409 U.S. 844 [1972]).

35. Quoted in 484 F. 2d 279–80 (concurring and dissenting opinion of Judge Wallace Kent).

36. In the words of counsel for intervenors, quoted in a dissenting opinion on the later appeal to the Sixth Circuit: "Seven days after allowing appellants to intervene, as a matter of right but subject to oppressive conditions, the trial court required the filing of written briefs on the legal propriety of a metropolitan plan of desegregation. . . . . The court did not require or permit oral argument. Less than 36 hours later the court" ruled that a metropolitan plan would be proper, "rejecting the contentions of Intervenor School Districts. Testimony regarding metropolitan plans commenced four days later (a weekend and Motion day falling between) at 10:10 A.M. Prior

to the noon recess, just two hours after Intervenor School District counsel had first appeared in the District Court and before completion of testimony of a single witness, the District Judge announced that counsel could stop by his office and pick up" a copy of his decision and opinion "wherein the court announced its intention to seek a more desirable racial mix by means of a Metropolitan Plan.

"Thus without any opportunity for oral argument, without opportunity to examine or cross-examine one witness, without opportunity to present one shred of evidence, and indeed, without opportunity to obtain copies of previous pleadings and testimony (let alone read same), the Intervenor School Districts had been effectively foreclosed from protecting their interests" (484 F. 2d 269).

37. The district judge's unreported opinion is quoted almost in full in 484 F. 2d 242–45.

38. 345 F. Supp. 914 (1972), 920, 918.

39. *Ibid.,* 925–26.

40. 418 U.S. 717 (1974), Brief for Petitioners, 74–75.

41. 345 F. Supp. 933–35.

42. *Ibid.,* 929, 919, 926, 929, 926.

43. *Ibid.,* 931.

44. *Ibid.,* 929–30.

45. *Ibid.,* 930.

46. 418 U.S. 717 (1974), Record, IVa, 18. The "safer" but smaller-capacity "diesel transit vehicle" cost "about $32,000 to $35,000 per vehicle" (*ibid.*).

47. 345 F. Supp. 930.

48. *Ibid.,* 931, 919.

49. *Ibid.,* 939, 933, 932, 939, 933, 932.

50. *Ibid.,* 935–36, 919, 936, 919–20.

51. *Ibid.,* 938.

52. 484 F. 2d 270.

53. *Ibid.,* 252.

54. *Ibid.,* 222, 235–37, 237–38.

55. *Ibid.,* 238–41. The court purported to recognize at the outset of its opinion that "the State of Michigan as such is not a party to this litigation." All "references thereto," it said, "should be read as references to the public officials, State and local, through whom the State is alleged or shown to have acted" (*ibid.*, 220). In this way, the court both disposed of the Eleventh Amendment objection that the state could not be sued and remained free to refer thereafter to the acts of "the State" or state institutions—for example, "the State Legislature"—without having to consider whether or how those acts could be said to be the acts of the particular individuals named as parties defendant.

56. *Michigan Compiled Laws Annotated,* 388.851 (1967): "Public or

private school buildings; construction requirements, waiver"; "Historical Note"; 340.77 (1967).

57. 484 F. 2d 238.

58. *Ibid.*, 231, quoting testimony of the Detroit school superintendent; 418 U.S. 717 (1974), Record, Va. 186.

59. 484 F. 2d 231; 418 U.S. 750; 484 F. 2d 238.

60. 484 F. 2d 242–45. The court "distinguished" the Fourth Circuit's decision in *Richmond* from this one on the ground that the district judge there had "ordered an actual consolidation of three separate school districts," while the judge here had only "directed a study of plans for the reassignment of pupils in school districts comprising the metropolitan area of Detroit," and on the ground that different state constitutional and statutory provisions were involved (*ibid.*, 250–51).

61. *Ibid.*, 275–76.

62. 418 U.S. 738, n. 18.

63. *Ibid.*, 752, 745.

64. *Ibid.*, 738.

65. It is true, of course, as Justice Powell pointed out in *Keyes*, that the "desegregation" rationale for requiring racial balance does not explain the result of *Swann* on the basis of its facts, but that defect must be taken as showing only that the Court there misperceived those facts, as, indeed, the *Swann* opinion amply attests.

66. 418 U.S. 739–40.

67. *Ibid.*, 740–41 (Chief Justice Burger's italics).

68. *Ibid.*, 788, n. 1; 741, n. 19; 747, n. 22.

69. *Ibid.*, 741–44.

70. *Ibid.*, 744, 741, 744–45.

71. *Ibid.*, 746.

72. *Ibid.*, 748–52.

73. *Ibid.*, 748–49.

74. *Ibid.*, 749–51.

75. *Ibid.*, 752–53.

76. *Ibid.*, 753, 754, 756.

77. *Ibid.*, 756, n.2.

78. *Ibid.*, 757–58.

79. 411 U.S. 1; 418 U.S. 761, 762.

80. *Ibid.*, 763, 770, 785, 782, 801.

81. *Ibid.*, 792.

82. *Ibid.*, 763, 768, 769, 772, 775, 776, 777, 781.

83. *Ibid.*, 770, 745–46, 764, 767, 777.

84. *Ibid.*, 765.

85. *Ibid.*, 771.

86. *Ibid.*, 779–80.

87. *Ibid.*, 782, 808, 814.

88. *Ibid.*, 782, 784.

89. *Ibid.*, 784, 789–90.

90. *Ibid.*, 790–91; a footnote says, "See Mich. Comp. Laws § 388.851 (1970)."

91. The closest the district judge came to making such a finding was his statement: "In view of our findings of fact already noted we think it unnecessary to parse in detail the activities of the local board and the state authorities in the area of school construction and the furnishing of school facilities. It is our conclusion that these activities were in keeping, generally, with the discriminatory practices which advanced or perpetuated racial segregation in these schools" (338 F. Supp. 589).

92. On the page cited by Justice Marshall, the court of appeals stated: "Under Michigan law, M.S.A. §15.1961, M.C.L.A. 388.851, school building construction plans must be approved by the State Board of Education. Prior to 1962 the State Board also had specific statutory authority to supervise school site selection. The proofs concerning the effect of Detroit's school construction program are therefore largely applicable to show State responsibility for the segregative results."

93. See above, pp. 226–27.

94. 418 U.S. 791.

95. *Ibid.*, 792; a footnote says, "See Mich. Comp. Laws §§388.629 and 340.600."

96. *Michigan Compiled Laws Annotated*, 388.629 (1967): "The secretary of the board of education of each district enrolling nonresident pupils shall certify to the superintendent of public instruction on forms furnished by the superintendent of public instruction, the number of nonresident pupils enrolled in each grade on the fourth Friday following Labor Day of each year, the districts in which the nonresident pupils reside, the amount of tuition charged for the current year, and any other information required by the superintendent of public instruction." *Ibid.*, 340.600: "The superintendent of public instruction shall have authority by himself or someone designated by him, to review, confirm, set aside or amend the action, order or decision of the board of any school district with reference to the routes over which pupils shall be transported, the distance such pupils shall be required to walk, and the suitability and number of the vehicles and equipment for the transportation of the pupils."

97. 418 U.S. 792, 793.

98. *Ibid.*, 785–86.

99. *Ibid.*, 798.

100. *Ibid.*, 802.

101. *Ibid.*, 806–807.

102. *Ibid.*, 799, 756, n. 2.

103. *Ibid.*, 799, n. 19. Justice Marshall argued, in the remainder of the same footnote, that "a racially neutral 'neighborhood school'

attendance plan" was rejected in *Swann* because of "extensive residential segregation" regardless of whether this residential segregation was caused by state action." He overlooked the fact that in *Swann* the Court expressly assumed and argued at length, however unpersuasively, that the "residential segregation" involved in that case had been caused by the prior dual system. Justice Marshall had just conceded, however, that he was not assuming that Detroit's schools were blacker or the suburban schools whiter than they would have been except for the constitutional violation that was found.

104. *Ibid.*, 805.

105. *Ibid.*, 802. Justice Marshall's further argument that the "racial identifiability" of Detroit's schools would result not only from "their high percentage of Negro students" but also from the racial make-up of the surrounding area (*ibid.*, 803–04) is of no help to him for the same reason: his concession that he did not claim that the Detroit-suburban racial disparity was one of the "vestiges of state-imposed segregation."

106. *Ibid.*, 806.

107. *Ibid.*, 809, 810, 812–14. After the Court's decision, some members of the Detroit board considered adopting an integration plan that would permit some schools to be 50 percent white. The NAACP, however, insisted on complete racial balance "despite the belief it could accelerate the flight of whites to the suburbs." The chief attorney for the NAACP in the case was "surprised that a majority-black board of education would even consider" lesser integration, for "it would represent yielding to white attitudes and would only continue the privileged place of whites in the public school system." In his view: "If there were only two white schools left and busing meant that those whites moved out of the city, then so be it" (Austin (Texas) *American-Statesman*, Aug. 19, 1974, p. 2).

108. 418 U.S. 814.

109. *Board of School Commissioners of City of Indianapolis* v. *United States*, 421 U.S. 931 (1975); *Board of Education of Louisville, Kentucky* v. *Haycraft*, 421 U.S. 929 (1975).

110. *United States* v. *State of Missouri*, 515 F. 2d 1365 (8th Cir., 1975) (consolidation of districts required despite *Milliken*); *United States* v. *Board of School Commissioners of City of Indianapolis*, 503 F. 2d 68 (7th Cir., 1974) (interdistrict busing not precluded); *Haycraft* v. *Board of Education of Louisville, Kentucky*, 510 F. 2d 1358 (6th Cir., 1974) (companion to *Newburg Area Council, Inc.* v. *Board of Education of Jefferson County, Kentucky*) (same); *Tasby* v. *Estes*, 517 F. 2d 92 (5th Cir., 1975) (further busing in Dallas); *Hart* v. *Community School Board of Education, New York School District No. 21*, 512 F. 2d 37 (2d Cir., 1975); *Spangler* v. *Pasadena City Board of Education*, 519 F. 2d 430 (9th Cir., 1975); *United States* v. *School District of Omaha*, 521 F. 2d 530 (8th Cir., 1975).

Chapter 11. *Effects of the Supreme Court's Attempt to Compel School Racial Integration: A Self-Defeating Requirement*

1. William Rodgers, "A Holding of 'Not Unconstitutional': Law Reform through Judicial Abstention," *Washington Law Review* 44 (1969) 609.

2. *The Supreme Court and the Idea of Progress* (New York, 1970), 11–12.

3. *Lochner* v. *New York*, 198 U.S. 45, 76 (dissenting opinion).

4. 416 U.S. 312 (1974). Daniel Boorstin, *Democracy and Its Discontents* (New York, 1974), 58–60: "Recently, for the first time in our history, we seem almost to be making an effort to Balkanize this great nation"; "When before has it been respectable for American politicians to declare themselves the candidates for their race, for Americans to accept uncritically a racial caucus in the Congress of the nation?"; "We must return to the ideal of equality. We must recognize that many of the acts committed in the name of equal opportunity are in fact acts of discrimination. We must reject reactionary programs, though they masquerade under slogans of progress, which would carry us back to Old World prejudices, primitive hatreds, and discriminatory quotas."

5. 82 Wash. 2d 11, 507 P. 2d 1169 (1973).

6. 416 U.S. 336, n. 18. It should be noted, however, that Justice Douglas' condemnation of racial discrimination in this context seems half-hearted at best and that the bulk of his opinion is devoted to suggesting that the school achieve its racial objectives by somewhat less open means. Thus, although the school must, he stated, proceed *"in a racially neutral way,"* he saw no objection to the school's "setting minority applications apart for separate processing," (*ibid.*, 334; italics in the original). See also Lino Graglia, "Special Admission of the 'Culturally Deprived' to Law School," *University of Pennsylvania Law Review* 119 (1970) 351.

7. *Keyes* v. *School District No. One, Denver, Colorado*, 413 U.S. 189, 247–48 (1973) (separate opinion).

8. "Is Busing Necessary?" *Commentary*, 53 (March 1972) 45.

9. *Keyes*, 248 (separate opinion).

10. See *Equal Educational Opportunity—1971: Hearings before the Select Committee on Equal Educational Opportunity of the United States Senate*, 92d Cong., 1st sess. (1971); *School Busing: Hearings before Subcommittee No. 5 of the Committee on the Judiciary, House of Representatives*, 92d Cong., 2d sess. (1972); *Busing of School Children: Hearings before the Subcommittee on Constitutional Rights of the Committee on the Judiciary, United States Senate*, 93d Cong., 2d sess. (1974).

11. *Equal Educational Opportunity—1971*, 9018 (Nashville); *ibid.*, 9026 (Tampa); *Busing of School Children*, 274 (Kalamazoo); *School Busing*, 930 (Dallas).

12. At the 1972 congressional hearings on school busing, Congressman Fletcher Thompson of Georgia testified that in his congressional district "a 6-year-old high school, which cost about $1 million, [had] to be abandoned" to further integration. From a survey he conducted of other school districts, he learned of 356 schools that had been closed for this reason. The 274 of these schools about which cost data were available

had a total cost or value of $52,443,104. Data later submitted to Thompson by HEW showed 1,224 schools closed for "desegregation" in fourteen southern and border states from 1954 to 1969 (*School Busing*, 21–29). Before 1969, of course, busing to achieve racial balance had hardly begun.

13. *Wright* v. *Council of City of Emporia*, 407 U.S. 451, 469 (1972).

14. Glazer, 48.

15. *Keyes*, 246 (separate opinion).

16. *Swann* v. *Charlotte-Mecklenburg Board of Education*, 402 U.S. 1, 28 (1970). "Bus transportation has been an integral part of the public education system for years . . . a normal and accepted tool of educational policy" (*ibid.*, 29). In rural areas, where longer-distance busing is most common, the losses as well as the gains may be different from those in the city. For example, distance may be less meaningful, and there may be no significant community interests to preserve in an area smaller than that covered by the bus.

17. See NAACP Legal Defense and Educational Fund, Inc., *It's Not the Distance, "It's the Niggers"* (New York, 1972).

18. Edward Banfield, "Race: Thinking May Make It So," in *The Unheavenly City*, (Boston, 1968): Almost everything said about the problems of the Negro tends to exaggerate the purely racial aspects of the situation. . . . The importance of [purely racial] factors is exaggerated implicitly by any statement about the Negro that fails—as almost all do—to take account of such "nonracial factors [as], especially, income, class, education, and place of origin (rural or urban, Southern or not)" (69)."Much of what appears (especially to Negroes) as race prejudice is really *class* prejudice or, at any rate, class antipathy. Similarly, much of what appears (especially to whites) as 'Negro' behavior is really lower-class behavior" (76)." 'Whatever their origin,' writes sociologist Urie Bronfenbrenner, 'the most immediate, overwhelming, and stubborn obstacles to achieving quality and equality in education now lie as much in the character and way of life of the American Negro as in the indifference and hostility of the white community' " (85).

19. See Ben Wattenberg, *The Real America* (Garden City, N. Y., 1974), ch. ix. In the 1960s, black family income increased by 99.6 percent, while white family income increased 69 percent (*ibid.,*125). If the "middle class" is defined as consisting of persons having a family income of at least $7,000 a year, 51 percent of all black families were middle class in 1972, compared to 76 percent of white families (*ibid.*, 126). However, in 1972 the income of black families was still only 62 percent of that of white families (*ibid.*, 125), and 33 percent of all black families were "broken"—i. e., headed by a woman (*ibid.*, 137). Perhaps most important, "in 1971, of the 10.6 million on welfare, 43% were Negro—4.5 million. The black population in 1971 was 23 million. The percentage of blacks on AFDC [Aid to Families with Dependent Children], then, was 19%—up from 8% eleven years earlier. When other welfare programs

are added to the AFDC numbers, about 25% of the blacks are now on welfare—one in four! The white rate is 4%" (*ibid.*, 138).

20. Christopher Jencks *et al.*, *Inequality* (New York, 1972), 81-82. See also James Coleman *et al.*, *Equality of Educational Opportunity* (1966), 20-21, and Frederick Mosteller and Daniel Moynihan, "A Pathbreaking Report," in *On Equality of Educational Opportunity*, Mosteller and Moynihan, eds. (New York, 1972), 23.

21. See p. 145, above. Beloine Young and Grace Bress, "A New Educational Decision: Is Detroit the End of the School Bus Line?" *Phi Delta Kappan*, April 1975, p. 518: " 'There is no doubt that our classes for the intellectually gifted would have been totally segregated . . . if we had continued them,' says the superintendent of Community School District 22 [New York City]. Another district has banned all classes for academically talented children on the ground that they would not have the 'correct' racial balance."

22. *Our Nation's Schools—A Report Card: "A" in School Violence and Vandalism: Preliminary Report of the Subcommittee to Investigate Juvenile Delinquency to the Committee on the Judiciary, United States Senate,* 94th Cong., 1st sess. (1975), 3-5.

23. *New York Times*, Feb. 9, 1970, p. 1. "Many white teachers are convinced that there is a carefully plotted conspiracy for a black 'takeover' of the high schools." The "African-American Teachers Association" called "for support of black students who 'seek "through any means necessary" to make these educational institutions relevant to their needs.' " The chairman of the "African-American Students Association" stated that "violence was the only power students had to 'back up what they say,' comparing it to the power of the [teacher's union] to strike." "A shop teacher, identified in the minds of some students as a supporter of George C. Wallace, was assaulted by young blacks who squirted his coat with lighter fluid and set it on fire." This "which was followed by the threat of a teacher walkout, led to the placing of a strong police detachment in the school and the dropping of 678 students—mostly blacks—from its register, an action later declared illegal by a Federal judge" (*ibid.*, 42).

24. "A Scholar Who Inspired It Says Busing Backfired," *National Observer*, June 7, 1975, p. 1. Ray Rist, "Busing White Children Into Black Schools: A Study in Controversy," *Integrated Education*, July 1974, p. 13, reported that when the principal at a 90 percent black school from which blacks were being bused was asked whether whites should also be bused in, he replied: "The idea . . . is unthinkable. . . . This school has a strong pecking order in which physical prowess and the ability to socialize according to the rules of urban Black culture are the main determinants of status. Most white students, even those strong enough to defend themselves physically, aren't used to the social rituals of a black school—the dancing, the clothing, the jive." Ben Wattenberg and Richard Scammon, "Black Progress and Liberal Rhetoric," *Commentary*, 54 (April

1973), 40: "As for the problem of crime, it hardly needs repeating, and scarcely needs to be documented, that crime rates—particularly violent crime rates—are high among blacks. Blacks comprise only about a ninth of the U.S. population, yet more blacks were arrested for crimes of violence in 1970 than whites—105,000 versus 96,000. This means, essentially, that the rate of violent crimes among blacks is about ten times the rate among whites."

25. Glazer, 46. When Kenneth Clark (see above, p. 27) a leading proponent of compulsory integration, was asked why he sent his children to private schools, he replied, "My children have only one life and I could not risk that" (Walter Goodman, "Kenneth Clark's Revolutionary Slogan: Just Teach Them to Read!" *New York Times Magazine*, March 18, 1973, p. 14). When federal District Judge Robert R. Merhige, Jr., who ordered the consolidation of the Richmond, Virginia, schools with those of the surrounding counties, was asked the same question, his reply was "When I'm on the bench, I'm a judge and when at home, I'm a father" (Paul Harvey, "The Advocates of Busing Preach But Don't Practice"; quoted in *Busing of School Children*, 272). "Of the leaders of the [New York City] school system itself, the nine-member Board of Education and the 20-odd deputy and associate superintendents, only a handful have children who attend or ever did attend the New York City public schools. Even worse, the Negro middle class has almost entirely disappeared and of the Negro leaders of the integration drive, the Wilkinsons and the Clarks, the Farmers, the Joneses and the Rustins, the Youngs and the Galamisons, not one has or ever had a child in the New York City public schools" (Martin Mayer, "Close to Midnight for New York Schools," *New York Times*, May 2, 1965; quoted in *School Busing*, 167). "In a study of the political supporters of Louise Day Hicks, the Boston School Committee's champion of the neighborhood school and *de facto* segregation, it was noted that those most likely to support integration are also least likely to expose their own families to it. . . . The Boston liberals have given their most sincere judgment by the residential location of their families: They have voted with their feet" (John Scott and Lois Scott, "Not So Much Anti-Negro as Pro-Middle Class," in *Prejudice and Race Relations*, ed. Raymond Mack [Chicago, 1970], 65).

26. "Ask Sen. Ted Kennedy where his son goes to school, he will tell you 'that's a private matter.'

"His private practice does not parallel his public position.

"His son attends a private school. It costs him $2,400 a year to send his son there. He can afford it. . . .

"And Sen. George McGovern has blasted the President for opposing compulsory busing saying, 'the President has encouraged contempt for the law. . . .'

"McGovern, when he lived in the suburbs, sent his daughter to a private Catholic high school. Now living in the District the daughter is sent daily to a

Bethesda high school, tuition for nonresidents, $1,450. Percentage of blacks, about 3 percent. In District public schools the percentage is 95 per cent black. . . .

"Interestingly, the first black appointed to the Supreme Court, Justice Thurgood Marshall, sent his two youngsters to this private school where the tuition may be from $1,600 to $2,000." Mentioned among other leading proponents of busing who "buy a way out" for their own children were Senator Walter Mondale of Minnesota and Senator Philip Hart of Illinois (Harvey, quoted in *Busing of School Children*, 271).

"Last week on CBS, Mike Wallace's Sixty Minutes revealed for the first time on television how rank hypocrisy is on the school question among Washington liberals. . . .

"What Mike Wallace showed here . . . was an array of black and white liberals who managed to keep their own children out of Washington's heavily black schools by sending them to private or suburban schools. . . .

"As Mrs. Donald Fraser, whose husband is Minnesota's most liberal congressman, put it to Wallace: 'Your children get educated only once.' . . . She told Wallace that her daughter was used to having white people around in school. . . .

"Commentators, national correspondents, and the great lamas of journalism, columnists, also are hypocritical on this score. One sardonic columnist for the Washington Post, interviewed by Wallace, said, 'Nobody wants to make their children pay for their own social philosophy.' The columnist's own son is in private school and he admits the rich can 'buy out.'

"Then why do liberals support integration and busing if they really don't believe in it down deep? The Washington Post columnist told Wallace:

" 'The lines get drawn in such a way that you end up supporting something that you think is unwise, perhaps unworkable, simply because of its symbolic content, simply because you get a bunch of rabid mouth-foaming racists opposing it, so you're forced to support it' " (Nick Thimmesch, "Where Do Liberals Enroll Their Kids?"; quoted in 117 *Cong. Rec.* 45616 [1971]).

27. David Armor, "The Double Double Standard: A Reply," *Public Interest*, No. 30 (Winter 1973) 119-20: "One expectation stands out above all others: Integrated education will enhance the academic achievement of minority groups, and thereby close (or at least substantially reduce) the achievement gap"; Elizabeth Cohen, "An Experimental Approach to School Effects" (unpublished paper presented to the Western Sociology of Education Association at Asilomar, Calif., Feb. 1, 1974), 1: "The size of the difference in test scores ["between blacks and whites and between other ethnic minorities and whites"] when social class is uncontrolled is enormous. The difference is unthinkable and unbearable to

a generation of intellectuals nurtured on the idea of environmental difference as the major sources of IQ differentials."

28. Jencks *et al.*, 103: "Advocates of desegregation are seldom very interested in its effects on advantaged students. Some actually hope that desegregation will depress advantaged students' achievement, so as to narrow the gap between them and the disadvantaged." Young and Bress, 518: "Prematurely discouraged with the results of the sixties' inadequately monitored innovations (many of which were oversold) many city school systems have, in effect, given up on the goal of producing equal educational results through 'equalizing upwards,' i.e., by raising the achievement of poor and minority students to meet the white average. Perhaps without realizing it, they are attempting to 'equalize down' by discouraging excellence. Some New York City schools have eliminated courses like calculus, enriched English, etc., that attract primarily a high-achieving white middle-class enrollment."

29. See Coleman, *Equality of Educational Opportunity*, 307.

30. "The Evidence on Busing," *Public Interest*, No. 28 (Summer 1972) 90, 96 (italics in the original). Thomas Pettigrew and others replied in "Busing: A Review of 'The Evidence,' " *Public Interest*, No. 30 (Winter 1973) 88. Armor in turn replied in "The Double Double Standard: A Reply," *ibid.*, 119. Pettigrew, after years of attempting to persuade courts, largely successfully, that compulsory integration was beneficial, if not necessary, to black academic achievement, here asserted that it was not a matter of "social scientists' opinions" but of the "courts' interpretation of the 14th Amendment" (*ibid.*, 113–14). Armor indignantly pointed out in reply (*ibid.*, 130): "The double standard here is obvious. One willingly applies social science findings to public policy if they are in accordance with one's values, but declares them irrelevant if they contradict one's values."

31. Armor, "The Evidence on Busing," 99–101. Because high school grade-point average is a prime determinant of eligibility for college admission, usually without regard to the quality of the high school attended, this result tends to diminish college opportunities for blacks.

32. *Ibid.*, 101-02.

33. *Ibid.*, 102.

34. Nancy St. John, *School Desegregation* (New York, 1975), 119.

35. Jencks *et al.*, 102, 106. See also Frank Goodman, "De Facto School Segregation: A Constitutional and Empirical Analysis," *Calif. L. Rev.* 60 (1972) 275, 400-435 ("The influence of biracial schooling upon the achievement of black students is highly *uncertain*" [426; Goodman's italics]); and Richard Light and Paul Smith, "Accumulating Evidence: Procedures for Resolving Contradictions among Different Research Studies," *Harvard Educational Review* 41 (1971) 429, 443 ("The contradictions among the studies are more striking than the similarities"). "Educational Inequality: A Preliminary Report to the Carnegie Corporation of New York" (mimeo-

graphed), quoted in *School Busing*, 1434, asserts: "Policy with respect to racial integration should" not be made "on the basis of integration's alleged effect on the short term careers of either white or black students. Such effects are at best problematic, certainly modest and possibly nonexistent."

36. See above, Ch. 2, "The Justification for the *Brown* Decision." From 1960 to 1971, black voter registration doubled in the eleven southern states, from 29.1 percent to 58.6 percent; white registration in 1971 was 65 percent. In 1974 nearly 3,000 blacks held elective office nationwide (*U.S. Statistical Abstract* [1974], 436). Major cities with black mayors include Los Angeles; Detroit; Washington, D.C.; Dayton, Ohio; Newark, New Jersey; Atlanta; and Gary, Indiana.

37. The superintendent of schools of Dallas, Texas, Nolan Estes, testified (*School Busing*, 930): "The truth of the matter is, when students with similar backgrounds and needs are spread throughout the city, the educational treatment is more difficult to deliver. In fact, most federally-funded approaches to compensatory education hinge upon a critical mass and concentration of effort. Some programs would have to be eliminated by federal regulation if the concentration of certain types of students was dissipated. We've already seen the grief of students who were no longer eligible for ESEA [Elementary and Secondary Education Act of 1965, 20 U.S.C., sect. 241a (1969)] Title I benefits because they were reassigned from their inner city schools to more affluent schools." See also, to the same effect, the testimony of a member of the board of education of Pasadena, California (*ibid.*, 1443–44).

38. "A Pathbreaking Report," 8-9. The authors continued: "The *Summary Report*, issued slightly in advance of the [Coleman Report] itself, seems to be at heart a political document designed to ease the blow of the findings, even perhaps to deflect them somewhat." Godfrey Hodgson, "Do Schools Make a Difference?" *Atlantic Monthly* 231, (March 1973) 38: "The Office of Education, which realized all too clearly how explosive the report was, didn't exactly trumpet the news to the world. The report was released, by a hallowed bureaucratic stratagem, on the eve of July 4, 1966. Few reporters care to spend that holiday gutting 737 pages of regression analysis and standard deviations. And to head off those few who might have been tempted to make the effort if they guessed that there was a good story at the end of it, the Office of Education put out a summary report which can only be described as misleading."

39. "A Pathbreaking Report," 15.

40. "De Facto School Segregation," 365. Goodman also pointed out: "Desegregation and compensatory education make competing demands upon the same limited fund of resources; a dollar spent on busing is one that might otherwise have been invested in remedial programs or smaller classes in slum schools. Politically, moreover, middle-class parents whose children are being bused to slum schools under court order may well conclude that they have sacrificed enough to the education of the

disadvantaged and that the balance of the school budget be spent on programs affording at least equal benefit to their own children. Indeed, court-ordered desegregation has been known to create such bitterness that communities, in protest, have voted down an otherwise acceptable tax increase or bond issue" (*ibid.*).

41. *Swann* v. *Charlotte-Mecklenburg Board of Education,* 379 F. Supp. 1102, 1105 (1974): "The attitude or state of mind at the top, among the Board of Education, is far more important than the physical details or logistics of pupil assignment. If that attitude or policy is negative or technical, the children know it and feel it; then 'ratios' and 'bussing' assume unwanted but unavoidable significance." The Civil Rights Commission found that "public statements by Mayor White" of Boston in 1974 and 1975—such as "I'm for integration but against forced busing"—"confused the public and constitute a disservice to the rule of law." The mayor "did take the position that he would uphold the law," but "a lawful court order . . . should be given affirmative support by public officials sworn to uphold the Constitution" (U.S. Civil Rights Commission, *Desegregating the Boston Public Schools: A Crisis in Civic Responsibility* [Washington, D.C., 1975], 29–30.

42. See Bruce Porter, "It Was a Good School to Integrate," *New York Times Magazine,* Feb. 9, 1975, p. 15. Madison High School in Brooklyn, New York, was a high-quality school in a neighborhood "dominated by middle-class Jews, largely Democratic and loosely liberal." "If integration would work any place," it was thought, "it would work at Madison." One day, however, "two students, one black and one white, accidentally bumped into each other in the doorway of the second-floor washroom, and instead of apologizing they started a fight that precipitated a school race war. Fighting between blacks and whites lasted three days. One boy was stabbed; another was clubbed. Twice, the terrified blacks had to be bused out of the neighborhood past crowds of angry white students waving sticks and shouting, 'Nigger go home.' Nearly 150 policemen were brought in to keep the races apart, and the school was closed down."

43. Statement by a former principal of a New York City school, quoted by columnist William Raspberry, Austin (Texas), *American-Statesman,* Sept. 25, 1975, p. 4.

44. Nolan Estes stated (*School Busing*, 930): "There appears to be a feeling of distrust between black and white students—partly due to economic and social differences, and also because of understandable frustrations and anxieties. The end results of these deep-seated problems are reflected in a growing number of disruptions, a sharply rising suspension rate, and an unprecedented wave of teacher abuse."

45. Armor, "The Evidence on Busing," 102.

46. *Ibid.,* 103, 105. St. John, 119: "The immediate effect of desegregation on interracial attitudes is sometimes positive but often negative."

47. Armor, 115-116. Two of the studies reviewed by Armor indicated positive results from integration by means of busing in one area. They showed that a much higher percentage of the bused black students entered

college than of an unbused black control group and that they entered higher quality institutions (regular four-year colleges or universities). One of the studies (data were not available for the other) showed, however, that because of a high drop-out rate, "towards the end of the sophomore year the bused students were not very much more likely to be enrolled full-time in college than the control group" (*ibid.,* 105).

48. According to *Facts on File,* Sept. 23, 1973, 808E2, "The Gallup Poll reported on Sept. 8 that while a large majority of the nation favored integration of public schools, only 5% (9% of the blacks and 4% of the whites) favored busing as a means of achieving integration."

49. "Crowded Bandwagon: In Michigan Contest, the Big Issue Is Who Opposes Busing Most," *Wall Street Journal,* Oct. 23, 1972, p. 1. After racial cross-district busing was ordered by the district judge in Detroit, busing became the overwhelming issue in Michigan elections. Candidates for offices having no control of the schools were nonetheless required to take a stand against busing, for it "was the only thing people wanted to know." "Let me know," one said, "when you find somebody who is for busing." "You can't," another stated, "take the position that there's a good argument on each side. They are too excited and too knowledgeable to buy that." The mayor of a Detroit suburb was "singing sweet music" to the voters' ears: "America, America, we don't want it this way, / No, No, No, No bus for us. / No, No, No, No bus for us." Governor George Wallace of Alabama, "an outspoken foe of busing," won the Michigan Democratic primary "by a landslide." Factory workers planned work stoppages and a boycott of businesses that contributed heavily to the NAACP. Residents of "posh Grosse Pointe," able to take more direct and effective action, made plans by which a private school could be set up in "about a month or six weeks."

The *Christian Science Monitor,* Nov. 20, 1972, 1, reported on the "growing number of school officials across the U.S. to lose their jobs over school integration." In San Francisco a school superintendent was "chased out of a Chinatown hall in February by parents angry over his integrationist views who shouted, 'Kill him, kill him!' "

50. Statement by the associate national director of the Congress of Racial Equality (CORE), *School Busing,* 1036–38. The convention also adopted a proposal for an amendment to the United States Constitution prohibiting school racial assignment (*ibid.,* 1037).

51. Since 1971, more than one hundred such measures have been introduced in both houses of Congress. See CCH *Congressional Index,* 92d, 93d, and 94th congresses.

52. 118 *Cong. Rec.* (1972), 8928, 28915-16, 35330.

53. 20 U.S.C., sect. 1652(a) (Supp, IV, 1974). Sect. 1652(b) provides, *inter alia,* that HEW, "including the Office of Education," shall not "by rule, regulation, order, guideline, or otherwise . . . urge, persuade, induce or require" the use of state or local funds "for any purpose, unless constitutionally required, for which Federal funds appropriated to carry out any applicable program may not be used."

54. 20 U.S.C.A., sect. 1653 (1974 Supp.). It was further enacted, in refutation of *Swann*, that the provisions of Title IV of the 1964 Civil Rights Act denying authority to require transportation to achieve racial balance were to "apply to all public school pupils and to every public school system, public school and public school board, as defined by Title IV, under all circumstances and conditions and at all times in every State, district, territory, Commonwealth, or possession of the United States regardless of whether" such pupils, systems, or schools are "in the northern, eastern, western, or southern part of the United States" (20 U.S.C., sect. 1656 [Supp. IV, 1974]).

55. *Weekly Compilation of Presidential Documents*, 8 (June 26, 1975) 1084, 1085.

56. *Drummond* v. *Acree*, 409 U.S. 1228 (1972). "At most," Justice Powell stated, "Congress may have intended to postpone the effectiveness of transportation orders in 'de facto' cases and in cases in which district court judges have misused their remedial powers."

57. Harold Spaeth, *An Introduction to Supreme Court Decision Making* (San Francisco, 1972), 3: "The religiously motivated founding of most of the colonies north of Virginia resulted in governments that were based upon sectarian interpretations of the Bible or natural law." Later "the need for a less parochial fundamental law became apparent. The solution, of course, was the enshrinement of the Constitution as American society's secular substitute for Holy Writ." Alexander Bickel, in *The Supreme Court and the Idea of Progress* (New York, 1970), 15, quotes a famous statement made in 1913 by a leader of the New York bar: "Our great and sacred Constitution, serene and inviolable, stretches its beneficent powers over our land . . . like the outstretched arm of God himself. . . . The people of the United States . . . ordained and established one Supreme Court—the most rational, considerate, discerning, veracious, impersonal power."

58. Alexander Bickel, *The Least Dangerous Branch* (Indianapolis, 1962), 258: "The Supreme Court's law . . . could not in our system prevail—not merely in the very long run, but within the decade—if it ran counter to deeply felt popular needs or convictions, or even if it was opposed by a determined and substantial minority and received with indifference by the rest of the country. This, in the end, is how and why judicial review is consistent with the theory and practice of political democracy." But, Clifton McCleskey responded in "Judicial Review in a Democracy: A Dissenting Opinion," *Houston Law Review* 3 (1966) 358, "it simply is not enough to assert without satisfactory proof that 'ultimately' the popular will always prevails under judicial review. We have known at least since David Hume that all governments—even the dictatorial ones—rest 'ultimately' on the consent of the governed, but the democratic theory we have outlined nowhere contemplates 'ultimate' popular control. The whole logic of that theory denies the propriety of resorting to such a subterfuge—democracy is an attempt to provide popular control here and now, not ultimately." Bickel later considerably revised his views of the Court. See Bickel, *The Supreme Court and the Idea of Progress*. See also George Braden, "The Search

for Objectivity in Constitutional Law," *Yale L. J.* 57 (1948) 571; Learned Hand, *The Spirit of Liberty,* ed. I. Dillard (3d ed., New York, 1960), 155; and Morris Cohen, *The Faith of a Liberal* (New York, 1946), 175.

59. One element of this insulation is the fraternity of professors of constitutional law, something of a College of Cardinals in the practice of constitutional religion. Most members of this group are no less willing than the Court to pronounce, under the guise of constitutional expertise, on questions about which they have no degree of special competence. They form a nearly solid phalanx of articulate and influential resistance to all attempts to limit the Court's power. At the 1972 busing hearings, for example, they and other law professors were virtually unanimous in advising Congress that a constitutional amendment prohibiting compulsory integration would be highly inappropriate and that limiting legislation would likely be unconstitutional (*School Busing,* 56–68, 1084–87, 1941–50). Little or no guidance was offered as to how compulsory integration might effectively be stopped.

60. *Furman* v. *Georgia,* 408 U.S. 238 (1972). Despite Justice Marshall's confident assertion, concurring in *Furman,* that "capital punishment is morally unacceptable to the people of the United States at this time in their history" (*ibid.,* 360), a Gallup poll of November 1972 showed that it was favored—57 percent to 32 percent (*New York Times,* Nov. 23, 1972, p. 18). Of course, if capital punishment were in fact unacceptable to the American people, there would presumably be no need for the Court to prohibit it in the face of a Constitution that twice (Amends. V, XIV) explicitly recognizes it. But, Justice Marshall also found, "American citizens know almost nothing about capital punishment" (408 U.S. 362).

61. *Pierce* v. *Society of Sisters,* 268 U.S. 510 (1925). The right does not apply, however, to public school teachers whose children are needed in the public schools to increase racial integration (*Cook* v. *Hudson,* 511 F. 2d 744 [5th Cir., 1975]).

62. See *Griswold* v. *Connecticut,* 381 U.S. 479 (1965); *Wisconsin* v. *Yoder,* 406 U.S. 205 (1972); *Roe* v. *Wade,* 410 U.S. 113 (1973); *Norwood* v. *Harrison,* 413 U.S. 455, 461 (1973) ("In the 1971 Term we reaffirmed the vitality of *Pierce*").

63. They already have been by the Fourth Circuit, in *McCrary* v. *Runyon,* 515 F. 2d 1082 (4th Cir., 1975).

64. Scott and Scott, 66. Three months prior to *Milliken,* the House adopted a very strong antibusing measure by an overwhelming vote (380 to 25) (120 *Cong. Rec.* H2270; daily ed., March 27, 1974). Six days after *Milliken,* however, the House acquiesced in a much milder "compromise" reached by a House-Senate conference committee (120 *Cong. Rec.* H7418; daily ed., July 31, 1974).

65. By the fall of 1973, the public school system was majority-black in, for example, Chicago (58 percent), Philadelphia (61), Detroit (70), Baltimore (70), Washington (96), Cleveland (57), Memphis (68), St. Louis (69), New Orleans (77), Kansas City, Missouri (56), Atlanta (81), Newark (72),

Oakland (62), Louisville (52), and Birmingham (62) (*U.S. News and World Report*, Aug. 11, 1975, p. 26). An HEW survey of 77 of the nation's 100 largest school districts showed that the percentage of blacks increased in 66 of the districts from 1970 to 1971 (118 *Cong. Rec.* 564 [1972]).

66. "A Scholar Who Inspired It Says Busing Backfired," *National Observer*, June 7, 1975, p. 1. Coleman also found that there is some "white flight from cities of all sizes, simply as a consequence of the proportion of blacks in the city. That is, the more blacks, the faster the white migration." He stated that compulsory integration does not seem to increase this movement in smaller cities. It is unfortunate indeed, however, that Coleman did not discover the evils of busing until after years of urging courts—he testified for the plaintiffs in, for example, *Keyes* v. *School District No. 1, Denver, Colorado*, 313 F. Supp. 90, 94 (D. Colo. 1970)—and Congress to greater efforts to increase integration. Harold Kurz, "Court Mandated Integration and White Flight in Los Angeles County," reprinted in *School Busing*, 1429-30, says that the greatest rates of decline in the number of white students (30.9 and 22.5 percent in two years) took place in the two, out of twenty-eight, school districts that had "extensive programs of racial balance, mandated by court order." However, some "white flight [is] normally encountered in the presence of minority enrollments equivalent to certain specified percentages of total enrollment, even in the absence of racial balance." *Our Nation's Schools* states (21): "A report prepared for the Boston School Committee has revealed that since the implementation of the desegregation order, at least 10,000 students, most of them white, have left Boston's public schools. School officials have stated that several of the city's 200 schools may be forced to close and cutbacks in teaching and other staffs made necessary. The withdrawals represent more than 10 percent of Boston's 94,000 elementary and secondary school students. Some 7,529 students are no longer in the public school system; 3,047 have transferred to private or parochial schools; 927 have been discharged to seek employment, and 3,555 are listed as dropouts." From September 1974 to September 1975, Boston's public schools lost some 15,000 white students and became majority-nonwhite (Nick Thimmesch, "Boston's Busing Travail," Austin (Texas) *American-Statesman*, Oct. 14, 1975, p. 4).

67. Scott and Scott, 66-67.

68. See n. 49, above.

69. See *Dred Scott* v. *Sandford*, 19 Howard 393 (1857); and *Civil Rights Cases*, 109 U.S. 3 (1883).

Table of Cases

Cases discussed in some detail are listed in italics.

Index

DISASTER BY DECREE

Designed by R.E. Rosenbaum.
Composed by Payne Printery, Inc.,
in 10 point Phototronic Baskerville, 2 points leaded,
with display lines in Baskerville bold.
Printed offset by Payne Printery.
on Warren's Number 66 text, 50 pound basis.
Bound by Vail-Ballou Press, Inc.,
in Joanna book cloth
and stamped in All Purpose foil.

Library of Congress Cataloging in Publication Data

Graglia, Lino A
  Disaster by Decree.

  Includes bibliographical references and index.
  1. Discrimination in education—Law and legislation—United States—Cases.
  2. School children—Transportation—Law and legislation—United States—Cases.
  I. Title.
KF4154.G7   344'.73'0798   75-36997
ISBN 0-8014-0980-2